The Sitwells

National Portrait Gallery, London

The Sitwells

and the Arts of the 1920s and 1930s

Published for the exhibition:
The Sitwells and the Arts of the 1920s and the 1930s,
held at the National Portrait Gallery
from 14 October 1994 to 22 January 1995

Published by
National Portrait Gallery Publications,
National Portrait Gallery, 2 St Martin's Place,
London WC2 0HE
reprinted, 1996

PAPERBACK ISBN 1 85514 141 8

A catalogue record for this book is available from
the British Library

Co-ordinated and edited by Joanna Skipwith
Assisted by Katie Bent
Designed by Atelier
Printed in Italy by Amilcare Pizzi

Cover illustration
The Sitwells
By Maurice Beck and Helen MacGregor, 1924
Copy print from lost original (detail)

Frontispiece
Osbert, Edith and Sacheverell Sitwell
By Cecil Beaton, 1927
(see 3.43)

Childhood at Renishaw

London and the War

Façade and the Twenties

Edith

Osbert

Sacheverell

Contents

This exhibition, devoted to the lives of the Sitwells and their relationship to the arts of the 1920s and 1930s, is the first whose progress I have been able to observe since becoming Director in January. It has been exciting to witness the rapidity with which the idea has taken shape through the energies of Robin Gibson and Honor Clerk, the two curators whose idea it was and who have overseen the project from beginning to end, working long hours assembling relevant material, negotiating loans and writing catalogue entries.

I hope that the exhibition will provide an opportunity for the public to see a wide range of works of art from the 1920s and 1930s in a social and artistic context that is very distinct from that of Bloomsbury: more cosmopolitan, more highly aestheticised, perhaps more chic. And as someone who belongs to a generation for whom the life and works of the Sitwells is largely unfamiliar (although Sacheverell Sitwell's *British Architects and Craftsmen*, *A Survey of Taste, Design and Style during Three Centuries 1600 to 1830* was the first work of architectural history I ever owned and I remember being recommended to read the works of Osbert Sitwell by an English master at school), I am looking forward to seeing how far their contemporary fame was deserved and what light the exhibition casts on the art, music and literature of their period.

We are indebted to many people for their help in mounting this exhibition, but above all to the members of the Sitwell family who have rallied to the cause with an enthusiasm that would have delighted the previous generation. We are also extremely grateful to the Trustees of the 29th May 1961 Charitable Trust for their generous grant and to *Harpers & Queen*, which, through the agency of Rupert Christiansen and Jamie Bill, has agreed to act as media sponsor.

Charles Saumarez Smith
Director, National Portrait Gallery

Foreword

Most exhibitions involve far more people than the public are aware of, and this exhibition particularly so. In putting together what we hope will be the definitive exhibition about the three Sitwells, there have been many people without whom this would not have been possible. First and foremost among these must be the sons of the late Sir Sacheverell Sitwell: Sir Reresby Sitwell and Francis Sitwell. Together with their wives, Penelope and Susanna, they have offered us more support, help, advice, hospitality and the freedom of their houses, Renishaw and Weston, than we could possibly have hoped for. They have lent by far the greatest number of exhibits and we are profoundly indebted to them, as we are to Alexandra Hayward and to George and William Sitwell.

In mounting the exhibition we were at all times reliant on the Sitwell biographies of John Pearson, Victoria Glendinning and Sarah Bradford. We have mercilessly raided these for our catalogue entries, which are a pale reflection of three of the most erudite and yet entertaining biographies of recent years. We are greatly indebted to Sarah Bradford and John Pearson for their essays, which are the backbone of the catalogue, and indeed for much helpful advice in putting together the exhibition. We must also thank Jonathan Fryer for stepping into the breach at short notice and writing two of the essays.

A number of people and institutions have been particularly helpful with information and loans. For assistance above and beyond the call of duty we most heartily thank Debra Armstrong-Morgan, Cathy Henderson and Sue Murphy (Harry Ransom Humanities Research Center, The University of Texas), Josie Adams and David Buchanan (Scarborough Art Gallery), Andy Cowan (Hamiltons Galleries), Lydia Cresswell-Jones (Sotheby's Beaton Archive), Helen Faulkner (BBC Music Library), Margaret Harmsworth, Bruce Hunter (David Higham Associates), Leela Meinertas and Andrew Kirk (Theatre Museum), Michael Meredith (School Library, Eton College), Lewis Morley, Robin Muir (British *Vogue*) and Anthony Rota (Bertram Rota Limited). Ian Carroll and Vivien Hamley both undertook research voluntarily for the catalogue; without their assistance many items of information would have gone untraced.

We are no less grateful to all the following who gave time, information or assistance in various ways: Rosalind Adams, Ian Anstruther, Nicolas Barker, Sybille Bedford, John Bernasconi (University of Hull Art Collection), Bryan Berryman (Scarborough Library), Richard Buckle, Father Philip Caraman SJ, Judith Collins (Tate Gallery), Kate Eustace (Ashmolean Museum), His Honour Judge Geddes, Victoria Glendinning, Anne Goodchild and Ian Bell (Graves Art Gallery, Sheffield), Irving Grose (Belgrave Gallery), John Handford (Macmillan), Sir Rupert Hart-Davis, Derek Hill, Mrs F. L. Hope, Gillian and Neville Jason, Susanna Kerr (Scottish National Portrait Gallery), Alberto de Lacerda, Richard Morphet, John and Virginia Murray, Maureen Murray, Lawrence Mynott, Quentin Newark, Michael Parkin, Lady Quennell, Richard Nathanson, Gillian Raffles (Mercury Gallery), Ben Read, William Reese, John Roberts, Pam Roberts (Royal Photographic Society), John Saumarez Smith, David Scrase (Fitzwilliam Museum), Richard Shone, Kenneth Snowman and Lady Walton.

Both the catalogue and the exhibition itself have involved a considerable number of our colleagues at a particularly busy time for the Gallery. We are grateful to our former Director, John Hayes, for his early support of the exhibition and to Charles Saumarez Smith for continuing it. Of those directly involved with the exhibition, Kathleen Soriano has been a tower of strength in the exhibitions office, producing lists and constructive assistance at the drop of a hat. Caroline Brown threw herself into the difficult task of designing a complex exhibition on a shoe-string budget with enthusiasm, as did Joanna Skipwith into the equally difficult task of producing a catalogue under the same conditions. We would also like to thank all the following for their assistance in various ways: Katie Bent, Lesley Bradshaw, Robert Carr-Archer, Emma Floyd, Stephanie Hopkinson, Sarah Kemp, Tim Moreton, Carole Patey, Terence Pepper, Jill Springall, Lisi Streule and Kai Kin Yung.

Robin Gibson
Honor Clerk

Acknowledgements

Sir Reresby Sitwell Bt 1.1, 1.2, 1.5, 1.6, 1.7, 1.8, 1.9, 1.11, 1.13, 1.14, 1.15, 1.16, 1.17, 1.18, 1.19, 1.20 (a), 1.22, 1.24 (c-d), 1.28, 1.29, 1.30, 1.31, 2.6, 2.13, 2.15, 2.18, 2.19, 2.29, 2.30, 2.34, 2.36, 2.37, 2.43, 2.57, 2.65, 3.4, 3.5 (a-d), 3.14, 3.26, 3.42 (b), 3.47, 3.50, 3.51, 3.52, 3.60, 3.64, 3.65, 3.68, 3.75, 3.78, 4.2, 4.6, 4.44, 4.53, 4.63, 4.69, 4.74, 4.77 (a), 4.78 (a), 5.7, 5.11, 5.13, 5.14, 5.15, 5.17, 5.22 (b), 5.23, 5.24, 5.25, 5.26, 5.27, 5.30, 5.31, 5.36, 5.39, 5.47, 5.49, 6.28, 6.35, 6.36, 6.41

Lady Sitwell 4.40 (b)

Mrs Richard Hayward 4.18, 4.61

Francis Sitwell 1.10, 1.24 (b), 1.25, 2.28, 2.42, 2.61, 2.62, 2.63, 2.66, 3.7, 3.9, 3.10, 3.12, 3.16, 3.17, 3.18, 3.19, 3.25, 3.32, 3.48, 3.59, 3.63, 3.69, 3.70, 3.71, 4.7, 4.11, 4.13, 4.16, 4.31, 4.33, 4.34 (a), 4.40 (a), 4.41, 4.45, 4.51, 4.52 (a), 4.57, 4.58, 4.59, 4.71, 4.73, 4.78 (d-m), 5.1, 5.8, 5.43, 5.44, 5.50 (a, c-i), 6.1, 6.2, 6.5, 6.7, 6.11 (c-d), 6.13, 6.14, 6.16, 6.17, 6.18, 6.19, 6.22, 6.23, 6.24, 6.25, 6.27, 6.29, 6.34, 6.37, 6.42, 6.43, 6.45, 6.50, 6.51 (b, d-l, n-q)

Susanna Sitwell 4.40 (a), 6.51 (m)

George Sitwell 6.30

William Sitwell 6.32

Warden and Fellows of All Souls College 4.26

Victoria Art Gallery, Bath City Council 4.30

Royal Pavilion, Art Gallery and Museum, Brighton 5.9

British Broadcasting Corporation 3.56, 3.58, 3.61, 4.75

Janet Cooper 2.31

Courtauld Institute Galleries, London (Fry Collection) 2.20

Doncaster Museums & Art Service 2.35

Master, Fellows and Scholars of Downing College 4.25

The Provost and Fellows, Eton College 2.11, 2.24, 2.69, 4.67, 5.10, 5.38

Syndics of the Fitzwilliam Museum, Cambridge 2.5, 3.35

His Honour Judge Geddes 3.27

Hamiltons Galleries Ltd 5.28

Sir Rupert Hart-Davis 2.8

Harvard University Portrait Collection, Harvard University Art Museums 4.21

Mrs F. L. Hope JP 4.32

University of Hull Art Collection 1.23

The Hulton Deutsch Collection 4.4, 4.15, 4.24, 4.77 (b), 5.29, 6.11 (b)

The Trustees of the Edward James Foundation 4.10

Jason & Rhodes 3.2, 3.3

Russel I. Kully, Los Angeles 4.5

Alberto de Lacerda 4.54, 4.72

Maggs Bros Ltd 3.55

Manchester City Art Galleries 3.28

The Mansell Collection 2.9, 2.10

David Mayou 2.12

Mercury Gallery, London 2.54

Lawrence Mynott 3.62, 4.78 (b), 6.28

Richard Nathanson, London 4.55, 4.60

National Buildings Record 1.20 (b)

National Gallery of Victoria, Melbourne, Australia 2.27

National Portrait Gallery, London 1.3, 1.4, 1.24 (a), 2.14, 2.17, 2.21, 2.23, 2.38, 2.39, 2.40, 2.45, 2.46, 2.47, 2.48, 2.50, 2.51, 2.52, 2.70, 3.1, 3.5 (f), 3.8, 3.22, 3.24, 3.30, 3.31, 3.38, 3.39, 3.40, 3.41 (a), 3.42 (c), 3.43 (a), 3.44, 3.67, 3.74, 3.76, 3.77, 4.1 (b-d), 4.8, 4.19, 4.20, 4.23, 4.27, 4.28, 4.29, 4.35, 4.43, 4.47, 4.48, 4.49, 4.50, 4.52 (b), 4.62, 4.64, 4.65, 4.78 (c), 5.3, 5.4, 5.5, 5.12, 5.20, 5.22 (a), 5.33, 5.35, 5.37, 5.46, 5.48, 6.8, 6.9 (a), 6.20, 6.33, 6.46, 6.47, 6.48, 6.49, 6.51 (a)

Michael Parkin Fine Art Limited 3.45, 6.39

John Pearson 1.26, 6.4, 6.11 (a)

Polunin Family 2.1

Private Collection 2.3, 2.7, 2.25, 2.41, 2.44, 2.59, 2.72, 3.23, 3.49, 4.68, 5.19, 5.34, 6.21, 6.31, 6.38, 6.51 (c)

William S. Reese 3.36

Bertram Rota Limited 2.67, 3.53, 4.17, 5.50 (b)

The Royal Photographic Society 2.53, 3.20

Scarborough Art Gallery, Scarborough Borough Council 2.64, 3.6

Scarborough Reference Library 1.21

Scottish National Portrait Gallery 5.41

Scottish National Gallery of Modern Art, Edinburgh 3.33

Fiona Searle 4.66

Sheffield City Art Galleries 2.22

Bob Simm 4.76

Mrs A. Kenneth Snowman 4.40 (c)

Sotheby's, London 2.73, 3.41 (b-d), 3.42 (a, d), 3.43 (b-h), 4.1 (a), 4.3, 4.12, 4.14, 4.37, 4.52 (c-f), 5.6, 5.32, 6.6, 6.9 (b), 6.10, 6.12, 6.15, 6.26

Tate Gallery, London 2.26, 3.29

Art Collection, Harry Ransom Humanities Research Center, The University of Texas at Austin 2.16, 3.34, 3.46, 3.66, 4.9, 4.36, 4.46, 5.2, 5.16

Harry Ransom Humanities Research Center, The University of Texas at Austin 3.54, 4.22, 5.18

Theatre Museum: Courtesy of the Board of Trustees of the Victoria and Albert Museum 2.2, 2.4, 2.55, 2.56, 3.21 (b), 3.37, 3.72

Ulysses Bookshop, London 2.68

Vogue, The Condé Nast Publications Limited 3.5 (e), 3.11, 4.39, 6.44

The William Walton Trust 3.15

Mrs Wendy Ward 4.42

Francis Wyndham 2.49

Lenders to the exhibition

The catalogue is divided into six chapters, each with an introductory essay followed by catalogue entries. Works are numbered within each chapter. Not all works in the exhibition have been illustrated but a complete catalogue list is given on page 220, with full details of measurements, inscriptions and lenders.

Two scrapbooks of press cuttings compiled by William Beaumont Morris, now in Francis Sitwell's collection, have been cited. These are referred to as the 'Sitwelliana' and 'Of Dame Edith Sitwell' scrapbooks.

A useful select bibliography is given in Sarah Bradford's biography, *Sacheverell Sitwell, Splendours and Miseries*, 1993.

The following abbreviations have been used throughout the catalogue:

ES	Edith Sitwell
OS	Osbert Sitwell
SS	Sacheverell Sitwell
NPG	National Portrait Gallery, London
FWGC	Sacheverell Sitwell, *For Want of the Golden City*, 1973
GM	Osbert Sitwell, *Great Morning*, 1948
LHRH	Osbert Sitwell, *Left Hand Right Hand!*, 1945
LNR	Osbert Sitwell, *Laughter in the Next Room*, 1949
NE	Osbert Sitwell, *Noble Essences*, 1950
ST	Osbert Sitwell, *The Scarlet Tree*, 1946
TCO	Edith Sitwell, *Taken Care Of, an autobiography*, 1965
Bradford	Sarah Bradford, *Sacheverell Sitwell, Splendours and Miseries*, 1993
Fifoot	Richard Fifoot, *A Bibliography of Edith, Osbert and Sacheverell Sitwell*, 1971
Glendinning	Victoria Glendinning, *Edith Sitwell, A Unicorn among Lions*, 1981
Lehmann	John Lehmann, *A Nest of Tigers, Edith, Osbert and Sacheverell Sitwell in their times*, 1968
Pearson	John Pearson, *Façades, Edith, Osbert and Sacheverell Sitwell*, 1978
Ritchie	Neil Ritchie, *Sacheverell Sitwell, an annotated and descriptive bibliography, 1916-1986*, 1987
Salter	Elizabeth Salter, *The Last Years of a Rebel, A Memoir of Edith Sitwell*, 1967

Catalogue note

An early law suit records that in 1301 Simon Sitwell was living at Ridgeway in the parish of Eckington, north-east Derbyshire. His descendants – first ironmasters, later coal owners, recently poets and authors – have lived in the area ever since. In 1540 Robert Sytwell moved to Staveley Netherthorpe, three miles to the south of Eckington, and it was he who acquired the site of Renishaw Hall, the family home. In 1625 George Sitwell, first to be described as 'of Renishaw', built a modest H-shaped manor house in the 'Pennine' style (the central nucleus of the present Hall), which he garrisoned for the King during the Civil Wars. Continually fined as a 'persistent delinquent' under Cromwell, he survived, thanks to the iron works he started that greatly enhanced the family fortunes.

The early squires of Renishaw were Whigs, quiet and scholarly country gentlemen who collected books and pictures, improved the estate, amassed rents from farms and royalties from iron, and married heiresses. By the end of the eighteenth century the male line had come to an end. Francis, fourth owner of Renishaw and the oldest of three bachelor brothers, was succeeded by the younger of two unmarried first cousins, William, who had grown rich through commerce in the City and trade with the American colonies. William loved music and the theatre and lived mainly at Bath and in London, where he indulged in favourite philanthropical and charitable activities. In time he adopted his orphaned nephew Francis, son of his sister Catherine and her husband Jonathan Hurt. In 1777 Francis Hurt succeeded to the Renishaw estates and a fortune of £500,000, and changed his surname to Sitwell.

The earlier Sitwells, worthy and relatively long-established, were followed by three generations who lived hard and died young, for the Hurts brought new blood with a wilder streak. Scholarly squires of Stuart and Georgian times were followed by great sportsmen, and Whigs by Tories with Jacobite sympathies; vast sums were spent on building and entertaining, and eventually the money ran out.

Francis Hurt Sitwell, as he is usually known, inherited his uncle's taste for music, and played both flute and violin. He married Mary, the 'Beauty of Bath', daughter of Canon Warneford – one of eight brothers, all clergymen. Later he inherited further large estates in Northumberland, Shropshire and south Yorkshire, which he parcelled out among his three sons. In 1792 he sold the ironworks and died the following year.

His eldest son, Sitwell Sitwell, was a man of exceptional energies. He married twice, had several mistresses, and kept a racing stud and hunters and hounds that once chased and killed two Royal Bengal tigers which had escaped from a menagerie in Sheffield. He added vast wings to the old Hall, built the classical stables that now house the new museum and arts centre, and created various follies in and around the park. In 1808 he added the ballroom and entertained the Prince Regent. He died, however, in 1811, aged only forty-one, and was succeeded by his only son, the 'first' Sir George.

The trustees sold the racing stud but Sir George kept the hunters and hounds. He married Susan, eldest sister of Archibald Campbell Tait – first of many Scotsmen to become Archbishop of Canterbury. Encouraged to go to Scotland for the shooting, Sir George leased Birkhall and later Balmoral, before Queen Victoria 'discovered' the Highlands.

Disaster struck! Farm rents had fallen, a solicitor robbed Sir George of a fortune, and he fought and lost an expensive election; finally the Sheffield bank failed. Much of the estate and contents of the house were sold, and Sir George's income reduced from £12,000 to £700 a year. He died in 1853.

Sir Reresby, third baronet, succeeded at the age of thirty-two. Overwhelmed by worry and misfortune, the former carefree young Life Guards officer died like his grandfather aged forty-one, in 1862. His widow, Louisa Lucy, fourth daughter of Colonel the Honourable Henry Hely-Hutchinson, a veteran of Waterloo, had intense religious inclinations but sound business sense. Her wise stewardship during the long minority of her son, helped by discovery of coal in large quantities below the southern fringes of the park, restored the family fortunes for the benefit of the 'eccentric' Sir George, creator of the garden and lake at Renishaw and father of the literary trio to whom this exhibition is devoted.

Reresby Sitwell

Introduction: A Brief Family History

5.22

Entrance to the Wilderness, Renishaw

By Bill Brandt, 1945

DH. Lawrence remarked of the Sitwells that their childhood had been 'as isolated as if they had lived on a desert island'. Nowhere was this isolation more marked than at Renishaw, their ancestral Derbyshire home, which had such a formative effect on their artistic development. They spent only a few months of the year at Renishaw and the remaining time at Wood End, their home in Scarborough; but the great house, which Anthony Powell described as 'melancholy, even sinister', its gardens and the surrounding countryside, represented a brooding presence in their early lives as powerful as that of Manderley in Daphne du Maurier's *Rebecca*. 'I was very fond of it and rather frightened of it', Sacheverell, youngest of the trio, wrote. 'There was something of the extinct monster about it.'

The house itself, three-storied, grey and battlemented, dominates the crest of a hill above a deep valley to the north-east of Chesterfield. Sitwells had lived in the area for some three centuries before the Cavalier George Sitwell built the original manor and moved there with his bride in 1625. He established an ironworks nearby and by the late 1600s the Sitwells were the principal producers of iron nails in the world. In the eighteenth century, having inherited a fortune and land from a cousin, the family became sporting squires with their own racehorses and packs of hounds. One of them, Sitwell Sitwell, embellished the house with a grand dining-room and drawing-room, and a ballroom specially designed for the reception of the Prince of Wales. Such extravagant hospitality did not go unnoticed, and he was made a baronet as a result. The sporting Sitwells came to grief in 1846, when the first Sir George lost all his money in a bank crash. Renishaw was closed and an auction held of much of the contents. And so it remained, haunted by ghosts, until inherited by Sir George, father of the trio, in 1862, at the age of two.

It was the discovery of coal in the park that enabled Sir George's careful mother to restore the family fortunes and provide her son with the wherewithal to create the lake and classical gardens and furnish the house with elaborate baroque furniture. The Arcadian surroundings were to some extent an illusion, however. The mining villages of Eckington and Renishaw were hidden from sight by majestic trees, but the façade of the house and the lawns were blackened by smuts from the coal-mine stacks. Industrial Sheffield with its steel blast furnaces was only six miles away, and two railway lines ran through the valley. Sir George liked to pretend that these aesthetically embarrassing objects did not exist. 'There is nothing between us and the Locker-Lampsons', he loftily told Evelyn Waugh.

At Renishaw the past was always present. Ghosts inhabited one empty wing but did not, however, confine themselves to that part of the house. Resenting the intrusion of the family, who normally occupied the house only during the months of August and September, they would venture out to frighten guests in bedrooms already rendered sepulchral by Sir George's baroque four-poster beds with their swagging curtains and dusty plumes. Guests were warned to hug the wall as they descended the principal stairs in case a malevolent phantom pushed them over. A gentler ghost, that of a boy drowned more than a century before, would appear in ladies' bedrooms and kiss their hands as a smell of damp river weed pervaded the room. The sinister atmosphere noted by Powell was enhanced by the fact that there was no electric light; the long winding passages were lit by flickering oil lamps while the old house creaked at night.

Surrounded by ghosts and portraits of their ancestors, it was hardly surprising that the Sitwell children should have been imbued with a strong sense of the past and infected with the ancestor worship which was their father's religion. They could not but be aware of Sitwell children who had lived in the house over the past 300 years. The rocking horse, which stood outside the nursery and featured in Sacheverell's first childhood memory (when he was photographed riding it aged about two), appeared in an 1826 water-colour of Sitwell children by Octavius Oakley. One of the finest paintings in the house, which hung in the dining-room, was a group portrait by John Singleton Copley painted in 1787, showing Sitwell children (including Sitwell Sitwell, the first baronet) playing in a sunlit room (fig. 1).

The childhood memories of Edith, Osbert and Sacheverell were far from sunlit, principally due to the oppressive atmosphere engendered by their father, the eccentric Sir George, and by the state of war which existed between him and his beautiful feckless

Childhood at Renishaw

1.19
The Sitwell Family
By John Singer Sargent, 1900

Imperial Portrait.

George one of the great comic figures of English literature, neither his personality nor his intellect were negligible. He did well both at Eton and at Oxford (which was more than could be said of either of his sons), and became famous at the age of twenty for exposing a fake medium at a spiritualist séance. He represented Scarborough as a Conservative MP from 1885 to 1886 and from 1892 to 1895; owned a local newspaper and a private printing press; was chairman of the *Saturday Review* when Frank Harris was editor; a member of the Statistical Society; a borough magistrate; and a colonel of local volunteers. In 1900, after a nervous breakdown, he spent nine years travelling extensively in Italy, observing Renaissance gardens, and published the results of his observations in his master-work, *On the Making of Gardens*, in 1909. He blazed the trail which his sons later followed to the southern baroque towns of Puglia (counting eighty-eight mosquito bites on one forearm during a night spent on the Gargano Peninsula), and introduced Osbert and Sacheverell to Venice. In 1909 he acquired, for £4,000, the vast medieval castle of Montegufoni in Tuscany, an Italian counterpart to the ancestral grandeurs of Renishaw. Sir George's taste – Italianate, at times impeccable, at others tending towards the florid – influenced both Osbert and Sacheverell, although they liked to represent themselves as springing, an unexpected flowering of genius, from a long line of hard-headed sporting squires.

Sir George's passion for ancestry and consequent dynastic ambition was to lead to his own personal downfall and the unhappiness of his children. He saw himself, according to Osbert, as 'the great Sir George', not only the embellisher of Renishaw but the founder of a dynasty which would raise the Sitwell name to new heights. To further this dynastic project he searched for a wife with the same scientific care which he exercised on other subjects – one eminently suitable candidate was rejected by him because of the shape of her nose. He found what he thought would be the ideal mate in the Honourable Ida Denison. She was beautiful, with a fashionably straight nose. Her father was extremely rich (with rumours of illegitimate royal descent through Lady Conyngham, mistress of George IV, whose wealthy though plebeian brother had left her son all his money) and her mother

wife, Lady Ida.

The fact that Sir George had succeeded to the baronetcy at the age of two deeply impressed him, and he was only too eager to impress this upon others. Aged only four, the infant snob replied to the question 'Who are you?' with the reply: 'I am Sir George Sitwell, baronet. I am four years old and the youngest baronet in England.' There was more to Sir George, however, than mere snobbery. He was a man of taste, intellectual energy and creative talent who influenced his children more than they cared to admit. Although his eldest son, Osbert, created in Sir

1.2
Sir George Sitwell
Attributed to Canon Frederick Harford, issued by
A & G Taylor, 1876

impeccably aristocratic (daughter of the 7th Duke of Beaufort and therefore descended from the Plantagenet kings of England). He married her, although she was almost uneducated, only seventeen, and they had, according to Sacheverell, 'only met twice at luncheon'. The result was disastrous. Lady Ida, 'the poor young creature, married against her will into a kind of slave-bondage', as Edith put it, ran back to her family after a few days but was ruthlessly returned to her husband. The pleasures of sex did not feature on the long list of Sir George's interests: procreation was the aim. In order to achieve the best possible results Sir George would read an improving book, announce 'Ida I am ready' before indulging in the deliberate act, and the procreation of another Sitwell genius would take place.

Unfortunately for Sir George, neither his wife nor his children were to prove ideal partners in his dynastic plans. Lady Ida's extravagant, self-indulgent Denison blood was uppermost in her character and was to lead to anguish and a retreat into eccentricity for her husband, and a traumatic experience for her children. She was cruel to Edith, whose intelligence and independence both puzzled and irritated her, but indulgent to

1.18
Renishaw Hall from the South
By an unknown photographer, *c.* 1910

both her sons who, in their youth at least, adored her. Sacheverell described her as:

> Tall and thin, and dark and beautiful, with straight Grecian nose, small mouth, dark brown eyes, and little shell-like ear, set close to her head ... and a straight thin neck that was exquisite in its pose upon her shoulders. She had a wonderful way of carrying herself and, thereby, an extraordinary distinction ... Her character ... was a compound of natural high spirits, and a sort of palace bred or aristocratic helplessness, as of one who was made ... to wear gloves indoors in order that [she] should have white hands, was scarcely allowed to put foot to the ground, and could not add up ...

To Sir George, who had a positive passion for double-entry book-keeping, this last deficiency in his wife was one of her most irritating characteristics. The thought of debt and a repetition of the disaster of 1846 was a recurrent nightmare which Ida's inherited extravagance kept constantly alive; to his chagrin, Sir George detected signs of the same failing in his children.

Sir George and Lady Ida had nothing whatsoever in common. Where she was gregarious and pleasure loving, he was austere and solitary. Where his humour was heavy-handed and ironic, hers was witty and quick. She lay late in bed every morning in a bedroom heavy with the scent of discarded gardenias and tuberoses, reading French novels, newspapers and letters, or playing patience on a flat-folding leather card-tray. She was addicted to cards and would play bridge endlessly every afternoon she could. Sir George meanwhile would be shut up in his study, which smelt of strong Egyptian cigarettes (he smoked twenty or thirty a day), reading scientific journals and indulging his multifarious intellectual interests by keeping his notebooks up to date. These might be headed 'Rotherham under Cromwell', 'Court Formalities at Constantinople', 'The Correct Use of Seaweed as an Article of Diet' or 'The Sacheverell Pedigrees'. According to Osbert, he contemplated publishing a history of the fork and, having experimented with a variety of positions designed to combat insomnia, an illustrated pamphlet entitled 'The Twenty-Seven Postures of Sir George R. Sitwell'.

The gulf between husband and wife reflected the utterly different ethos of their respective families. Lady Ida's parents were friends of the Prince of Wales and at the top of the social tree. Her father, created 1st Earl of Londesborough in 1887, was the prototype of an Edwardian 'swell'. He spent his enormous fortune lavishly, dropping £30,000 in 1873 on a musical extravaganza called *Babil and Bijou*, and Pavlova danced at a private party he gave at his huge Regent's Park house, St Dunstan's. Like the rest of the Marlborough House set surrounding the Prince of Wales, he was a sporting philistine, fond of actresses, racehorses and enormous shooting parties; and Lady Ida enjoyed pointing out the superiority of her father's social position and the magnificence of his way of life to the detriment of her husband's. 'A baronet', she would say, 'is the lowest form of life', and would boast of the way her father could spend a million pounds without noticing. Her mother, Lady Londesborough, was only too aware of her ancient royal blood. Arrogant and, like her daughter, given to violent rages, she lived, according to Edith, 'in luxury like a gilded and irascible wasp in a fine ripe nectarine'. Her granddaughter resembled her, 'beaked like a harpy' with 'queer-roofed Byzantine eyes'; both Edith and Sacheverell looked like the images on Plantagenet tombs. After their grandfather died in 1900 of psittacosis, probably caught from one of the exotic birds of which his wife was so fond, Edith and Osbert and later, briefly, Sacheverell, spent their Christmases with their Uncle Francis, now the 2nd Earl, and his wife Grace ('Aunt Gracie'), daughter of the Earl of Westmorland. They stayed at Blankney, the Londesborough country house in Lincolnshire.

Despite their own sporting ancestry, the young Sitwells loathed these occasions; they never rode, and detested the hunting and shooting set. The women spent their time changing their clothes in the intervals of vast and interminable meals while the men passed the day slaughtering everything that moved in the surrounding countryside. Osbert and Edith named them 'the Golden Horde', hating them as insensitive philistine snobs.

Nothing could have been more different from Sir George's family. His widowed mother, Louisa, Lady Sitwell, born a Hely-Hutchinson, was the epitome of Victorian piety. 'My grand-mother', Sacheverell wrote of her, 'was a lady of much character,

1.7

Lady Ida Sitwell

By Sir William Blake Richmond, 1888

but of pious proclivities as powerful and tyrannical as any form of drug addiction.' She and her spinster daughter, Florence, lived surrounded by curates, elderly servants and ancient dogs; their idea of a treat was a visit to Lambeth Palace to see their relation, Archibald Campbell Tait, Archbishop of Canterbury. (Edith unkindly referred to them as 'Lambeth Palace Lounge Lizards'.)

Apart from prayer, Lady Sitwell's pleasures were flowers and gardens; at Wood End, her house in Scarborough, the conservatory was filled with huge palms, orchids and exotic birds. Like many women of her age and class she was a hypochondriac, a tendency which reached almost manic proportions in her son and was passed on to her grandchildren. Her husband's early death, attributed to his passion for shooting regardless of his health, was held up as a dreadful example. As a result Sir George and his children were pathologically afraid of colds; to give a cold to a Sitwell was regarded as a heinous crime, its perpetrator always identified and pilloried. Osbert even contributed an essay on 'The History of the Cold' as an appendix to one of his volumes of autobiography.

Sir George possessed none of his mother's religious enthusiasm

(he was a resolute atheist) but he did inherit her dominating disposition and the acute business sense which had enabled her to rescue the family fortunes during his long minority.

The two families did not and could not mix amicably. The Londesboroughs liked to mock Sir George's aristocratic pretensions and his penny-pinching ways. The publication of *On the Making of Gardens* finished him in their eyes. He had betrayed his class; a 'gentleman' did not write books, still less publish them. Sir George for his part, constantly aware of the abyss into which his family had once peered, was ever watchful for the reappearance of his wife's family's financial irresponsibility. He did not have long to wait; Lady Ida's naïvety and longing for 'fun' on the scale which her family enjoyed, and which her husband's carefulness denied her, soon began to get her into trouble. She gathered round her a collection of female toadies only too willing to flatter an earl's daughter. These women, nicknamed contemptuously 'the fun brigade' by Osbert and Edith, battened on to her; mischievously, and to curry favour, they encouraged her to despise her husband's frugality and his literary and aesthetic interests. She gave them clothes and jewellery, and

1.11
Edith Sitwell
By W. D. Brigham, Scarborough, *c.* 1890

1.14
Osbert Sitwell
By Cromack, Scarborough, *c.* 1896

1.15
Sacheverell Sitwell
By Cromack, Scarborough, 1899

ran up debts at bridge while he became increasingly solitary, eccentric and paranoid. In his longing to be known to family history as 'the great Sir George', he indulged his passion for embellishing first Renishaw and then Montegufoni (in 1911 he sold the family Perugino to Pierpont Morgan to finance his architectural dreams). Temporary wooden towers were built at vantage points in the Renishaw grounds so that Sir George, whose day began at sunrise according to Renaissance precepts, could view the prospects through his telescope and order improvements. He created the garden terraces, imported the Italian statuary to grace them, and made the lake and island in the valley floor below the house. One day, walking with Osbert in the grounds, he indicated a site and said: 'And here, Osbert, I intend to have two great erections.'

In the spring of 1900 Sir George commissioned John Singer Sargent to paint a family group, and thereby immortalise the great patron, his beautiful aristocratic wife and the dynasty, represented by his three children (1.19). After exhibition at the Royal Academy, where it was admired by Sergei Diaghilev among others, the painting was intended to be hung at Renishaw as a companion to the Copley portrait (fig. 1). The symbolism was there for all to see: Sir George (who seldom rode) wore polished riding boots, an allusion to his sporting ancestry, while Lady Ida was the picture of the dutiful wife, elegantly arranging flowers in a silver bowl (something she would never have done; at Renishaw as in all grand houses the flowers were arranged by the head gardener). The family was posed against carefully chosen Sitwell heirlooms brought down from Renishaw to the artist's Chelsea studio. These included one of the panels of Brussels tapestry, and the commode designed by Robert Adam and made by Chippendale and Haig for the marriage of Francis Hurt Sitwell in 1776. As the elegant projection of an image, the painting was a triumph – the dominant father, his hand resting protectively on his daughter's shoulder, the beautiful wife absorbed in her domestic task, the heir and his brother playing contentedly – but as a representation of a happy family it was pure fantasy.

Edith later described herself as 'white with fury and contempt, and indignant that my father held me in what he thought was a tender paternal embrace'. Tenderness was something which she never experienced from either of her parents. Two days before she was born a violent row had taken place between her Londesborough grandparents in her mother's bedroom; her grandmother had discovered that the emeralds which her husband had recently been showering upon her were guilt offerings for his affairs with showgirls. This, said Edith, precipitated her birth on 7 September 1887, tactlessly in the middle of the grand luncheon of the Scarborough Cricket Festival of which her grandfather was patron. 'I was unpopular with my parents from the moment of my birth', she wrote. 'I was in disgrace for being a female, and worse, as I grew older, it was obvious that I was not going to conform to my father's standard of feminine beauty.'

Edith, 'Little E' as she was then known, had no doubts, however, about her intellectual destiny. Aged four, when asked by one of her mother's friends what she was going to be when she grew up, the precocious child replied 'a genius', and was promptly removed from the drawing-room and sent to bed in disgrace. Rejected by her parents, she endured a lonely childhood. For comfort she turned to birds: a puffin with a wooden leg, a baby owl which had fallen from its nest and the lone Renishaw peacock. She soon learnt the fickleness of love: when the Sitwells bought 'Peaky' a mate he lost interest in Edith. In her loneliness she ran away from home but, having no money and being incapable of buttoning her own boots, she was soon recaptured and returned. Later she was subjected in the schoolroom to a 'devoted, loving, peering, inquisitive, interfering, stultifying middle-class suffocation, on the chance that I would become "just like everybody else".' To this mental torture were added orthopaedic structures designed to straighten her spine and even her nose, blighting a period which she called her 'Bastille existence'.

All efforts to make Edith 'just like everybody else' were doomed to failure. Every Saturday afternoon she was 'kept in' as a punishment for her refusal to learn by heart *The Boy stood on the Burning Deck* (she would not pay lip-service to 'this idiotic episode'). Her poetic taste was already formed; by the age of thirteen she had memorised the whole of Pope's *The Rape of the Lock* – 'the only poem of genius to be found in Wood End'. Its effect on her was seminal, as Edith wrote in *Taken Care Of*:

> From the thin, glittering, occasionally shadowed, airy, ever-varying texture of that miracle of poetry, the instinct was instilled into me that not only structure, but also texture, are parents of rhythm in poetry...

Edith's passionate love of poetry was stimulated by the arrival in 1904 of Helen Rootham as her governess. Helen was a lifeline, a companion and protector who was interested in music and the arts. She was a gifted pianist; from the moment she arrived, Osbert recalled, 'the music of Chopin and Schumann, Brahms and Debussy, flowered as a constant background to our hours of leisure, and became associated at Renishaw with every expanse of water, every vista seen through green trees'. She not only coached Edith, who had musical talent, at the piano, she also introduced her to the French symbolist poets, to Verlaine, Rimbaud and Baudelaire, widening her poetic horizon beyond the writers she already knew and loved – Shakespeare, Swinburne, Shelley and Keats. It was Helen who was to provide Edith with her eventual escape route: with Helen as chaperone, Edith was allowed to go to London. Her first, temporary, flight took place in 1913; a year later she left for good.

Edith's love of poetry and music greatly influenced her brothers, even though they were so much younger than she was. As Sacheverell later recalled in 'Serenade to a Sister':

> You could read a poem, and inspire one to poetry
> By the inflection of your voice ...

Osbert, the longed-for heir born in December 1892, was psychologically the most complex of the trio and, from Sir George's point of view, the most disappointing, dashing all his hopes for a glorious proconsular dynasty of Sitwells. After his death a furious note was found among his papers indicating the depth of his resentment against his eldest son: 'There *is* no such person as Captain Osbert Sitwell.' Osbert adored his mother and admired what he called the 'Bourbon' magnificence and extravagance of the Londesboroughs. Increasingly he was to become his mother's champion in the deepening war between his parents which began as he reached adolescence. Mother and son would collaborate on 'teases'. Playing on his father's well-known loathing of colour in the garden, Osbert would ostentatiously cultivate a rhododendron of a particularly flamboyant hue, while his mother arranged for a vulgar rustic pergola to be erected, as a 'surprise' for her husband, and smothered it in bright, suburban pink roses of a variety which Sir George particularly abominated. Sent to Eton in his father's footsteps, Osbert stated that he liked Eton apart from the boys and the masters, the work and the games. Later his entry in *Who's Who* read: 'Educated during holidays from Eton.' Not surprisingly he did badly there, thus falling at the first step on the path to glory.

Osbert's closest relationship, despite the difference in their ages, was with his brother Sacheverell, born in November 1897. Sacheverell had an altogether easier row to hoe, as far as his parents were concerned, than either of his elder siblings. Since he was not the immediate heir, less was expected of him by his father than of Osbert. Until her increasing money troubles drove her to drink, Sachie, as he was known by his family, loved his mother passionately. Their relationship, he wrote, was one of companionship: they were on the same level. As a child he was happy, open and affectionate; in Scarborough he would embarrass his parents by inviting strangers in off the streets to lunch with them. At Renishaw he sat at Edith's feet as she read poetry to him, and the three of them would wander in the gardens and the woods absorbing a deep love of the countryside which never left him.

Looking back, Sacheverell wrote of his childhood at Renishaw in extremely gloomy vein. He described it as 'a long dark tunnel', in which the only 'beacon of hope' was provided by the Copley portrait, evidence that the possibility of happiness did exist. This was certainly exaggerated as far as his early years were concerned. He hated being sent away from home to school, writing of 'sad partings at sunset' when he and Osbert would bury personal mementoes under the mulberry tree and swear eternal loyalty to each other. At Eton, where he was initially unpopular and lonely, he fared better than Osbert. He spent hours in the library devouring books on subjects which interested him and overspending his meagre allowance on his avant-garde interests: magazines and books devoted to the Russian ballet, Japanese

prints and gramophone records.

For the Sitwell children, as for many upper-class children at the time, servants were the mainstay of their lives. Nurse Edith Davis, described by Edith's biographer as 'the one wholly reliable and affectionate adult in Edith's life', remained with them until Sacheverell was four. Davis was a countrywoman and taught the children the names of the wild flowers in the Derbyshire countryside. Osbert wrote of her that placidity and a comforting belief in the beneficence of God and man were her chief characteristics. 'Her wisdom was of the blood, not of the mind, and she possessed a great understanding of young people, young animals, and of birds and wild flowers.' She remained a warm, stable presence, unruffled by the storms of Lady Ida's sudden fits of rage or the icy remoteness of Sir George.

The largest place in their lives was filled by Henry Moat, Sir George's butler-valet, a huge Yorkshireman whose bulk matched his great height. Edith described him as 'an enormous purple man like a benevolent hippopotamus' with a 'voice like a fog-horn endowed with splendour'. He came of a long line of whaling captains from Whitby and had eighteen brothers all as large and strong as himself. He acted as a buffer between his employers and

Fig. 1
The Sitwell Children
By John Singleton Copley, 1787
Oil on canvas, 156.2 x 180.3
Collection of Sir Reresby Sitwell Bt

their children, telling Edith, 'You'd better run, Miss Edith. Her ladyship is in one of her states and is looking for you.' Osbert and Sacheverell liked to listen to Moat in the pantry, which was his kingdom, imitating some guest whom they particularly disliked, or telling stories of the sea and singing shanties in his deep bass bellow. Henry's was an earthy presence; he was fond of drink and women and notorious for getting Lady Ida's maids pregnant. He enjoyed teaching Sir George's sons the kind of worldly wisdom they would certainly not learn from their father, as he later wrote to Osbert after reading a cutting about his famous entry in *Who's Who* ('Educated during holidays from Eton'):

> Well, Sir, I make bold to claim some of that, because whether you were at Scarboro', Renishaw or abroad, if you or Master Sachie wanted to know anything about things on the earth, the sea, or under the earth or in the air above, you generally came to me, even when you had a tutor, and often the tutors came too.

Years later, Evelyn Waugh, when a guest at Renishaw in 1930, was surprised at the terms of familiarity on which the Sitwells lived with their servants. Moat's relationship with Sir George as described by Osbert was one of the great comic turns:

> He and my father [were] mutually critical and at the same time appreciative. My father always referred to Henry as 'the Great man', and Henry, for his part, mixed with feelings of the utmost disrespect, cherished towards him as well, sentiments approaching veneration. He realised his quality, both mental and physical, and that he was an uncommon, if difficult, character.

Moat served Sir George for forty-two years, with periods of absence usually occasioned by some particularly eccentric behaviour on the part of the baronet. 'Henry,' Sir George remarked one day, 'I've a new idea – knife-handles should be made of condensed milk!' 'Yes, Sir George,' the disgusted Moat replied patiently, 'but what if the cat gets at them?'

Another household figure at Renishaw was Sacheverell's tutor, Major A. B. Brockwell, who figures as Colonel Fantock in Edith's eponymous poem about their childhood at Renishaw, as Fantock again in Sachie's autobiographical *All Summer in a Day* and as

Major Viburne in Osbert's *Tales My Father Taught Me*. Osbert and Moat despised Brockwell, an impoverished military man whom they regarded as an old fake. 'This paladin was disinterred from time to time and chartered by my father to oversee the household, muddle the accounts and misorder the food. Major Viburne posed as a warrior and a gourmet but in both instances his experience was limited', wrote Osbert. Sacheverell genuinely loved him, and both he and Edith left sympathetic descriptions of him. In her poem, 'Colonel Fantock', Edith writes of his gallant struggles with poverty and old age:

Old military ghost with mayfly whiskers,

Poor harmless creature, blown by the cold wind,

Boasting of unseen unreal victories ...

Sacheverell watched the old man dressing for dinner at Renishaw, carefully unwrapping his ancient clothes from layers of tissue paper: 'this evening suit that he tended so carefully was the symbol of life, and if he were forced to give it up, then all the pretensions on his part that made living endurable on such straitened means would break down, and he would be as dead as anything, save the actual touch of death, could make him'.

'Colonel Fantock' was an example of Edith's myth-making skills. In it she wove fantasy portraits of herself and her brothers as they walked in the sunlit gardens of Renishaw:

But Dagobert and Peregrine and I

Were children then; we walked like shy gazelles

Among the music of the thin flower-bells ...

All day within the sweet and ancient gardens

He [Fantock] had my childish self for audience -

Whose body flat and strange, whose pale straight hair

Made me appear as though I had been drowned ...

And Dagobert my brother whose large strength,

Great body and grave beauty still reflect

The Angevin dead kings from whom we spring;

And sweet as the young tender winds that stir

In thickets when the earliest flower-bells sing

Upon the boughs, was his just character;

And Peregrine the youngest with a naïve

Shy grace like a faun's, whose slant eyes seemed

The warm green light beneath eternal boughs.

His hair was like the fronds of feathers, life

In him was changing ever, springing fresh

As the dark sounds of birds ... the furry warmth

And purring sound of fires was in his voice

Which never failed to warm and comfort me.

The image, despite obvious absurdities (no one who knew Osbert well could have described him as 'sweet' or his Hanoverian looks as 'the grave beauty' of Angevin kings), was powerful and, for a time at least, convincing. Anthony Powell, who knew them in the late twenties, described them as 'pale, attenuated courtiers from a medieval tapestry'.

'We all have the remote air of a legend', Edith had written in 'Fantock'. Remoteness from life was a characteristic of the Sitwells in their personae as well as their work. Both Edith and Sacheverell wrote of being 'outside life', observers of a curious pageant whose emotions they did not share. This remoteness stemmed from the circumstances of their childhood, their isolation and their sense of existing as beings apart. Sacheverell's descriptions of local miners whom they encountered while out on walks are incurious, dismissive: 'Soon, like smuts in the air, they had drifted away with their curious hob-nailed, lumbering walk.' The miners' children had watched in amazement as the three tall Sitwells plucked blackberries from the tops of bushes which they could not reach, but once these children had disappeared from view and their 'shrill sharp voices' could no longer be heard, 'they were out of the world altogether, underneath the earth, perhaps, like mushrooms before the summer nights' warm rain'. The realities of these people's existence were of absolutely no interest. The sights and sounds, trees and wild flowers of the Derbyshire countryside seemed infinitely more real. 'I lived in my green world of growth, companioned by the animals and the plants', Edith wrote of her Renishaw childhood. The Arcadian woods and gardens at Renishaw were also a source of poetic inspiration to Sacheverell, one to which he returned again and again until the end of his life in poems like 'Derbyshire Bluebells', 'The Lime Avenue', or 'The Eckington Woods'.

The Sitwells were attracted to the exotic rather than the

mundane. Things had to be extraordinary, beautiful, mad or macabre. Their own most un-ordinary family represented a hermetic world in which their baroque imaginations ran rampant, and the atmospheric old house – its furnishings, some shabby, some magnificent – were all imbued with significance. It was a world in which reality had very little place and myth became reality.

Among the objects in the house which influenced the children most were the five fabulous panels of Brussels tapestry hanging in the drawing-room and ballroom. These attracted them far more than any of the hunting or racing scenes favoured by their sporting ancestors. They represented, Sacheverell wrote, 'a world of suavity and opulence ... elephants and black slaves, bell-hung pagodas and clipped hornbeams ... clouds tacking like fleets of sailing-ships ... terraces with pots of orange trees ... and continual fountain jets'. This world lived in the children's imagination more vividly than the huddled stone miners' cottages in the valley or the prim terraces of Scarborough.

By 1910 when Edith was twenty-three, Osbert eighteen and Sacheverell thirteen, dark clouds had begun to mass on the Renishaw horizon. The following summer Lady Ida's debts amounted to £2,000, a sum which she was quite unable to pay yet which she nonetheless struggled to keep from her husband. Since Sir George's return from his extensive travels in Italy in 1909, the marital relationship had become increasingly strained, with Sir George's eccentricity and remoteness from his family ever more marked. Lady Ida, who had reached the perilous age of forty in 1909, turned to alcohol in her boredom and despair.

The children thought only of escape from the tyranny of their father and the violent mood swings of their mother. Edith now had the support of Helen Rootham and in 1913 was to make her first escape to London. Osbert was in the 11th Hussars and soon to join the Guards. Sacheverell, up at Eton since the autumn of 1911, was left to bear the brunt of holidays with his parents mostly alone, writing to Osbert of 'these 2 basilisks Father & Mother. Collectively & in practice I hate them'.

In a naïve effort to help his mother extricate herself from her financial difficulties, Osbert had unwittingly introduced her to the instrument of her final disgrace. This was Julian Osgood Field, a well-born American with a shady past of which Osbert, dazzled by Field's acquaintance with Proust and other figures of the Parisian *haute-monde*, knew nothing. Field, an experienced confidence trickster (who, unknown to Osbert, had served three months in prison for forgery in 1901 and was an undischarged bankrupt), ensnared Lady Ida with promises of cash in return for easy social introductions. Foolish and frantic, Lady Ida fell in with his plans, embroiling in the process some of Osbert's fellow officers, and young Yorkshiremen with expectations. The first of a series of lawsuits involving her began in 1912 and continued over the following years. Sir George rescued her once, paying off her debts to the trustees of one of her victims, but finally and disastrously he refused to pay what she owed to the heirs of the money-lender with whom Field had involved her, on the grounds that Field had been convicted of fraud and should suffer the consequences. The worldly-wise Londesboroughs pleaded with him to settle; self-righteously he would not budge. The result was that in March 1915, while Osbert was in the trenches (from which he was given leave to attend his mother's case) and Sachie at Eton, Lady Ida was convicted of fraud and sentenced to a period of detention in Holloway. The headlines blared: 'Earl's Daughter – horrible fraud'.

For the Sitwell children their mother's sentence was traumatic. The wreck of their parents' marriage had resulted in the ultimate and public disgrace. Faced with the condemnation and sneers both of the middle classes and 'the Golden Horde', the three young Sitwells formed what Osbert dubbed a 'closed corporation', shield to shield against the outside world and, indeed, against their parents, the source of the disgrace. The pathetic marital situation was to be concealed, the mini-tragedy turned into a running comedy act, expressive of the currently fashionable war of the Young against the Old. More importantly and publicly, the philistines who had condemned their mother had to be confronted and routed. The Londesborough women and 'the fun brigade', who had jeered at books and even at Sargent, should be confronted with the War poets and Picasso. The three Sitwells, standing shoulder to shoulder, resolved to take up the pen as a sword in the battle against the philistine.

Sarah Bradford

1.1

Lady Sitwell with Florence and Sir George
By George du Maurier, *c.* 1881

Sir George Sitwell succeeded to his father Sir
Reresby's title in 1862, aged two. 'The youngest
baronet in England' and his sister Florence were
brought up in Scarborough by their mother, Lady
Sitwell (née Louisa Lucy Hely-Hutchinson), and
made only occasional visits to the ancestral home.
It was her careful economies, however, that laid
the foundations for a revival in the family finances
and enabled Sir George to return to Renishaw.

A pervasive and at times straitening evangelical
piety characterised the household of Lady Sitwell.
In later life it took so strong a hold on Florence
that hopes of a prospective suitor were dashed
when Lady Sitwell reported her daughter 'so
much taken up with heavenly things that she
could not gain her attention'.[1] Sir George's youth
was spent in a freer spirit of intellectual pursuit,
immune to the religious atmosphere surrounding
him despite his mother's best endeavours and
frequent visits to his great-uncle, Archbishop Tait
of Canterbury. Edith, much loved as a child by
her grandmother and aunt, wrote in later life that
'both ladies smelt faintly of long-used prayer-
books and the red cloth of hassocks'.[2]

The drawing by the *Punch* cartoonist and
illustrator George du Maurier (1834–1896) shows
the Sitwells in the conservatory at Wood End at
some time before Sir George's marriage; Sir
George is wearing the blazer of the Hovingham
cricket club. Edith, describing the drawing in her
autobiography, did not miss the occasion to scoff:
'My father was dressed as a cricketer and was
carrying a bat. He never played cricket, but it was
obvious from the drawing that he was, for some
reason, inseparable from the bat, and that he had
just returned from a match in which the triumph
was his alone'.[3] Du Maurier probably met the
Sitwells while he and his family were on holiday
in Whitby. He later became a great admirer of
Sir George's wife, Lady Ida, and used her as the
model for several illustrations in his novel *Peter
Ibbetson* (1895).

1. Quoted in LHRH, p. 158
2. TCO, p. 62
3. *Ibid.*, p. 28 [Sir George *did* play cricket, however.]

1.2

Sir George Sitwell
Attributed to Canon Frederick Harford, issued by
A & G Taylor, 1876
(illustrated on page 14)

Sir George's sister Florence noted in her diary in
1876: 'In the afternoon I sat out in the garden
with Mother, while George went to be
photographed in a suit of armour by Canon
Harford'.[1] Although he may have been
photographed on other occasions wearing armour,
it seems likely that this is the photograph to which
Florence refers. Canon Harford, a Minor Canon
of Westminster, may have been one of Lady
Sitwell's numerous ecclesiastical acquaintants
and his amateur photograph would have been issued
by A & G Taylor as an Imperial-sized print for
the family to distribute.

1. Quoted in H. Bridgeman and E. Drury, *The British Eccentric*, 1975, pp. 51-2

1.3

**Archibald Campbell Tait, Archbishop
of Canterbury**
By James Jacques Tissot ('Coïde'), 1869

Archbishop Tait (1811–1882) was the youngest
brother of Sir George's grandmother. Sir George's
guardian and the flagship of Lady Sitwell's clerical
world, he succeeded Dr Arnold as headmaster of
Rugby and served as Dean of Carlisle and Bishop
of London before becoming Archbishop of
Canterbury in 1869. Admired as a fair-minded
and statesmanlike administrator, he suffered a
cataleptic seizure (brought on by overwork) in
November 1869 and this caricature, published in
Vanity Fair, was accompanied by an encomium on
his good works and thanksgiving for his restored
health. Osbert bore him a posthumous grudge for
habitually gargling with the Renishaw 1815
vintage port to disinfect his sore throat.

1.4

**Randall Davidson, Baron Davidson
of Lambeth**
By Sir Leslie Ward ('Spy'), 1901

Randall Davidson (1848–1930) was resident
chaplain to Archbishop Tait, and on marrying the
Archbishop's daughter was inevitably drawn into
the Sitwell orbit. He became Dean of Windsor
and Queen Victoria's domestic chaplain in 1883,
Bishop of Rochester in 1891 and Bishop of
Winchester in 1895. During his time as
Archbishop of Canterbury (1903–1928), a flow of
Sitwell relations visited Lambeth Palace, including
the youthful Edith and Osbert, who remembered
a particularly austere dinner of 1914 (lemonade
and cutlets) disrupted by suffragettes directed to
the Palace by the Bishop of London.

1.5

'The Capture of a Spirit', *The Graphic*, 7 February 1880

An exploit of which he was so proud that it featured in his *Who's Who* entry until his death, was Sir George Sitwell's unmasking of a fake medium. During his Christmas vacation from Oxford in 1880, he and Carl Von Buch set out to discredit a 'well-known', though curiously unnamed, medium in the very temple of spiritualism, the British National Association of Spiritualists. Although the American-born vogue for spiritualism had already taken hold in Britain, there had been no significant exposé and it was not until two years later that the Society for Psychical Research was founded expressly to test claims of paranormal events.

It took Sir George (illustrated fourth from the right in the top group) and Von Buch three sessions to establish the truth. The medium claimed to sit behind a curtain throughout the séances. On the first visit she was tied into her chair by Sir George and Buch, and there was no evidence of spectral activity. On the second occasion the medium was secured under the direction of 'an official connected with the institution'. The spirit of a twelve-year-old child, 'Marie', duly appeared but the rustling of clothes behind the curtain, the extraordinary levity of the ghost's pronouncements and the fact that she seemed to be wearing stays, aroused the suspicions of the investigators. It was during a third visit, with further witnesses, that 'Marie' was seized by the wrist and the curtain was torn aside to reveal the medium's empty chair and scattered clothes. The story was widely reported and Sir George's actions applauded. 'Spiritualism, as an imposture, is the more shameful because it trades on grief. From small beginnings and an obscure propaganda it now impudently assumes the dignity of a religion',[1] declaimed the *Daily Telegraph* in its report. Osbert, writing sixty-five years later, was also impressed. 'Previous to this, it had been given out by the members of the faith that anyone touching a manifestation would die, so that my father's action in holding the "spirit" and preventing her from escaping had required courage and enterprise.'[2]

1. *Daily Telegraph*, 13.1.1880
2. LHRH, p. 27

1.6

Electioneering ephemera

During the sixteen years of his political career Sir George served two terms as Conservative MP for Scarborough (1885-1886 and 1892-1895) and contested, unsuccessfully, five further elections. His first term as MP was brought to an end by the election of Joshua Rowntree, and in 1895 the Liberal candidate defeated him by twenty-four votes. His further defeat in 1900 was thought to have contributed to his nervous breakdown. In 1906 he became a Liberal.

THE CAPTURE OF A SPIRIT

SKETCHES AT A RECENT SPIRITUALISTIC SÉANCE IN GREAT RUSSELL STREET FROM NOTES SUPPLIED BY SIR G. SITWELL AND MR. VON BUCH

1.7

Lady Ida Sitwell

By Sir William Blake Richmond, 1888
(illustrated on page 17)

Sir George Sitwell married the Honourable Ida
Denison, the seventeen-year-old daughter of the
future Earl of Londesborough, in November 1886.
As Osbert relates in *Left Hand Right Hand!*, the
occasion appears to have precipitated Sir George
into a flurry of artistic patronage. After a wedding
present of a conventional outdoor portrait of
Lady Ida in a chaise by Heywood Hardy, he
commissioned a series of drawings of himself and
his wife from Lillie Langtry's favourite artist
Frank Miles. By September the following year, he
was considering approaching two of the leading
painters of the classical revival, Lawrence Alma-
Tadema and William Blake Richmond, for a
larger painting which would do justice to his
young wife's Grecian features. In early 1888 he
wrote home to his agent Peveril Turnbull:
'[Richmond] wishes to paint her in an amber
dress of a loose and rather aesthetic character and
totally unlike in every particular to the style and
feeling of those she wears.' And three weeks later:
'Richmond gave up of his own accord his dress
after it had been made and looked hideous. Now,
he has begun a portrait of Ida in one of his
lolling-back positions. I have told him I dislike it,
I wonder if he will kick?' Osbert observes: 'the
eventual portrait ... not sitting in "one of his
lolling-back positions", but uncomfortably upright,
dressed in a turquoise-blue coat and playing a
zither, an instrument she had never seen in her
life until she sat to Richmond – is very hideous
and insignificant, although a pretty likeness. My
father, on receiving it was anxious to cut out the
head, frame it as a small oval picture, and "burn
the rest".'[1]

1. LHRH, p. 211

1.8

Sir George Sitwell

By Henry Tonks, 1898

Sir George sat in white tie to Henry Tonks, the
surgeon turned painter who was already teaching
at the Slade School. Tonks's pupils were to include
the majority of British artists of note in the first
half of the century, from Augustus John and
Wyndham Lewis to Sir William Coldstream and
Richard Eurich.

The artist stayed for 'some time' at Renishaw
and although the painting was completed, the visit
was not deemed a success (Osbert suspected a
clash of temperament). A curious view of the
artist, renowned as an opinionated and scathing
critic with 'the commanding presence of a
nineteenth-century cardinal'[1], emerges from
Osbert's recollection of him: 'I remember ... his
appearance, so lank, damp and forlorn, as he
came back to the house one afternoon, when the
punt he had been sailing on the lake had capsized.
A sudden squall had swung the sail right over, and
he had been immersed. I have never seen a figure
that looked more wet, almost as though clothed in
water weeds.' But despite the impression of a
humourless situation, Tonks evidently found some
amusement and confessed to Osbert that one
morning when he had been about to start
painting, Sir George 'had looked across at him
and said, "Don't paint the hair today: it's not
quite in its usual form".'[2] In later years Tonks
became friendly with both Osbert and Sacheverell:
'The younger Sitwell ... is a charming companion.
I like him partly because he really seems to like
the society of his elders and uses his eyes and looks
about.'[3]

1. M. Holroyd, *Augustus John*, 1974, p. 41
2. Quoted in LHRH, p. 213
3. Letter from H. Tonks to A. M. Baniel, 25.10.1924, quoted in J. Hone,
The Life of Henry Tonks, 1952, p. 203

1.9

**Edith Davis with Osbert, Edith and
Sacheverell Sitwell**

By Cromack, Scarborough, 1898

Edith Davis had been nursery maid to Lady Ida
and looked after Edith, Osbert and Sacheverell as
children. For Edith in particular she provided
warmth in an emotionally barren home; 'her real
name was comfort'[1], she was to write at the end
of her life. Davis left the family after a violent
argument with Sir George when Sacheverell was
four, Osbert about to be committed to school and
Edith already in the charge of governesses. Osbert
remembered her with great fondness and she sent
him birthday cards for several years after moving
to her new home in Newbury.

1. TCO, p. 27

1.10

Edith Sitwell with her Mother

By John Thomson, *c.* 1888

Edith was born on 7 September 1887 at Wood End. Not only was she not the male heir required by Sir George, she was not, as she sensed from her parents' attitude, even pretty: 'I was rather a fat little girl: my moon-round face ... surrounded by green-gold curls.' She saw herself as a baby Tiresias, with 'the eyes of someone who had witnessed and foretold all the tragedy of the world'.[1] As she grew up Edith's appearance became a source of deep insecurity, which the classic and uniformly acknowledged beauty of her mother only made worse. There was a hostile, unloving relationship between the two throughout Edith's childhood and it was not until after her mother's prison sentence, when Edith was twenty-five, that any softening in their attitudes could be discerned.

The reputation of the photographer John Thomson (1837-1921) rests mainly on his studies of the Far East and of London street life, but by the mid-1880s he was well established as a portraitist with a royal warrant. The photograph of Edith with her mother would have been taken in his studio in Grosvenor Street, Mayfair.

1. TCO, p. 27

1.11

Edith Sitwell

By W. D. Brigham, Scarborough, *c.* 1890 (illustrated on page 18)

In healthy contrast to Edith's self-perception, her Aunt Florence recorded the childhood of her unusual but by no means freakish niece: 'Baby is just like a child in a story book in appearance, with fat cheeks, sometimes like pink campions, blue eyes and fair curls, a dear little person, touchingly devoted to her dog, Dido.'[1]

1. Quoted in LHRH, p. 85

1.12

Edith Sitwell at Art Class in Scarborough

By an unknown photographer, *c.* 1898-1900

At the age of about eleven or twelve Edith's lessons with her governess, Miss King-Church, were supplemented by art classes. 'Having discovered that I had no talent whatsoever for the pictorial arts, he [Sir George] determined that I should be forced to learn to draw at the local Art School, which specialised in a damping-down process of an extraordinary proficiency. Michael Angelo [*sic*] and Leonardo could emerge living from this tuition but I doubt if any lesser painter could have survived it.'[1] The class was given by Miss Alberts, 'a kind, woolly, tea-addicted elderly maiden ... who was always garbed in green serge' and who 'did not hate art, she simply ignored it'.[2] Edith, with a fringe and long frizzed hair in the centre of the photograph, seems awkwardly conscious of the photographer.

1. TCO, pp. 49-50
2. *Ibid.*

Childhood at Renishaw   27

Edith Sitwell
By W. D. Brigham, Scarborough, *c.* 1904

In an interview for the *Yorkshire Post* in 1936 Edith described herself in her first evening dress made of white tulle: 'With my face remorselessly "softened" by my hair being frizzed and then pulled down over my nose, I resembled a caricature of the Fairy Queen in a pantomime.'[1]

At seventeen Edith was tall (she reached six foot) and slim, and shows no signs in studio photographs of the idiosyncratic style she would later cultivate. Although this was the year in which Helen Rootham replaced Miss King-Church as Edith's governess, opening up her intellectual and geographical horizons, an enforced and eccentric conformity coloured life outside the schoolroom. The most spectacular evidence of this must have been Edith's twenty-first birthday party, organised by her father to coincide with the September Doncaster race meeting despite the fact that both he and Edith loathed racing. Two years in planning, it involved massive redecorations at Renishaw, and of the thirty guests, none of whom knew each other, only two were Edith's age.

1. Quoted in Glendinning, p. 37

1.14

Osbert Sitwell

By Cromack, Scarborough, *c.* 1896
(illustrated on page 18)

Osbert was born on 6 December 1892 at
3 Arlington Street, Piccadilly, a house taken by
his father in order to attend to his parliamentary
duties. The welcome news was recorded by Aunt
Florence in her diary: 'Yesterday morning a
telegram to Mother announced the birth of a son
to George and Ida. Rejoicing in the town, and
bells ringing. Today, in a letter to Mother, Lady
Londesborough describes the little boy as healthy,
lively, compact and plump – also pretty.'[1]
Osbert's childhood was in almost every respect
the antithesis of Edith's. Loved and indulged by
both his parents and by the servants, educated at
home by a governess, there was scarcely a cloud
on the horizon until, at the age of nine, he was
sent briefly to a day school in Scarborough and
then to Ludgrove, a boarding school in New
Barnet. 'Bloodsworth', as he calls it in *The Scarlet
Tree*, was chosen because the headmaster was 'the
most famous dribbler in England', a perplexing
reason for the young Osbert, better informed
about table manners than football.

1. Quoted by OS in LHRH, p. 91

1.15

Sacheverell Sitwell

By Cromack, Scarborough, 1899
(illustrated on page 18)

The youngest of the Sitwell trio, Sacheverell was
born on 15 November 1897 in his parents' house,
5 Belvoir Terrace in The Crescent, Scarborough.
His was a childhood even more indulged than
Osbert's, more at a remove from Edith's. As the
reserve heir, his responsibilities were less onerous
than Osbert's and the paternal lectures
correspondingly fewer. His infancy was spent in
mutual infatuation with his mother, an idyllic
relationship recollected forty-five years later in
Splendours and Miseries, and one which, even at
such a distance, struck Edith as both
misremembered and personally offensive to her.

1.16

Osbert Sitwell

By Cromack, Scarborough, *c.* 1902
(left)

Another pose from this sitting was used by Osbert
in *The Scarlet Tree* to illustrate the account of his
life at Ludgrove School, a chapter he ironically
entitled 'The Happiest Time of One's Life'. He
gives full rein to the unhappy memory: in being
'thus obliged to concentrate my mind upon it, the
sensation amounts almost to physical nausea, to
the feeling of being lost, isolated, of waking up in
a strange place and wondering who and where
you may be'.[1] Home-sickness, bullying, beating,
desiccated teaching and (most objectionable) the
instilling of middle-class values, seem to have
been offset only by copious supplies of food from
tender relatives:

'Granny Sitwell said something about another
hamper, but I hope she wont send me any more
figs, as the others were not as good as they might
have been and the aples were nearly as good as
the figs. Your Chocolate Cake and Barley Shugar
are so good.'[2]

1. ST, p. 119
2. OS to his mother, 8.3.1903, quoted in ST, p. 138

1.17

Sacheverell Sitwell

By Sarony, *c.* 1908
(left)

Osbert described Sacheverell as 'resembling in
appearance a lion cub, with his broad face, green
eyes and tawny hair, or perhaps King Henry VIII
as he may have looked as a child'.[1]

The firm of Sarony was founded by Oliver
Sarony, a Canadian of great charm, who settled
in Scarborough in 1857 and built up the most
successful provincial photographic business in the
country. The seasonal visitors to Scarborough
flocked to his huge gothic studio in the
eponymous Sarony Square where he was reputed
to conduct a sitting with eight different poses and
have the subject out of the studio within ten
minutes. The firm continued to operate for a
further seventy years after Sarony's death in 1879.

1. ST, p. 273

1.18

Renishaw Hall

By an unknown photographer, *c.* 1910

a) from the south
(illustrated on page 15)
b) from the north
(below)

Throughout its long history Renishaw was subject to the fluctuations in the Sitwell fortunes and it was only thanks to the sound economies of Sir George's mother that the house was re-established as a summer family home after the marriage of Sir George and Lady Ida.

Sir George's great contribution to Renishaw was the laying out of the gardens, inspired by Italian Renaissance designs. It became an obsession, and for all the vistas, pools and fountains that were achieved there were many projects, like the Lake Pavilion, that remained a gleam in his eye. In later years Osbert unkindly pointed out his father's tendency to flout the very precepts of organic planning that he had advocated: 'He abolished small hills, created lakes, and particularly liked ... to alter the levels at which full grown trees were standing. Two old yew trees in front of the dining-room window at Renishaw, were regularly heightened and lowered; a process which I believed could have been shown to chart, like a thermometer, the temperature of his mood.'[1]

1. OS, 'Hortus Conclusus', in *On the Making of Gardens*, 1949

1.19

The Sitwell Family

By John Singer Sargent, 1900
(illustrated on page 13)

As early as 1895 Sir George was contemplating the commission of a family heirloom, although at that date he inclined rather towards a china dessert service decorated with caricatures by Harry Furniss ('One can use china as ornament when not on the table, and political caricatures by Furniss would reproduce also for fireplace tiles, illustrations to a book, and one might make a book-plate')[1]. Over the next few years his ideas developed and by the end of the decade he had decided that the commission of a companion piece to John Singleton Copley's *The Sitwell Children* of 1787 (fig. 1, p. 21), would be more appropriate. The hunt for a suitable artist involved the critic and painter D. S. MacColl, and both Jacques Emile Blanche and Hubert Herkomer were considered and rejected before Sir George fixed on Sargent, to whom he was introduced by his cousin George Swinton, whose wife Sargent had already painted. The artist was summoned to Renishaw, was much impressed by the Copley painting, and the commission was duly settled at £1,500. Osbert recalls in *Left Hand Right Hand!* that on this visit Sargent painted a virtuoso water-colour of Lady Ida, Sacheverell and himself that was accidentally used by a housemaid to light the fire.

For the first few months of 1900 the Sitwell family decamped to 25 Chesham Place, Belgravia, to be on hand for sittings in Sargent's studio in Tite Street, Chelsea. One of the vast Brussels tapestries, the Chippendale commode, a silver bowl won by an ancestor at Chesterfield races and the Copley portrait were also transported from Renishaw to Tite Street. With an empire table and Chelsea figures lent by Sir Joseph Duveen, the setting was eventually arranged by Sir George and Sargent, and the sittings, which were to continue on alternate days for five or six weeks, began on 1 March.

Sargent bore Sir George's constant interference with exemplary patience and showed great kindness to the children, particularly Edith. Osbert recounts that Sir George had asked Sargent to emphasise Edith's crooked nose but that the incensed artist had depicted her nose as straight while developing an angle in Sir George's. In *Taken Care Of* Edith not only describes her fury at the 'tender paternal embrace' in which she is shown, but demolishes her parents' poses: 'My father was portrayed in riding-dress (he never rode)[2], my mother in a white-spangled low evening gown and a hat with feathers, arranging, with one prettily shaped, flaccid, entirely useless hand, red anemones in a silver bowl (she never arranged flowers, and in any case it would have been a curious occupation for one wearing a ball-dress, even if, at the same time, she wore a hat).'

The painting was shown privately to friends of the family in Sargent's studio in April. The artist, in a gesture of considerable generosity, had made a gift of a frame to match the Copley. The following year the group was exhibited at the Academy, arousing considerable interest in the press. Osbert thought he detected his father's hand in one article defending the painting: 'One or two critics have complained that the children and the heads of the two principal figures are disproportionately small. The explanation, of course, is that both Sir George and Lady Ida come of a tall race and are much above the common height.'[3]

In wider terms the portrait has been seen as the prototype of the Edwardian group, 'conjuring up', as Richard Ormond states, 'a picture of Edwardian life as surely as Devis's puppet-like figures evoke the eighteenth century.'[4]

1. Sir G. Sitwell to P. Turnbull, 21.3.1895, quoted in LHRH, p. 211
2. Sir George must have ridden occasionally. Osbert discusses his father's Arab charger in LNR, p. 270
3. LHRH, pp. 238-9
4. R. Ormond, *John Singer Sargent*, 1970, p. 63

1.20
Wood End

a) Lady Sitwell in the conservatory
By an unknown photographer, *c.* 1890s
b) Wood End from the garden
Photographed for the National Buildings Record, 1981

During the siblings' early years the Sitwell and Londesborough families were prominent residents of the elegant Italianate villas and regular terraces of The Crescent, Scarborough. Belvoir House at the western end was the winter home of Sir George and Lady Ida during the 1890s and it was there in 1897 that Sacheverell was born. At a stone's throw was Londesborough Lodge bought by Lady Ida's family in the mid-nineteenth century and next door but one to The Lodge, Wood End (now a natural history museum), built in the 1830s and bought by Sir George's widowed mother in 1870.

Much of Sir George's youth was spent at Wood End and Edith was born here in 1887, but it was not until 1902 that Lady Sitwell (by now established at Hay Brow outside Scarborough and at Gosden in Surrey) formally gave Wood End to her son. From then until the outbreak of the First World War, Wood End as much as Renishaw was

the Sitwells' home. Osbert, who found 'something evil' about the house, describes it disdainfully as being 'of orange-yellow stone, in what I believe was known as the incised Boeotian Style'.[1] Wood End's principal feature, the huge central conservatory, was added to the house by Sir George's mother. In her day it was lit by Chinese lanterns and filled with exotic, and in some cases finicky, birds (the Peking nightingale preferred its food on a pink plate). It housed one of the most flourishing palm trees in England and the roof was continually being raised to accommodate its increasing height. Beyond the conservatory Sir George in his turn built an extension in imitation of the library at Renishaw. It was in this wing that Osbert slept as a child, frightened and cut off from the rest of the house.

During the naval bombardment of Scarborough in December 1914 Wood End was damaged by shrapnel. Soon after, the Sitwells retreated to Renishaw, leaving the house unoccupied until Osbert returned to campaign as Liberal candidate in the general election of 1918.

1. ST, p. 85

1.21
The Esplanade, Scarborough, at Noon
By George Washington Wilson, *c.* 1890s

Most of the Sitwell trio's childhood was spent in Scarborough. A town embattled against the elements in winter, in 'the season' it was a crowded and fashionable resort with 'bracing air, an equable temperature, mineral springs of high medicinal value, splendid sands, romantic cliffs, excellent bathing, boating and fishing, a good system of drainage, great freedom from zymotic diseases, a low death-rate and an excellent train service.'[1]

The view from the Esplanade shows the bulk of the Grand Hotel, 'as prominent', wrote Sacheverell, 'in any memory of Scarborough as is Vesuvius in any view of the town and bay of Naples.'[2] The line of buildings to the left of the Grand marks the front line of genteel Scarborough; among the terraces and elegant houses behind lay The Crescent with Wood End and Belvoir House, the Sitwells' early homes.

1. 1899 Guide to Scarborough, quoted by B. Berryman in *Vintage Scarborough*, 1976
2. FWGC, p. 70

1.22

Henry Moat and Reresby Sitwell

By an unknown photographer, Scarborough,
August 1936

Henry Moat entered service with the Sitwells as a
footman in 1893 and remained with the family,
principally as Sir George's butler-valet, until his
retirement in the spring of 1936. He was
photographed later that year with Sir George's
grandson. Known to Sir George as 'the Great
man', Henry conducted himself in true Sitwellian
style, campaigning in a lifelong battle of wills with
his employer, whom he treated, according to
Osbert, with 'the utmost disrespect' and
'sentiments approaching veneration'.[1] Serious
ruptures in their relationship led to the occasional
hiatus in Henry's service, but they 'never failed to
gravitate towards each other again, as if
influenced by the working of some natural law'.[2]
Henry accompanied Sir George on his extensive
travels abroad, and moved with his employers to
Italy when they settled in Montegufoni. In one of
the most bizarre revelations of *The Scarlet Tree*,
Osbert recounts Henry's membership (the only
English member) of the proscribed Italian secret
society, the Camorra.[3]

1. LHRH, p. 95
2. *Ibid.*
3. ST, p. 288

1.23

'He gained a fortune but he gave a son'
Portrait of Henry Moat
By Christopher Richard Wynne Nevinson, 1918

The artist apparently used Henry Moat as the
model for this moralising study on the ethics of
war. The wealthy profiteer sits with a mournful
air amid the evidence of his material success – the
fine fireplace, gilt picture frame and bell-push.
A photograph of his lost son stands on the
mantelpiece. The painting was shown in
Nevinson's exhibition at the Leicester Galleries in
March 1918 and reproduced under the title
Bourgeois by Henry Wood Nevinson, the artist's
father, in a chapter on the middle classes in *Rough
Islanders* (1930).

   The ironies inherent in the situation are
legion. Henry's physical appearance may have
struck Nevinson as appropriate, but as a servant,
an unmarried man (yet the father reputedly of a
number of illegitimate children) and a member of
the Army Service Corps during the First World
War, it is difficult to conceive of anyone less
qualified for the role of bereaved profiteer. The
painting was made during Henry's longest
'absence' from Sir George's service, and while he
was in the army. It is not known when or whether
he sat to Nevinson.

1.24

Montegufoni

By Alinari, Florence, *c.* 1905

a) South front and east baroque façade
b) South front entrance (right)

Montegufoni had five courtyards, three terraces, a grotto and more than a hundred rooms, including a chapel and a seventeenth-century frescoed bathroom. The eleventh-century seat of the Acciaiuoli family, later Dukes of Athens, it housed about 300 Italian peasants when Sir George bought it in 1909 (in Osbert's name) for £4,000. 'The roof is in splendid order,' he wrote to Osbert, 'and the drains can't be wrong, as there aren't any.'[1]

Over the next fifteen years most of the peasants were induced to move out, and the castle and gardens slowly but dogmatically restored

under Sir George's intermittent supervision. In 1925, although it was still without heating or electricity, he and Lady Ida moved in for good and life at Montegufoni became in essence much like life at Renishaw, Sir George absorbed in the house and gardens, Lady Ida absent-mindedly entertaining, and Edith, Osbert and Sacheverell making regular visits with friends.

Montegufoni remained Sir George's home until the Second World War forced him to Switzerland. The house was used during the war to store some of the most famous paintings from the Uffizi and in 1946 Osbert returned to find it in good condition. Both he and Edith were often there in the 1950s, and in 1965 Osbert made it his permanent home. After his death it passed not to Sacheverell, who had hoped to live there, but to Sacheverell's son Reresby. It was sold by him in 1974.

1. Letter from Sir George Sitwell to OS, quoted in GM, p. 76

1.25

On the Making of Gardens
By Sir George Sitwell, 1909

Of all the literary projects that preoccupied Sir George, his essay, *On the Making of Gardens*, was the most successful and the first to be commercially published. It was also therapeutic. By May 1902 he was suffering so badly from the effects of a nervous breakdown that he found it intolerable to spend two successive nights in the same house. Endless changes failed to cure him and it was not until a doctor suggested foreign travel that his spirits improved. So began the convalescent's tour, visiting the Renaissance gardens of Italy: 'lovely sunny days spent in his own company, which he greatly enjoyed, with Henry and the luncheon basket discreetly within call'.[1]

Sir George's essay deals with the decadence of garden design in post-Renaissance Europe. His targets are Augustan formalism and the mock Romantic landscape, his inspiration the genius of the Italian garden: 'in all the world there is no place so full of poetry as the Villa d'Este which formalist and naturalist united to decry'.[2] The essay is in effect an argument for imaginative thought in garden planning: 'to make a great garden, one must have a great idea or a great opportunity'. The secret, in practical terms, lies in recognising the potential of existing natural features.

The book was published in 1909, its cover bearing a garden design of trite and relentless symmetry that would not have looked out of place as an Edwardian theatre set. The author fumed: 'Murrays have managed to contradict with it every lesson I inculcate.'[3]

1. OS, 'Hortus Conclusus', in *On the Making of Gardens*, 1949
2. Sir G. Sitwell, *On the Making of Gardens*, 1909
3. Quoted by OS in 'Hortus Conclusus', op. cit.

1.26

Sir George Sitwell leaving the Old Bailey
Photographed for the *Daily Sketch*, 12 March 1915

From the early days of their marriage Sir George tried to instil in his wife a sense of financial responsibility, but their divergent interests and lifestyles, and his frequent absences abroad, left him ignorant of the extent to which she was running up debts. A passion for flowers (she ordered six dozen tuberoses in one day), a lavish generosity in entertaining friends and a tendency to lose at cards, had resulted by 1911 in her owing £2,000. She fell neatly into the snare laid for her by the confidence trickster Julian Osgood Field, who seemed to offer the solution to her dilemma by obtaining a loan from a rich Miss Dobbs, whom Lady Ida was to introduce into polite society in return.

The unthinkable climax of Lady Ida's involvement with Field was her prosecution in March 1915 for conspiracy to defraud Miss Dobbs. Sir George, who seemed to have a misplaced confidence in the outcome of the trial, refused to settle the case out of court on the grounds that Field was already a convicted criminal. Lady Ida was duly sentenced to three months in Holloway.

The photograph shows Sir George with the recently cultivated beard that gave rise to the nickname 'Ginger', used freely behind Sir George's back by his children.

1.27
Facsimile from the *News of the World*, 14 March 1915

The scandal of Lady Ida's trial and imprisonment was not wasted by the press, but could well have made even more impact had it not coincided with the revelation of the 'Brides in the Bath' murders. Sacheverell, then at Eton, first learnt of his mother's imprisonment through a report in the *Sunday Express*.

1.28
Lady Ida Sitwell
By Bassano, 1904

Another pose from this session by Bassano was cannibalised by the *Daily Mirror* and used to illustrate the report of Lady Ida's court appearance in 1915.

Edith's rage and humiliation over the whole affair can be gauged from the draft of a letter she wrote to her cousin, Brigadier General William Henry Sitwell.[1] After her mother's statement in court that she was raising money to pay Osbert's debts, Edith was keenly aware of the potential damage to Osbert's career. In desperation she appealed to the Brigadier, an exact contemporary of her father and a veteran of the Afghan, Ashanti and Boer wars, to set the record straight. 'It is very difficult for me to write, for I am so filled with rage and loathing, that it is almost impossible to express myself clearly, as though they had not done enough to ruin their children before this last action. I do feel that no-one but a man can deal with this, and as you share with us the name that mother is doing her best to dishonour, and, unlike the rest of the family, are not afraid of Father, I am writing to ask you to do it.'

1. Unpublished, undated draft, Renishaw papers

London during the early years of this century was still the metropolitan heart of a great empire. Though the death of Queen Victoria in 1901 seemed to herald a new era, London Society retained many of its old formalities and hierarchies. The mansions that lined Park Lane and other parts of Mayfair had not yet been demolished or converted into offices or hotels, and households of even quite modest means felt unable to function without servants. The more affluent middle classes changed for dinner each evening, while the inquisitive poor would gather at the entrances of the grander houses during the Season, to watch the finely dressed guests arrive. Hostesses vied with each other in the sumptuousness of their entertaining and the brilliance of the men and women they could parade at their salons.

Not that London was immune to change. Just as the motor car was beginning to alter the streets and atmosphere of the city for good, so new schools of thought, art and design began to transform more enlightened circles, not least in Bloomsbury. Roger Fry's first Post-Impressionist exhibition in 1910 paved the way for an indigenous revolution in the arts and its impact slowly filtered through to home-grown movements such as Vorticism and the more domestic concepts of the Omega Workshops. The theatre, too, was enjoying a golden age with the heyday of George Bernard Shaw and Granville Barker, and in 1911 the arrival of the Russian ballet seemed to many to synthesise all that was modern and progressive in the arts.

Founded by the brilliant Russian impresario, Sergei Diaghilev, the *Ballets Russes* had taken several European cities by storm, thrilling and scandalising conventional critics and theatre-goers. Part of Diaghilev's genius lay in his ability to combine the phenomenal talents of different composers and artists (Debussy, Ravel and Stravinsky, Picasso, Derain and Cocteau) with those of his Russian dancers, choreographers and designers. It was, as Osbert wrote in *Great Morning*, the flowering of an art form, witnessed only once a century. As he followed the movements of the greatest dancer of them all, Vaslav Nijinsky, he realised that he was 'watching a legend in [the] process of being born'.

Such stimulation offered a heady brew for an impressionable young man, even one who had emerged from as sophisticated and eccentric a background as Osbert Sitwell's. Osbert had left Eton in 1911 a failure in the eyes both of Sir George and the school authorities. He had loathed this factory for producing 'that boring and emasculate commodity, the English Gentleman', but out of self-protection had learnt to dissimulate his real feelings and interests. Sir George, thwarted in his desire to have a son and heir of whom he could be proud, punished Osbert by denying him the opportunity of going up to Oxford. Instead, after months of miserable disputes with his father, Osbert was packed off to a military crammer in Camberley, to prepare for the Sandhurst entrance examination.

Osbert was dismayed, yet on another level the absurdity of the situation seems to have appealed to his sense of humour. His unsuitability for a conventional military career was blatant, but to his surprise the crammer was actually less disagreeable than being at home. Nobody censored his reading and he was free from his father's oppressive presence. When he failed the exams he must have thought that he had escaped the army, but Sir George was not to be defeated. He arranged a commission in a Yeomanry regiment, and Osbert found himself seconded to the 11th Hussars, based at Aldershot.

The cavalry, with its deification of the horse, was singularly inappropriate for a young man with Osbert's aesthetic leaning. He cites his cousin, a fellow officer in the mess at Aldershot, as the ideal member of the regiment: 'a routine of port and a fall on his head once a week from horseback kept him in that state of chronic, numb confusion which was then the aim of every cavalry officer.' Only the kindness of his soldier-servant, later his butler, Robins, relieved the situation. Osbert savoured what few moments of solitude he could seize, listened to gramophone records and buried himself in Arnold Bennett's *Clayhanger*.

He craved London. 'Though only thirty-six miles away,' he wrote, 'the capital seemed infinitely distant.' At last in June 1912 he was given a few days' leave. He booked a seat on his own at Covent Garden where the *Ballets Russes* happened to be performing. The evening he chose was the London première of *The Firebird*, with Karsavina in the title role. It was Osbert's first encounter both with contemporary dance and with the music of

London and the War

2.4
**Poster for the *Ballets Russes* at the
Théâtre des Champs-Elysées** (detail)
By Jean Cocteau, 1913

2.3

Tamara Karsavina as the Firebird

By Bertram Park, 1912

Igor Stravinsky, and he was captivated by the whole production. It was shocking and provocative in the most constructive way, beckoning the audience to enter an uncharted 'dominion of the senses'. 'Directly the overture began to be played,' Osbert wrote, 'I came to life.' The music and the movement, as well as the brilliant costumes, awoke his latent sensuality. Furthermore, they made him realise that art could be not just beautiful but powerful, able to vanquish the huffing ranks of the philistines. 'Now I knew where I stood', he declared, announcing what was to become the creed for all three Sitwells: 'I would be, for so long as I lived, on the side of the arts.' Over the years Osbert came to know personally many people associated with the ballet company, though at first he was deeply in awe of them. He was so overcome by emotion when he met Debussy in London in the summer of 1914, that later he could remember absolutely nothing about him.

Osbert's elation was short-lived, however, or rather it alternated with bouts of depression brought on by Aldershot and by his mother's growing debt crisis. Within a matter of weeks of seeing *The Firebird* he suffered a nervous breakdown and had to be given compassionate leave. He fled to Italy, where his parents were then staying, to beg his father to allow him a change of career. Half-hidden within a mosquito net on a bed in a Florence hotel, Sir George harangued him for his 'defects and delinquencies'. Yet this respite in Italy was a happy time and there were moments of tenderness between father and son as they set out for long days together at Montegufoni.

It was not only the idea of being an army officer that Osbert loathed. As he confessed in *Left Hand Right Hand!*, he did not want to be an ambassador or a prime minister either. Rather, he wished to be left alone, to be master of his own time and activities, sampling all the wonderful pleasures of life. In defiance of his background and his imposing physical appearance, he had acquired the vocation of an aesthete. Nevertheless, on his return to England that November he was transferred to the Grenadier Guards. It was, thankfully, a different world from the dumb hostility of Aldershot. His fellow officers were aristocrats or the scions of wealthy families, accustomed to privilege and fine-living.

While they ran up debts through hunting or riding, Osbert overspent on books and opera tickets. When asked by the Captain of the King's Guard if he liked horses, he replied: 'No, but I like giraffes – they have such a beautiful line.' Such mannered eccentricity was greeted with affection, and the warmth of the friendship that Osbert found in the mess helped lift him from his earlier despair. 'December 1912', he wrote, 'was the month in which my life, my own life, began.'

Conveniently situated at Wellington Barracks in Central London, Osbert's posting with the Grenadier Guards gave him the opportunity to circulate in London Society. He was quickly taken up by a number of influential and conscientious hostesses. *La vieillesse dorée*, as he called them, included the indomitable Margot Asquith, wife of the Liberal Prime Minister; and Osbert became a frequent visitor to 10 Downing Street, then at its zenith as a meeting-place not only for politicians, but for writers, academics and presentable young men.

Grander still were the salons open to Osbert through family ties. However much he might mock his father, he was not above using his parents' connections to further his own social advancement. His charming manners, his attentiveness, his impeccable dress (and the very fact of belonging to an historic regiment with royal duties) all made Osbert a most welcome guest in fashionable houses.

One of his favourite haunts was the house of the late King Edward VII's former mistress, Mrs Keppel, now ensconced in opulent surroundings in Grosvenor Street. A friend of Sir George and Lady Ida, she kept a motherly eye on Osbert and later Edith. It was at her house that Osbert met Diaghilev and Mrs Keppel's daughter, Violet (Trefusis), who was to become a lifelong friend. Even more imposing was the mansion in Chesham Place belonging to the septuagenarian Lady Brougham. Lady Brougham found no stimulation either in politics or in intellectual pursuits, but Osbert cherished her for her debonair and jaunty manner, her gossip and her wit. She had none of the leaden boorishness of the dreaded 'Golden Horde' of the Sitwell siblings' childhood.

In 1913 Edith also found a form of liberation in London, albeit in very different circumstances from Osbert's. Unlike her

now consider herself a professional poet and as such she clearly needed to transfer herself to the centre of literary life in London. Helen Rootham handled the practical side of things, and she and Edith decamped from Renishaw, to the sound of Lady Ida's angry protests and dire warnings.

Edith's life style in London was startlingly different from Osbert's; her private income was extremely modest in comparison. While Osbert drank champagne and patronised fine restaurants, Edith and Helen lived off tea, bone broth, white beans and glazed penny buns. 'Although undernourished,' Edith wrote, 'I was never hungry.' Things improved a little when they moved from a dingy boarding house to a small flat of their own in Moscow Road, Bayswater. It was on the fifth floor of Pembridge Mansions, an unprepossessing block described by the poet Brian Howard as looking like an 'inexpensive and dirty hospital'. Edith and Helen had a sitting-room each, furnished distinctively to disguise the grim anonymity of their new home. It was a far cry from the elegant Mayfair salons frequented by Osbert, but Edith managed to entice an extraordinary range of people to Bayswater. W. B. Yeats, Robert Graves, T. S. Eliot and Ezra Pound were among those who trudged up the dreadful stairs for tea and stimulating conversation.

Partly to help pay the rent, Edith took a job in the pensions office in Chelsea at the outbreak of the war, earning 25 shillings (£1.25) a week, plus five shillings war bonus. Appalled by the smell of cooking fat in the staff canteen, she would take herself off to a large store in Sloane Square at lunchtime, for milky coffee, bread rolls and butter.

The war affected the Sitwells in starkly different ways. Sir George saw it as a personal affront and became convinced that the Germans were specifically out to get him. Typically, this did not stop him from developing a deep admiration for the Kaiser, with whom he shared a birthday. Nevertheless, towards the end of 1914, while Sir George and his wife were staying at Wood End, three German cruisers loomed out of the mist in Scarborough's bay and opened fire on the town. Shell fragments hit the house as Sir George sheltered in the cellar. Lady Ida remained defiantly in bed.

brothers, she had until then lived almost exclusively at Renishaw or with relatives, inwardly fuming at her mother for bringing sordid tragedy on the family. Living under the same roof as Lady Ida had become intolerable to Edith, and her governess-turned-companion, Helen Rootham, saw escape as the only way of enabling her to let her personality and her literary interests develop.

Incongruous though it now seems, the *Daily Mirror* gave Edith the impetus to make her break with home, publishing her first poem to appear in print 'Drowned Suns', on 13 March 1913. She was paid two pounds by the newspaper, which went on to publish ten more of her poems over the following three years. She could

2.20
Nina Hamnett
By Roger Fry, 1917

2.26
The Editor of *Wheels*
By Alvaro Guevara, *c.* 1919

The bombardment precipitated elaborate plans for retreat. Should the Germans invade, Sir George would retire to the thatched hut built for waterfowl on an island in the public park below Wood End, and be perfectly happy 'with a few books [sent] down from time to time from the London Library'.

The war had one benefit for Osbert: it scotched the next career move that Sir George had arranged for him in the Scarborough Town Clerk's Office. Recalled to his regiment in August, he was sent to France in December. Osbert was even less suited to trench warfare than most of his companions. He hated discomfort, had no real interest in the mechanics of soldiering, and saw the war not so much as an exciting challenge as a tragic end to a whole way of life. The increasing desolation of the battlefield and the senseless loss of young lives only deepened his gloom. To make matters worse, Osbert felt bored for most of his time at the front.

Not that he had to endure it for very long. Early in 1915 he was summoned back to London to attend his mother's trial. Almost as difficult to endure as the long hours spent in the courtroom was the forced levity of Sir George, who, apparently oblivious to his wife's ordeal and his family's anguish, attempted to enliven several luncheons and dinners by discoursing on 'The History of the Fork'. When Lady Ida was sentenced in March and sent to Holloway, Osbert was given further extended leave and did not return to the front until July.

Edith's reaction to her mother's downfall was one of anger, evoking in her a strong determination not to let it ruin her own life. She saw the scandal as a grotesque mirror-image of what was happening on the other side of the Channel: a 'dwarfish imitation of the universe of mud and flies', as she later put it. The affair encouraged her to redouble her efforts to establish an independent literary career. She sent her first book of poems for private publication, at her own expense, to Basil Blackwell in Oxford; significantly, it took its title, *The Mother*, from a violent poem describing a matricide.

Back in France, Osbert found preparations for the Battle of Loos in full swing. Gung-ho senior officers, with an uncanny resemblance to Sir George and his cronies, assured the men that the Germans had no idea what was in store for them. But in the event, the Hun, far from naïve, was ready and waiting. For Osbert the resultant carnage was incontrovertible confirmation of the dangerous folly of arrogant elders who believed that they knew best. In *Laughter in the Next Room* he describes the devastating slaughter with bemused detachment: 'the bodies of friends and enemies lay, curious crumpled shapes, swollen and stiff in the long yellow grass under the chicory flowers'. Among the dead claimed by the war were Osbert's two closest friends in the Guards, Ivo Charteris and Wyndham 'Bimbo' Tennant.

After the disastrous offensive Osbert was promoted to the rank of captain and given command of a company. Far from bringing the expected challenge of new responsibilities, the early months of 1916 proved to be a tedious period of waiting while the generals decided what to do next. In fact, Osbert never saw battle again; he contracted blood-poisoning from an injured foot and was repatriated late in the spring of 1916. After several weeks of being looked after by a private nurse at Renishaw he was assigned to Chelsea Barracks. Far earlier than he could ever have hoped, he was able to savour London Society once more.

Among the *beau monde* of Mayfair and Chelsea Osbert had all the kudos of an officer invalided home from the front. Far more important for his siblings, however, was the fact that he, too, had written a poem, entitled 'Babel'. Moreover, its publication in *The Times* was a literary début of considerable distinction. 'My muse', wrote Osbert of this coup, 'was born with a silver pen in her mouth.' A fortnight before, *The Times* had carried Julian Grenfell's poem 'Into Battle'. 'Babel' is essentially anti-war, decrying how 'all we came to know as good / Gave way to Evil's fiery flood'. It does not bear comparison with the best of First World War poetry, but its symbolic value (for the Sitwell trio, at least) was immense. Osbert had accomplished the magic transformation from advocate of the arts to practitioner, and as he later wrote: 'From the moment of my beginning to write, my life, even in the middle of war, found a purpose.'

It was possibly at this time that Osbert also found a different kind of fulfilment, though we cannot know for sure; he remained discreet over certain personal matters until the end of his days.

What we do know is that he now became an habitué of a different kind of *vieillesse dorée*: the ageing survivors of Oscar Wilde's circle, of whom the most justly celebrated was Robert Ross, Wilde's one-time lover and faithful friend. Ross entertained in rooms in Half Moon Street, off Piccadilly, and although he had long since lost his looks he dazzled Osbert with his memories and his worldliness. Through Ross, Osbert met a number of fascinating gentlemen of a certain age, who were as enchanted with him as were the society hostesses. Osbert moved with ease from the drawing-rooms of mainstream cultivated society to the more intimate parties of a tight, self-protecting band of well-connected bachelors.

Not that all of Osbert's wide circle of friends were elderly, by any means. He had become an enthusiastic patron of the Eiffel Tower restaurant in Fitzrovia, that northern extension of Soho that for the next twenty years or so was to be the headquarters of London's Bohemian society. Decorated with Vorticist murals and patronised by writers and artists (Wyndham Lewis and William Roberts, Augustus John and his models), the Eiffel Tower was also a magnet for the fast and furious children of Osbert's glamorous drawing-room world.

Lady Cunard's daughter, Nancy, like Edith, was finding her own means of expression, not only in words, but also in the way she presented herself to the world. Both she and Edith increasingly drew attention to themselves by their unusual clothes and jewellery, though their lives could hardly have been more dissimilar. While Edith developed an aura of virginal medievalism, Nancy was a self-liberated soul, the outrageous herald of the Roaring Twenties. What united them was a deep disdain for much of the fashionable verse of the day and in particular for what Osbert termed the 'lark' school of War poetry. Although they had several friends and acquaintances among that diverse band known generically as the Georgian Poets (who included at various times such writers as Walter de la Mare, Robert Graves, D. H. Lawrence and John Masefield), they were highly dismissive of much of the Georgians' output and of Edward Marsh, editor of *Georgian Poetry*. Edith later proclaimed sniffily that 'to these men rhetoric and formalism were abhorrent, partly, no doubt, because

to manage either quality in verse, the writer must have a certain gift for poetry.'

Edith had little time for what she saw as poetic indiscipline. Accordingly, she and Nancy Cunard founded a vehicle to promote an alternative literary trend: the periodical anthology *Wheels*. Although named after a poem by Nancy that appeared in the first issue, or 'cycle', in 1916, *Wheels* developed as the brainchild of Osbert and Edith. At the outset it drew heavily on the talents of close friends, including work by Helen Rootham and giving Sacheverell his first appearance in print. In later issues, poems by Wilfred Owen and Aldous Huxley lent credence to Middleton Murry's judgement that the publication had established itself as a 'radical opposition' to the 'coalition government' of the Georgians. The six cycles of *Wheels* were self-consciously modern in tone, propounding not only an advanced literary cynicism but also the radical talent of contemporary artists. Yet as the critic John Press has written, Edith's own poetry smacked of 'the world of the opulent Edwardian nursery into which have been smuggled the ballet designs of Bakst and drawings of Aubrey Beardsley.'

Edith and Nancy Cunard had another common interest: the talented (and promiscuously bisexual) young Chilean painter Alvaro 'Chile' Guevara. Seven years Edith's junior, Chile had come to England as a boy and had later studied at the Slade School of Fine Art. He appreciated Edith's poetry and was intrigued by her particular brand of beauty, but he was in love with Nancy Cunard. For Edith, drawn to him more intensely than she had been attracted to any man until then, this was a severe blow to her self-confidence. An accomplished amateur boxer, Chile exuded the irresistible combination of animal vitality and artistic sensibility. In later life Edith claimed she would have married him had it not been rumoured that he had contracted a venereal disease, but this notion of matrimony may well have been wishful thinking on her part.

At the same time Edith was nurturing a more platonic enthusiasm for Aldous Huxley, whom she hoped would contribute to *Wheels*. Her persistence paid off, and Huxley was represented by no less than nine poems in the second cycle, which appeared in December 1917. This was despite the fact that his attitude to

the Sitwells was distinctly ambivalent. He nicknamed them the Shufflebottoms, 'each of them larger and whiter than the other ... Their great object is to REBEL, which sounds quite charming; only one finds that the steps which they are prepared to take, the lengths they will go are so small as to be hardly perceptible to the naked eye.' It may have been only a timid revolution, but the Sitwells were making their name as self-publicists, noisily challenging the Establishment, while their standing in literary London was undoubtedly growing.

Osbert was able to enhance his own position considerably when he acquired suitable Chelsea premises in which to entertain. Sir George took a lease for him on 5 Swan Walk, an attractive little house overlooking the old Physic Garden. One of Osbert's earliest guests was the celebrated hostess (and butt of many

2.17
Osbert Sitwell
By Nina Hamnett, *c.* 1920s

writers' caricatures), Lady Colefax, who in later years was cruelly dubbed 'the Coalbox' by the Sitwells. Sybil Colefax was a thick-skinned literary lion-hunter who had considerable success in attracting to her salon the very people who mocked her; they came because they knew that other fascinating people would be present. One of her gatherings, in December 1917, helped put the Sitwell siblings firmly on the literary map. According to an account of the evening given by Aldous Huxley, Edmund Gosse chaired a series of predominantly embarrassing readings by poets as diverse as Robert Nichols and T. S. Eliot, as well as the Sitwells themselves. However dismissive Huxley was about the Shufflebottoms' performance, they had evidently 'arrived'. As their friend, the flamboyant painter Nina Hamnett, wrote in her autobiography: 'Every time that the public thought they had vanished from sight, they cropped up again, new poems, new books, they were like corks floating.'

Sacheverell, precociously, was by now a fully-fledged member of the Sitwell literary corporation. He had followed in Osbert's footsteps to Eton and the Guards. He shared his brother's artistic and literary enthusiasms; if anything, he was even more carried away by the *Ballets Russes* than Osbert, becoming one of Diaghilev's most loyal supporters in Britain after the war and eventually collaborating on a ballet for his company. In June 1918 his first solo book of poetry, *The People's Palace*, was published by Blackwell, receiving an enthusiastic review from T. S. Eliot, among others. Huxley went so far as to hail the author as 'le Rimbaud de nos jours'.

With their star firmly in the ascendant, and with Osbert's readiness to spend lavishly on food and drink, the Sitwell brothers had little difficulty in persuading the great and the good to come to Swan Walk for cocktails or dinner. On Armistice Night their dinner guests were Diaghilev and Léonide Massine, whose return to London with the *Ballets Russes* the previous month seemed the first omen of peace. As the acknowledged champions of the *Ballets Russes* in London, the Sitwells were able to take full advantage of the prestige this gave them among late converts to the ballet's powers, not least the Bloomsbury Group. Now, on Armistice Night, having fed Diaghilev and Massine, Osbert accompanied

2.31
**The Drawing-room at 2 Carlyle Square,
Chelsea**
By Ethel Sands, *c.* 1920-1925

them through the crowds of revellers to a party given by the art collector Monty Shearman at his rooms in the Adelphi. Here, as Osbert put it, 'the Bloomsbury Junta was in full session'. A swirl of painters and writers included Roger Fry, Mark Gertler, Lytton Strachey and D. H. Lawrence; 'soldiers, Bloomsbury beauties, and conscientious objectors – all except Diaghilev – danced.'

The end of the war only heightened Osbert's anger at the terrible waste of life and years. This gave him fresh energy to take on the world, initially in the unlikely guise of a prospective Member of Parliament. He was nominated to fight his father's old seat of Scarborough, in the Liberal cause. Too much of an individualist to be a true party man, he had for some time judged politicians mainly on the single issue of whether they were for or against the war. This did not stop him from throwing himself into the general election campaign, however, or enlisting his siblings' help. As Edith wrote to one of her favourite protégés, Robert Nichols: 'we are all a little bit vague about our principles, but ever so staunch'. Having thoroughly disapproved of the 'war-monger' Lloyd George, Osbert stood as a 'Squiffite', loyal to the former Liberal leader Asquith. The campaign, for which he was given three weeks leave by the War Office, brought him into contact with a wide range of local people but 'nobody ... in the neighbourhood was in the least curious about the particular new world I wanted to help build, and had thought to be a chief and abiding interest for English people!' His Conservative opponent won.

Sachie, meanwhile, had been flirting with Bolshevism. At Eton he had refused to have a 'fag' to run his errands for him, and his short time in the army had reinforced his dislike of the more pompous members of the British Establishment. Fortunately he was able to escape the Grenadiers and, like many other ex-servicemen, resumed his education. Shortly after Christmas he went up to Balliol College, Oxford. After his experience of life in London, Oxford seemed rather flat, though he soon found opportunities to develop his as yet unsuspected talent for patronage.

One beneficiary was the notoriously precious master of the English novella, Ronald Firbank, then living as a virtual recluse in orchid-filled rooms opposite Magdalen. When Osbert visited Sachie in February 1919, they decided together to rediscover this curious throwback to the 1890s. With Siegfried Sassoon they arranged a dinner in Firbank's honour at the Golden Cross. Firbank, who on the occasion of another celebratory meal ate a single pea, arrived with the dessert and read extracts from his unfinished novel, *Valmouth*. 'You have no idea', Firbank sighed to Osbert, 'how difficult it is to keep up one's interest, when writing of a heroine who is over a hundred and twenty years of age.' Osbert was so impressed that he published an extract from *Valmouth* in the periodical *Art and Letters*, of which he was now co-editor, having bought into the publication with financial help from Arnold Bennett in 1918.

With their hands firmly on the tillers of both *Art and Letters* and *Wheels*, the Sitwells were in a strong position to influence literary taste – to create, as Cyril Connolly put it, their own alternative Bloomsbury. This was done largely by a well-thought-out campaign of publicly denigrating enemies, or those of whom Edith, in particular, had a low esteem, while at the same time building up 'discoveries' who showed special talent.

The Sitwells were magnificent, though exhausting, champions, but poisonous foes. The *London Mercury*, and in particular its editor J. C. Squire, was a regular target for their disapproval at this time. Exposing the nepotism of awards such as the Hawthornden and other literary prizes, the Sitwells awarded their 'Stuffed Owl' for the dullest literary work of the year to, among others, Squire, Edward Shanks and Harold Nicolson. In 1921 Osbert followed this with *Who Killed Cock Robin?*, a brilliant polemic on the Squirearchy. 'Poetry', he wrote, 'is *not* the monopoly of lark-lovers, or of those who laud the Night Jar, any more than it belongs to the elephant or the macaw.' For those in favour, however, there were almost no lengths to which the Sitwells would not go, as the young music student William Walton was to discover when he was taken up by Sacheverell at Oxford.

The first spring and summer of peacetime allowed both Osbert and Sachie to get away from England and to make new discoveries on the continent. Osbert had been suffering from recurring flu and gratefully accepted an invitation to accompany one of his generous patronesses, Mrs Ronnie Greville, on a recuperative holiday to Monte Carlo. 'Aunt Maggie', as Osbert called her, had a malicious tongue that distressed many people, including Sachie, but Osbert relished her lively company and was amused by her sycophantic interest in royalty. From Monte Carlo he moved on to Biarritz, where Sacheverell joined him, enthusing over modern pictures he had seen in Paris. These included works by Braque, Matisse, Picasso and, above all, Modigliani, whose studio he had visited, armed with an introduction from Nina Hamnett. Modigliani's studio was squalid, the artist and his girlfriend desperately poor, but stacked up against the walls were marvellous paintings and drawings. In later years Osbert and Sachie related a variety of tales describing how Sir George's parsimony had denied them the chance to acquire, for a relatively small sum, a substantial number of works by Modigliani.

Sachie returned late to Oxford and after the excitements of Paris and the new Diaghilev season at the Coliseum, abandoned his university career for good. He moved in permanently with Osbert at Swan Walk, soon to be joined by William Walton, and set about promoting the works of the painters he had so admired in France. With Modigliani's agent, Leopold Zborowski, the Sitwell brothers hatched a plan to stage two complementary exhibitions: one of English Vorticist paintings in Paris and another of contemporary French art in London. The first of these foundered owing to lack of time, but the second was realised in an exhibition staged in August 1919 at Heal's Mansard Gallery in Tottenham Court Road. The catalogue, with a prefatory note by Arnold Bennett, lists 177 paintings and sculptures and a further 141 drawings by a total of thirty-nine artists. The international spectrum of Paris studios was well represented with Russians, Poles, Spaniards and Italians in addition to native French artists. There were two works by Picasso, four by Matisse and six by Derain. Raoul Dufy, Chaïm Soutine, Fernand Léger, Maurice de Vlaminck, Othon Friesz and the sculptors Alexander Archipenko and Ossip Zadkine were also included, but according to Osbert it was the little-known works of Modigliani and Maurice Utrillo that caused the greatest stir. The Sitwell brothers commuted to the exhibition each day from Mrs Greville's house, Polesden Lacey,

and took turns with Herbert Read to man the desk and sell catalogues. The exhibition was hailed by Roger Fry as the most representative show of modern French art seen in London for many years. 'Anyone who cares for art ...' wrote Clive Bell in the *Nation*, 'will be thankful to those enterprising poets, the two Mr Sitwells, and to M. Zborowski for bringing over from Paris just what he wanted to see.' 'A collection of grotesques', spluttered another correspondent, signing himself 'Philistine'.

Despite their precarious financial position, the Sitwell brothers were building an impressive collection of contemporary art. In addition to a Modigliani bought at cost from Zborowski, they owned a Picasso drawing and paintings by Juan Gris and de Chirico, as well as pictures by London-based avant-garde artists like Henri Gaudier-Brzeska, William Roberts and Wyndham Lewis, whose work had been reproduced in *Wheels* and *Art and Letters*. Now widely seen as arbiters of artistic as well as literary taste, Osbert and Sachie needed grander premises to house their collection and to serve as a base from which to run their campaign to educate the British public. An admirably suitable house was found in Carlyle Square, just off the King's Road. It had a fine first-floor drawing-room, with plenty of space to entertain. Osbert filled it with Victorian *bibelots* and amusing objects, while the walls were covered with silks and hung with pictures and ethnic sculpture. Under the watchful eye of their housekeeper, Mrs Powell, glittering dinner parties were organised in the famous sub-aqueous dining-room.

With Edith and Sacheverell in attendance, Osbert presided at the French marble table. 'Taking at random the names of friends who have sat round its soft gold and peach-coloured surface,' he later reflected, 'it would murmur Arnold Bennett, W. H. Davies, Maurice Ravel, Sergei Diaghilev, Maynard Keynes, Lydia Lopokova, Walter Sickert, Clive Bell, Roger Fry, Virginia Woolf, Léonide Massine, George Gershwin, Harold Acton, Arthur Waley, T. S. Eliot, and many others, not to mention William Walton.' No longer just a frequenter of memorable London salons, Osbert now had one of his own.

Jonathan Fryer

2.1
Sergei Diaghilev
By Elizabeth Polunin, *c.* 1920

'He could charm a dead man to life,' Sir Charles Cochran wrote of Diaghilev (1872-1929), though others were less tolerant of his manipulative style. 'With his burly, tall, rather shapeless figure,' Osbert wrote, 'he seemed formed, like a bear, to wear a coat of fur, but his clothes were smart and well cut. His black hair carried a badger's stripe of white in it, and he was of an impressive and alert appearance, with a robust elegance'. The Russian impresario had already introduced Parisians to Russian painting and opera when he launched the first season of the *Ballets Russes* in 1909. For the next twenty years Diaghilev's ballets influenced artistic developments throughout Europe and America, extending beyond the musical, theatrical and visual arts to writers, couturiers and interior designers.

The Sitwells were no exception. Indeed Osbert, one of the élite who had known the pre-First World War Diaghilev seasons, could be patronising about those whose first exposure came with the return of the company to London in the autumn of 1918. It was only at this time that the friendship between Diaghilev and the Sitwell brothers began, an association which led to *The Triumph of Neptune* (see 3.37).

Both Elizabeth Polunin and her husband Vladimir were scene painters for Diaghilev's company and the portrait of Diaghilev is based on a photograph taken in Vladimir's studio in 1919.

1. C. B. Cochran, *The Secrets of a Showman*, 1925, p. 368
2. GM, p. 246

2.2
Igor Stravinsky playing *The Rite of Spring*
By Jean Cocteau, 1913

Throughout all the Sitwells' writings the name of the Russian born Igor Stravinsky (1882-1971) recurs as a reminder of what is best in the Modern movement. 'No sooner has he evolved and made perfect one kind of thing', wrote Sacheverell, 'than he shakes off all the qualities he may have acquired during its creation in order to arrive fresh and empty-handed in front of some new object of his curiosity.' The three major pre-war ballet scores he wrote for Diaghilev were each in their way a milestone for Osbert: *The Firebird*, the formative cultural experience of his life; *Petrouchka*, to Osbert's mind the greatest of the pre-war productions; and *The Rite of Spring*, living proof, in the riots that greeted its première in Paris, of the power of art.

The anarchic multi-talented Cocteau was closely involved with Diaghilev and in addition to designing the Ballet's first posters (see 2.4) conceived for him two of the company's best-known ballets: *Parade* (1917) and *Le Train Bleu* (1924). The drawing, a vivid attempt to capture the angular rhythms of *The Rite of Spring*, dates from the year of the ballet's first performance.

1. SS in *Radio Times*, 8.7.1927, p.55

2.3
Tamara Karsavina as the Firebird
By Bertram Park, 1912
(illustrated on page 38)

'Genius ran through the whole of this ballet', wrote Osbert of the 1912 Covent Garden production of *The Firebird*. 'Karsavina ... was then at the height of beauty and of her career, the greatest female dancer that Europe had seen for a century. The very poise of her lily-like neck was unforgettable, and there was about her shape and movements a perfection of grace that for the first time made me realise how near are the Russians, for all their hyperborean extravagances and childish glitter, to the ancient Greeks.' The production was choreographed by Michel Fokine and designed by Alexander Golovine, though the costumes of the Firebird, the Prince and the Tsarevna were by Léon Bakst.

Karsavina was photographed both by Bertram Park and by Emil Otto Hoppé in the Firebird role in London. She is wearing the high feathered head-dress of Bakst's original design.

1. GM, pp. 140-1

2.4

Poster for the *Ballets Russes* at the Théâtre des Champs-Elysées
By Jean Cocteau, 1913

The French impresario Gabriel Astruc had organised the first appearance of the *Ballets Russes* in Paris in 1909 and when appointed Director of the new Théâtre des Champs-Elysées in 1913 he invited Diaghilev to give a season there. Cocteau's poster shows Vaslav Nijinsky in *Le Spectre de la Rose*, a role that Osbert, who saw him dance it in London, described as 'the climax of romantic ballet'. 'This great dancer', he wrote in *Great Morning*, 'seemed to hold all physical laws in abeyance and for an instant of time to remain, at the height of his leap, poised and stationary; when asked how he achieved this defiance of the law of gravity, he replied, "It's very simple: you jump and just stop in the air for a moment."'[1]

For the Sitwells, as for many of their progressive outlook, Cocteau was a revered source of inspiration and though they knew him well his name crops up, like that of Picasso, as something of a trophy in their literature. In 1957 Cocteau sent Edith two drawings inscribed with his thanks for her *Collected Poems*, 'un cadeau royal dans une époque sordide'.

1. GM, p. 242.

2.5

Lydia Lopokova
By Pablo Picasso, 1919

The Russian *première danseuse*, Lydia Lopokova (1892-1981), succeeded Karsavina in the affections of London audiences. Although she had danced with the Diaghilev Ballet in Europe and America, it was not until September 1918 that she was first seen in London, as Mariuccia in *The Good Humoured Ladies*. This was a role well suited to her naturally vivacious character: 'her wit', as Osbert put it, 'entered into every gesture, into everything she did'.[1] It was probably at the party thrown by the Sitwells for the Russian Ballet at Swan Walk in October 1918 that she first met her future husband, the economist Maynard Keynes.

The following year's repertoire included *La Boutique Fantasque*, in which Lopokova triumphed; and *The Three Cornered Hat*, designed by Picasso. The drawing of Lopokova was made during the three months that Picasso spent in London supervising Vladimir Polunin's painting of the set. It is one of three portrait drawings and many sketches of her by Picasso that survive, and was owned by the ballet critic and historian Cyril Beaumont. It was acquired by the Fitzwilliam Museum in 1989, with help from the National Art Collections Fund.

1. LNR, p. 14

2.6

Sacheverell Sitwell
By Maurice Beck and Helen Macgregor, 1924

Sacheverell left Eton in December 1916, precociously cultured, already a bibliophile and collector. In the New Year he joined Osbert in the Grenadier Guards and became part of his brother's glittering social world. He was based at Chelsea Barracks, then for the last year of the First World War at Tadworth and Aldershot. His siblings waited out the war in a fever of apprehension that he would be sent to the front, but in the event he remained in Britain, witnessing the dispatch of other young men. 'I well remember', he wrote in later life, 'the band playing "The British Grenadiers" and the Commanding Officer saying in a broken voice that few of them would be living in a few weeks' time'.[1] But these were also heady days and in the last month of the war Sacheverell was swept up in the fever that greeted the return of the Russian Ballet to London. His evenings were frequently cut short by the need to return to camp, prompting Diaghilev to ask him, 'Qu'est-ce que c'est cette Aldershot – c'est une femme?'[2]

1. SS, quoted in Bradford, p. 85
2. GM, p. 128

2.7

Violet Trefusis

By Sir John Lavery, *c.* 1920

The daughter of one of Osbert's most cherished elderly acquaintances, Mrs George Keppel, Violet (1894-1972) was a lifelong, if sometimes trying, friend to the Sitwells. Her announcement in 1913 that she and Osbert were engaged took no one more by surprise than Osbert. It was a joke she enjoyed for many years, referring to him as her 'ex-fiancé'. She later annoyed Sacheverell and Georgia by precipitously revealing their engagement. Despite her marriage to Denys Trefusis in 1919, Violet pursued a passionate affair with Vita Sackville-West that had begun the previous year, and it may have been at about this time that Lavery, an old friend of the family, painted Violet's portrait. After Trefusis's death in 1929 she lived in France and at the family villa, l'Ombrellino, in Florence, writing novels in English and French. In the minefield of expatriate Tuscan life, Violet was glad to have Osbert as a neighbour at Montegufoni. 'Let snobs and Americans pay court to Berenson,' she wrote, 'I have the Sitwells.'[1]

1. Quoted in P. Julian and J. Phillips, *Violet Trefusis, Life and Letters*, 1976, p. 124

2.8

Lady Cunard with George Moore in her Grosvenor Square Drawing-room

By Sir John Lavery, 1925

Few of the salons on Osbert's social round could boast a more impressive array of writers, artists, musicians and thinkers than the house of the American-born Lady Cunard (1872-1948). Having jettisoned her husband, Sir Bache, Lady Cunard was later associated with Sir Thomas Beecham, and was a well-connected promoter of all music, in particular the opera.

Lady Cunard was a friend of the artist's wife, Hazel, and owned a portrait of her by Lavery. The painting is set in the drawing-room of Lady Cunard's house in Grosvenor Square, the scene of Guevara's portrait of her daughter Nancy (2.27). The painter can be seen reflected in the mirror at the end of the room. Seated with Lady Cunard is the Irish novelist George Moore, an intimate friend (some thought he was Nancy's father). Sacheverell and his wife Georgia were often in Lady Cunard's company and in her will she left Sacheverell her letters from George Moore, 'to use as he thinks fit'.

2.9

Lady Diana Cooper

By Emil Otto Hoppé, January 1916

The fabled beauty of her time, Diana Manners (1892-1986), daughter of the Duke and Duchess of Rutland, was the familiar of Iris Tree at the Slade School of Fine Art and Nancy Cunard at the Eiffel Tower restaurant. She was a friend of the Prime Minister and a catch for every society hostess, moving in both Bohemian and upper-class circles with an ease that even Osbert would have found hard to emulate. They met at Lady Cunard's in 1914, Diana Manners surprised to find a 'Guardee' who discussed Stravinsky. 'Our friendship quickly ripened,' he wrote, 'but this was due to her, for she is the most inspiring as well as the most steadfast of friends.'[1] The photograph of her that Osbert carried with him in the trenches remains in its battered leather case on his desk at Renishaw.

She was in demand with portrait painters and photographers from early childhood and continued to excite attention as an actress of international renown and the wife of the diplomat Duff Cooper, later Viscount Norwich. She sat to Hoppé two years before he photographed Osbert (2.10). The exclusive Munich-born photographer owed much of his success in attracting well-known sitters to the efforts made on his behalf by Lady Lavery and Margot Asquith.

1. GM, p.257

2.10
Osbert Sitwell
By Emil Otto Hoppé, 1918

Increasingly voluble remonstrances from his father punctuated Osbert's idyllic existence in the Guards before the outbreak of war. In July 1914, fearing that his son was living wildly beyond his means, Sir George arranged for Osbert to leave the Guards and take up a position in the Town Clerk's Office at Scarborough. Within a month, however, war was declared and Osbert was summoned back to his regiment. He left for France in December 1914, the day after the German naval bombardment of Scarborough that his parents had experienced. Arriving in the front-line trenches he was handed a letter from his father. Sir George declared that although it was unlikely Osbert would encounter 'anywhere abroad' the 'same weight of gunfire that your mother and I had to face', he was in any case sending him the benefit of his experience. He advised Osbert, directly he heard the first shell, to retire to the 'undercroft', to keep warm, eat plenty of nourishing food at frequent intervals and to take a nap in the afternoon.[1]

Osbert is on the whole reticent about his war experience in his autobiography: 'In the trenches one day was sad, cold and hopeless as the next.'[2]

1. LNR, p. 78
2. *Ibid.*, p. 81

2.11
Osbert Sitwell
By Geoffrey Gunther, 1918

G. R. 'Giffy' Gunther (1899-1918) had been a friend of Sacheverell's at prep school and followed him to Eton where his career was considerably more impressive than that of either of the Sitwell brothers. He left at Easter 1917, joined the 3rd Battalion, the Grenadier Guards, and must have come across Osbert in London at about the time when a second edition of *Wheels 1916* was being published. He was sent to France where he earned a Military Cross before being killed on 4 November 1918, the same day as Wilfred Owen. His obituary in the *Eton Chronicle* paid tribute to his courage and compassion and noted that drawing had been his favourite pastime; the caricature of Osbert was one of a number he drew of fellow 'Guardees'. Gunther art prizes are still awarded at Eton in his memory.

2.12
The Winstonburg Line
By Osbert Sitwell, 1919

The Winstonburg Line, consisting of three anti-Churchill satires (two written anonymously for the *Daily Herald* and a third under the pseudonym 'Miles' for the *Nation*) was published in September 1919 by the pro-Bolshevik Frank Henderson of the Bomb Shop, 66 Charing Cross Road. Churchill's interventionist attitude to Russia in 1919 ('my nice new war')[1] was as inimical to Osbert as his policies had been during the First World War. The satires send up the Churchillian monologue and were apparently based, in part, on a conversation between Churchill and Siegfried Sassoon.

Osbert had nursed his dislike of Churchill since his family had stayed in London for the sittings with Sargent (see 1.19). The house they rented had belonged to a sister of Lady Randolph Churchill and the boudoir was crammed with photographs of the young Winston, 'in long clothes and short, in frocks and infant knickerbockers, in sailor suits, as a small schoolboy, as a Harrovian, as a young officer. Wherever we looked, that face ... followed us with intent gaze, determined and dramatic. It was impossible to work while those eyes followed us, and my sister was obliged several times to screen them with newspapers and exercise-books.'[2]

1. OS in 'A Certain Statesman', *The Winstonburg Line*
2. LHRH, p. 219

2.13

Siegfried Sassoon

By Pirie MacDonald, *c.* 1920

The erratic relationship between the Sitwells and the writer Siegfried Sassoon (1886-1967) began in 1917. Both as a poet and as a soldier-pacifist of great courage, he was a man in whom Osbert found much to admire, and with whom he had much in common. As literary editor of the *Daily Herald* in 1919, Sassoon was responsible for publishing a number of Osbert's anti-war satires. He was instrumental, too, in the Sitwells' best-known act of patronage. It was he who introduced Sacheverell to William Walton at Oxford.

Relations between Sassoon and the Sitwells must have been strained over the tussle to publish Wilfred Owen's work after his death, but it was the appearance in *Wheels* of pseudonymous attacks by Osbert on two of Sassoon's closest friends that led to a total rupture between 1921 and 1924. When relations were restored in 1925 Sassoon seems to have behaved with generosity towards all the Sitwells, particularly Sacheverell.

The photograph by the New York 'Photographer of Men', Pirie MacDonald, may have been taken on Sassoon's 1920 lecture tour in the United States.

2.14

Wilfred Owen

By John Gunston, 1916

Osbert was introduced to Owen (1893-1918) in September 1917 by Robert Ross, who in turn had been asked to look after the neurasthenic poet by Siegfried Sassoon. Over the next few months Osbert and Owen exchanged letters and poems and met on several occasions. Osbert recalled in particular a summer afternoon in 1918 when, together with Sassoon and Owen, he had listened to Violet Gordon Woodhouse (see 2.53) playing the harpsichord and eaten raspberries at Swan Walk. The idyll was short-lived. Owen returned to France and was killed a week before the armistice.

The chapter devoted to Owen in Osbert's *Noble Essences* is illustrated with a detail from this photograph by the poet's uncle. Osbert records his and Owen's aversion to the war: 'a link of nonconformity that in those years bound together the disbelievers with almost the same force with which faith had knitted together the early Christians'.[1] Owen had been asked to contribute to the 1918 edition of *Wheels*, but was posthumously published in the following, fourth cycle, which was dedicated to his memory. After corresponding with Owen's mother Edith began the task of editing Owen's war poems for publication and was disappointed when the project was taken over by Sassoon.

1. NE, p. 89

2.15

Ivo Charteris

By Langfier Ltd, *c.* 1915

Though younger than Osbert, Ivo Charteris (1896-1915) and his cousin Wyndham Tennant were his closest friends in the Guards. Both had joined at the outbreak of the war and both were killed in France, Ivo in the autumn of 1915, shortly after his nineteenth birthday, and 'Bimbo' Tennant almost exactly a year later. Their deaths left a great void in Osbert's life.

Ivo's death was a blow not only to Osbert, but also to Sacheverell, an Eton friend, and to Edith: he had been one of the very earliest guests to tea at her flat in Pembridge Mansions. Osbert was also a friend of Ivo's mother, Lady Wemyss, who lost not only her youngest son Ivo in the war, but her oldest, Hugo, as well.

2.16

Edith Sitwell

By Nina Hamnett, 1915

Edith sat to Nina Hamnett on at least three occasions. This mask-like portrait of 1915 is among the earliest of the extant drawings. A sitting in 1918 produced further drawings, including another in the collection at Texas University and one acquired by Sickert. Only one painting of Edith by Nina Hamnett is recorded and its whereabouts are unknown. Described by various critics who saw it in the National Portrait Society exhibition in 1919, it showed Edith in a rainbow-coloured jacket and with 'kaleidoscopic breasts'. Edith also sat to Nina Hamnett for a drawing in the 1920s when the artist was collaborating with Osbert on *The People's Album of London Statues*, published by Duckworth in 1928.

2.17

Osbert Sitwell

By Nina Hamnett, *c.* 1920s
(illustrated on page 44)

Nina Hamnett had painted Osbert in his Grenadiers' uniform and although the artist pronounced it a failure[1] it was shown with her portrait of Edith at the National Portrait Society exhibition in 1919. 'I painted another of him', she says of this second portrait in *Laughing Torso*, 'in a small "John Bull" top-hat, a head and shoulders, and that was much better.'

Osbert renewed his friendship with Nina Hamnett when she returned to London from Paris in the mid-1920s. Admiring her illustrations for Seymour Leslie's novel *The Silent Queen*, he proposed that they collaborate on a book of London statues. 'Whiskered and forgotten peers in top-hat and classical togas should be our aim' he wrote to her.[2]

1. Whereabouts unknown
2. Quoted in D. Hooker, *Nina Hamnett, Queen of Bohemia*, 1986, p. 185

2.18

Osbert Sitwell

Attributed to Nina Hamnett, *c.* 1920s

From stylistic and circumstantial evidence it seems likely that this is a sketch for Nina Hamnett's portrait of Osbert (2.17). Wearing the same top-hat and cravat that appear in the painting, and with similarly drawn almond-shaped eyes, Osbert is shown seated with his left hand resting on a dog's head. Over his left shoulder can be seen one of the many glass domes that featured prominently in the house in Carlyle Square.

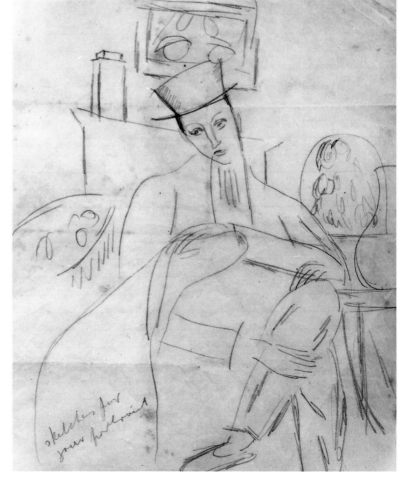

2.19

Omega Screen

By an unknown artist, *c.* 1919

The fact that the Omega Workshops artists operated anonymously has preserved the identity of the painter who decorated this screen. It is known to have been in the family collection at the time Beaton photographed Georgia sitting in front of it in 1927 (see 6.6), but may well have been acquired by Osbert many years earlier. Osbert knew several of the Omega artists. In addition to Roger Fry, there were Nina Hamnett, who painted his portrait twice; Edward Wolfe, who took him to Charleston[1]; and Dora Carrington, who was treated to tea and a glimpse of Osbert's striped silk underwear at Swan Walk in November 1918.

Any of these artists may have had a hand in decorating the screen. The linear outlines suggest Edward Wolfe and there are similarities with Nina Hamnett's *The Ringmaster*.[2] Fairs and circuses were popular subjects for Omega though here the style of composition is not readily attributable, lying somewhere between Carrington's breezy fairground scenes and the tight sophistication of Mark Gertler's *Merry-Go-Round* of 1916 (Tate Gallery).

1. See photograph of OS in R. Shone, *Bloomsbury Portraits*, 1976, p. 195
2. See D. Hooker, *Nina Hamnett, Queen of Bohemia*, 1986, p. 96

2.20

Nina Hamnett

By Roger Fry, 1917
(illustrated on page 40)

The painter Nina Hamnett (1890-1956), the acknowledged 'Queen of Bohemia', was the passport for many of her compatriots to the artistic community in Paris just before and after the First World War. It was her letter of introduction that enabled Sacheverell to visit Modigliani's studio in Paris in 1919. Born in Tenby, Wales, Nina studied in Dublin and in London and worked for Roger Fry's Omega Workshops before moving to Paris in February 1914. She became a familiar figure in Montparnasse, her acquaintances among the avant-garde including Modigliani, Zadkine, Foujita and Brancusi. The outbreak of war forced her to return to London and it was between the late autumn of 1914 and her return to Paris in 1920 that she got to know the Sitwells. Osbert described her as having 'a particularly fine flair for people'[1], and a habit of bestowing introductions, as though they were gifts, between people she thought likely to make friends.

Roger Fry's portrait is one of several he made of Nina Hamnett in 1917 when they were enjoying a brief affair.

1. NE, p. 207

2.21

Roger Fry

By A. C. Cooper, 28 February 1918

Edith described the critic and painter Roger Fry (1866-1934) as a delightful, courteous and learned companion; an espouser of lost causes; a man with a gift for friendship and a cavalier disdain for the details of ordinary life, 'incapable of noticing any but a spiritual discomfort'.[1] Fry was a friend of the Sitwells from their earliest days in London and as well as making portraits of Edith (2.22), advised on the colour scheme in the drawing-room in Carlyle Square (see 2.33). He also decorated, in Omega style, an old kitchen table that in later years was taken to Renishaw and became Osbert's writing desk. As the 'hierophant' (Osbert's word) of modern art and the organiser of the two Post-Impressionist exhibitions in London in 1910 and 1912, Fry provided a lead that Osbert and Sacheverell were to follow with their exhibition of Modern French Art in 1919.

The photograph shows Fry seated in an Omega chair in the study at Durbins, the house he designed for himself in Guildford.

1. TCO, p. 83

Edith Sitwell
By Roger Fry, 1918

In her autobiography Edith writes that she sat to Roger Fry for 'several portraits'. This, and another in a collection in Connecticut, are the only two completed paintings that survive, but it seems probable that this is the one to which Edith refers in *Taken Care Of*. 'For one of these [portraits] I wore a green evening dress, the colour of the leaves of lilies, and my appearance in this, in the full glare of the midsummer light of midday, in Fitzroy Square, together with the appearance of Mr Fry, his bushy, long grey hair floating from under an enormous black sombrero, caused great joy to the children of the district as we crossed from Mr Fry's studio to his house for luncheon.'[1]

The date inscribed on the painting is indistinct and may be read as 1915 or 1918 although on stylistic grounds it has been assigned to the later year.[2] There is, however, the suggestion of a personality still not fully formed. The fashionable evening dress she is wearing contrasts sharply with the bright Omega design in the background; in later portraits her appearance would be more carefully tailored to suit a champion of Modernism.

1. TCO, p. 83
2. F. Spalding, *Images of Edith*, exhibition catalogue, Sheffield Polytechnic, 1977, p. 7, footnote

Alvaro Guevara
By George Beresford, 1920

The painter and South American amateur boxing champion Alvaro 'Chile' Guevara (1894-1951) came from a rich Valparaiso family. Intended for the family business, he was sent to Bradford Technical College to learn the wool trade, but on showing an aptitude for drawing, he was encouraged by William Rothenstein to attend evening classes at Bradford College of Art. He moved on to the Slade and from 1912 to 1916 made extensive acquaintances among his fellow students and the wider art world. It may have been through Roger Fry or Sickert that he came into contact with the Sitwells. The tall, good-looking, bisexual Guevara is presumed by Edith's biographers to be the first of two unrequited loves, and their close friendship survived his obsession with Nancy Cunard (see 2.27). In 1927 Edith wrote introducing Chile to Gertrude Stein: 'He is a painter, and also a writer, of real genius – not one of those dear little intellectuals ... It would be an awful thing if a man with a mind like his had to have it fretted away by the vulgar little clothes-moths that sit drinking and pretending to be geniuses in the cafés.'[1] Guevara's portraits are probably his best-known works, but the Chilean paintings he exhibited at the Leicester Galleries in 1926 (with a catalogue introduction by Osbert) were admired at the time. After his marriage to Meraud Guinness in 1929 and the vicissitudes of his later life, spent mostly in France, the Sitwells had little contact with him.

1. Quoted in D. Holman-Hunt, *Latin Among Lions*, pp. 165-6

Brian Howard
By an unknown photographer, *c.* 1925

Brian Howard (1905-1958) was one of the earliest, and one of the least able of Edith's literary protégés. From Eton the precocious aesthete dispatched his poems to Edith, noting in his diary on 15 February 1921: 'In the morning I received a *wonderful* letter from Edith Sitwell. She encloses me back my poems but compliments me tremendously and writes 4 pages advising me, and asking for more and other poems. I *am* so encouraged. I go to bed with a slight temperature.'[1] Under the *nom de plume* of 'Charles Orange' one of his poems was included in the final volume of *Wheels*. Howard's first rush of enthusiasm for Edith cooled somewhat on visiting her in Moscow Road ('an uninviting Bayswater slum') where he was given 'one penny bun and three quarters of a cup of rancid tea in a dirty cottage mug'.[2] Her visit to Eton in 1922 was an occasion of acute embarrassment: 'She whispered her speech into a table, and as a result it was horribly difficult to hear anything at all ... the beastly old Vice-Provost, Macnaghten – got up and advised Edie to speak louder in the future!'[3] Both Osbert and Sacheverell contributed poems to *The Eton Candle*, the single-issue anthology edited from school by Brian Howard and Harold Acton in 1922.

1. B. Howard, unpublished diary, School Library, Eton College
2. Letter from Brian Howard to Harold Acton, quoted in M. J. Lancaster, *Brian Howard*, 1968, p. 90
3. *Ibid.*, p. 96

2.25
Iris Tree
By Vanessa Bell, 1915

Iris Tree (1897-1968) and her sister Viola, the daughters of the great actor-manager Sir Herbert Beerbohm Tree, were both friends of the Sitwells. Iris, 'fast', rebellious and clever like her close friend Nancy Cunard, briefly attended (with Diana Cooper) the Slade School of Fine Art,[1] where they were fellow students with 'Chile' Guevara. A poet and actress as well as a painter, Iris contributed poems to the first four volumes of *Wheels* and later toured with Diana Cooper in *The Miracle*. She married the American photographer and painter Curtis Moffat.

Iris sat to many artists. As a child she had been painted by Sir William Nicholson. While Vanessa Bell was making this portrait at 46 Gordon Square, Duncan Grant was also painting her (the portrait is now in the Reading Museum and Art Gallery), and Roger Fry painted her in the same year. She also sat to Epstein and Augustus John, and to Guevara after his paintings of Edith and Nancy Cunard.

2.26
The Editor of *Wheels*
By Alvaro Guevara, *c.* 1919
(illustrated on page 41)

Guevara's portrait of Edith was exhibited at the International Society in October 1919. It both impressed and puzzled critics at the time: 'There is colour with real light in it, and arranged in a real design; and, besides this, there is real character in the sitter. With so many realities there is danger of an imperfect harmony among them; and we are not sure that this quiet, peculiar colour, this slanting, unexpected design, and this intense character are harmonized ... one must put a note of interrogation against a most exciting picture.'[1] Edith is seen seated on an Omega Egyptian dining-chair in her flat at 22 Pembridge Mansions.

No documentary evidence is given to support the date of 1916 often ascribed to this work. Guevara's association with *Wheels* was limited to the third and fourth cycles, both published in 1919 (2.28) and it seems unlikely, had the portrait been finished in 1916, that it would have remained unexhibited for three years.

1. *The Times*, 9.10.1919

2.27

Nancy Cunard

By Alvaro Guevara, 1919

The epitome of the outrageous *jeunesse dorée*, Nancy Cunard (1896-1965) is punctiliously described by Osbert in *Great Morning* as having 'ineffable charm and distinction of mind'.[1] She called out more fulsome epithets from others: 'incomparably bewitching', according to Raymond Mortimer; a head 'carved in crystal with green jade for eyes' said Harold Acton; 'skin as white as bleached almonds' recalled David Garnett. A poet who was credited by some, but not her biographer, as the instigator of *Wheels*, she also ran a private printing press in the later 1920s. She was wild, promiscuous and uninhibited where Edith was affectionate, loyal and chaste.

Nancy turned the heads of many of Edith's male friends, including Aldous Huxley, Robert Nichols and, most significantly, 'Chile' Guevara. Chile and Nancy were introduced to each other by Iris Tree at the focal point of bohemian London, the Eiffel Tower restaurant. Writing many years later Nancy recalled the meeting: 'I was nonplussed by the tall, rather slouchy South American dressed in a black suit somewhat short in the arm. But I was struck by his fine, sensitive hands, which he always kept thrust deep in his pockets as he shambled down streets, with, of all things, a bowler hat on his fine massive head.'[2]

The affair between Nancy and Chile was fostered by Lady Cunard, who also encouraged the painting of Chile's portrait of Nancy in the winter of 1919 when 'hours of silence would slip away as the day dropped into December murk'.[3] Nancy had recently left her husband, Sydney Fairbairn, and the portrait is set in her mother's drawing-room in Grosvenor Square where she was living at the time. Looking back in 1955 on her youthful diaries Nancy described the portrait as 'unending' and 'awful'. She quickly tired of Chile's attentions and her rejection of his proposals prompted him to return to his native country for an extended painting session. The portrait was first exhibited at the Modern Society of Portrait Painters exhibition in February 1920, and acquired by the National Gallery of Victoria, Melbourne, in 1954.

1. GM, p. 256
2. Quoted by D. Holman-Hunt in *Latin Among Lions*, 1974, p. 76
3. *Ibid.*

2.28

Wheels

The six volumes, or 'cycles', of the poetry anthology *Wheels* were published between 1916 and 1921 as a Modernist counterblast to Edward Marsh's *Georgian Poetry*. The title poem in the first cycle is by Nancy Cunard. Her contemporary, Nina Hamnett, thought that *Wheels* owed its inspiration to her: 'Nancy Cunard, who was often at the Eiffel Tower, started a poetry magazine called *Wheels*. Three young poets called Sitwell wrote for it.'[1] Whatever the original division of labour, Edith alone is acknowledged as the editor in the four volumes from 1918. After the cliquish collection of writers included in the 1916 volume (described by the *Evening Standard* as a 'Society Anthology'), *Wheels* broadened its scope to include Aldous Huxley and, most notably, Wilfred Owen in 1919. From the second cycle onwards the reviews of previous cycles were published at the end of each volume. The majority were favourable and reflect an increasingly appreciative view of the anthologies, but Edith doubtless enjoyed including her detractors, too: the critic of the *Pall Mall Gazette* complained that 'the foetidness of the whole clings to the nostrils'.

1. N. Hamnett, *Laughing Torso*, 1932, p. 98

a) *Wheels*: *An Anthology of Verse*
Published by B. H. Blackwell, Oxford, 1916

The first *Wheels* includes poems by Nancy Cunard, Iris Tree, Osbert and Edith as well as Sacheverell's first published poem, 'Li-Taï-Pé Drinks and Drowns'. It also saw the posthumous publication of three poems by Osbert's Grenadier friend, 'Bimbo' Tennant, killed in 1916, and an elegy, 'The Great Adventure', written to his memory by Helen Rootham. A second edition published in April 1917 includes an anonymous preface by Osbert entitled 'In Bad Taste'.

b) *Wheels: A Second Cycle*
Published by B. H. Blackwell, Oxford, 1917

The 1917 *Wheels* includes nine poems by Aldous Huxley. The cover was designed by C. W. Beaumont. This was the cycle Wilfred Owen bought when he was considering the Sitwells' request for poems from him.

c) *Wheels 1918: A Third Cycle*
Published by B. H. Blackwell, Oxford, 1919
Edited by Edith Sitwell

The cover for the 1918 *Wheels* is *The Sky Pilot* by Laurence Atkinson (1873-1941), a self-taught artist who had joined Wyndham Lewis's Rebel Art Centre in 1914. The endpapers for this cycle were designed by Alvaro Guevara (see 2.23) who also contributed translations of two Spanish poems to this and the subsequent volume.

d) *Wheels 1919: Fourth Cycle*
Published by B. H. Blackwell, Oxford, 1919
Edited by Edith Sitwell

Wheels 1919 is dedicated to the memory of Wilfred Owen and includes seven of his poems: 'The Show', 'Strange Meeting', 'A Terre', 'The Sentry', 'Disabled', 'The Dead Beat' and 'The Chances'. The cover, *Gun Drill*, and endpapers are by William Roberts.

e) *Wheels 1920: Fifth Cycle*
Published by Duckworth, London 1928
Edited by Edith Sitwell

The first edition of *Wheels 1920*, dedicated to Mrs Arnold Bennett, was published by Leonard Parsons in October 1920 with a cover and endpapers designed by Gino Severini (see 3.16). Duckworth's 1928 re-issue uses the same design but omits the wheel device on the title page. In the first edition this had included Wyndham Lewis's name on one of the spokes, although he was not a contributor.

f) *Wheels 1921: Sixth Cycle*
Published by C. W. Daniel Ltd, London, 1921
Edited by Edith Sitwell

The cover for the final volume of *Wheels* was, like that for the fourth cycle, designed by William Roberts. The price of *Wheels* seems to have fluctuated dramatically with the change of publisher. From 2/6 for the first volume, it rose to 6/- for the 1919 and 1920 editions, dropping to 3/6 for the slimmer 1921 *Wheels*.

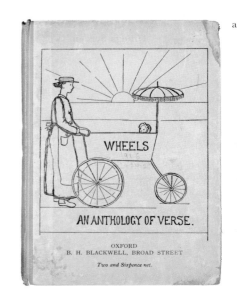
a

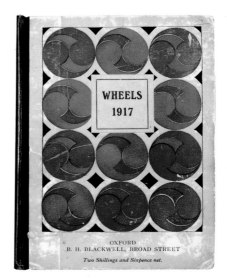
b

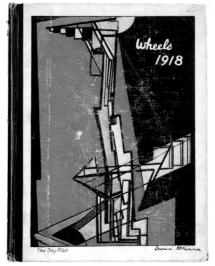
c

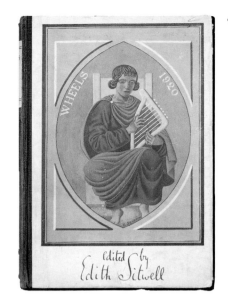
e

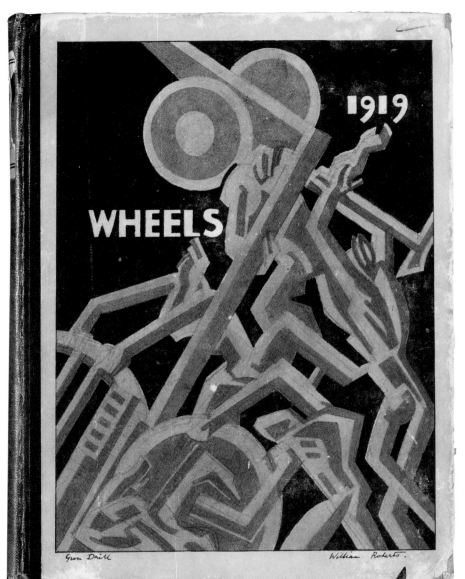
d

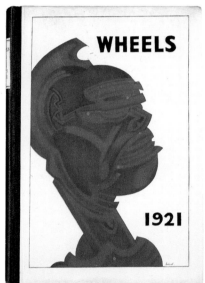
f

d, title page illustration

d, endpapers

2.29

A Shell Dump

By William Roberts, 1919

William Roberts (1895-1980) studied at the Slade School of Fine Art from 1910 to 1913, a fellow student with C. R. W. Nevinson, Stanley Spencer, David Bomberg, Adrian Allinson, Paul Nash and Alvaro Guevara. As a regular diner at the Eiffel Tower restaurant, he also knew Nancy Cunard and Iris Tree, and must have come across Osbert among the smarter members of London's Bohemian society. He was called up in April 1916 and spent three years as a gunner in the Royal Field Artillery, including seventeen months at a

stretch in France. In the summer of 1918 he became an official artist for the Canadian War Records Office. After painting *Gas Attack* for the Canadians, Roberts was commissioned by the British Ministry of Information and chose as his subject an ammunition dump. The massive painting, *A Shell Dump* (Imperial War Museum), was completed shortly after the end of the First World War. The water-colour owned by Osbert was one of a number of early works by Roberts in his possession and though related in subject matter, post-dates the canvas in the Imperial War Museum.

From an Office Window

By Christopher Richard Wynne Nevinson, 1917

C. R. W. Nevinson (1889-1946) was one of several
Slade students advised by his tutor Henry Tonks
to abandon art as a career. Humiliated, he
transferred his talents from 1912-1913 to the
Académie Julian in Paris and for a time shared a
studio with Modigliani. One of his closest friends
in Montparnasse was Gino Severini (see 3.16) and
it was with Severini's help that the Italian Futurist
Marinetti visited England in June 1914. His
manifesto, co-signed by Nevinson, was published
in the British press that summer. Despite Tonks's
warning, Nevinson enjoyed huge success with his
Modernist war paintings and street scenes, which
were immediately popular in exhibitions in both
London and New York.

Nevinson served in the First World War as an
ambulance driver and with the RAMC before
being appointed an Official War Artist. He met
Osbert in 1916 and readily fell under the Sitwell
spell, finding them 'in love with all the finer
achievements of man, yet full of wit and diabolical
cynicism'.[1] Curiously, he also describes them as
'tolerant'. In later years Nevinson drew portraits
of Edith (see 4.5) and Georgia as well as making
oil studies of Renishaw. It is not known exactly
when Osbert acquired *From an Office Window*, but
it hung prominently in his house in Carlyle
Square (see 2.33). He included a lyrical
description of it in his book on Nevinson
published in 1925 in the *Contemporary British Artists*
series: 'The angles and curves of pale blue smoke,
those cylindrical chimney-pots that turn in the
wind with the sound of a ghost in chains and
clanking armour'.[2] In 1947 it was lent to
Nevinson's memorial exhibition at the Leicester
Galleries for which Osbert also wrote a catalogue
preface. Nevinson produced a mezzotint of the
same subject in 1918.[3]

1. C. R. W. Nevinson, *Paint and Prejudice*, 1937, p. 89
2. OS, *C. R. W. Nevinson*, 1925
3. Illustrated in *Avant-garde British Printmaking*, exhibition catalogue,
British Museum, 1990 (30)

2.31

The Drawing-room at 2 Carlyle Square, Chelsea

By Ethel Sands, *c.* 1920-1925
(illustrated on page 45)

Osbert and Sacheverell moved into 2 Carlyle
Square from Swan Walk in November 1919. The
American painter and socialite Ethel Sands was a
frequent visitor; indeed for much of the year they
were also neighbours, for Sands lived with her
friend, the painter Nan Hudson, two streets away
at The Vale. Osbert became her particular friend
and the relationship lasted from 1917 until her
death in 1962.

The drawing-room at Carlyle Square was on
the first floor and was painted blue, pink and
violet, colours apparently chosen by Roger Fry
who, according to Osbert, also helped to paint the
ceiling. Sands's painting shows the back part of
the L-shaped room and in it can be seen some of
the Victorian glass that Osbert moved from Swan
Walk in 'terrifying prismatic journeys in cabs'.[1]
Over the fireplace hangs the Modigliani *Peasant
Girl*, which he showed to his father with the
(hopeless) intention of persuading him to purchase
the contents of Modigliani's studio. After the sale
of the Modigliani, its place was taken by a Juan
Gris painting. Dobson's curtain (see 3.11) hung
across the entrance to this part of the room when,
on the night of 24 January 1922, the first
performance of *Façade* was given to a small invited
audience of friends.

1. LNR, pp. 157-61

2.32

Photograph of the wardrobe painted by Ethel Sands in 1924

By Lewis Morley, 1963

'Ethel Sands decorated a wardrobe for me,' wrote
Osbert in *Moving House*, 'and on the outside she
painted a replica of the inside, shelves of ties,
collars, shirts, shoes and shoe-trees, a shiny black
tall hat and a long cane with a tortoiseshell
handle.'[1] The wardrobe is still in the possession of
the Sitwell family.

1. OS, *Queen Mary and Others*, 1974, pp. 170-1

2.33

The Drawing-room, 2 Carlyle Square

Copy print from the *Illustrated London News*,
16 October 1926

This view of the drawing-room is taken from
beside one of the front windows. Visible at the
back of the L-shaped room is Wyndham Lewis's
A Reading of Ovid (3.33): its frame can also just be
made out in Ethel Sands' painting (see p. 45).
Nevinson's *From an Office Window* (2.30) hangs
above a table with Chinese gilded flowers in
Bristol blue glass jars and a glass dome containing
a white feather flower arrangement.

The photograph is one of a number
illustrating an article on London interiors.
Captioned 'A well-known Modernist Poet's taste
in furniture and decoration', it is a modest
contrast to the other rooms featured, which
include the first and second drawing-rooms in
Lord and Lady Louis Mountbatten's house in
Park Lane.

2.34

Interior of 2 Carlyle Square
By E. J. Mason for *Homes and Gardens*,
January 1936

a) Dining-room
The dining-room or 'the shed', as Osbert called it
in an interview with Ronald Blythe, was a
separate structure in the garden. 'How can
photography present anything but a travesty',
gushed *Homes and Gardens*, 'of a dining-room with
dark green iridescent walls with Baroque consoles
of heavy gilded carving and the writhing gold of
dragons, scarlet lacquer and green opalescent
Venetian glass?' The marble top of the dining-
table was supported on four bronze lions that had
come from a chiffonier in Carlton House Terrace.
The painting to the right is *Prize-Fight* by William
Roberts.

b) Drawing-room
A Tchelitchew portrait of Edith hangs over the
fireplace. On either side of it stand African
sculptures against strips of 'petunia-coloured
ribbon'. To the right are grouped the Severini
gouaches (see 3.16).

c) Back room, ground floor
The ground-floor room had pink walls and
lacquer-red woodwork. The drawings are
described as ranging from 'Rowlandson to
Gaudier-Brzeska and Picasso', though the
Romneys to the right of the window are most
easily discernible in the photograph. Dominating
the room is the carved wooden bowl containing
the Sitwells' press cuttings.

2.35
Edward Marsh
By Frank Dobson, 1938

The Sitwells' antagonism to Edward Marsh
(1872-1953) was a complicated affair. As a patron
of modern art and literature he was a potential
ally, and many of the authors who contributed
to his biennial anthology, *Georgian Poetry*, from its
inception in 1912, were also commended by the
Sitwells. But as an establishment figure (he
was knighted in 1937) who promoted the Rupert
Brooke school of War poetry, and more
particularly as Winston Churchill's private
secretary, he was 'The Enemy'. Osbert's cruel
portrayal of him in *Triple Fugue* severed friendly
relations. As Mr Matthew Dean, he was easily
recognisable with 'eyebrows tilted up like the
eaves of a Japanese temple', 'a patron of
advanced art ... as long as it has not advanced too
far to make safe its retreat', and a man whose
position 'behind the scenes in politics helps his
prestige as a connoisseur of art'.

The sculptor Frank Dobson was one of the
many young artists whose work was collected by
Marsh around the time of the First World War.
The bust, made some twenty years later, was
exhibited at the Academy in 1939 and acquired
by Doncaster Museum and Art Gallery as a gift
from the Contemporary Art Society in 1963.

2.36
Art and Letters
Nos 1-4 (new series), 1918-1919

Art and Letters was founded by Herbert Read and
Frank Rutter. The first issue appeared in June
1917. The following year Osbert and Sacheverell
expressed an interest in buying into the magazine
and Read recorded his first meeting with them at
the Café Royal: 'aristocratic, wealthy, officers in
the Guards ... *also* furious socialists, good poets
(Sachie very good) and very young'.[1] Osbert
became a one-third partner and co-editor of *Art
and Letters* from November 1918 until the demise of
the quarterly in 1920. The list of contributors,
many already recruited by Read, indicates a
publication in a different league from *Wheels*.
Among the writers are T. S. Eliot, Ezra Pound,
Dorothy Richardson and Siegfried Sassoon; there
is music by Bernard van Dieren and E. J. Moeran
and illustrations by Picasso and Modigliani as well
as many English avant-garde artists.

Though Read helped the Sitwell brothers with
the Heal's exhibition in 1919, in later years their
friendship became somewhat strained, not least
when Geoffrey Grigson observed parallels between
Edith's *Aspects of Modern Poetry* and Read's earlier
Form in Modern Poetry. 'I can't go on saying that I
don't believe a word of what Grigson wrote',
Read told Denton Welch. 'You know what these
things are. One can never put them right it seems
– especially with the Sitwells. Conceit isn't the
word to describe their attitude. It's a sort of
arrogance due, I think, to their loveless
childhood.'[2]

1. Quoted in Pearson, p. 126
2. Quoted in J. King, *The Last Modern, A Life of Herbert Read*, 1990, p. 144

2.37
Who Killed Cock-Robin?
By Osbert Sitwell, 1921

The amiable, tweedy J. C. Squire (1884-1958),
champion of the ordinary man, of England,
cricket and Rupert Brooke, featured prominently
in the Sitwell demonology. He was in fact
anathema to a broad range of the literary élite,
'that little worm' according to Lytton Strachey,
and 'more repulsive', spluttered Virginia Woolf,
'than words can express'. As literary editor of the
New Statesman Squire had been responsible for a
review of *Wheels, Third Cycle* that described Edith's
talent as 'charming and rather trivial'. In his new
magazine, the *London Mercury*, founded in 1919, he
was still unreformed, denouncing Osbert as 'an
ordinary immature writer of verses'. *Who Killed
Cock Robin?* was Osbert's most succinct diatribe
against the 'Squirearchy', here re-named the
'Mammon Poets', and consists of a series of
gnomic and epigrammatic utterances in the style
of Jean Cocteau's *Le Coq et l'Arlequin*. It bemoans
in particular the debased Tennysonian verse of
his contemporaries, personified as 'Eunuch
Arden', 'a putrescent corpse' who 'walks abroad
"singing" ... in a high falsetto voice'.

2.38
Robert Ross
By Elliott and Fry, *c.* 1914

The lover of Oscar Wilde and chief guardian of his memory and literary reputation, Robert Ross (1869-1918) is seen here with a copy of *De Profundis*, which Wilde wrote in prison. As an ex-art editor of the *Morning Post*, Ross was an established pundit, but it was his role as literary godfather that was of primary importance to the Sitwells. Osbert had met Ross before the First World War at 'Hill', the home of Mrs Charles Hunter, and during the war years got to know him well. Ross's bachelor rooms at 40 Half Moon Street are nostalgically recalled in *Noble Essences* and it was through him that the Sitwells met, among others, Edmund Gosse, Arnold Bennett, Siegfried Sassoon and Wilfred Owen.

2.39
Sir Edmund Gosse
By John Russell and Sons, *c.* 1916

Osbert described Edmund Gosse (1849-1928), the Grand Old Man of literary London, as 'the lingering, final spark of the pre-Raphaelite comet which had flashed through the darkness of the Victorian small hours'. He was more prosaically described by Lord Clark as 'a cross between an old tom-cat and an octogenarian pirate'. Edith wrote of dining with the Gosses as a pleasure 'not unmingled with terror for one could never foresee exactly what Sir Edmund was going to do to one conversationally.'

1. NE, p. 35
2. Quoted in Pearson, p. 110
3. TCO, p. 95

2.40
Arnold Bennett
By Howard Coster, 1929

Arnold Bennett (1867-1931) was one of several members of the older literary generation who cultivated, and were cultivated by, the Sitwells. Osbert was introduced to him by Robert Ross in the spring of 1918 at the Reform Club and within a short space of time he had become 'Uncle Arnold' to all three Sitwells and dined regularly with Osbert and Sacheverell. Liberal with money (he helped the Sitwells buy into *Art and Letters*), he was also generous in lending his prestige as a novelist and critic: his preface to the 1919 French Art exhibition catalogue added considerable weight to the project. 'Battle', he wrote famously of the Sitwells, 'is in the curve of their nostrils. They issue forth from their bright pavilions and demand trouble. And few spectacles are more touching than their gentle, quiet, surprised, ruthless demeanour when they get it.' An interruption in their friendship occurred when Edith fell out with Bennett's young French wife, Marguerite (to whom *Wheels* 1920 was dedicated), over the Anglo-French Poetry Society that had been initiated by the Bennetts but hijacked by Edith. Marguerite had 'impertinently' criticised Helen Rootham. Contact was resumed after Bennett left Marguerite and it was at a dance at his house in 1924 that Osbert met Georgia Doble.

1. *Adelphi*, August 1923

2.41

Woman, Harlequin and Pierrot
By Pablo Picasso, 1918

Sacheverell had been 'especially impressed by the work of Picasso'[1], which he had seen in Paris in March 1919, and later in the year he visited the artist in London during the painting of the *Tricorne* backdrop in Vladimir Polunin's studio. Picasso's dropcloth for the Cocteau-Satie ballet *Parade*, also seen in London for the first time that summer, he considered a masterpiece, recognising that the artist's interest in the *commedia dell'arte* struck a deep chord with a long-held fascination of his own. In the autumn he and Osbert began discussions with Picasso about painting frescoes at Montegufoni (see 3.16). The drawing was in Osbert's collection and it is likely that he acquired it at about this time. It is not in Christian Zervos's *Pablo Picasso, Oeuvres de 1917 à 1919* (1949), but was probably made while Picasso was on honeymoon, staying in Madame Errazuriz's villa in Biarritz.

1. LNR, p. 51

2.42

Mother and Child
By Amedeo Modigliani, *c.* 1914-1916

It is not clear when Sacheverell acquired this drawing by Modigliani, but the inscription suggests that it was originally a gift to Zborowski from the artist. In *For Want of the Golden City* (1973), Sacheverell recalled that on his visit to Paris in March 1919 he 'bought two full length oil-paintings ... and several drawings for a pound apiece'.[1] Osbert wrote in *Laughter in the Next Room* that Sacheverell arrived in Biarritz with 'a fine drawing by Modigliani', though it is uncertain whether this 'fine drawing' was that torn up and used by the hotel valet to pack his shoes. Neither is it known whether the Sitwells bought any of the 'sheaf' of Modigliani drawings sold for a shilling each at the Heal's exhibition in 1919. Compositions similar to *Mother and Child* are in the Frans Hals Museum in Haarlem and the John S. Newberry Collection in the Museum of Modern Art, New York, and suggest a date between 1914 and 1916.

The Sitwells' ownership of Modigliani paintings poses a more difficult puzzle. In *Laughter in the Next Room* Osbert writes about the *Peasant Girl*, which he and Sacheverell were allowed to purchase at cost (£4) from 'the Parisian dealers who owned the majority of Modigliani's work in the [Heal's] Exhibition'. As none of the nine Modigliani paintings in the exhibition bore this title, it may not have been exhibited. The work, described in detail by Osbert, was sold by him 'some five or six years later', and then resold twice within a few months. The identity of this painting is not now known though it can be seen sketchily in Ethel Sands's painting of the Carlyle Square drawing-room (2.31). There is more of a problem with the two paintings mentioned by Sacheverell in *For Want of the Golden City*. He says that one of these 'is now in the Tate Gallery', but his ownership is not recorded in the provenance of any of the Tate's Modiglianis, though the gallery's *The Little Peasant* (5269) was exhibited as no. 41 in the Heal's exhibition.

1. FWGC, p. 392

2.43

At the House of Mrs Kinfoot
By Osbert Sitwell, 1921

In the four satirical poems included in this elegant pamphlet, privately published in an edition of 101 by The Favil Press, Osbert lampoons as 'Mrs Kinfoot' his erstwhile hostess and guest at Swan Walk, Sibyl Colefax.

The endpapers, by William Roberts, reflect the widespread interest among artists and collectors of the time in sculpture from Africa and Oceania. Two figurines from Osbert's collection are visible in photographs of his house in Carlyle Square (2.34).

2.44

To the Lord of Song
By William Roberts, *c.* 1913-1914

The Sitwells made two gestures of homage to great singers: all three of them offered bay and myrtle to the Italian soprano Madame Tetrazzini; and, probably in 1913 or 1914, Osbert and Sacheverell presented 'an enormous laurel wreath' to the Russian singer and actor Feodor Chaliapin, who was staying at the Savoy. It seems likely that Roberts's drawing illustrates this occasion and shows Chaliapin on the left with the Sitwells proffering a wreath. As neither Edith's nor the artist's presence at the Savoy is recorded, the drawing is probably based on an account given to Roberts later.

The wreath party, which consisted of William Walton, Francis Birrell, Raymond Mortimer and David Garnett in addition to the Sitwell brothers, was kept waiting for Chaliapin the entire morning. When he arrived 'the great Russian seized the wreath and with extraordinary *savoir-faire* did not even glance at it but sent it spinning away behind him across the polished floor. Then, taking Osbert into his bear's hug, he embraced him warmly, kissing him on each cheek and then holding him at arms' length, gazed with delight at seeing a poet so close.'[1]

1. D. Garnett, *The Familiar Faces*, 1962, p. 24

2.45

Robert Nichols
By Augustus John, 1921

In the now-forgotten verse of Robert Nichols (1893-1944), Edith sensed a poet of real promise, providing him with encouragement during a long and sustained correspondence. But though his *Ardours and Endurances* (1917) won him a temporary reputation as a War poet, the verdict of Nancy Cunard (see 2.27), with whom he was infatuated, that he was a 'shocking poet', was widely held. In America, however, he enjoyed success with a play, *Wings over Europe* (1928). Relations with the Sitwells deteriorated and in 1934 Nichols erupted into print with *Fisbo*, a monumental poem in rhyming couplets attacking Osbert on every conceivable front, including the furnishing of Carlyle Square:

> A Regency bed, wax fruit à la Victoria,
> Three chairs constructed from the bones of sauria,
> A poor Picabia, a worse Kandinsky,
> A caricature in waxwork of Nijinsky.

2.46

Virginia Woolf

By Vanessa Bell, 1912

'The company of Bloomsbury', wrote Edith disingenuously in her autobiography, 'were kind-hearted, and from time to time I entered it on sufferance.' In fact the Sitwells were thrown together with the Bloomsbury writers and artists on numerous occasions although they eyed each other askance in private. In the 1950s Edith dismissed Virginia Woolf the novelist as 'a beautiful little knitter',[1] but there was a mutual affection and a degree of respect between the two *grandes dames*. 'Of course you are a good poet,' Virginia Woolf wrote to Edith, 'but I can't think why.'[2]

In her diary Virginia Woolf noted meeting the Sitwell brothers for the first time at 46 Gordon Square on the day before the Russian Ballet party at Swan Walk in October 1918. Coincidentally her review of Edith's poems had appeared in *The Times* the same morning. The novelist's keen eye is responsible for some of the most memorable descriptions of Edith and she wrote of her at length in her diary on 20 May 1925. 'I thought she was severe, implacable & tremendous; rigid in her own conception. Not a bit of it. She is ... very kind, beautifully mannered ... Edith is humble: has lived in a park alone till 27, & so described nothing but sights & sounds; then came to London, & is trying to get a little emotion into her poetry – all of which I suspected, & think promising.'

Vanessa Bell's portrait is one of four she made of Virginia in the year of her marriage to Leonard Woolf. The artist herself had rather less contact with the Sitwells than her sister, but she designed the wrapper for Edith's *Poetry and Criticism*, published by the Hogarth Press in 1925.

1. Quoted in Pearson, p. 221
2. *Ibid.*

2.47
Giles Lytton Strachey
By Nina Hamnett, *c.* 1917

The fact that the critic and biographer Lytton Strachey (1880-1932) was a frequent guest of the Sitwells, in England and in Italy, did not prevent mutual sniping behind the scenes. After a grim evening at the Anglo-French Poetry Society in 1920 Strachey wrote to Dora Carrington that Edith, 'her nose longer than an ant-eater's', read some of 'her absurd stuff'.[1] Edith retaliated in her autobiography that Strachey 'seemed to have been cut out of very thin cardboard'[2] and she must have taken satisfaction when the *Observer* praised her *Victoria of England* (1936) as 'broader and warmer' than Strachey's earlier biography.

1. Quoted in Pearson, p. 166
2. TCO, p. 86

2.48
Walter Richard Sickert with his wife Thérèse Lessore
By Cecil Beaton, 1941

Edith, at the age of seventeen ('so shy that my hands were glued to my sides')[1], was the first of the Sitwells to meet Sickert (1860-1942). She was taken to tea with him by her cousin Mrs George Swinton and given a music-hall drawing by Sickert that remained one of her most treasured possessions. In later years Osbert got to know Sickert well, being asked to breakfast parties in Fitzroy Street and reciprocating with invitations to Swan Walk and later to Carlyle Square. He also owned a painting by Sickert's third wife, Thérèse Lessore. After Sickert's death Osbert edited a book of the artist's writings entitled *A Free House!* (1947).

1. TCO, p. 88

2.49

Ada Leverson

By Rita Martin, *c.* 1911

When, as children, the Sitwells first observed the writer Ada Leverson (1862-1933), in a hotel in Mayfair, she must have had the ethereal beauty caught by Rita Martin. A decade later, when they knew her well, she was stout, deaf, and dressed in black with a large hat; but nothing was ever dull in her company, as Osbert wrote in her obituary. Her 'Edith Ottley' novels about contemporary Edwardian London life enjoyed a revival in the 1960s, but she is more enduringly remembered as a friend to Oscar Wilde at the time of his trial and after his release from prison. It was Wilde who dubbed her 'the Sphinx'. Although a contemporary of their parents, the Sphinx was a close friend of the Sitwell trio from their meeting in 1918 and they spent many winters in each other's company in Italy. She was devoted to Osbert, who saw her on a daily basis in London in the years after the First World War and wrote at length about her in *Noble Essences*. Edith described her as 'a very wise owl entangled in a bush of singularly thick, singularly bright forsythia'[1]; and Sacheverell's third book, *The One Hundred and One Harlequins* (1922) was dedicated to her.

1. TCO, p. 84

2.50

Ronald Firbank

By Augustus John, *c.* 1915

Osbert had noticed the writer Ronald Firbank (1886-1926), looking like 'a witty and decadent Red Indian', some years before he and Sacheverell called on him in Oxford in 1919. They were, apparently, the first people to whom the reclusive Firbank had spoken, apart from his charlady and a guard on the London train, in two years. Edith had drawn their attention to *Vainglory* in 1915, and all the Sitwells admired the aesthetic prose style of this 'reincarnation of all the Nineties', as Wyndham Lewis called him. He later became a friend in London and in Italy, where he had a villa in Fiesole.

Augustus John was also a friend of Firbank and designed frontispieces for *Caprice* (1917) and *Valmouth* (1919). After Firbank's death Osbert contributed a memoir to the first volume of his works and this was reprinted, with an essay by Augustus John, in Ifan Kyrle Fletcher's *Ronald Firbank, A Memoir* in 1930. John's drawing was used by Osbert to illustrate his chapter on Firbank in *Noble Essences*; a second drawing is in the collection of the University of Texas.

2.51

Harold Monro

By Jacob Kramer, 1923

Harold Monro (1879-1932), poet and editor, was the founder of three literary magazines between 1912 and 1919, but it was his Poetry Bookshop in Devonshire Street that put him on the literary map. Here, in the comfortable panelled rooms above his shop, the London literati met regularly, read poetry and discussed new ideas. 'He would often of an evening bring together whole schools of poets of the most diverse faith, opinions and temperament ... Sometimes there would be battle, but always one heard the literary news.'[1] Both Harold and his wife Alida were friends of the Sitwells and stayed at Renishaw.

The artist Jacob Kramer may have met Monro through his friend Jacob Epstein, who rented rooms above the Poetry Bookshop. The mask-like portrait indicates the influence of African and Oceanic artefacts on Kramer's work at the time. It was reproduced as the frontispiece to Monro's posthumously published *Collected Poems* in 1933.

1. LNR, p. 34

2.52

William Henry Davies

By Augustus John, 1918

By the time the Sitwells met the Welsh-born writer W. H. Davies (1871-1940), shortly before the First World War, his reputation was already established with the publication of *The Autobiography of a Super-Tramp* (1908). 'He seemed only to make new friends, never new enemies', Osbert wrote of him in *Noble Essences*, recalling the affection in which he was held among the artistic and literary circles of the time. He was a frequent and often unexpected visitor of Edith's and Helen's at Pembridge Mansions and a regular at Swan Walk and Carlyle Square. After his marriage in 1925 he lived in Gloucestershire, a neighbour of Violet Gordon Woodhouse. Sickert, who was introduced to Davies by Osbert, said of him: 'I never find anyone who understands a single thing I'm aiming at, and then you bring along an old tramp with a wooden leg, and he at once understands everything I've ever attempted.'[1] After Davies's death Osbert wrote an appreciation of him for *Life and Letters To-day* and an introduction to his *Collected Poems* in 1943.

Two years before Augustus John's drawing Davies sat to Jacob Epstein for a sculpture, a cast of which is also in the collection of the National Portrait Gallery.

1. NE, p. 232

2.53

Violet Gordon Woodhouse

By Herbert Lambert, 1929

Both Sacheverell and Osbert wrote that they had known only two women of genius. One was their sister, the other was the musician Violet Gordon Woodhouse (1872-1948). A harpsichordist, clavichordist and pianist, she met Osbert at one of the Sunday afternoon concerts she gave at her house in Ovington Square during the First World War. She became a close family friend and all three Sitwells stayed with her at Nether Lypiatt, her home in Gloucestershire, and visited her in Mount Street, Mayfair. Osbert and Sacheverell were both present on the occasion in 1943 when she played there for George Bernard Shaw.

The series of photographs of Violet Gordon Woodhouse, deriving their inspiration from seventeenth-century Dutch interiors, are among the finest examples of Herbert Lambert's work. Many of the photographer's subjects were musicians; Violet Gordon Woodhouse and her teacher Arnold Dolmetsch (also photographed by Lambert) would have been of particular interest as Lambert was himself a clavichord maker.

On a January night in 1922 a mystified audience of 'friends and artists' were crammed into the icy drawing-room of Osbert's house in Carlyle Square, to hear what the badly typed programme called 'Miss Edith Sitwell on her Sengerphone with accompaniments, overture and interlude by W. Walton'. The mouth of the Sengerphone, a sort of overgrown megaphone, protruded through a painted curtain hung at the far end of the room; and while the willowy W. Walton attempted to conduct his mutinous sextet the hidden poetess intoned a number of her latest poems through the Sengerphone to the music. These included 'Madame Mouse Trots', 'Said King Pompey' and 'Jumbo's Lullaby'.

The performance left much to be desired, and the audience must have been grateful for the hot rum punch with which the evening ended. Yet if one had to pick a moment when the public legend of the Sitwells really started, it was during this cold, uncomfortable evening, which saw the first performance of the 'verse and music entertainment' that Edith had entitled *Façade*.

Until then, all three Sitwells had been pursuing their separate lives and ambitions to a greater extent than is often realised. Edith had still to write the poetry on which her reputation rests, but she had established her vocation as a poet, emphatically not a poetess, and was desperate for wider recognition. She was jealous of her position as co-founder and 'editor' of her avant-garde poetry annual, *Wheels*, and had a widespread network of her own admirers and friends on whom she could rely to boost her work.

For a nun-like figure, married to the sacred cause of Poetry, the gloom and apparent poverty of her famous flat in Pembridge Mansions was not entirely inappropriate, and certainly added to her air of dedication to her art. Moscow Road was a more magical address for a poet than Mayfair, and on her allowance from the family of £400 a year Edith managed to create something of a private salon for the writers and artists who appealed to her. According to the writer Geoffrey Gorer:

… those tea-parties of hers really were one of the most extraordinary literary affairs of the twenties when you think of them. For there she was, all but penniless, in a dingy little flat in an unfashionable part of London. All she could offer

was strong tea and buns. Yet, because of who she was, she attracted to that flat almost every major literary figure of the twenties.

Even so, nothing could seem further from all of this than the lives Osbert and Sacheverell were leading in their elegant house in Carlyle Square. Despite the lack of heating in the drawing-room, theirs were fashionable, almost pampered, lives compared with Edith's. From a family trust Osbert received a princely £2,000 a year. His housekeeper, Mrs Powell, looked after the brothers with absolute devotion, and up to a point their activities inevitably overlapped. They shared their friends, their travels and most of their enthusiasms. Italy, in particular, was common ground between them, partly because of their annual visits to Montegufoni, but more importantly because of their travels through southern Italy and the period they spent together every winter, writing in the Hotel Capuccini in Amalfi. Their work, however, like their characters, was quite distinct and very different.

The most dynamic member of the Sitwell trio was undoubtedly Osbert. If anything he was too dynamic. He was already a poetic satirist of some distinction, publicist, polemicist, and editor of the influential magazine, *Art and Letters*. With his first short story, *The Machine Breaks Down*, he had recently begun his career as a fiction writer; but his greatest role was as what he termed a self-appointed 'paladin', a champion fighting to defend 'the artist' against the forces of 'the Philistine'. Needless to say, the artists he was most intent on saving and protecting were the other two members of the Sitwell trio, Edith and Sacheverell.

Sacheverell seemed particularly at risk, for unlike his siblings he was as gentle as he was unaggressive, and as precocious as he was inexperienced. He was also a natural connoisseur, whose eye for the still-unfashionable baroque of Southern Italy would lead to his original and highly influential book, *Southern Baroque Art*, to be published in 1924. Most remarkable of all was the confidence with which he was already pursuing a self-appointed role as a sort of eighteenth-century patron and impresario of the arts. In 1919 he had a brain-wave that must rank among the greatest might-have-beens of modern art. In London he had come to know Picasso, and actually engaged him to fresco the great hall at Montegufoni

Façade and the Twenties

3.16

Three *Commedia dell'Arte* **Musicians**

By Gino Severini, 1922

for a fee of £1,000. The result in that enormous room might have been miraculous, and one can still sympathise with Sacheverell's anger when his father, rich Sir George, typically refused to consider it.

A more effective, and equally original, piece of patronage was the way that, as a nineteen-year-old undergraduate at Oxford, Sacheverell had 'adopted' the sixteen-year-old 'genius', William Walton. Walton, the son of a singing teacher from Oldham, was a music scholar at Christ Church at the time, and Sacheverell was so impressed by his abilities that he persuaded Osbert to invite him to live with them at Carlyle Square. Walton stayed on with the Sitwells for fourteen years as a friend and member of the family. There were no strings attached, except that he worked at his music. According to Osbert they simply wanted 'to be of use to him, and advance his chances and genius'.

As Walton said, 'had I been a writer, things might have been uncomfortable, but as a musician I just had my own room with my piano at the top of the house, and I was left in peace to get on with my work'. The redoubtable Mrs Powell mothered him and darned his socks, his keep was free, and when the Sitwells went to Italy or Renishaw he travelled with them. His greatest benefits were freedom and sophistication. As he said, 'for a raw young composer who knew nothing about anything it was an extraordinary education simply to be with the Sitwells, and especially to meet their friends who came to Carlyle Square'.

On that January night, none of the Sitwells can have possibly foreseen the extraordinary way in which *Façade* would become part of their legend. It is a strange tale, and because of this it is hard to disentangle the precise facts of its genesis from the fictions that surround them. What is indisputable is the degree to which all three Sitwells were involved. The verse was Edith's and the music William Walton's, but the whole inspiration and development of *Façade* into a key-work of the twenties was a remarkable combined achievement. And, as so often happened when all three Sitwells worked together, the whole affair got curiously out of hand.

For some time Edith had been attempting to establish herself as a great poetic presence – yet not succeeding as she might

have wished. Few of the earlier poets she had promoted in *Wheels* had stayed 'faithful', and despite her teas in Pembridge Mansions she was finding it harder to maintain her presence as embattled 'poetess'.

Her poetry was changing, too. She had recently become increasingly involved in experimental poetry as she moved away from the heavy realism of her earlier verse, and began evolving a style akin to abstract art. She made a lot of what she called her personal, poetic 'technique', and was absorbed by such things as the 'texture' of words, using assonance, dissonance, rhythm and repetition to produce particular effects. She had begun performing what she would term her poetic 'exercises': conscientiously teaching herself to use words much as a composer uses notes and phrases in his music. Music had always meant a lot to her, and according to Osbert she was experimenting in order to obtain

3.40
William Walton
By Cecil Beaton, 1926

'through the medium of words, the rhythm of dance measures such as waltzes, polkas, foxtrots'.

This naturally interested Walton as a composer, and according to what Edith told her secretary, Elizabeth Salter, 'Willie gave me certain rhythms and said, "There you are, Edith, see what you can do with that." So I went away and did it. I wanted to prove that I could.' She added, not unimportantly, that she first wrote the poems in *Façade* 'for fun'.

Walton's memory of what occurred was completely different, although he confirmed the distinctly casual way *Façade* began. He always maintained that he had no recollection of providing Edith with her 'rhythms'. 'It was simply that Edith had written a number of poems already which were calling out for music. When I began writing it, it was just one big experiment.' And, certainly, Edith had already published more than half the poems that were included in the first production of *Façade* before the idea of writing any music to accompany them was even mooted.

According to Walton the real impulse came from Osbert and Sacheverell, 'who both became extremely excited and involved with it once we started. They, not Edith, were the ones who were really keen on making me continue with the music. I remember thinking it was not a very good idea, but when I said so, they simply told me they'd get Constant Lambert to do it if I wouldn't – and of course I couldn't possibly let that occur.'

As usual, Osbert and Sacheverell were very much aware of what they were up to. Ever since Schoenberg composed music to accompany Albert Giraud's *Pierrot Lunaire* ten years earlier, the whole idea of having verse declaimed to music had become something of a cliché in the Modern Movement. The real precedent had been Jean Cocteau's *Parade*, with décor by Picasso and music by Erik Satie, which had caused such notable furore when performed in Paris in 1917. Cocteau's career – as poet, artist, impresario and dandy – had long been a potent source of inspiration, and envy, to Osbert. The idea of creating a similar artistic triumph and issuing an artistic challenge to the die-hards and the philistines in the midst of London, must have been irresistible to him. Here with *Façade* perhaps he had his chance.

As work on *Façade* progressed, there was a sense of the

Sitwells' patronage of Walton beginning to pay off. By now all three of them were taking it extremely seriously; and Osbert has described the long sessions Edith and Walton spent together going over her poems again and yet again, 'while he marked and accented them for his own guidance, to show where the precise stress and emphasis fell'.

Theoretically their aims were most ambitious: to achieve a fusion of poetry and music and get through for once to 'that unattainable land which, in the finest songs, always lies looming mysteriously beyond, a land full of meanings and of nuances, analogies and images'. More to the point, much of the Sitwells' own sense of fantasy and 'fun' was wonderfully preserved within the poems and the music, as was something of their attitude to life – magical, witty and stylish to an extraordinary degree.

3.14
**Edith with Neil Porter at the
New Chenil Galleries**
By Pacific and Atlantic Photos Ltd, April 1926

Walton's music matched the mood and rhythms of the poetry so perfectly that one feels that only a composer who was virtually a member of the family could have managed it. In composing the music for *Façade*, the only modern work he ever admitted having influenced him was Stravinsky's *The Soldier's Tale*. This had been performed first in Switzerland in 1918 and, working directly with his librettist, Ramuz, Stravinsky had composed an extraordinarily complex score that included a waltz in Viennese style, a ragtime serenade, an Argentinian tango and a Bach-like chorale.

It was a difficult model for an inexperienced young composer to attempt to follow, and it inevitably took time – and quite a number of rehearsals, fiascos and performances – before *Façade* could hope to be completed. But Walton had the determined Osbert and Sacheverell to spur him on. Sacheverell solved the problem of how the poetry should be declaimed by discovering the Sengerphone: a large papier mâché megaphone with an elaborate mouthpiece. It had been invented by one Herr Senger, a Swiss opera singer, to enable him to sing the part of Fafner the dragon with great clarity and resonance at Bayreuth. It was, said Walton, 'a lovely instrument', with a mouthpiece covering the lower part of the face, and it allowed the poetry to be spoken clearly and impersonally. It was Osbert's idea that the Sengerphone, the speaker and the orchestra should all be carefully concealed from the audience behind a painted curtain.

The resemblance of the whole production to that of Cocteau's *Parade* was growing: Cocteau had even had the idea of using a hidden megaphone for declaiming words above the ballet, and Picasso would have been ideal to paint the dividing curtain for *Façade* just as he had painted Cocteau's scenery. But the days were over when the Sitwells could afford to commission him. Instead Osbert picked Frank Dobson, who had been working on a Brancusi-like portrait bust of him in brass (3.2). His studio was just around the corner from Carlyle Square in Manresa Road, and together they devised a large drop curtain with a huge mask in the centre with an open mouth – through which the Sengerphone projected.

Then there was the question of a title for the unnamed work. Various versions of its origins have developed over the years, as

3.15
Curtain design for *Façade*
By John Piper, 1942

things had a habit of doing with the Sitwells, but Walton firmly insisted that it came from Edith's char-lady at Pembridge Mansions. 'All this carry-on is just one big façade', she is supposed to have grumbled, a remark that only a Sitwell char-lady could have uttered, and which Edith certainly appreciated.

There were a number of experimental performances of *Façade*, and with each the production, poetry and music were improved. After the first performance at Carlyle Square a second was held, again in private, at Mrs Mathias's house on 7 February 1922. During the next fifteen months the Sitwells, and especially Walton, rallied round 'to smooth out the imperfections of the entertainment' for a full public performance. This memorable event was scheduled for the afternoon of 12 June 1923 at the Aeolian Hall.

The Aeolian Hall (or the A-E-I-O-Ulian Hall, as Noël Coward christened it) was in Bond Street, and the performance that took place became central to the whole mythology of the Sitwells. According to the 'official' Sitwell view, as expressed by both Edith and Osbert in their memoirs, it was the nearest they ever came to actual confrontation with the embattled philistine. A large part of the audience were there to indulge their favourite English sport of 'artist-baiting' and were so incensed at their contact with artists in the flesh that they became infuriated as *Façade* continued and 'manifested their contempt and rage', first by hissing, and finally by threatening to attack poor Edith, who had to wait until the hostile crowd dispersed. She used to claim that she was nearly lynched by the 'inevitable old woman', symbol of the enemy, who had waited, umbrella raised, to smite her.

Next day the popular papers took up the battle and continued to insult the Sitwells in their sacred role of artists. Osbert's wartime hatred of the yellow press revived when he read in one gossip column, in an article under the headline 'Drivel They Paid To Hear', an interview with the fireman at the Aeolian Hall who was quoted as saying, quite reasonably in the circumstances, 'that never in twenty years' experience of recitals at that hall had he known anything like it'.

'For several weeks subsequently', wrote Osbert, 'we were obliged to go about London feeling as if we had committed a

murder'; and from then on the battle of the Aeolian Hall seemed to epitomise all that was obscurantist, vulgar and ill-natured in the way society at large reacted to the artist.

But was it really? Walton's friend, the musician, Angus Morrison was there and remembered something very different from the scenes described by Osbert and by Edith. As he described it:

> Everyone was perfectly good-mannered and no one objected violently at all. There were certainly no boos or catcalls. On the other hand there wasn't much enthusiasm either. As a performance, the Aeolian Hall *Façade* simply wasn't very good, and then a hot summer afternoon in a stuffy London hall isn't the place to listen to a new production like *Façade*. The hall wasn't very full, and the whole thing fell distinctly flat.

Two future writers, Evelyn Waugh and Harold Acton, both keen Sitwellians, were also in the audience and neither mentioned any demonstration of 'contempt and rage'. Nor did Virginia Woolf, who was also there and who wrote rather weakly, 'I understood so little that I could not judge.'

As for William Walton, he freely admitted that 'the performance at the Aeolian Hall was a shambles. It was badly performed and the music wasn't right. By the time of the next

3.4
Osbert Sitwell
By Hugh Cecil, *c.* 1925

performance at the Chenil Galleries, we got it right, and it was all a great success, but at the Aeolian Hall it was disastrous.' It is interesting that he also claimed to have been 'terribly upset – far more so than Edith and Osbert, who really loved a fight, and saw this as a chance to weigh in against the opposition'.

The truth of what occurred that afternoon is that the first public performance of *Façade* was actually a flop and not a battle; and faced with failure, Osbert and Edith's first reaction was always to reach for an opponent they could blame it on. In this way even failure could be reinvented in terms of that pattern of betrayal and aggression that life had taught them. Given their confidence and taste for conflict, this was a source of considerable strength to them both; and much of their energy and wit, their social life and even their writing, was fuelled by the constant need to fight back at a dimly comprehended enemy. If, as then, there simply was no enemy, an enemy had to be invented.

At the end of his account of the affair in his autobiography, Osbert congratulates himself on the fact that 'we had created a first-class scandal in literature and music', a somewhat strange remark until one recalls again the all-important precedent of Cocteau's *Parade*. For one of the great achievements of *Parade*, when originally performed in Paris, was the amount of sheer controversy it aroused. Indeed, it produced *un scandale*: jeers, catcalls, critics up in arms, and a full-scale battle in the stalls between the impassioned enemies of the work and its supporters. It shocked the bourgeoisie and the reactionaries, showed where the lines of battle lay, and instantly established Cocteau's name at the centre of the Modern Movement.

Façade at the Aeolian Hall was simply not *un scandale*. Osbert did his best to make it one but sadly, unlike the French, the secret weapon of the English philistine is not aggression but indifference. The performance would have been quietly forgotten but for the sleek young man whom Angus Morrison saw walking out 'a little more ostentatiously than perhaps he need have done', just before the end of the performance.

Osbert had got to know Noël Coward a few months before that afternoon, at the house of Mrs Beatrice Guinness. Although penurious, more or less unknown, and still only twenty-three, the

author of *The Young Idea* was, as his biographer Cole Lesley said, by now always in demand in the houses of the rich and famous, thanks to his conversation and the songs he sang at the piano.

Early that summer Coward was writing a revue for Gertrude Lawrence and Maisie Gay, and a few days before the Aeolian Hall performance Osbert had met him lunching at the Ivy. According to Coward's recollection, Osbert remarked, 'I hear you're doing a review. What fun!' He then invited him to come to see *Façade* with what would prove to be the ominous words, 'It might give you some ideas.' Coward went, and according to Cole Lesley, 'Noël always told me that he did *not* walk out of *Façade*. "I wouldn't have missed a minute of it for anything in the world",

3.20
Noël Coward
By Dorothy Wilding, 1925

were, I am afraid, the words he used.'

Whether he did or not hardly matters, for Coward saw enough to give him what he needed. He had been looking for material for Maisie Gay, and when *London Calling!* opened at the Duke of York's Theatre at the beginning of September 1923 the hit of the show was her performance as the poetess Hernia Whittlebot, in a sketch entitled 'The Swiss Family Whittlebot', reciting her 'poems' with her two brothers, Gob and Sago Whittlebot.

If Osbert was really longing for publicity, he had got it now. The three Whittlebots were unmistakably the Sitwells and there was a compliment of sorts in being singled out as *the* representatives of modern English poetry. But Maisie Gay was just a little too successful. Her round face with its comedienne's pop eyes could hardly have been less like Edith's, but it was not difficult to send up the way that Edith spoke *Façade*, and Miss Gay was soon out-Sitwelling the Sitwells with 'poems' like 'Peruvian Love Song' and 'Sonata for Harpsichord'.

In point of fact, the 'poems' Coward wrote for her were not particularly Sitwellian – nor particularly witty. One of the most memorable, 'Poor Shakespeare', began:

Blow, blow thou winter wind

Rough and rude like a goat's behind

And there was another that which went simply,

Your mouth is my mouth,

And our mouth is their mouth

And their mouth is Bournemouth.

But everything depended on the way they were delivered, and even William Walton, who made a point of visiting the show, had to admit that 'The Swiss Family Whittlebot' was 'really not unfunny'. Then came trouble. As Coward himself related:

During the first two weeks of the run I received, to my intense surprise, a cross letter from Osbert Sitwell; in fact, so angry was it, that at first I imagined it to be a joke. However, it was far from being a joke, and shortly afterwards another letter arrived, even crosser than the first. To this day I am a little puzzled as to why that light-hearted burlesque should have aroused him, his brother and his sister to such paroxysms of fury.

Coward was being more than a little disingenuous when he wrote this, for, as he must have known, there were several reasons for the Sitwells' anger. Possibly the worst of them was sheer frustration. Osbert had been all set to face the artistic scandal of *Façade* and to perform his usual act of ridiculing his reactionary opponents as he had ridiculed his enemies the Georgian poets, the generals, the press lords, and of course, Sir George. Instead, the reverse had happened. At the Duke of York's it was the Sitwells and modern poetry that were being ridiculed – and the philistines, instead of being laughed at, were now laughing very loudly in their turn. A mere actor from the London suburbs, and the lower-middle classes, had taken on *their* role of mockery – at their expense. Worst of all, the Sitwells were in the situation Edith always dreaded – of having someone being most impertinent to her and not being able to retaliate.

Osbert was always a great believer in the prompt despatch of lawyers' letters, but in this case legal action was impossible. For apart from the cost of a full-scale libel suit, one can imagine what a field-day Coward and the irrepressible Miss Gay would have had in the witness box. In the circumstances, the advice that the writer Beverley Nichols says he would have given them was probably the best: 'Yes, Noël should be stopped; but darlings, if you ask for it in *la Vie de Bohème* you get it, and you have asked for it ... and you should all rise above it.' This was one thing that Edith and Osbert were never very good at, and in the months that followed their indignation mounted as *London Calling!* went on to become the hit show of the season.

Edith never saw the show. Perhaps it would have been better if she had, although, as William Walton said, 'she would have made such a scene in the theatre that anything could have happened then'. As it was, she obviously received wildly exaggerated reports of Maisie Gay's antics, until she genuinely believed that she was depicted in the sketch with extraordinary obscenity. She was abnormally sensitive over her appearance, and was convinced that Maisie Gay had also insinuated that she was a lesbian.

For Edith, whose dignity and angry sense of pride covered the childhood scars left by Sir George's snubs, this must have been a harrowing experience. In the autumn of 1923 she fell ill, first with her usual nervous troubles, then with an acute attack of jaundice that left her more or less prostrated for the remainder of the year.

The long-term effect of the affair on her was even worse. Edith had always been insecure and touchy, but it was now that the idea of being assailed by what she called 'gross public insult' started to obsess her. It would do so, off and on, for the rest of her life. As late as 1947 she would complain bitterly to John Lehmann about the way Noël Coward had attacked her in a 'sketch of the utmost indecency, really filthy. Nobody helped me, and I had to put up with having filthy verses about vice imputed to me and recited every night and three afternoons weekly for three months.' Osbert, too, was extraordinarily bitter over *London Calling!*, blaming Coward for its effect upon his sister. Suddenly there were shades of the Lady Ida scandal and, as in 1915, the siblings drew together to defend themselves in the face of public insult.

Coward replied to Osbert's angry letters with a well-simulated air of puzzled apology and the remark that he had merely taken the idea of the sketch from the performance of *Façade*, as Osbert had in fact suggested. Osbert replied with scarcely veiled fury:

> We are delighted to have been the means of suggesting an idea to you. It is always as well to have one, even if it isn't your own; it must be a novel experience to you. All you want, now, is a little self-confidence – and, of course, to use your voice more.
>
> Insulting my sister is a fine beginning for you. We look forward to other triumphs. Have you tried cheating at cards?

Sacheverell, as usual, did his best to calm things down. Like William Walton, he believed that these violent controversies and feuds were self-defeating and upsetting, and should be avoided at all costs. But Osbert strongly disagreed and the vendetta was bitterly maintained for years. One gathers something of the venom that he felt for Coward from a short – and wisely unpublished – poem that he wrote called 'The Missing Link':

> In one smug person, Coward sums
> Up both the suburbs and the slums;
> Before both, nightly boasts his race
> By spitting in a lady's face.

Coward's private view of the Sitwells was perhaps more telling. He dismissed them as 'two wiseacres and a cow'.

What was so ironic in all this was that Osbert never seemed to realise that the fuss stirred up by Coward and by *London Calling!* was the nearest he would ever get to the artistic *scandale* he had been banking on from that June's production of *Façade*. Indeed, with the spiralling success of *London Calling!*, publicity for the Whittlebots became immense. Coward repeated the offence, with Joyce Carey impersonating Hernia Whittlebot at a theatrical garden party. He even issued some slim volumes of her poetry. However furious Osbert might have been, the incident put the Sitwells on the map as nothing ever had before – or would again.

3.26
Edith Sitwell
By Rex Whistler, 1929

Earlier that year a correspondent writing in the London *Star* had announced: 'Plain people are now writing to the *Star* asking, "Who are the Sitwells?"' Answering their question, the *Star* replied in words that must have gladdened Osbert's heart, despite himself. 'They are all poets. But they are more than that. They are a cult.'

The critic Martin Green was pitching their claim a little high when he described the Sitwells as 'the major preceptors of the post-war generation', but they were certainly precursors, particularly over taste; and for the influential, mainly Oxford-educated young ('dandy aesthetes' like Harold Acton, Evelyn Waugh, Peter Quennell and Kenneth Clark) the Sitwells possessed irresistible allure.

Another writer of this generation, Cyril Connolly, placed their claims still higher. 'For all their faults,' he said, 'the Sitwells were a dazzling monument to the English scene. They absolutely enhanced life for us during the twenties, and had they not been there a whole area of art and life would have been missing.'

It was extraordinary how acute the Sitwells' cultural antennae had been to what would fascinate this post-war generation. Their passion for the figures of the nineties; their affinities with Cocteau and Diaghilev; their contempt for Cambridge-orientated Bloomsbury intellectualism; and their attacks upon the paternal wisdom of the old aroused increasing respect.

Desmond MacCarthy, who was no great admirer of the Sitwells, compared Osbert with Comte Robert de Montesquiou, the great Parisian dandy and model for Proust's Baron de Charlus; and Harold Acton, following and then surpassing Osbert's style and manner, rapidly became the cynosure of Oxford. It was he who caused many a hearty Oxford eyebrow to be raised by reciting Edith's poems through a megaphone from his college window. *Façade* had made megaphones, and Edith's poetry, intellectually fashionable, and 'Sitwellism' had suddenly become a banner to be waved against the tedious, the puritanical, the insular and the old. As a result many of these young Oxford aesthetes seemed to be fighting the old Sitwell battles on their own account.

More than this, the Sitwells – and Sacheverell in particular – were becoming what Connolly called, 'trail-blazers in the arts, setting new fashions with the range of their enthusiasms'. For the young aesthete Kenneth Clark, 'it was wonderful to find people so liberated from accepted thought and values – particularly from those of Bloomsbury, and the domination of Roger Fry and all that muddy-coloured, pseudo classicism.'

It was Connolly who actually called the Sitwells 'an alternative Bloomsbury', for they had something else that Bloomsbury lacked – undoubted glamour. Loelia Ponsonby, who became Duchess of Westminster, met them during this time:

... and believe me, it really was something to meet the Sitwells for the first time in those days. They were so utterly unlike anybody else, and held a position in the arts that no one aspires to today. The nearest to it, I suppose, would be some very elevated cultural pop-star, but they excited far more awe than any pop-star ever would. They were so extraordinarily clever and funny and there were three of them which made them still more disconcerting.

It was against this background that work on a much-updated and revised version of *Façade* continued. After the nightmares and near nervous breakdowns that had accompanied the earlier performances, it says much for the collective courage of the Sitwells that they were still willing to place themselves in the firing-line with another full-scale public performance. But courage – particularly when faced with the chance of a fresh dust-up with the philistine – was something they had never lacked, and on 27 April 1926 *Façade* received its second public performance at the New Chenil Galleries in London. 'And this time', as Walton gratefully remarked, 'we finally got it right, and I can remember seeing the music critic, Ernest Newman, banging his umbrella on the ground with excitement.'

Façade had arrived and was being hailed as a genuine popular success; a few days later in the pages of the *Sunday Times* Newman himself, the greatest musical panjandrum of the day and a dedicated protagonist of Wagner, reiterated the enthusiasm of his umbrella by comparing the musical technique of *Façade* with that of *Pelléas* and *Tristan*, and praising the whole performance as 'the jolliest musical entertainment of the season'.

fitting, all three Sitwells were there to join in the success. They took their bows before a cheering audience, but as they did so they were also bowing out upon that unique 'embattled trio' that they had created.

The combined performance that had helped create *Façade* was all but over. Sacheverell had married; as a poet Edith would increasingly follow her own unique career; and Osbert, the movement's self-appointed 'paladin' would be fighting other battles of his own before he found himself a fresh vocation. *Façade* would henceforth have to be the trio's monument.

John Pearson

For the Sitwells there was more to it than that. Unlike the Aeolian Hall disaster three years earlier, this was a performance on their own home ground in Chelsea, and it was a potent demonstration of the support and enthusiasm that their name could now excite among so many of the capital's artistic élite. Diaghilev himself was in the audience; and Cecil Beaton found the hall so crowded that he could not get a seat and had to stand 'along with masses of other thrilled and expectant people. Half the audience seemed nicely arty and the other half merely revoltingly arty.'

For once the nicely arty and the revoltingly arty were united in their enthusiasm. There were repeated encores and, as was

3.6
Mr Osbert and Mr Sacheverell Sitwell
By Max Beerbohm, 1923

3.1
Edith Sitwell

By Maurice Lambert, *c.* 1926-1927

Maurice Lambert (1901-1964) was probably drawn briefly into the Sitwell orbit through his brother, Constant Lambert (see 3.22). Osbert may well have seen Maurice's head of William Walton in the exhibition of works by young artists at the Goupil Gallery in 1925 (see 3.8) and decided to commission the portrait of Edith in the rather advanced medium of aluminium. The apparently unique original cast remains with the family. This version is one of two further casts made from it in 1984; a third was made in 1994.

Lambert included the head of Edith in his first one-man exhibition at the Claridge Galleries in June 1927. Both the exhibition and the head attracted considerable attention and for a short time Lambert was considered to be one of the most promising of the up-and-coming sculptors. He had been apprenticed to the neo-classical sculptor Derwent Wood, from *c.*1919 to 1924, but obvious sources for the head of Edith must be Vorticist works like Wyndham Lewis's painting and drawings of her (see 3.29 & 3.30) and Frank Dobson's head of Osbert (3.2). *The Times* admired the head but felt that Lambert was more of 'a talented craftsman in metal than a creative sculptor'.

3.2
Osbert Sitwell

By Frank Dobson, 1921-1922

Osbert sat to Dobson (1888-1963) for this remarkable Brancusiesque head nearly every day for three months during preparations for *Façade*, for which Dobson also painted the backdrop (see 3.11). It has often been inferred that the head was commissioned by T. E. Lawrence, who lent a cast to the Tate Gallery in 1923, and that it dates from that year (it was subsequently presented to the Gallery). It was, however, almost certainly commissioned by Osbert, who owned the first cast (now in the collection of the Fondazione William Walton); and as *Façade* was first performed on 24 January 1922 the bulk of the work must have been completed by then. Lawrence described the work as 'appropriate, authentic and magnificent ... as loud as the massed bands of the Guards'[1] and with some justification, certainly in terms of British sculpture, as 'the finest portrait bust of modern times'.[2] Osbert says that three copies were cast although, to date, only two have been traced.[3] It is the Tate cast that is illustrated here. The cast included in the exhibition was made in 1994 from the original plaster.

1. *The Modern British Paintings, Drawings and Sculpture I*, Tate Gallery, 1964, p., 151
2. LNR p. 186
3. *Ibid.*

3.3
Osbert Sitwell

By Frank Dobson, 1921-1922

The original plaster model for 3.2 was apparently rescued from Dobson's studio after the Blitz and was sold at Christie's on 23 November 1993. It shows more clearly that as well as being an outstanding piece of sculpture it was also an extremely perceptive portrait of the young Osbert.

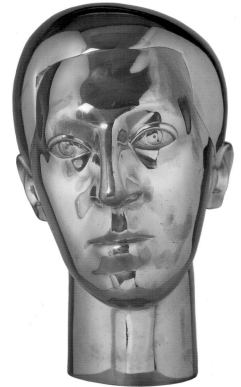

3.4

Osbert Sitwell

By Hugh Cecil, *c.* 1925
(illustrated on page 80)

The fashionable photographer Hugh Cecil may
have been suggested to Osbert by Diana Cooper,
of whom Cecil took some of the best early
photographs. Here he makes the most of Osbert's
'Hanoverian' profile, in his usual understated
manner, against the opulent furnishings of his
Grafton Street studio. Beaton, who was to
displace Cecil over the next few years, would later
dismiss him as an imitator of the photographs of
Baron de Meyer and as 'an irascible man and a
door-slammer, who was easily bored and in an
indefensibly rude manner was apt to show his lack
of interest in his more ordinary sitters'.[1]

1. C. Beaton and G. Buckland, *The Magic Image*, 1975, p. 273

3.5

**Photographs by Maurice Beck and
Helen Macgregor**

a) Osbert, 1924
b) Sacheverell, 1924
c) Edith, 1924

It was soon after the first performance of *Façade*
that a positive deluge of photographs and features
on the Sitwells began to appear in the illustrated
magazines of the period.

The rough-and-ready old Rugbyian engineer
Maurice Beck (1886-1960) and the determined
small Scottish spinster Helen Macgregor – an
unlikely partnership – were the chief photographers
for British *Vogue* from 1922 until August 1927 when
they were firmly displaced by Cecil Beaton. Their
first photograph of Edith seems to have been the
one used by *Vogue* to illustrate its review of the

Aeolian Hall performance of *Façade* in the issue of
15 July 1923. The series shown here was taken for
Vogue in 1924, presumably in one sitting with all
three Sitwells, and probably in connection with the
publication of Sacheverell's *Southern Baroque Art*, and
used thereafter on several occasions.

The work of Beck and Macgregor had
considerable influence on Cecil Beaton and
foreshadows some of his best-known photographs
of the Sitwells (see 3.43). Indeed, as he recalls in
his diary for 15 April 1926, a visit to Helen
Macgregor (who was 'rather like an apple that
has been kept for a long time in a loft') was
absolutely crucial for his development as a
photographer. 'She'd inspired me with all sorts of
notions for getting amusing textures by varnishing
cheap brocades and canvas or taking photos of
people reflected in piano tops.'[1]

1. C. Beaton, *The Wandering Years: Diaries 1922-1939*, 1961, pp. 80-84

3.6

Mr Osbert and Mr Sacheverell Sitwell

By Max Beerbohm, 1923

(illustrated on page 85)

With an introduction from Ada Leverson, Osbert and Sacheverell first met Beerbohm (1872-1956) at Rapallo on their journey to the south of Italy with William Walton in the spring of 1922. Rapallo became a regular point of call on their journeys south and Beerbohm drew four caricatures of them both, the last in 1930.[1]

Although Beerbohm had met the brothers only once when he drew this caricature, it is perhaps the sharpest of the four; the words issuing in mutual admiration from the parrots' mouths are 'Bravo, Sacheverell!' and 'Well done, Osbert!' The drawing was included in Beerbohm's exhibition at the Leicester Galleries at the time of the first public performance of *Façade* in June 1923 and was noticed by Hannen Swaffer in his vitriolic review (see 3.13).

1. R. Hart-Davis, *A Catalogue of the Caricatures of Max Beerbohm*, 1972, nos. 1545-1550

3.7

Mr Osbert and Mr Sacheverell Sitwell

By Max Beerbohm, 1925

Beerbohm's second caricature of the brothers was drawn when they were staying at Rapallo early in 1925, and beginning work on *All at Sea* (see 3.47). Both the original drawing and the sketch for it, which is on notepaper from the Villino Chiaro[1], Beerbohm's house, are in the Sitwell family collection. According to Hart-Davis this version is a copy made by Beerbohm for Sacheverell, possibly as a wedding present.[2] The original version was included in Beerbohm's exhibition at the Leicester Galleries in 1925.

1. Lehmann, repro. f.p. 54

2. R. Hart-Davis, *A Catalogue of the Caricatures of Max Beerbohm*, no. 1547

3.8

William Walton

By Maurice Lambert, *c.* 1925

The composer William Walton (1902-1983) won a place as a chorister at Christ Church, Oxford, in 1912, and by 1918 had been squeezed in as an undergraduate at the age of sixteen. Through his friendship at Oxford with Siegfried Sassoon (who continued to support him financially for many years), he had been introduced to Sacheverell, who used to take the young music student out to lunch. When it became clear that Walton must leave Oxford and be rescued from the prospect of continuing his studies at the Royal College of Music, Osbert and Sacheverell invited him to come and live with them in London. Together with the Dean of Christ Church, Dr Thomas Strong, Sassoon and Lord Berners, they guaranteed him an income of £250 a year and in June 1919 Walton arrived at Swan Walk. In November he moved with the brothers to Carlyle Square, occupying a room at the top of the house, and he remained with them for the next fourteen years.

Walton's near-contemporary, Constant Lambert, became part of the entourage in 1923 and through him Walton would have met Constant's brother, the sculptor Maurice (see 3.1). Maurice's futuristic head of Walton was finished by the time of his first public exhibition and was one of fourteen of his works included in the mixed show at the Goupil Gallery in April 1925.

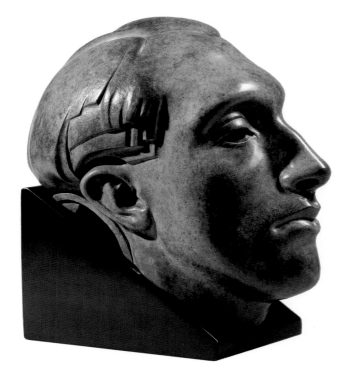

3.9

Harlequin and Pulcinella in the Snow
Illustration for the frontispiece of *Façade*
By Gino Severini, *c.* 1921

Severini's book illustrations for works by the Sitwells seem to have been largely requested by post, and, probably owing to Sacheverell's mutual interest with Severini in the *commedia dell'arte*, all involve harlequins and pulcinellas, apparently with the minimum of symbolism (see 3.18 and 3.19). It is difficult to see any particular relevance in this frontispiece either to the performance of *Façade* or to the poems in the volume unless the snow represents the five works grouped under the heading 'Winter'. Harlequin and Pulcinella with, respectively, mandolin and guitar are clearly 'artists' following the footsteps of an unknown precursor towards the door in a brick façade.

3.10

Façade
By Edith Sitwell, 1922

The first performance of *Façade* was held at Carlyle Square on 22 January 1922, before an invited audience of friends. They were given typewritten programmes as they arrived, and served hot rum punch afterwards to revive those 'who had lost their bearings on a voyage of discovery, and had arrived back feeling somewhat confused, concussed and self-conscious'.[1] The programme contained the following note: 'All these poems, and some additional ones, will appear in a book called *Façade* which Miss Sitwell is publishing privately in a limited edition with a special frontispiece in colour by Gino Severini – at the Faril [*sic*] Press, Kensington.'[2] 150 numbered copies duly appeared the following month though the one shown here was an unnumbered copy belonging to Edith. Only eleven of the seventeen poems from the first programme were in fact included, the additional ones forming the first section of the book under the heading 'Winter'. The elegant boards with their printed brick pattern presumably reflect the title of the work, while Severini's frontispiece seems to belong more to the 'Winter' section (see 3.9).

1. LNR, p. 191
2. Fifoot, EA6, pp. 24-5

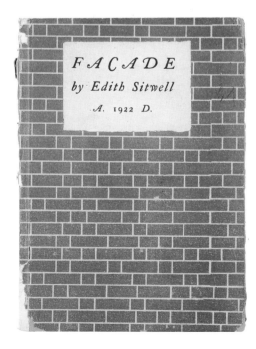

Curtain design for *Façade*

By Frank Dobson, 1922

None of the three curtains commissioned by the
Sitwells for performances of *Façade* now survive.
Osbert relates how it was he who had thought of
presenting *Façade* behind a curtain with the use of
a mask through which Edith would recite the
poems. Sacheverell and Walton were despatched
to Hampstead to borrow the Sengerphone, a
glorified megaphone, from its inventor, Mr
Senger, to aid the sound projection.[1] While sitting
to Dobson for his portrait in 1922 (see 3.2), Osbert
had gossiped about their plans and Dobson
offered to design a suitable curtain with masks.[2]

The curtain was used for all the British
performances, including the first private
performance at Carlyle Square on 24 January
1923, until replaced by Severini's new curtain in
1928. The Dobson curtain was stretched across
the double doorway into the back part of the
drawing-room and from behind it Edith
declaimed with the Sengerphone through the
large hole in the central mask while Osbert acted
as master of ceremonies through the smaller mask
on the right. A second private performance was
given two weeks later for the patroness, Mrs
Robert Mathias, at her house in Montagu Square
on 7 February.[3]

1. LNR, p. 186
2. *Ibid.*, p. 187
3. *Ibid.*, p. 190

**Autograph manuscript of the 'Valse'
from *Façade*,**

By Sir William Walton, *c.* 1922-1923

Most of Walton's manuscripts are now in the
Humanities Research Centre, The University of
Texas at Austin, but this copy of the 'Valse' was
sold anonymously at Christie's in 1976.[1] The
'accompaniment' for Edith's poem 'Waltz', it was
one of those written between the first private
performance of *Façade* on 24 January 1922 and the
public performance on 12 June 1923 at the Aeolian
Hall. Although there were press reports of twenty-
eight numbers in the newly reconstituted *Façade*
in 1923, no programme for the occasion was
produced and documentation suggests that only
twenty-four numbers were given, with Edith doing
all the recitation.[2] Walton and Edith had
produced thirteen new numbers since early 1922,
including some of those that are now best known.
Eight of the old numbers were dropped and not
used again until reconstituted separately as *Façade
Revised* in 1977 and *Façade 2* in 1979.[3] 'Valse' is no.
16 in the definitive version of *Façade*, performed in
1951, and was included both in the 1931 Frederick
Ashton ballet and the Orchestral Suite. Edith's
poem 'Waltz' was subsequently published in *Vogue*
in late December 1924 as 'Valse Maigre, 1843',[4]
and is self-evidently one of those poems
intentionally conceived in a dance rhythm.

1. Christie's, 7.12.1976 (34)
2. S. Craggs, *William Walton: A Catalogue*, 1990, p. 21
3. *Ibid.*, p. 27
4. Fifoot, EA6, p. 26

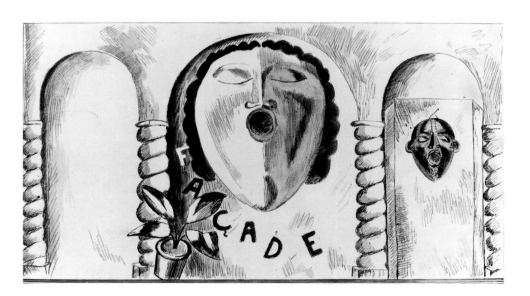

3.13

Review of the first public performance of *Façade* at the Aeolian Hall, London, 12 June 1923

Facsimile of the *Daily Express*, 13 June 1923

Blanket press invitations ensured at least nine reviews for the first public performance of *Façade* at the Aeolian Hall. Only one is actively hostile and none give any indication of the riot that both Osbert and Edith remembered. 'The attitude of certain of the audience was so threatening that I was warned to stay on the platform, hidden by the curtain, until they got tired of waiting for me and went home', remembered Edith in *Taken Care Of*.[1] 'The front rows, especially, manifested their contempt and rage ... albeit a good deal of applause countered the hissing', wrote Osbert, continuing by quoting in full the only fully-fledged attack, that of Hannen Swaffer in his 'Mr London' column from the *Daily Graphic*.[2] Under the eye-catching heading, 'Drivel They Paid To Hear', Swaffer calls on expert opinion to back up his knee-jerk reaction to this new artistic venture, quoting the duty fireman at the Hall who had 'never in twenty years' experience of recitals at that hall ... known anything like it'. 'Surely', thundered Swaffer in true gossip-column fashion, 'it is time that this sort of thing were stopped.' *Vogue* concluded on 15 July: 'Not all who visited the Aeolian Hall ... heard the brazen call of the tiger lily or saw the gleaming purple of the nightingale's song.'

1. TCO, p. 122
2. LINR, pp. 193-4

3.14

Façade at the New Chenil Galleries, April 1926

By Pacific and Atlantic Photos Ltd, 1926

a) Edith, Osbert and Sacheverell (below)
b) Edith with Neil Porter
(illustrated on page 77)

For the second public performance of *Façade*, at the New Chenil Galleries, Chelsea, on 27 April 1926, Edith and Walton had continued to revise and rewrite, producing seven new or reconstituted numbers and including a few of those they had dropped from the Aeolian Hall presentation. *Façade* now included the popular 'Foxtrot: Old Sir Falk' and 'Tango: I Do Like to be Beside the Seaside' which are among its most enduring numbers, and the whole affair was a great success.

The decision to recruit Neil Porter (1895-1944), a professional actor, was presumably made to add both variety and polish to the recitation of the poems. Neil Porter was the actor/producer son of Caleb Porter and had made his first appearance at the Old Vic as Cassio in 1924. By 29 June, when a repeat performance of *Façade* had been scheduled at the New Chenil Galleries, it seems likely that Porter was involved in a tour of *Dr Syn* and unable to take part.[1] The twenty-year-old Constant Lambert was recruited in his place.

1. *Who's Who in the Theatre*, 1936, p. 1191

3.15

Curtain design for *Façade*

By John Piper, 1942
(illustrated on page 79)

The first 'definitive' performance of *Façade* was not given until 29 May 1942 in the Aeolian Hall, the scene of the disastrous first public performance nineteen years earlier. Constant Lambert recited on his own, and used for the first time the order of performance of twenty-one numbers in seven groups of three that appeared in the published score in 1951. One of the most striking additions to the performance was a new curtain designed by John Piper (1903-1992), whom Osbert had 'discovered' after reviewing the artist's *Brighton Aquatints* (1939) in *The Listener*.

This lithograph is an accurate reproduction of Piper's original gouache and collage design and was made later under his supervision for the William Walton Trust.[1] Faithful in spirit to Dobson's original design with a central mask, the hole in the middle was now destined to hold a microphone and there is no auxiliary mask for a Master of Ceremonies. The 'gothick' air of romantic melancholy is, however, an age away from the aggressive modernism of the original *Façade*. It is close in atmosphere to Piper's designs for William Walton's ballet *The Quest*, which was based on Spenser's *Faerie Queene* and first performed by Sadler's Wells Ballet the following year.

1. Original design exhibited in *John Piper*, exhibition catalogue, Tate Gallery, London, 1983, no. 63

POETRY THROUGH A MEGAPHONE.

ONE-NOTE CONCERT BY MISS SITWELL.

If Miss Edith Sitwell considers that the best way to recite her poems is through a megaphone in a tragic voice on one note, that is her affair. She wrote them, and ought to know best.

The Æolian Hall was half filled yesterday to hear her do it.

Across the platform was stretched a curtain representing, chiefly, a piebald face, one half red, the other white. Mr. Osbert Sitwell introduced this as "Venus." Where the mouth should have been a gaping megaphone protruded. Miss Sitwell called it a senger-phone.

There were twenty-eight items on the programme, but only one note came

MISS EDITH SITWELL.

3.16

Three *Commedia dell'Arte* Musicians
Design for a fresco at Montegufoni
By Gino Severini, 1922
(illustrated on page 75)

One of some thirty small gouaches and drawings by Severini (1883-1966) in the collection of the Sitwell family, this is an exact design (or just possibly a repetition) of the largest fresco at Montegufoni, a Sitwell commission that was to become Severini's major achievement of the early 1920s. Many of the small Severinis acquired by the Sitwells at that time can be seen in photographs of Carlyle Square and comprise drawings and gouaches for the Montegufoni frescoes, some rejected or related designs in gouache, and designs for book jackets. Two larger Severini gouaches of *commedia dell'arte* figures that belonged to Sacheverell may be those he acquired from Severini's dealer Léonce Rosenberg in the autumn of 1919. Sacheverell and Osbert had hoped that Picasso would undertake the frescoes at Montegufoni, but the scheme seems to have foundered with Sir George refusing to pay Picasso's fees some time late in 1920. Rosenberg probably then approached Severini on the brothers' behalf.[1]

In his autobiography Severini implies that he did not meet the Sitwells until after he had signed Sir George's contract (dated 8 February 1921).[2] He finally met Osbert and Sacheverell by appointment at their Italian agents in Florence on the way to Montegufoni in April.[3] The designs for *Wheels* in 1920 (see 2.28) must presumably have been arranged through Rosenberg, and certainly later designs for book jackets (see 3.18 and 3.19) were probably commissioned by post. As owners of two Severini *commedia dell'arte* subjects, it seems likely that Sacheverell and Osbert had already set their hearts on the same theme; the scheme was agreed with the artist on the spot and they soon set off for Rapallo and Lecce.[4]

The room to be decorated at Montegufoni was a narrow *salotto* on an upper floor joining one wing of the castle to the other. In line with the theories Severini had developed in Paris during his evolution from Synthetic Cubism to what he termed 'réalisme classicisant' (in his treatise *Du Cubisme au Classicisme*, 1921), he first worked out the structure of his designs by dividing the wall panels into harmonious units.[5] He worked from cartoons, designs for which were found at Montegufoni when the castle was finally sold. The scheme comprises seven panels, two of which are still-lifes with views of Montegufoni and the

surrounding country, and a ceiling decoration in the roman style. The three musicians – Harlequin, Scaramouche and Tartaglia – are seen at the base of the fortified walls with the Montegufoni lion, and are quite closely based on those on the title page of Callot's *Balli di Sfessania*, with which Sacheverell was well acquainted.[6] Apart from drawings in the Sitwell family collection there are eleven other preliminary studies for the frescoes in the collection of Severini's daughter.[7]

1. Bradford, p. 107
2. M. Caiger Smith, 'Gino Severini – The Montegufoni Frescoes', unpublished M.A. report in the library of the Courtald Institute, London, 1983. M.C.S. reproduces the contract in full.
3. G. Severini, *Tempo de l'Effort Moderne*, 1968, pp. 186-7
4. Bradford, pp. 108-9
5. D. Fonti, *Gino Severini: Catalogo Ragionato*, 1988, pp. 42, 353. This design is no. 390B
6. FWGC, p. 186
7. M. Caiger Smith, op. cit.

3.17
The Serenade
By Gino Severini, *c.* 1922
(left)

Severini worked on the Montegufoni frescoes
throughout 1921 and had finished them by the
summer of 1922. As he declares in his
autobiography, he remained grateful to the Sitwells
for the rest of his life.[1] Apart from securing his
return to Italy from Paris, the commission enabled
him to put his new aesthetic theories into practice
on a large scale and provided an idyllic year for
him and his family in the Tuscan countryside.
Severini continued to work on the subject of the
commedia dell'arte, and at the end of his life he
presented Sacheverell and Georgia with his 1959
lithograph of a Cubist harlequin and pulcinella.

A number of gouaches of *commedia dell'arte*
figures refer to the castle at Montegufoni but bear
no relation to the completed frescoes. The *trompe-
l'oeil* surround of this gouache suggests that it was
an idea for a fresco, but it may be an independent
composition purchased at the time by Osbert and
Sacheverell. The Sitwells were certainly on the
look-out for paintings that could double up as book
jackets or illustrations.

1. G. Severini, *Tempo de l'Effort Moderne*, 1968, pp. 186-7

3.18
Design for the dust jacket of
The Thirteenth Caesar
By Gino Severini, 1924
(below left)

After the completion of the Montegufoni frescoes
Severini undertook numerous small commissions
for the Sitwells, including a 1923 New Year
greetings card and book-plate for Osbert and
Sacheverell,[1] and a gouache greetings card for Sir
George. In 1924 Sacheverell requested Severini to
produce a drawing in 'coffee, brown and grey' for
the cover of his third volume of poetry to be titled
Actor Rehearsing.[2] The original title, from one of the
poems in the book, makes better sense of Severini's
sinister masked pulcinella, strutting the stage and
plucking his stringless guitar.

Following hard on the heels of *Southern Baroque
Art*, the publication of the retitled *The Thirteenth
Caesar* in October 1924 further helped to make
Sacheverell a celebrity in his own right. Writing to
thank him for a copy of the book, his friend Arthur
Waley described him as 'certainly the best poet in
England and perhaps ... the best living poet
anywhere'.[3]

1. See F. Meloni, *Gino Severini: Tutto l'Opera Grafica*, 1982
2. Ritchie, A7, pp. 40-1
3. Bradford, pp. 124-5

3.19
Design for the dust jacket of
The Cyder Feast
By Gino Severini, 1927
(below right)

Severini's last book jacket for the Sitwells is an
appropriately atmospheric design of a pulcinella
stealing apples, and marks the end of the *commedia
dell'arte* theme of Sacheverell's book covers. The
dedication of the book includes Sacheverell's first
child Reresby, and is dated the day of his birth,
15 April 1927.[1]

Severini's final commission for the Sitwells
came in September 1928 when he was asked to
design a new curtain for *Façade*, to be performed
at the Siena Festival with Constant Lambert.
Osbert was delighted with the festival and wrote
to David Horner: '*Façade* went extremely well ...
Willie [Walton] a success beyond his merits (as a
person). He was referred to as "Il world-famous
Wanton" in one paper.'[2] Walton also benefited
from the Sitwells' patronage of Severini, and his
scores, including *Belshazzar's Feast* (1931), used
Severini's striking design for the jackets.

1. Ritchie, A12, pp. 49-50
2. Pearson, p. 248

3.20
Noël Coward

By Dorothy Wilding, 1925
(illustrated on page 81)

Osbert's patronising invitation to Noël Coward
(1899-1973) to attend the performance of *Façade*
and the ensuing feud described in John Pearson's
essay were in the long run of greater consequence
to Edith, who regularly tortured herself with the
supposed insult to her in 'The Swiss Family
Whittlebot' for nearly forty years. Coward met
Osbert three years later in New York and, while
refusing to accede to Osbert's request that he
should 'apologise publicly to Edith in all the
papers', was under the impression that a truce
had been called.[1] A reconciliation seems finally to
have been effected by the Queen, a mutual friend,
who invited them both to Buckingham Palace in
1947, after which Osbert felt obliged to remove all
mention of the feud from *Laughter in the Next Room*
when it appeared the following year.[2]

Coward's hand-written apology to Edith in
1926 was coldly received by her with a one-line
acceptance. Finally, in 1962, Coward, who had a
passion for books about Elizabeth I, sent Edith a
message of congratulation for *The Queens and the
Hive* via George Cukor. Partly, no doubt, because
of Edith's admiration for Cukor, the right note
had at last been struck and Coward received a
telegram inviting him to her 75th birthday concert
and supper at the Royal Festival Hall with the
note: 'FRIENDSHIP NEVER TOO LATE'. They met for
tea and corresponded, exchanging books and
mutual praise, and Coward gave her one of his
paintings. The friendship continued until Edith
became too frail, and Coward's Swiss address duly
appears in her last address book, immediately
before 'Coroner (murdered tramp) Southwark'
and 'Cat Torturers'.

1. C. Lesley, *The Life of Noël Coward*, 1976, p. 104
2. *Pearson*, pp. 392-3
3. Glendinning, p. 82
4. C. Lesley, op. cit., p. 424

3.21
'The Swiss Family Whittlebot'

Facsimile from *The Sketch*, 26 September 1923

Noël Coward's sketch for the Charlot review
London Calling! was more than just a skit on the
Sitwells and *Façade*, and gave vent to his deep-
rooted dislike of modern verse. Indeed, as Cole
Lesley points out, Hernia Whittlebot's poem
'Beloved it is Dawn, I rise' had already been
published the previous year in Coward's collection
of satires *A Withered Nosegay*. *The Sketch*
photograph of 'The Swiss Family Whittlebot' at
the Duke of York's Theatre, 'quite one of the
wittiest items in the show and ... a clever parody
of a certain well-known family of poets', shows the
line-up of an 'Introducer', Gob and Sago
Whittlebot (played by the brothers Leonard and
William Childs) and the poetess Hernia played by
the well-known actress and vocalist, Maisie Gay.
Gob is seen playing a spoof modern instrument
called a 'cophutican'. Hernia, whom the stage
directions describe as 'effectively and charmingly
dressed in undraped dyed sacking', produces a
megaphone before being removed from the stage
by the stage manager at the end of the sketch.

Coward's effective satire on the Sitwells did
not end with the sketch, and he repeated the
'insult' at a theatrical garden party with Joyce
Carey reading some of Hernia Whittlebot's
poems, which he had published the same year in
a slim volume. The book contains a spoof errata
slip and a caricature of Maisie Gay as Hernia by
'E. Loin MacNaughtan'.

1. C. Lesley, *The Life of Noël Coward*, 1976, p. 77
2. *The Sketch* says *Og* but this is presumably a misprint for *Gob* quoted in
all other sources
3. Glendinning, p. 8

3.22
Constant Lambert

By Christopher Wood, 1926

Constant Lambert (1905-1951) was a near
neighbour of Osbert and Sacheverell in Chelsea
and lived at his parents' house (his father,
George, was the distinguished Australian painter)
at 25 Glebe Place until 1926. A student of
composition at the Royal College of Music under
Vaughan Williams and Sir George Dyson, he was
only seventeen when he enterprisingly presented
himself on the doorstep of Carlyle Square in
1922. His good looks ensured that he was invited
in by Osbert, and he was to remain a friend of all
three Sitwells until his death. He quickly became
a close friend and colleague of William Walton
(*Façade* was dedicated to him), and he cultivated
the Sitwells' other musician friends such as
Bernard van Dieren and Lord Berners. He
maintained a greater independence from the
Sitwells than Walton and was not above making
jokes at their expense; it was he who spread the
rumour that Walton was the illegitimate son of
Sir George Sitwell by Dame Ethel Smyth.

In 1923 he set two of Sacheverell's poems to
music and invited Osbert and Sacheverell to the
first performance at the Royal College on
6 March 1924. When Neil Porter was unable to
appear at the June 1926 performance at the New
Chenil Galleries it was Lambert who stepped in
to fill the breach. Osbert remembered him as
'... the perfect instrument of this performance, a
speaker *sans pareil* of the verse, clear, rapid,
incisive, tireless, and commanding vocally an
extraordinary range of inflection, from menace
and the threat of doom to the most debonair and
jaunty inconsequence'. He became the Sitwells'
favourite performer in *Façade*, doing the honours
at the Siena Festival in 1928 and recording seven
numbers with Edith for Decca in 1929. He was
also the reciter in the first complete broadcast of
Façade from the Central Hall, Westminster, in
March the following year. He was a regular guest
at the Renishaw summer gatherings, valued for
his humour and piano playing, and in 1926 he
finished writing his ballet *Pomona* there. His major
collaboration with a Sitwell was *The Rio Grande*,
written in 1927, a setting of Sacheverell's poem
that both came to dislike, though for different
reasons (see 3.23).

Lambert shared Sacheverell's passion for Liszt
and was a major influence and adviser on the
biography published in 1934. As Conductor and
Director of Music at the Vic-Wells Ballet from
1931, he presided over the transformation of

The Rio Grande and *Façade* into ballets. Increasing problems with diabetes and alcoholism dogged the end of his short career. Four weeks after the devastating reviews of his ballet *Tiresias* at Covent Garden in July 1951 Lambert collapsed and died. Osbert used his obituary of Lambert in the *New Statesman* to accuse the critics of 'felling' Lambert; and Edith, who had dined with him the previous week, also took up the cudgels in his memory.[5]

Christopher Wood's portrait derives from an earlier episode in Lambert's life, his commission for the ballet *Romeo and Juliet* from Diaghilev in 1926. He had been introduced to the Russian impresario not by the Sitwells but by the artist Edmund Dulac,[6] and Christopher Wood, who was then considered in Paris to be the only acceptable English Modernist, had been recommended to Diaghilev by Picasso for the sets and costumes. Lambert, still at the Royal College, visited Wood in Paris in the winter of 1925-1926 to work on the ballet, and despite Wood's condescension ('I have this little musician staying ... He got dreadfully on my nerves')[7] conceived a sort of hero-worship for the opium-smoking artist. A first, rather unfinished, portrait of Lambert, looking like a schoolboy in his blazer, was made in 1925 and now belongs to the Royal Opera House. This version, completed some time during the following year, is perhaps Wood's portrait masterpiece, combining a Modigliani-like elegance and stylisation with a telling characterisation of the mingled primness and sensuousness of his youthful sitter. A third portrait entitled *The Composer*, showing a semi-nude young man reclining with violin on the beach, dates from 1927 and though said to represent Lambert can at best be no more than a symbolic portrait.

1. OS, 'Portrait of a Very Young Man', in *Queen Mary and Others*, 1974, p. 77
2. Bradford, p. 90
3. LNR, p. 197
4. S. Craggs, *William Walton: A Catalogue*, 1990, pp. 24-5
5. R. Shead, *Constant Lambert*, 1973, p. 173
6. *Ibid.*, p. 48
7. A. Motion, *The Lamberts*, 1986, p. 146

3.23

The Rio Grande

Miniature score of a poem by Sacheverell Sitwell, set to music by Constant Lambert, 1929

Lambert had already set two of Sacheverell's poems to music in 1923 and took the text of *The Rio Grande* from *The Thirteenth Caesar* (see 3.18). Possibly Lambert's masterpiece as a composer, it is an ambitious setting for chorus, orchestra and solo piano that won the composer overnight fame after its first public performance on 12 December 1929. Sacheverell's poem, which is an evocation of a carnival in a South American port, provides an exotic setting and highly rhythmic words on which Lambert structured his musical ideas.

Both Lambert and Sacheverell later resented being pigeonholed as the authors of *The Rio Grande*, Sacheverell referring to it as 'by far the worst poem I have ever written'[1]; and Lambert feeling it typecast him as a 'jazz-inspired' composer. Like the other Sitwell musical collaborations, *Façade* and *Belshazzar's Feast* (the monumental oratorio for which Osbert had produced the libretto), it became a regular feature of British musical life and was staple fare at the Proms for many years. The miniature score was not published until 1942 but still carries the John Banting decoration (dated 1928) that appeared on the original publication. Banting (1902-1972), the young British Surrealist painter, was a friend of Lambert's and designed the sets and costumes for his ballets *Pomona* in 1930 and *Prometheus* in 1936.

1. Ritchie, B10, p. 226

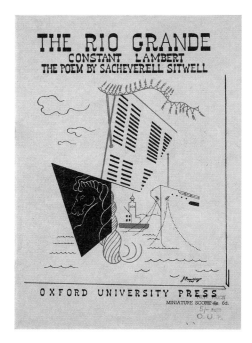

3.24

William Walton

By Rex Whistler, 1929

Life with Osbert and Sacheverell at Carlyle Square had many advantages for the young composer, despite Osbert's occasional disapproval of his piano playing, which 'never very much improved'.[1] They regularly took him abroad with them and spared no effort to further his career. An introduction to Diaghilev came to nothing,[2] but Lord Berners and Constant Lambert became firm friends of Walton and in 1923 Walton, Osbert and Sacheverell joined Berners in Salzburg for the International Festival of Modern Music where Walton's string quartet was to be performed. At Salzburg they also encountered Alban Berg and Arnold Schönberg, while in London Walton introduced the Sitwells to Philip Heseltine and George Gershwin.[3]

By 1929 Walton was enjoying his *succès d'estime* as the composer of *Façade* in the same way that Whistler was known as the painter of the Tate Gallery restaurant murals (1927). They both formed part of the circle of 'bright young things' round Stephen Tennant, with whom Whistler had formed an association at the Slade. In the spring of 1929 Tennant invited them all to Garmisch in Bavaria to stay with him at Haus Hirth, a sort of aristocratic guest house run by Walter and Johanna Hirth, where Tennant was undergoing treatment for his health. While Walton put the finishing touches to his Viola Concerto, Whistler relaxed and drew a little, including this portrait.[4]

The drawing was apparently damaged in an air raid in 1940 and on Whistler's death in Normandy in 1944 it passed to Osbert Sitwell, who used it to illustrate *Laughter in the Next Room*,[5] and subsequently presented it to the National Portrait Gallery.

1. LNR, p. 176
2. Pearson, p. 212
3. LNR, pp. 178-9, 182
4. L. Whistler, *The Laughter and the Urn*, 1985, pp. 136-8
5. LNR, f.p. 176

3.25

Bath

By Edith Sitwell, 1932

When Edith wrote her first full-length prose work
in the late 1920s, it was to her childhood
inspiration, Alexander Pope, that she returned.
The original impetus for *Bath*, Edith's second
money-making prose work, is not recorded. It was
mostly written in Paris in the summer of 1931 at
the Hôtel de la Bourdonnais with books sent from
the London Library.[1] Structured round the life of
Beau Nash, a great many extended quotations are
linked by passages of the historical impressionism
at which she excelled. Dedicated to her parents,
Bath was published in May 1932 and in July went
into a second printing, though Edith still
described it to Georgia as 'the rottenest book on
this earth'.[2] The jacket design is by Rex Whistler.

1. Glendinning, p. 149
2. *Ibid.*, pp. 167-8

3.26

Edith Sitwell

By Rex Whistler, 1929

(illustrated on page 83)

The young Rex Whistler (1905-1944) probably met
Osbert, Sacheverell and Georgia at Stephen
Tennant's house party at Wilsford in the summer
of 1927 (see 6.9) but he would almost certainly
have been known to Osbert from his friend Henry
Tonks as the promising young Slade student who
had been selected to paint murals for the Tate
Gallery restaurant. The following year Osbert
commissioned his book-plate from Whistler and in
August invited him to Renishaw with his friend
Edith Olivier for the first of several memorable
house parties.[1] Although the portrait is dated 1929
on the reverse there is no published record of
either Edith or Rex Whistler visiting Renishaw
that year. It is possible that they were at
Renishaw over the New Year (1928-1929) or paid
an unrecorded visit there during the summer.

   This was one of Whistler's earliest portraits
and he was clearly fascinated by the great
Venetian rococo chair, one of a pair still at
Renishaw. Edith's quizzical expression probably
owes something to the Beaton photographs of
1926, but already foreshadows her role as the
grande dame of English letters rather than Beaton's
dreamy revolutionary (see 3.41).

1. Bradford, p. 188

3.27

**Caricature portraits of Osbert, Edith
and Sacheverell Sitwell**

By Rex Whistler, 1929

Osbert, pompous with cigar; Edith declaiming in
long dress; and Sacheverell the eternal sightseer
with coat and hat on his arm: Whistler made his
witty drawings of the trio on the back of
restaurant bills, undoubtedly to amuse his friends
at Haus Hirth in Bavaria where he was staying as
the guest of Stephen Tennant in the spring of
1929 (see 3.24). Walton, Sassoon and Edith
Olivier were also staying there, and the Sitwells
would certainly have been a frequent topic of
conversation. Whistler gave the drawings to Frau
Hirth, Tante Johanna as she was known to all her
guests, and she subsequently presented them to
the Princess of Hesse together with Whistler's
thank-you letter of 18 May 1929.[1] There is no
evidence that Frau Hirth ever met the Sitwells.

1. Information from the present owner, 31.3.1994

3.28

Portrait of the Artist as the Painter Raphael

Self-portrait by Wyndham Lewis, 1921

By the time the writer and artist (Percy) Wyndham Lewis (1882-1957) met the Sitwells, probably during the summer of 1918, he was already a well-established and contentious figure, having quarrelled with Roger Fry, seceded from Omega, founded the Rebel Art Centre, produced *Blast* and exhibited in the Vorticist exhibitions of 1915 and 1917. Although he spent a great deal of time with the Sitwells in the early years of their friendship, he seems to have mistrusted them from the start, putting his friend Herbert Read on his guard when Osbert and Sacheverell were negotiating to buy into *Art and Letters*. Lewis, however, designed the cover for Osbert's first issue of the magazine and contributed drawings and prose to further numbers. The proposed Paris counterpart of the Heal's exhibition was to have focused on his work, and in September 1919 the Sitwells encouraged a scheme for him to design a ballet based on Rowlandson for Diaghilev, with music by Walton. In 1922 he stayed at Renishaw and in the same year he met up with the Sitwells in Venice.

His self-portrait as Raphael dates from these friendly years. It was painted in April 1921 and exhibited together with *A reading of Ovid* (3.33) in the *Tyros and Portraits* exhibition in the Leicester Galleries. On looking at the portrait in later years with Michael Ayrton, Lewis pointed out that he had painted the eyes without highlights, saying that they would have given the wrong kind of life to the head.

His relationship with the Sitwells may have soured because of the portrait of Edith (see 3.29), but its failure seems inevitable. Lewis belonged to an older generation and the Sitwells' youth combined with their arrogation of artistic standards must have annoyed him as much as the intellectual stranglehold of the 'Bloomsburys', which he described as 'the time-honoured technique of social superiority, but put to the uses of *intellectual* superiority: to be socially snobbish about the possession of taste'.[1] It is not difficult to understand his hostility. Although educated at public school, Lewis had a rough and rootless youth behind him and a current lifestyle that depended on demeaning acts of patronage. The solid evidence of his treachery appeared in the 600 pages of *The Apes of God* in 1930. Lewis's attack was along a broad front, but the Sitwells came in for special treatment as Lord Osmund (a 'licking, eating, sniffing, fat-muzzled machine'); Lord Phoebus ('gigantically Fauntleroy'); and Lady Harriet Finnian Shaw ('still making mudpies at forty'). Even Georgia, whom Lewis had never met, was included as a Jewish New Zealand heiress. The Sitwells' childish response to this outrage was a sustained attack of anonymous telegrams, postcards and parcels designed to work on Lewis's persecution mania.

1. Quoted in J. Meyers, *The Enemy*, 1980, p. 163

3.29

Edith Sitwell
By Wyndham Lewis, 1923-1935

When so many other enemies had 'come round', D. H. Lawrence and Lewis remained, irredeemably, posthumously, unforgiven. Whereas Lawrence provoked a reflex invective from Edith, Lewis brought out a more measured response. She wrote an unpublished essay on him in 1931 and depicted him in the character of Henry Debingham in *I Live Under a Black Sun* (1937). He also features as Stanley Esor in Osbert's *Those Were the Days* (1938). In *Blasting and Bombardiering* Lewis celebrated his status: Edith 'is one of my most hoary, tried, and reliable enemies. We are two good old enemies, Edith and I, inseparables, in fact.' It was a battle they both seem to have enjoyed; Lewis found Edith a worthy foe even

when she threw the Queensberry Rules to the winds. 'She once', he said, 'called me Percy.'[1]

The friction between them developed during Lewis's painting of Edith. The sittings began in 1923 and continued, Edith claimed, 'every day excepting Sundays for ten months'.[2] After that, and with the portrait incomplete, she refused to sit any more. The reason seems to be that Lewis had made a pass. He was 'seized with a kind of schwärmerei for me',[3] she told Elizabeth Salter. In later years Lewis went to some length to dispel any suspicion that he might have found Edith physically desirable. 'She had practically no hair' he wrote to Geoffrey Grigson. 'She was hollow chested, with a long frozen nose, down which she looked and sneered to show her father was a baronet.'[4]

According to Mrs Lewis, 'the head was, to all intents and purposes, finished, the coat largely finished and the legs in position when the painting

was abandoned. When Lewis took it up again in about 1935, he added the forearms and background, and slightly altered the coat.'[5] The hands, though, are still missing. Michel's argument that they 'would have introduced an excess of flesh in this disembodied appearance' is a convincing one, though there is a certain attraction in the idea that Lewis deliberately omitted Edith's best feature. The painting has an important place in the history of twentieth-century portraiture and may even be seen, as Tom Normand suggests, as an ironic criticism of 'an entire class of mock intellectuals'.[6]

1. W. Lewis, *Blasting and Bombardiering*, 1982, p. 92
2. ES in 'Hazards of Sitting for My Portrait', *Observer*, 27 11 1960
3. Quoted in E. Salter, *The Last Years of a Rebel*, 1967, p. 61
4. Quoted in J. Meyers, *The Enemy*, 1980, p. 115
5. W. Michel, *Wyndham Lewis, Paintings and Drawings*, 1971, p. 338 (P36)
6. T. Normand, *Wyndham Lewis the artist*, 1992, p. 188

3.30

Edith Sitwell

By Wyndham Lewis, 1921

This drawing and another of Edith inscribed *Throne* (in the collection of Francis Sitwell) are dated 1921 and show her in a helmet-like head-dress. In this portrait the delineation of the hooded eyes anticipates the expression in Lewis's painting (3.29). 'I think it is his best drawing,' Sacheverell wrote to David Piper shortly after Osbert gave it to the National Portrait Gallery, 'but not inspired by love, but hatred – though I don't know why.'[1] Two further undated Lewis drawings of Edith (National Gallery of South Australia, Adelaide, and Cecil Higgins Art Gallery, Bedford) are catalogued in sequence with these by Walter Michel.[2]

1. SS to David Piper, 2.8.1966, NPG archives
2. W. Michel, *Wyndham Lewis, Paintings and Drawings*, 1971

3.31

Edith Sitwell

By Wyndham Lewis, 1923

This later drawing by Lewis shows Edith with the hair-style familiar from Guevara's portrait (2.26, illustrated on page 41). Uncharacteristcally, she is wearing a flapper's *bandeau,* which may have inspired Maisie Gay's head-dress in 'The Swiss Family Whittlebot' sketch (see 3.21).

3.32

The Sitwell Brothers

By Wyndham Lewis, 1922

According to Sacheverell's recollection, this drawing was made in Venice in 1922. The Sitwells and Richard Wyndham had taken Victor Cunard's palazzo on the Grand Canal for a fortnight. Lewis was also in Venice, with Nancy Cunard, and they all met daily in a café. 'Osbert and Sacheverell Sitwell were both there,' recalled Lewis, 'the pleasant corpulence of the former vibrating to the impact of his own ... pleasantries; Sacheverell with the look of sedate alarm which at that period was characteristic of him.'[1] Although the drawing is squared up, Lewis made no painting of the two brothers; Richard Cork suggests that this may be because the following year Lewis's interest shifted to Edith.[2] He did, however, make a more polished pencil study of Sacheverell (6.1).

1. W. Lewis, *Blasting and Bombardiering*, 1982, p. 237
2. R. Cork, *Wyndham Lewis: The Twenties*, 1984, exhibition catalogue, Anthony d'Offay Gallery

Wyndham Lewis
(The Sitwell Brothers ; Osbert & Sacheverell)

3·33
A Reading of Ovid (Tyros)
By Wyndham Lewis, 1920-1921

'Satire is dead today' Lewis told a *Daily Express* reporter. 'There has been no great satirist since Swift. The reason is that the sense of moral discrimination in this age has been so blurred that it simply wouldn't understand written satire if it saw it. People are, in fact, impervious to logic, so I have determined to get at them by the medium of paint. Hence the Tyro.'[1] These vacuous creations, grinning lewdly over Ovid, are Lewis's symbols for the intellectual dishonesty he sensed among his contemporaries. 'Teeth and laughter...', he said, 'are the Tyro's two prominent features.'[2] The painting was included in the *Tyros and Portraits* exhibition at the Leicester Galleries in April 1921 and was presumably acquired by Osbert at that time. Lewis thought it would make 'a good Altarpiece'.[3] It can be made out in the photograph of the Carlyle Square drawing-room (2.31).

1. Quoted in W. Michel, *Wyndham Lewis, Paintings and Drawings*, 1971, p. 99
2. *Ibid.*
3. W. Lewis to J. Quinn, 2.5.1921

3·34
Edith Sitwell
By Albert Rutherston, 1928

Thomas Balston of Duckworth had been Edith's publisher since 1923 when he issued her *Bucolic Comedies*. He published Osbert's *Before the Bombardment* in 1926 and Sacheverell's *All Summer in a Day* the following year.[1] Albert Rutherston (1881-1953) had been commissioned by the Curwen Press in 1925 to do the drawings for the combined Sitwell anthology, *Poor Young People*;[2] and it was to him that Balston turned for portraits of the Sitwells for his bibliography of their published writings, *Sitwelliana* (1928). Rutherston drew Osbert and Sacheverell in 1927 and Edith the following year. This drawing was apparently a second version given by Rutherston to the artist Alfred Thornton.

1. Fifoot, p. 45
2. *Ibid.*, A8, pp. 42-3 (repro. plate 7)

3.35

A Comedy of Manners, London
Design for a fan
By Albert Rutherston, 1932

After Rutherston's portraits for his *Sitwelliana*
bibliography (see 3.34), Thomas Balston went on
to commission this extraordinary water-colour in
1929. Whether he intended it to be as satirical as
it now appears, and to what end, is not recorded,
nor is it known why Rutherston waited three
years to execute the commission. In Rutherston's
preferred medium of water-colour on silk, and in
the fan format he inherited from Charles Conder,
it cannot be read other than as a caricature.
Reports that the Sitwells were offended are
understandable, though there is no record of the
work being exhibited,[1] and it may well be no
coincidence that all three switched publishers in
the years following 1932. Sacheverell's quarrel
with Balston was ostensibly over money but, on
Edith's recommendation, he turned to Faber and
Faber for his *Canons of Giant Art* (1933) and the
biography of Liszt (1934),[2] while Osbert went to
Macmillan.

The portraits of the three are recognisably
drawn from Rutherston's drawings for *Sitwelliana*
and their presence on the stage with a cloth-
covered table almost certainly reflects their now-
famous poetry readings such as the series at the
Theatre Arts Club in the summer of 1928.[3] Also
identified by her initials in the cartouche on the
right is Sacheverell's wife Georgia, seen holding

up baby Reresby to an unenthusiastic Sacheverell
while their black nanny, Mary Cole, is seen
behind the proscenium column to the right. The
identity of the other figures is not recorded
though an informed guess might be hazarded.
Clearly identifiable to the left is William Walton
holding a small version of the fabled *Façade*
megaphone. Behind him could be other members
of the Wilsford House set, 'bright young things'
including Stephen Tennant, Rex Whistler, Cecil
Beaton and possibly the Jungman sisters, presided
over by the formidable Edith Olivier with perhaps
a bespectacled Roger Fry in the background. The
right-hand side is less easy but the sleeping
bearded man might be Lytton Strachey, with
other Bloomsburyish characters.

1. M. Rutherston, *Albert Rutherston*, exhibition catalogue, 180 New Bond
Street, London W.1., 1988, pp. 12-13, 23 (no. 11)
2. See Bradford, pp. 228-33
3. *Ibid.*, p. 184

3.36
'Sitwelliana'
Selection of caricatures by Siegfried Sassoon,
c. 1925-1950

Although it is still a mystery as to why only the
Sitwells should induce in Siegfried Sassoon a
compulsion to draw well over a hundred
caricatures of them (and apparently never of
anyone else), the recent discovery of the drawings
underscores the ambiguity inherent in his
relationship towards them, already apparent from
references in his diaries. There were 118 drawings
in the lot at the sale at Sotheby's from his library,
in addition to various drawings in other lots,
including one of Edith in her presentation copy of
Aspects of Modern Poetry as late as 1934.[1] Although
dated to *c.* 1925 in the sale catalogue, it is clear
that such a large number of drawings would
probably have been produced over a fairly
substantial period and, as *Aspects of Modern Poetry*
and other references indicate, later rather
than earlier.

Aptly described by the sale catalogue as
'schoolboyish', the more elaborate coloured
drawings are amusing and skilful pastiches of Max
Beerbohm. Occasionally verging on the
affectionate, and on the whole less obsessive than
might be expected from such an apparently
enduring preoccupation, they shed an
extraordinary light on Sassoon's feelings towards
Osbert and Edith in particular. Despite a well-
documented breach from 1921 to 1924, Sassoon
apparently enjoyed extremely cordial relations
with all three until the mid-1930s, though
references to him in their published works and
biographies gradually die out and his name
does not, for instance, appear in Edith's last
address book.

1. Sotheby's, 18.7.1991, lot 123

REGINA

'Just to keep the cold out.'

The Gipsy's Warning.
"You will be the fattest poet in England."

CHANSONS GRISES.

The Triumph of Neptune
Photographs by Sasha, 1926

a) Lubov Tchernicheva and Vera Petrova
b) Serge Lifar, Lord Berners and Alexandra Danilova

On 3 December 1926 Sacheverell's ballet, *The Triumph of Neptune,* with music by Lord Berners, was given its first performance at the Lyceum Theatre. It was the culmination of the Sitwells' involvement with Diaghilev.

The idea of collaborating on a ballet with Sacheverell had been Lord Berners's, but it was not until September 1926 that they and Diaghilev finally got together in Florence to work out a scenario. Described by Sacheverell in letters home to Georgia as 'tiresome' and 'too odd for words', Berners nonetheless produced the music for twelve scenes concocted by Sacheverell from a mixture of Victorian pantomime and modern surrealism.[1] The most hostile review described the 'libretto' as a 'nightmare story of Neptune and sailors and explorers and a magic telescope and ogres and Fleet-street and a drunken negro ... and the journalist who escapes before the end, and was sawn in half'.[2] The scenery and costumes by Prince Shervachidze were based on the Victorian style of Pollock's toy theatres, which had indeed provided the inspiration for the ballet; and when Diaghilev visited London later in the autumn he was taken by Sacheverell to Pollock's shop.[3]

Despite one or two critical reviews, the first night was a fashionable success and the ballet proved to be quite popular. Osbert was away on his American tour but among the smart crowd who turned out for the 'Berners-Sitwell' ballet was Edith escorted by Alvaro Guevara and Lord Glenconner. Constant Lambert and Walton had both helped Berners with the score and in the first interval Walton left the audience to conduct a suite arranged from *Façade.* The choreography was by Balanchine and the principal dancers were Lifar, Danilova and Sokolova, with Balanchine himself appearing as a black man and a beggar. Photograph b) shows Berners with Lifar as Tom Tug, the sailor hero, and Danilova as the Fairy Queen. Hannen Swaffer's review in the *Daily Express* attempted to make some amends for his attack on *Façade* (see 3.13): 'We saw at the Lyceum last night the beginnings of a British Ballet.'

1. Bradford, p. 161
2. Unidentified newspaper cutting in the Theatre Museum
3. Bradford, p. 161

3.38
Lord Berners
(Sir Gerald Tyrwhitt Wilson, 14th Baron)
By Rex Whistler, 1929

Osbert probably met Gerald Berners (1883-1950) towards the end of the First World War on one of his visits to Robert Ross in his rooms at Miss Burton's establishment in Half Moon Street where Berners was also a tenant.[1] The eccentric aristocrat, composer, writer and painter with his independence of spirit, disregard for convention and total dedication to the arts, became to a certain extent a role model for Osbert. He quickly established a close friendship with all three Sitwells, entertaining each other at Carlyle Square and at Berners's house in Halkin Street (where in mocking emulation of Osbert he had placed a huge bowl with one solitary press cutting in the entrance hall). They met on holidays abroad in Austria, Italy and Greece; at house parties at Sir Philip Sassoon's house, Port Lympne; and naturally at Renishaw, Weston and Berners's house, Faringdon.

It was Sacheverell, however, with his passion for music, who formed the closest ties with Berners, and collaborated with him on the Diaghilev ballet, *The Triumph of Neptune*, in 1926. In 1931 Sacheverell dedicated *Spanish Baroque Art* to Berners, and following one of the regular financial crises that beset Sacheverell and Georgia during this period they accepted Berners's invitation to go and live with him at Faringdon, taking Nannah and their first child Reresby with them.[2] The following February, when they all moved up to Berners's London house, William Walton joined them to make a foursome in the increasingly glittering social circles in which they were now moving.[3] In 1937 Georgia quarrelled with Berners over his disloyalty to Emerald Cunard during the abdication crisis[4] but the quarrel had been patched up by the outbreak of the war and visits to Weston were renewed.[5]

Rex Whistler had been offered an honorary scholarship to the British School in Rome in 1928, and that summer, with an introduction to Lord Berners (who had a house at 3 The Forum), found himself being chauffeured around Castel Gandolfo and Lake Albano in Berners's famous Rolls.[6] The following year, six weeks after his return from Bavaria, Whistler returned to Rome as Berners's guest for five weeks and produced a number of paintings, including this portrait of his host. 'Alas, only too like him! And so it cannot give much pleasure. He is so charming and kind', Whistler wrote home to his friend Edith Olivier.[7] Indeed the painting remained unsold until offered to the National Portrait Gallery by Laurence Whistler in 1975. On the back of the board is inscribed in the artist's hand *Lord Berners, started afternoon July 12th 1929/13th/Finished 14th*, showing the speed with which Whistler painted his apparently finely detailed works. Another painting of the same room at 3 The Forum (with a self-portrait of the artist at the easel and Berners seen on the balcony beyond) is at Faringdon.

1. LNR, p. 28
2. Bradford, p. 226
3. *Ibid.*, p. 233
4. *Ibid.*, p. 263
5. *Ibid.*, p. 287
6. L. Whistler, *The Laughter and the Urn*, 1985, p. 121
7. *Ibid.*, p. 146

3.39
Cecil Beaton
By Pavel Tchelitchew, 1934

Cecil Beaton (1904-1980) met the Sitwells when he was twenty-two at almost exactly the time he was deciding to take up photography as a career. The professional and personal relationship that developed, in particular between Beaton and Edith, was to become almost symbiotic as the mutual fame of photographer and sitter was regularly promoted and mirrored by his photographs.

The initial meeting in 1926 had been no accident (see 3.41). In later life Beaton remembered asking a friend, 'What on earth can I become in life?' 'Just become a friend of the Sitwells and wait and see what happens', had been the reply.[1] Beaton's initial enthusiasm rapidly secured a place for him in the Sitwells' social circle and they shared many friends in common, including Rex Whistler, Lord Berners and Tchelitchew. The introduction to Beaton's published diaries for 1928 is devoted almost entirely to each of the Sitwells in turn as he describes their impact on his artistic and social ambitions: 'the Sitwell brothers ... had established a mode of aesthetic existence that completely satisfied my own taste. No detail of their way of life was ugly or humdrum.' 'With their aristocratic looks, dignified manner, and air of lofty disdain, they seemed to me above criticism.'[2]

As well as being among his most obliging sitters and social mentors, the Sitwells promoted Beaton's career in numerous ways. It was thanks to Osbert that Beaton's first book, *The Book of Beauty* (1930), was commissioned from Thomas Balston of Duckworth and in 1935 Beaton was asked to design the sets and costumes for the Osbert/Walton/Frederick Ashton ballet, *The First Shoot*, for C. B. Cochran's revue, *Follow the Sun*, which opened in Manchester in 1935: 'my first living-picture in the theatre', as Beaton described it.[3]

Beaton did not meet Tchelitchew until 1931 when, in company with Lord Berners, he stopped off in Paris for Edward James's ballet season and found Tchelitchew designing the scenery for *Errante*.[4] Tchelitchew's gouache of Beaton, however, was probably painted at the end of 1934 when they were both in New York.

1. C. Beaton, *The Wandering Years*, 1961, p. 150
2. *Ibid.*, p. 163
3. *Ibid.*, pp. 228-9
4. *Ibid.*, p. 226

3.40
William Walton
By Cecil Beaton, 1926
(illustrated on page 76)

Beaton's first photographs of Walton, and indeed of Osbert Sitwell (3.41), are dated to 1926 when he was using the 'Cubist' background that he had painted himself and used for other photographs. The essence of photographic 'Modernism', they clearly reflect the popular success of the performances of *Façade* at the New Chenil Galleries that year. Both photographs were included in Beaton's first exhibition at the Cooling Galleries the following year. A variant image including Walton's hands is also known. Beaton's inscription on the reverse indicates that he was still using this photograph as a press print in 1928, the year in which *Façade* was performed at the Siena Festival.

3.41
Photographs of Osbert and Edith Sitwell
By Cecil Beaton, 1926

a) Osbert, b) Edith

Both the photographs of Osbert and William Walton against a 'Cubist' background are generally dated 1926 and there seems to be no reason to doubt this. All Beaton's photographs of the Sitwells over the next ten years have, however, been subject to miscellaneous datings, sometimes due to a simple misunderstanding; sometimes on the unreliable basis of publication dates in magazines; and sometimes, as in James Danziger's *Beaton* (1980), apparently at random. With information from both Sitwell and Beaton biographical sources, it is, however, possible to establish a rough chronology.

Beaton and Edith had a mutual friend, the wealthy Society beauty Allanah Harper (see 4.14), and on 7 December 1926 Beaton prevailed on Allanah to bring Edith to lunch. The visit to his house at Sussex Gardens and subsequent afternoon's photography are described in detail in his published diary. 'I must perpetuate the image in front of me, of a young faun-like creature sitting against my leaping-fawn [*sic*] design, looking surprisingly Victorian in her crudely-cut Pre-Raphaelite dress with her matador's jet hat, and necklace, her long medieval fingers covered with enormous rings ... As the afternoon wore on ... I even persuaded her to asphyxiate under the glass dome ... A Chinese torture she called it, but loved it all the same.' Two days later: 'Lately ... I've been giving Selfridge's photographic department nearly all the developing. This morning I traipsed there for the fifty millionth time to get the results of Edith Sitwell. The camera had leaked: light got in and spoiled a number of negatives. It would!'[1] The spoiled negatives may well have included those of Edith under the Victorian glass dome.

1. C. Beaton, *The Wandering Years*, 1961, pp. 148-50

Photographs of Edith, Osbert and Sacheverell Sitwell

By Cecil Beaton, 1927 (A)

a) Edith
b) Osbert, Sacheverell and Edith

It seems likely that the remainder of the early photographs of the Sitwells, which rocketed Beaton to fame, were taken either in two sittings at Beaton's house in London in the summer of 1927 or on his visit to the annual August house party at Renishaw in 1930 (see 4.1). Confusion between these two dates has sometimes arisen because in both years Edith wore the same or a very similar brocade dress. Other dates sometimes given reflect a publication date, either in *Vogue*, for which Beaton was now working, or in other periodicals.

Sacheverell appears for the first time in 1927. Sarah Bradford has shown that although Beaton had been 'following' the social lives of Sacheverell and Georgia, he did not actually meet them until they were all invited to Stephen Tennant's house party at Wilsford on 18 June that year.[1] Since Sacheverell and Osbert had left for Paris by 27 June and did not return again until October, several sittings may have taken place in the second half of June. It is of course possible, indeed likely, that Edith had separate sittings with Beaton. Three unidentifiable photographs of the Sitwells formed the high point of Beaton's exhibition at the Cooling Galleries in November, for which Osbert contributed the introduction to the catalogue.

In these exploratory photographs of the three photogenic Sitwells Beaton uses shiny oilcloth or lamé material, a device that he had picked up from his visit to Helen Macgregor (see 3.5) and with which he had been experimenting the previous year. In other versions of the triple-headed, lying-down group, Edith can be seen to be wearing a black choker and dark dress and Osbert a darker suit than in the next group of photographs.[2] The print exhibited here was made for an exhibition and may have been acquired from the Cooling Galleries show by Osbert. The photograph of Edith was published in the magazine *Eve* on 14 September 1927.

1. Bradford, p. 168
2. cf., photograph reproduced in H. Vickers, *Cecil Beaton*, ill. pp. 98-9

3.43

Photographs of Edith, Osbert and Sacheverell Sitwell

By Cecil Beaton, 1927 (B)

a) Edith (below left)
b) Sacheverell (below right)
c) Edith (opposite)
d) Osbert, Edith and Sacheverell (page 2)
e) Apotheosis of Edith attended by Osbert and Sacheverell (page 116)

In this group of photographs Edith wears the splendid brocade dress, a single ring on her left hand and a cord round her neck with a pendant (or just possibly an eyeglass). Osbert wears a lighter coloured suit, where visible, than in the previous group (3.42) and his 'Cubist' tie, or the leopard-effect dressing gown. Sacheverell appears in a magnificent heavily patterned silk gown. Apart from these indications of one particular sitting, the photographs mark a development in Beaton's ideas, with the Sitwells consciously acting out roles devised for them, especially in the recumbent photographs (c) and (d) and the 'apotheosis' (e).

In the most famous photograph of the series Edith is shown lying in state with attendant wooden cherubim on the black and white linoleum tiles that Beaton had acquired for just such an event (c). The present print is a splendid vintage exhibition print from Beaton's collection that is an unusual variant of the much-reproduced version with Edith lying diagonally across the composition. Here she is totally shrouded in a glittering fabric that sets off the spray of lilies to far greater effect than the brocade dress of the better-known shot. The photograph was the subject of an angry scene between Beaton and Edith's mother, Lady Ida, the following year

when they met at Georgia's bedside in the Paris clinic where Georgia was being treated. 'What do you mean by taking a photograph of my daughter in a coffin?' demanded Lady Ida in an exchange that nevertheless ended amicably with Beaton committing the unforgivable solecism of calling her 'Lady Sitwell'.[1]

The altarpiece-like apotheosis of Edith with Osbert and Sacheverell kneeling as 'donors' (e) was clearly planned very carefully and involved placing a folding screen on the console table in the green and gold drawing room at Sussex Gardens. Beaton's drawing (3.46) of the same composition includes one of Osbert's Italian shell 'grotto' chairs, two pieces of contemporary sculpture and a Victorian glass-domed shell arrangement from Carlyle Square, none of which appear in the photograph.

1. Bradford, pp. 177-8

The Sitwells
By Robert Sherriffs, *c.* 1927-1930
(illustrated on page 239)

The inter-war fashion for being publicly
caricatured in the latest 'Post-Cubist' styles is
amusingly satirised by E. F. Benson in his
description of Lucia's desperate attempts to be
drawn by Herbert Alton in *Lucia in London*.
Sacheverell's *Sitwelliana* scrapbook is full of more
or less recognisable caricatures culled from the
multitude of illustrated magazines of the period.
The cartoon by Robert Sherriffs (1906-1960) may
have been intended for *Tatler* or the *Sketch*, though
does not seem finished. It clearly mirrors a period
when the Sitwell aesthetic was under a cloud and
suggests that they, like George Bernard Shaw, will
weather the storm; a connection with the poor
reception of their only dramatic work, *All at Sea*
(see 3.47), seems plausible.

Osbert describes in reverent detail his first
meeting with Shaw in 1917 at a dinner at
Romano's hosted by the distinguished journalists
H. W. Nevinson and H. W. Massingham.[1] Shaw
seems to have known all the Sitwells slightly;
Georgia, who met him in the South of France in
1928, noted that he was 'very amiable about Edith
and "Sitwellism" in general'.[2]

1. LNR, pp. 110-12
2. Bradford, p. 189

'If the Sitwells indulged in the simple life'
By Adrian Allinson, *c.* 1928

The notoriety that early public performances of
Façade brought to the Sitwells is clearly reflected
in Allinson's cartoon with its reference to the New
Chenil Galleries on the upturned tea chest and
the gramophone horn next to Edith. A Cubist
landscape hangs on the tree outside the caravan
and what looks suspiciously like a Tchelitchew
portrait of Edith hangs on the tree behind her.

Allinson (1890-1959) worked variously for the
Bystander, the *Daily Express*, the *Graphic*, and the
Weekly Dispatch and although the cartoon is
inscribed *12 October* on the reverse, its publication
has not so far been traced.

Edith, Osbert and Sacheverell Sitwell
By Cecil Beaton, 1931

Beaton's drawing was published in *Vogue* on
5 August, which suggests that it was probably
sketched much later than the 'apotheosis'
photograph (see 3.43). The inclusion of modern
sculpture and of Osbert's grotto chair places the
Sitwells' taste and *modus vivendi* more firmly in
context than was possible in the photograph taken
in Beaton's drawing-room.

3.47

Design for the dust jacket of *All at Sea*
By Cecil Beaton, 1927

Osbert and Sacheverell began work on a play together in the summer of 1924. Work continued that winter in Rapallo, interrupted by Sacheverell's dashing off to sort out misunderstandings with Georgia Doble, with whom he was now tempestuously in love.[1] Draft manuscripts dated 1925 are in Sacheverell's hand, suggesting that it was mostly his work.[2] A press conference to announce the completion of the play was arranged by Osbert at the Savoy the following July and, bearing in mind his continuing resentment against Noël Coward, concluded with an inflammatory and totally unjustifiable attack on the social aspirations of actors: 'Golf is surely one of the great curses of the acting profession at the moment'. The ensuing controversy lasted well into the following year, further fanned by Osbert in a public dispute with the comedian Bobbie Hale; and, apart from failing to produce the impresario that the press conference had been designed to attract, may explain why nothing more was heard of the play until November 1927.[3] The text was published to coincide with the semi-private first performance of the play at the Arts Theatre Club on 27 November under what was now the third title, *First Class Passengers Only* (the first 1925 title was *Level Crossings*).[4]

Described as *A Social Tragedy in Three Acts* and by Osbert to Max Beerbohm as 'a satire on current silliness', the play was a noteworthy flop, apparently not very funny, and petered out entirely in the third act.[5] Somewhat Firbankian in tone rather than strictly satirical or comic, the action on board the SS *Inania*, somewhere between New York and London, involved a set of stock characters including a Sybil Colefax-like social climber, Lady Flinteye, and Lord Playstruck, a society pet. The 'hero', Peter Leach (played by S. Esmé Percy) went through a number of disguises including a Russian baroness and an 'advanced curate' who 'rehearses the Salome dance in the crypt of St Vitus's, though of course without the head'.[6]

Cecil Beaton's impeccably frivolous and period design for the book contrasts strangely with Osbert's lengthy foreword 'A Few Days in an Author's Life', in which he gives vent to all the bitterness he had accrued against critics and gossip columnists during the past three years.

1. Bradford, pp. 133, 140
2. Ritchie, A14, p. 53
3. Pearson, pp. 200, 208
4. Ritchie, A14, p. 53
5. Pearson, p. 242
6. Unidentified press cutting, the Theatre Museum

3.48

The Sitwells with the cast of *First Class Passengers Only*
By an unknown photographer, 1927

Several press prints issued were undoubtedly taken at rehearsals for *First Class Passengers Only* since the three Sitwells are seen in day-wear ostentatiously reading from the script. Osbert appeared during the performance as impresario and spokesman for the three, immaculately dressed with a tuberose in his buttonhole.[1] This shot, which was copied from an unidentified cutting in the 'Sitwelliana' album, shows the principals with Osbert, Edith and Sacheverell. Another press cutting includes Val Gielgud in the cast, though he is not credited in the programme. The 'crew', also not shown here, apparently included the young Arthur Jeffress, the American collector and art dealer.

Cecil Beaton's sets, probably his first public designs for the theatre, included stools covered with oilcloth that stuck to the cast, though it was probably for his increasingly camp appearance and behaviour that Osbert refused to dine with him and Stephen Tennant after the first night.[2]

1. Bradford, p. 173
2. *Ibid.*, pp. 172-3

3.49

'We Are Hopeless Gramophonists'

By Barbara Ker-Seymer for *Harper's Bazaar*,
January 1933

The original of this photograph by Barbara Ker-
Seymer was taken to illustrate a chatty article by
Osbert and Sacheverell for *Harper's Bazaar*. It
includes the Maurice Lambert head of Edith (3.1)
and the E. M. Ginn hand-made and hand-wound
gramophone that is still extant. In their article,
Osbert and Sacheverell make a plea for the
foundation of a Liszt Society and a Berlioz
Society, perhaps a piece of subliminal advertising
for Sacheverell's biography of Liszt that appeared
the following year. At a time when the Sitwells'
literary output was heavily under attack from
Geoffrey Grigson, Wyndham Lewis and others,
the lightweight tone and stagey photographs of
features like this one gave their enemies additional
ammunition.

3.50

The Sitwells

By Norman Parkinson, *c.* 1935

This and several variant photographs of the reassembled trio were evidently taken for a
magazine article, possibly in 1935 at the same
time as the young Norman Parkinson's
photograph of Osbert (5.17). No trace of
publication has been found, however, nor is there
any evidence that the location is the garden at
Carlyle Square with a fresco by Severini in the
background as has been stated.[1] This and the
photographs by Baron (3.51) do, however, provide
evidence of renewed public interest in the Sitwells
as a collective phenomenon after a period in the
doldrums in the first half of the 1930s.

1. N. Parkinson, *Lifework*, 1983, pp. 32-3.

3.51

Edith, Osbert and Sacheverell Sitwell

By Baron, *c.* 1937

The Sitwells were quick to take up any bright
young photographer and had possibly been
introduced to Baron by Rex Whistler, who had
been at Clifton College with him. Baron (born
Baron Nahum, 1906-1956) set up his studio in
London in 1936 at 23 Grosvenor Street where this
photograph was taken. The occasion for the
photograph is not known, but it appears to be a
dignified attempt to recapture something of the
spirit of Beaton's photographs of the siblings ten
years earlier and is among the photographer's
most memorable images.

Baron, whose burgeoning career was severely
interrupted by war service, later recalled being
summoned by Edith to Renishaw in 1948 to
photograph the three of them before she and
Osbert set off on their American lecture tour.
'She wouldn't dream, she said, of asking anyone
else to photograph her.'[1] In the event, the
photographs were taken in London. Various
individual photographs of all three continued to
appear until Baron's death in 1956. Sacheverell
contributed the foreword to Baron's bestselling
book of ballet photographs, *Baron at the Ballet*,
published in 1950.[2]

1. *Baron* by Baron, 1957, pp. 125-6
2. Ritchie, B43, pp. 255-6

Façade may have been the culmination of the siblings' family collaborations, but they continued to give poetry readings together and met frequently for family gatherings at Renishaw, Weston and Montegufoni. With Sacheverell's courtship of and eventual marriage to Georgia Doble and Osbert's hectic social life, Edith was increasingly consolidating her own position and fighting her own battles as the apologist of Modernist poetry.

From 1924 Edith and Helen Rootham were frequent visitors to Paris, staying with Helen's sister, Evelyn Wiel, in her small apartment at 129 rue Sainte-Dominique, in the seventh arrondissement. Edith had enjoyed her first taste of Paris as a girl of seventeen, improving her French under Helen's watchful eye. Paris meant escape for Edith: escape from overwork and the skirmishes of life in London. With her latest volume of poems, *Troy Park*, completed, she could pace her writing more gently, stay in bed and give her increasingly painful back more rest. In fact, wherever Edith was, she spent considerable amounts of time in bed, where she did most of her work.

Back in London in 1925, Edith found a valuable new friend and confidante in Allanah Harper, the vivacious daughter of a wealthy engineer who had taken his family with him on his assignments to Egypt and elsewhere. Allanah had been at school with Iris Tree and the Jungman sisters and, like them, had contributed to the wilder excesses of the 'Bright Young Things'. By the mid-1920s, however, she had relinquished parties and divided much of her time between England and France, satisfying her appetite for art and literature. In early 1925 she attended a poetry reading at Lady Mond's house and heard Edith reciting her work. 'Here was the beauty of a Piero della Francesca', Allanah wrote. 'Her flat fair hair was like that of a naiad, her hands as white as alabaster. On her long gothic fingers she wore huge rings, lumps of topaz and turquoise, on her wrists were coral and jet bracelets.' Even more captivating was Edith's beautifully modulated voice: 'she began to recite and a window opened onto an enchanted world. Each vowel and consonant flowed and she seemed to weave her poetry in the air. The world became heightened and transformed until I could see a whole landscape there behind her eyes.' A complimentary article by Allanah on all

three Sitwells in the avant-garde magazine *Le Flambeau* elicited grateful acknowledgement from Edith ('How nice it is to have people understand one's work like this') and an invitation to tea at Pembridge Mansions, in the company of T. S. Eliot. At a time when Helen Rootham was becoming increasingly difficult Edith needed just the sort of supportive friendship that Allanah could offer, on both sides of the Channel. They were able to discuss personal as well as literary matters, but their intimacy never altered Allanah's essentially deferential attitude to the poet.

Writers and artists of many nationalities converged on Paris in the 1920s and 1930s, attracted by the relatively low cost of living, relaxed morals, good food and wine, and the atmosphere of creative fervour. Many of these expatriates gravitated to the home of the American writer Gertrude Stein, who entertained with the aid of her gypsy-like companion Alice B. Toklas. The walls of their apartment in the rue de Fleurus were covered with paintings by contemporary artists including Cézanne, Matisse and Picasso. 'It was the job of Alice B. Toklas', wrote Edith, 'to entertain the wives and the less interesting of the guests', while Gertrude sat talking with the men. An exception was made for Edith. Gertrude thought she had 'the mind of a man' and was impressed by her unique appearance and bearing. Edith in turn became a champion of Gertrude's writing, admiring her idiosyncratic use of language: 'She threw a word into the air, and when it returned to the ground it bore within it the original meaning it bore before custom and misuse had blurred it.' Edith's championship provided more than encouragement: the Oxford and Cambridge lectures that the Sitwells arranged for Gertrude in the spring of 1926 did much to raise awareness of her work in Britain.

Through Gertrude, Edith broadened her circle of friends and acquaintances in Paris and it was at the rue de Fleurus that she met the young Russian émigré and painter Pavel Tchelitchew. 'The fact that you have met [him] at my house does not mean that I will be responsible for him', Gertrude warned. Edith's relationship with 'Pavlik', as he was known to his friends, was to become the most important, and in many ways most unsatisfactory, of her life. She first saw him in January 1927 in a theatre. 'During both entr'actes, I noticed a tall, desperately thin,

Edith

desperately anxious young man circling round me, staring at me as if he had seen a ghost.' When they met at Gertrude Stein's a few days later, Pavlik explained that Edith bore an uncanny resemblance to the Russian priest who had been his father's confessor.

Aged twenty-nine, eleven years younger than Edith, Pavlik was of noble descent and became known by Edith and her friends as 'the Boyar'. He displayed many of the characteristics of his background: charm, passion, energy, enthusiasm and wildly fluctuating moods, varying from childlike joy to deep depression and irrational resentment. Unfortunately for Edith, who quickly fell under his spell, Pavlik was homosexual, currently living *en ménage* with a young American pianist, Allen Tanner. It is uncertain exactly how much Edith understood or accepted Pavlik's sexuality (or indeed her brother Osbert's) and although circumstances conspired to surround her, throughout adult life, with friends, acquaintances and protégés who were homosexual, she found the implications distasteful, referring darkly to 'piggy things'. On the other hand she seems to have indulged flamboyantly camp behaviour and her nickname for Cecil Beaton was 'Maysie'.

What Pavlik sought in Edith was a muse, a model and a Maecenas, not a mistress. What Edith sought in Pavlik is uncertain: would she really have wanted to consummate their relationship? Wyndham Lewis's notorious but unspecified 'impertinence' while painting her portrait in 1923 left her bitter and angry. It seems to have been taken for granted by many people she knew that her celibacy was somehow inevitable. 'In other ages she would have been a cloistered nun', wrote Virginia Woolf, 'or an eccentric secluded country old maid.'

Edith's developing role as Pavlik's patron assumed new importance after Gertrude Stein fell out with him in 1928, relegating his pictures to a back room in the rue de Fleurus apartment, where visitors were not entertained. It was Edith who received the guests at the vernissage of Pavlik's exhibition at the Galerie Vignon in Paris in June 1927, and who made sure the artist spoke to influential critics. And it was largely Edith who arranged for Pavlik to hold a one-man show at the Claridge Gallery in London in July the following year, using all the Sitwells' powers of influence to generate a gratifying amount of coverage in the British press.

Not that Edith was neglecting her own work. Her poetry was heading in new directions, as *Gold Coast Customs* (1929) demonstrated. In this work rhythm was as important as in *Façade*, but nonsense and entertainment had given way to a political (though not Audenesque) seriousness. The gap between the lives of the rich and the poor was sharply depicted and there was biting criticism of Society hostesses like 'Lady Bamburgher' (unmistakably Emerald Cunard).

Much of Edith's reading and intellectual energy was directed towards the past, however, rather than the present. She researched and wrote a biography of Alexander Pope, published by Faber and Faber in February 1930. Like her later biographical prose studies, its approach to the subject and period was intuitive rather than scholarly. It was not just the academics who disapproved. The young critic Geoffrey Grigson, writing in the *Yorkshire Post*, berated Edith for arrogance, self-satisfaction and ignorance of psychology. Though it immediately secured him prominence among the ranks of The Enemy, Grigson's animosity could not cloud the fact that

4.1
Edith Sitwell
By Cecil Beaton, 1930
(previous page)

4.14
Allanah Harper
By Cecil Beaton, *c.* 1926
(above)

Edith's star was rising. Three months after *Alexander Pope* was published, Duckworth brought out the first edition of her *Collected Poems*, a prospect she described as 'a thrill'. On the whole it was well received and the death of the Poet Laureate, Robert Bridges, the month before publication prompted the odd journalist, not altogether facetiously, to propose Edith as his successor.

Domestically things were less happy. Edith, plagued with illnesses of various kinds herself, had more grounds for concern about Helen Rootham. In 1930 it was diagnosed that Helen had cancer, and as her health deteriorated, so, too, did her behaviour. She became increasingly demanding and selfish, and in 1932 decided that she would be better off going to live permanently with her sister Evelyn in Paris. Partly out of loyalty, and partly as she could not afford to keep the Pembridge Mansions flat on her own, Edith moved to Paris with Helen that September. In her autobiography Edith would write of her new Paris-based life as 'unmitigated hell'. Certainly the conditions in Evelyn Wiel's flat were cramped, making it impossible to avoid Helen's often unreasonable demands. Yet Edith was able to work sufficiently hard to compile her book, *The English Eccentrics*, with the help of reference books sent over by the London Library.

Edith's sense of 'unmitigated hell' can be partly attributed to the way that Pavlik was treating Allen Tanner, who was to find himself ousted in favour of the young American writer Charles Henri Ford. Edith, with her strong sense of fidelity, was appalled, but her interventions were met with reproof. Pavlik would fly into a rage when he felt that she was 'trying to wear the trousers' within their own relationship, and would punish her by depriving her of his company. Many years later she wrote that their friendship had been punctuated by 'rows of unbelievable ferocity'. On one occasion when painting her portrait he had threatened to kill her; and she was only rescued from the situation by Cecil Beaton arriving for tea. Pavlik clearly enjoyed the sadistic satisfaction of his power over Edith, yet there were still moments of uninhibited fun together, both in Paris and at the cottage at Guermantes that the painter Stella Bowen had made available to Pavlik, his sister Choura and Allen Tanner.

With hindsight it often seems as though Edith courted suffering,

in her work as well as in her personal life. In November 1934 her book *Aspects of Modern Poetry* came out, stirring up a hornets' nest of reaction. With provocative comments about some of her *bêtes noires* (F. R. Leavis, Wyndham Lewis and Geoffrey Grigson), it was bound to provide a new battleground. Aided by Osbert on the sidelines Edith threw herself into the ensuing campaign with gusto. But it was not a battle with much dignity. As her biographers have pointed out, Canute-like she railed against the coming Auden generation, in whom she could see little worth; and far from establishing herself as an authority, *Aspects* laid her open to serious charges of plagiarism.

Edith wrote very little poetry for the rest of the decade, concentrating instead on prose. Her *Victoria of England* (1936) hit just the right note with the British public, and became a bestseller.

4.13
Pavel Tchelitchew
By George Platt Lynes, *c.* 1935

"Lewis!"

During the research for the book, she had found a new London base for herself: the Sesame, Imperial and Pioneer Club in Grosvenor Street, W1. At first sight an unlikely roost for such an exotic bird as Edith, the Sesame Club in fact provided the ideal location for her to hold court, either at large cocktail parties or over more intimate meals.

Numerous young (almost invariably male) talents whom Edith wished to foster made the pilgrimage to see her at her Club. They included her Welsh wonder-boy Dylan Thomas, who had earlier referred to her work as 'virgin dung' but now savoured her patronage. Edith pushed him and promoted him and stood by him through thick and thin. She relished her part in defending him, as

she wrote in her autobiography: 'the air still seems to reverberate with the wooden sound of numskulls soundly hit.' She maintained that he always behaved with the utmost decorum in her presence, though there must have been times (such as the occasion at the Sesame Club when Dylan's wife Caitlin ordered the wheelchair-bound John Hayward, to lick ice-cream off her arm), when the Thomases tried her to the limit.

In 1937 Edith's mother, Lady Ida, died (while Edith's now-forgotten novel, *I Live under a Black Sun*, was at the printers). Lady Ida's departure from the world elicited no mercy from Edith, who looked back on her relationship with her mother with horror. The real or imagined trials of Edith's childhood made it impossible for her to forgive. When Helen Rootham died, however, in October 1938, Edith did experience real grief. As she told several friends, Helen had in many ways been a true mother to her. Disoriented, Edith started to pack up her things at the flat in the rue Sainte-Dominique, but lingered on there well into 1939. She was in Italy on holiday when Hitler's troops invaded Poland. Osbert sent a cable urging her to get back to England as soon as possible.

Edith returned to Renishaw, to live with Osbert and, when his R.A.F. duties permitted, with Osbert's companion, David Horner. Sir George stayed on at Montegufoni, only moving to the greater safety of Switzerland in 1942. Edith found the Second World War no more palatable than the First. For her, it was all such a cruel waste and a bore. Life at Renishaw did not help. The huge old house was freezing in winter and was still without electric light. When the artist John Piper went to stay there he found that Edith was spending her mornings in bed and fortifying herself with large glasses of neat gin. Alcohol would become an indispensable solace for Edith over the coming years, a means of keeping despair at bay, with inevitable consequences for her health.

The war years were far from wasted by Edith, however. She made some extremely important friendships, not least with the wealthy novelist 'Bryher', who lived in Lowndes Square with the poet 'H. D.' (Hilda Doolittle). Bryher, whose real name was Winifred Ellerman, was the daughter of a shipping magnate and had met Edith casually several times before Edith decamped for Paris. After several visits to Renishaw an intense friendship was

3.36
**Caricature of Edith Sitwell
from 'Sitwelliana'**
By Siegfried Sassoon, *c.* 1925-1950

4.12
Charles Henri Ford
By Cecil Beaton, 1930s
(opposite)

forged, and Bryher became an astonishingly generous benefactor to Edith over many years, not only reducing Edith's financial worries but also enabling her to distribute *largesse* herself to protégés and friends. Pavel Tchelitchew and Dylan Thomas, always on the look-out for prospective financial gain, assumed that Edith was rich in her own right, but that was far from the case. She received very little of the family fortune, even on Sir George's death in July 1943, and was consistently overdrawn at the bank. Only Osbert was really comfortably off. Sacheverell was so poorly provided for that when Edith went to stay with him at Weston for a period, she did so as a paying guest.

The bleakness of the war gave a new impetus to Edith's poetic creativity, and *Street Songs*, her first collection of poems for years, caught the public mood when it came out in January 1942. It included the powerful poem 'Still Falls the Rain', which Edith was to read with legendary effect during a flying bomb raid on London in the summer of 1944. More importantly, *Street Songs* relaunched Edith as a poetic force to be reckoned with. Fashionable editors such as Cyril Connolly and Stephen Spender at *Horizon* and John Lehmann at *Penguin New Writing* hailed her as a significant wartime voice.

During the war years Edith also planned and wrote a deliberately 'popular' account of the origins and youth of Queen Elizabeth I, with the aim of winning a degree of financial security as well as public acceptance. The book was eventually published by Macmillan in September 1946 as *Fanfare for Elizabeth*. Macmillan ordered what turned out to be a justifiably generous first print run of 20,000 copies. Whatever academic historians might think, the reading public on both sides of the Atlantic were captivated by Edith's graphic portrayal of Tudor England.

The warm reception accorded to *Fanfare for Elizabeth* in the United States made the prospect of visiting that country all the more alluring. Edith set sail for New York in October 1948, accompanied by Osbert and David Horner, for the first of their U.S. reading tours. Sacheverell was not invited. Osbert maintained that three Sitwells together would have been too much even for the Americans to stomach. But there was a more bitter reason. Since Sacheverell's marriage to Georgia there had been an estrangement between the two brothers. Edith expressed her love and loyalty to both, but despite the festering resentment she felt against David Horner she saw that her destiny was more closely linked to Osbert than to Sachie.

The first Sitwell tour was largely instigated by Charles Henri Ford, who had returned to the United States before the war, taking Tchelitchew with him. It was thoughtfully packaged and promoted; Edith's eccentricity and Osbert's ponderous Britishness made an intriguing and seductive combination. Moreover, Edith's steady stream of both prose and verse since *Street Songs* meant that there was substance behind her daunting demeanour. She relished the attendant publicity, the interviews and the clamour of invitations that started the moment her party landed in New York.

Less successful was Edith's reunion with Pavlik. Both of them seem to have viewed the prospect with a mixture of eager anticipation and dread. In the event, both were disappointed and hurt. *Hide and Seek*, his important new work, had been bought by the Museum of Modern Art; and Pavlik was eager to take Edith to see it. But Edith pleaded incapacity through lumbago the first morning that he suggested, and when she did manage to go with him she committed the cardinal sin of remaining totally silent. Pavlik was outraged. The fulsome letter of praise that Edith sent the following day did nothing to heal the wound. Insulted (and probably also jealous of the amount of attention Edith was getting in New York), Pavlik turned against her and sought opportunities to humiliate her. He was incensed enough to tell Charles Henri Ford that he would like to slap her in the face and 'have her kneel at my feet and crawl like a worm'.

The misunderstanding and bitterness with Pavlik soured what was otherwise a triumphant visit for Edith. She and Osbert received generous lecture fees, there were capacity audiences at Yale and Boston, and ten thousand people turned up at the New York Town Hall to hear them. Reviews of the celebrity performance of *Façade* at the Museum of Modern Art paid gratifying homage: 'Dr Sitwell's voice is an orchestra in itself, and it has a haunting quality, a range and power that are quite staggering.' When they were courted by the leading Society hostesses, Edith did not object. She had apparently grown out of her youthful disdain for fashionable salons. Pavlik was not alone in noting that she had changed; he observed the fanfare for Edith with derision.

Queen Edith would certainly have chosen the Americans as her subjects, not the British. Back in England in the Spring of 1949 she thundered to friends that only the Americans really understood her. This impression was strongly reinforced by the contrasting reviews of a new anthology of her poems, *The Canticle of the Rose*, published that September. In England they were short and tepid at best, while in the United States respected publications like the *New York Times* and the *Herald Tribune* produced lengthy commendations. 'I am so indignant', Edith told John Lehmann, 'that I will never, never allow the British public to see one of my poems again.'

Despite the diagnosis that Osbert had developed Parkinson's disease, Edith and he (with David Horner once more in tow) set sail on the liner, the *Queen Elizabeth*, for a second and even more ambitious American tour, starting in November 1950. They could hardly repeat *Façade*, so instead Edith dreamt up the idea of a Shakespeare recital centred on herself as Lady Macbeth, bedecked in a huge flowing dress, massive jewellery and a spiked gold crown. Several of her London friends wondered whether she had lost all self-critical faculties when they learnt of this extraordinary proposition. Evelyn Waugh, who happened to be in New York, was beside himself with glee at the thought. Yet even though Edith had had no formal theatrical training, and could never have competed with Shakespearean actresses, she somehow got away with it, thanks to the sheer authority and awesomeness of her presence.

Public awards followed one after another. These included not only the Royal Society for Literature medal for Poetry but also no less than three honorary doctorates, from the British universities of Leeds, Durham and Oxford. She learnt of the Oxford degree before she left America for England in March 1950, and considered it the crowning achievement in recognition of her poetic genius. Enjoying the situation in every respect, she henceforth styled herself 'Dr Edith Sitwell, D.Litt., D.Litt., D.Litt.' The novelist Ivy Compton-Burnett was not alone in feeling that

success had spoilt Edith, remarking: 'She's become a mixture of the Blessed Virgin Mary and Queen Elizabeth!' A fourth honorary doctorate was awarded by Sheffield University in 1955.

For many Americans, however, Edith's airs and graces were part of her appeal and had helped draw 2,000 people to a reading she and Osbert had given in Hollywood. Far from dismissing Tinsel Town for its vulgarity, Edith had found it glamorous and she enjoyed her encounters with film stars. One of her first engagements in Hollywood had been lunch with the film director George Cukor, who hoped to make a film of *Fanfare for Elizabeth*. He commissioned Edith to prepare a film treatment of her book, but when she began work on this back in England it soon became clear that she had no idea of what was required. The project caused her considerable anguish and amusement. She laughed with English friends about what the Tudor royals would have to do to make the film more acceptable to American audiences (not to mention the modern colloquial language the characters were meant to employ). Despite several script conferences in 1952 and 1953, and the best intentions of the script-writer Walter Reich, who was brought in to try to salvage it, like so many of the film world's enthusiastically promoted ideas it was eventually shelved.

Although Edith never collected newspaper cuttings as assiduously as Osbert, she did thrive on the oxygen of publicity. Even American journalists were not always flattering or accurate, however, and Edith took a particular dislike to the Hollywood gossip columnist Hedda Hopper, who made the mistake of referring to Edith, during her 1952-1953 sojourn in Hollywood, as a 'little old lady'. Edith took great delight in spreading the rumour that the current epidemic of rabies in the Los Angeles area had been caused by Hedda Hopper running around biting dogs.

Even more galling was the absurd story whipped up by the British press that Edith was going to bring Marilyn Monroe over to England. The two women had met and taken a liking to each other. The first time, in February 1954, they talked about the theories of the Austrian social philosopher Rudolf Steiner and giggled about 'ladies of only too certain an age' galloping around with large, bare, dusty feet over uncarpeted floors. Tired of repeated press enquiries back in England about whether she really

35

P. Tchelitchew

128 Edith

had asked the film star to visit her, Edith wrote curtly to the *Sunday Chronicle* that Miss Monroe was 'a very nice girl', but that she had merely suggested they have luncheon together should she pass through London. Just such a meal did indeed take place, at the Sesame Club, with Marilyn's husband, Arthur Miller, in attendance.

Less vexing was the deluge of press interest and letters from friends when Edith was made a Dame Commander of the British Empire (D.B.E.) in the Queen's birthday honours list in June 1954. As Edith told the South African writer William Plomer, one of the most satisfying aspects of this honour was that it had 'slapped down all the miserable little pipsqueaks in the *New Statesman and Nation* and *Spectator*, who have been persecuting me.' It is doubtful that her 'persecutors', such as the 'Movement' members Kingsley Amis and Philip Larkin, were much cowed; and it seems that Edith had forgotten how, as a young woman, she would have scoffed at the laurels bestowed on those whose work failed to meet her approval.

Few people would have realised that beneath Edith's public belligerence and majestic façade lay an insecure and profoundly vulnerable woman. She had never been partial to exercise; even getting her to walk in the gardens at Renishaw was a major achievement. She had put on a great deal of weight, through lack of exercise and her large intake of alcohol, and her legs had difficulty in supporting her. The final ten years of her life were marred by a series of falls (some of them undoubtedly after she had been drinking).

Osbert, physically in far worse shape, was dismayed by her mental deterioration and suggested that Edith might find some peace of mind if she joined the Catholic Church; neither of them had much respect for or interest in the dry Anglicanism of their forebears. David Horner had become a Catholic in 1944, which gave added irony to Edith's own conversion, as one of the main reasons for her frequent mental distress was David's presence at Renishaw and Montegufoni, where she was spending most of her summers and winters respectively. At times she felt positively murderous towards David, her fantasies of disposing of him fuelled by alcohol and the plots of detective stories that were her favourite

leisure reading. She would then suffer pangs of guilt, made all the more bitter by her realisation that Osbert relied far more on David than on her.

Edith was instructed in Roman Catholicism by Father Philip Caraman and was baptised at Farm Street Church in Mayfair in August 1955. Her godparents included Evelyn Waugh, Roy Campbell and Campbell's wife. Waugh had been worried that Edith might turn her baptism into a media event, but in fact only a very small party had been invited to the Church. Afterwards they were treated to a slap-up lunch at the Sesame Club. Father Caraman declared later that Edith was an eccentric Catholic, just as she was an eccentric woman. She certainly did not place much importance on attending Mass regularly. Indeed, she maintained (perhaps only half-jokingly) that the one good thing about having become a Catholic was that it had stopped her murdering David Horner.

Edith made her last U. S. tour in 1957, as usual in the company of Osbert and David. As David was currently consorting with a

4.11
Edith Sitwell
By Pavel Tchelitchew, 1935
(opposite)

4.35
Marilyn Monroe
By Cecil Beaton, 1956

painter, instead of faithfully staying at Osbert's side, Edith worked hard to ensure that he and his paramour were not received by top New York Society. However, not all of Edith's time and energy was spent on such machinations. She spoke profitably at the University of Texas at Austin (which later bought many of her manuscripts), and met the writer James Purdy, who was to become a cherished protégé.

In England that summer Edith learnt of Pavlik's death in Rome. For all the direct and indirect hurt she had received from him, the news came as a tremendous blow. She even felt guilty, without fully understanding why. The saddest aspect of her love for him was the knowledge that she could never have made him happy. Pavlik's death clouded what should have been an atmosphere of celebration over the second, updated edition of her *Collected Poems*, which had appeared only weeks before. The book won the Foyle Poetry Prize, but did not receive the clamour of attention that Edith would have liked.

Her fame, and subsequent demands on her time, now made it necessary for her to employ a secretary; she was fortunate enough to find the ideal person in the Australian crime-writer Elizabeth Salter. They had met at the Aldeburgh Festival, where Edith was giving a reading (and enjoying a burgeoning friendship with the composer Benjamin Britten). Elizabeth Salter was able to remove many of the practical worries of Edith's life, as well as acting as a filter for people who were trying to intrude on her time. She censored the distressingly frequent poison-pen letters that Edith received, mostly from women infuriated by the poet's exotic appearance. What to many people appeared noble eccentricity struck others as the egocentric posturing of someone set on attracting more media coverage than she deserved.

Edith's exoticism made a dramatic impact on thousands of British television viewers when she featured in May 1959 as one of the interviewees in John Freeman's remarkable *Face to Face* series. She proved herself a born performer. Even if some of the stories she told were fictitious, such as the one about an ancestor walking barefoot all the way from Leeds to London in order to found the family fortune, Edith won many new admirers that night, including people who had never read a single line of her verse.

Later that year at the Edinburgh Festival Edith discovered that the Scots love a fighter. When several people in the auditorium complained loudly that they could not hear her, she wagged a finger at them and retorted rudely: 'Get a hearing aid. I am not going to shout with my voice.' The interruptions continued until Elizabeth Salter wondered whether she ought to ask the management to bring the curtain down before there was a riot. By sheer will-power, however, Edith subdued the protesters and was given a rousing send-off when she left the theatre.

Having plotted for so long to oust David Horner from Osbert's affections and houses, Edith now found that David in turn was trying to get rid of her. He was telling people, including Georgia, that Edith had become deranged. Edith angrily rejected Osbert's suggestion that she consult a psychiatrist, but she could not keep treatment of her self-evident physical deterioration similarly at bay. Her kidneys had become infected and in the summer of 1960 her doctor insisted that she go into a nursing home in Sheffield for proper care. While there her alcohol intake was reduced and her appetite and strength picked up. The break also gave her the opportunity to view her situation more dispassionately. Aware that she was no longer welcome at Renishaw, Edith decided that she would live in London full-time.

For a while she stayed at the Sesame Club, where the bills inflated her already enormous overdraft. Characteristically, she dispelled her financial worries by organising large dinner parties for friends. Her bank manager became politely pressing, asking for manuscripts and other collateral to guarantee her debts. Mercifully, Elizabeth Salter had been over to Paris to see Evelyn Wiel and had brought back with her some of Edith's Tchelitchew paintings that had been stored there since before the war. These and other possessions of Edith's from Renishaw were sold at auction by Sotheby's in 1961, to meet tax demands and reduce her overdraft. Elizabeth subsequently recovered more Tchelitchews and a secret cache of Edith's notebooks that had been hidden behind a wardrobe in Evelyn's flat.

Elizabeth Salter and a nurse, Sister Doris Farquhar, took control over much of Edith's daily existence for the last few years of her life. She was moved into a small flat in Hampstead, under

Sister Farquhar's care, and submitted to a gentle but fixed routine devised by Elizabeth Salter. This ensured that she was properly looked after and that she could receive visitors without getting over-tired. Elizabeth Salter's organisational skills also helped Edith to finish a book on Queen Elizabeth and Mary, Queen of Scots, a sequel to *Fanfare for Elizabeth* called *The Queens and the Hive*, which was published in 1962. Her final volume of poetry, *The Outcasts*, was also published that year. Echoes of phrases and themes contained in her 1920s' verse had been reworked in the consciousness of her own mortality.

To mark Edith's seventy-fifth birthday a gala celebratory recital was organised by her nephew Francis in October 1962 at the Royal Festival Hall in London. She jokingly referred to it as her 'Memorial Concert'. Three thousand of her friends, family and admirers came along to hear her open the evening's entertainment with a short reading of her own poems, followed by Benjamin Britten's setting of 'Still Falls the Rain'. There was also a performance of *Façade*, conducted by William Walton. Edith sat in a wheelchair in the Royal Box, tears streaking her face as the audience turned to cheer her at the end of the performance. After that, her appearance on the television programme *This Is Your Life* would seem an anti-climax.

In 1963 Elizabeth Salter and Sister Farquhar thought it would do Edith good if she went on a world cruise, taking in Sri Lanka, Australia and the East Coast of the United States. Edith was not especially enamoured of life on board ship, but the voyage gave her the tranquility needed to work on a commissioned autobiography. She enjoyed herself in Australia, where she gave several memorable press conferences, and she was thrilled to learn that she had been made a Companion of Literature back at home. The journey across the Pacific was blighted by bad weather, however, and by the time the boat reached Miami she had a serious stomach upset and was vomiting blood. On doctors' advice she was put on a plane at Bermuda and flown back to London.

Edith's final home was a rented Queen Anne cottage that she named 'Bryher House', in Keats' Grove, Hampstead. There she lived surrounded by books and cats. Although she found it difficult to stay awake for more than short periods, she had the pleasure of seeing Malcolm Williamson's opera based on *The English Eccentrics*, and of being able to choose the photographs for her autobiography *Taken Care Of*. The book, posthumously published, was sadly inadequate and marred by the malice of hindsight. Its last line, anticipating her death, is unusually self-deprecating: 'Then all will be over, bar the shouting and the worms.' She died on 9 December 1964 and is buried near Sacheverell in the graveyard of the parish church at Lois Weedon, near Weston.

Jonathan Fryer

Edith Sitwell
By Cecil Beaton, 1930

a) illustrated on page 121
b) left

August 1930 saw one of the largest and grandest
Sitwell house parties at Renishaw and was the
occasion for Cecil Beaton's famous conversation
piece of the family (see 6.12) and some of his most
memorable photographs of Edith. While Sir
George and Lady Ida stayed at the Sitwell Arms,
the rest of the family was subject to the acute
observations of Evelyn Waugh who, as a guest
with his friend Robert Byron, recorded the
proceedings in his diary.[1] The constant stream of
guests also included Walton, Zita Jungman, Lady
Aberconway, Constant Lambert, Richard
Wyndham, Anthony Powell, Tom Balston,
Raymond Mortimer, Tom Driberg, Rex Whistler,
Harold Monro, Lord Berners, Francis Birrell,
Arthur Waley, Alastair Graham and, among the
older generation of Osbert's friends, Mrs Keppel
and Ada Leverson.[2] How Beaton managed to take
the photographs in this hectic month is not
recorded but Edith did not always see eye to eye
with Sacheverell's and Osbert's friends and was
presumably happy to be taken off by Beaton to
pose for him. In September, when Osbert and
most of the other guests had departed, she wrote
to Beaton: 'I simply can't tell you what excitement
there is at Renishaw about the photographs ... We
are all, including Mother, half off our heads with
excitement ... and are longing to have them
published in papers.'[3] Full-page reproductions of
Edith in bed and Georgia with her borzoi, Feo,
duly appeared in *Vogue* in October 1930.

Edith's biography of Alexander Pope had
appeared in March and seems to have influenced
Beaton's theatrical mimicry of the painter Zoffany,
a 1920s rediscovery and a later enthusiasm of
Sacheverell's. In a) young Reresby's black
'Nannah', Mary Cole, plays the part of the servant
to Edith, impassively receiving breakfast in one of
the famous four-poster beds, the caption in *Vogue*
noticing 'an interesting resemblance to certain
pictures of Cowper'.[4] Beaton's pictures of Edith as
solitary muse playing the harp (b) or in other
versions as startled sprite in front of one of the
magnificent Renishaw tapestries are among his
most poetic images.

1. M. Davie (ed.), *The Diaries of Evelyn Waugh*, 1986 edn, pp. 327-8
2. Bradford, pp. 217-9
3. *Ibid.*, p. 219
4. British *Vogue*, October 1930, p.72

4·2
Gertrude Stein
By Man Ray, 1926

Gertrude Stein (1874-1946) thought Edith had the most beautiful nose in the world. 'This friendship', she wrote, 'like all friendships has had its difficulties but I am convinced that fundamentally Gertrude Stein and Edith Sitwell are friends and enjoy being friends.'[1] Edith, less gracious, wrote that 'Gertrude was verbally very interesting, the more so as she invariably got everybody wrong. She looked rather like an Easter island idol, was immensely good humoured, and had a remarkable ability to work in the midst of any amount of noise.'[2]

They were introduced in Paris in late 1924 by Dorothy Todd, the editor of *Vogue*, for whom Edith had written a piece on Gertrude Stein that October. Alice B. Toklas recalled that at this first meeting Edith looked like a gendarme, dressed in a double-breasted coat with huge buttons.

Stein met Man Ray, the American Surrealist painter and photographer, in Paris in July 1921. He photographed her at various intervals, most memorably in 1922 posed in apposition to her portrait by Picasso. Man Ray reflected in his autobiography: 'Perhaps I was impressed by the staidness of her personality, but it never occurred to me to try any fantasy or acrobatics with her physiognomy.'[3] This pose has been dated to 1926 and the print is inscribed 'To Edith with much love from Gtde'.

1. G. Stein, *The Autobiography of Alice B. Toklas*, 1933
2. TCO, p. 136
3. Man Ray, *Self-Portrait*, 1963

4·3
Gertrude Stein and Alice B. Toklas
By Cecil Beaton, 1938

When Edith met Gertrude Stein in 1924 the American writer and pioneer of literary form was established with her lifelong companion Alice B. Toklas in Paris at 27 rue de Fleurus. It was here, surrounded by the superb collection of modern art that Stein had been accumulating since 1905 that Edith was entertained to tea and met the influential artists and writers of the day. Picasso was the brightest star of her salon and his portrait of her (now in the Metropolitan Museum, New York), hung among a dozen of his other works. Edith admired the 'revivifying' effect Gertrude Stein's writing had on the language and was flattered that Stein paid her the sort of serious intellectual attention she usually reserved for her masculine visitors. In the spring of 1926 Edith realised a long-held ambition when she and her brothers stage-managed Gertrude Stein's lectures at the Ordinary Society in Oxford and at Jesus College, Cambridge.

Stein's writing attracted little acclaim until the publication of *The Autobiography of Alice B. Toklas* in 1933. This was followed by Virgil Thomson's well-received opera, *Four Saints in Three Acts*, for which Stein had written the libretto; and by a successful lecture tour of America in 1934-1935. In later life Edith claimed it had been an oversight that she had failed to include any work by Gertrude Stein at the reading (held in Stein's presence) at Shakespeare and Company, but at the time it was seen as a deliberate insult.

In 1938 Stein and Toklas moved from the rue de Fleurus to 5 rue Christine where they were visited that summer by Cecil Beaton. He was given a tour of inspection and wrote in his diary that 'the Misses Stein and Toklas live like Biblical royalty: simply, yet in complete luxury.' They posed for him with their dogs Pépé and Basket (the poodle) in a room with blue and white pigeon-patterned wallpaper. 'I photographed also Toklas at her sewing', he went on. 'Determined not to talk this afternoon she nodded by way of understanding and said, "Interior".'[1]

1. C. Beaton, *The Wandering Years*, 1961, pp. 281-3

4.4

**Edith Sitwell reading from *Rustic Elegies*
for a 'Phonofilm', Clapham Studios**
By an unknown photographer, 1927

In the spring of 1927 Edith was filmed and
recorded by the pioneering 'Phonofilm' method
invented by Lee de Forest. According to the *Daily
Express*, which anticipated the event with an
article titled 'Woman Poet in a Film/Dramatic
recital for "Talking Picture"', she was to have
read two poems, one by herself and one by
Osbert, resulting in two eight-minute films
directed by Widgey R. Newman.

Although there are records of numerous short
films made by Newman for de Forest Phonofilms,
no trace can be found of Edith's recital. Edith is
wearing the black hat with trailing veils that she
wore at Sacheverell's wedding (see 6.4) and when
she sat to Nevinson for her portrait (see 4.5).

4.5

Edith Sitwell
By Christopher Richard Wynne Nevinson, 1927

Edith had been the first of the Sitwells to meet
Nevinson, in 1916, at the house of the art critic
Paul G. Konody, who was to write a book on
Nevinson's war paintings. The artist described her
as 'a grand woman, completely unlike the absurd
legends told about her by the envious and the
petty. Her courage has always been a tonic to me;
and her débonnaire wit, her feminine shrewdness,
and the nobility of her character make all her
vilifiers appear the most revolting of literary
parasites.'[1] The etching relates closely to a pastel
portrait the artist made of Edith.[2]

1. C. R. W. Nevinson, *Paint and Prejudice*, 1937, p. 88
2. Reproduced in E. Salter, *Edith Sitwell*, 1979, p. 69, and thought now
to be in a private collection, Australia

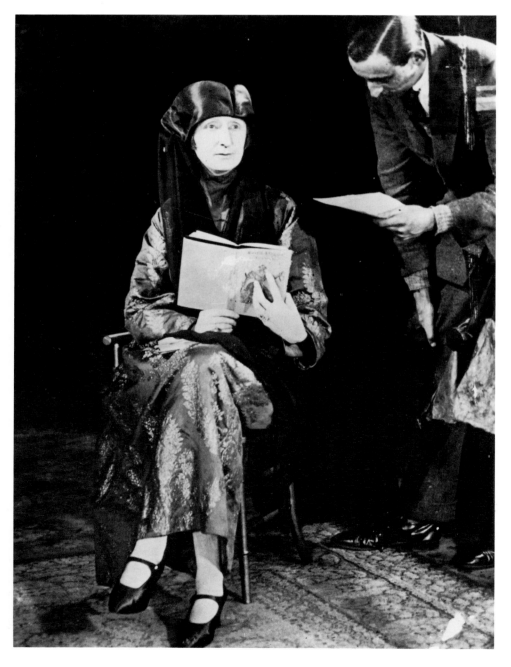

4.6
Pavel Tchelitchew
Self-portrait, *c.* 1933

Gertrude Stein introduced Edith to the Russian émigré painter Pavel Tchelitchew (1898-1957) in Paris in 1927. As Stein's enthusiasm for Tchelitchew's work waned, Edith stepped in to replace her as the painter's champion and muse. So began a relationship as frustrating and aggravating as it was rewarding to both of them. 'Nobody has ever understood you better, or come closer to you than I have,' Tchelitchew wrote to Edith, 'and nobody ever will.'[1] Their friendship developed as Edith visited, and eventually settled in, Paris in 1932. They maintained a regular correspondence, particularly after Tchelitchew's move to New York. The few letters that escaped the embargo placed on the collection held by the Beinecke Library at Yale University (until the year 2000) reveal a relationship of great intimacy. Their reunion after an interval of ten years, on Edith's first expedition to America in 1947, was a disaster of failed nerve and disappointed expectations from which their friendship barely recovered.

The self-portrait drawing inscribed to Edith is one of a pair; the other, entitled *My Face from Left* [2], was also in her collection and was sold by her at Sotheby's in December 1961 (lot 36).

1. Salter, p. 108
2. P. Tyler, *The Divine Comedy of Pavel Tchelitchew*, 1967, ill. f.p. 346

4.7
Pavel Tchelitchew
Self-portrait mask, 1929

'I couldn't read or draw – I was a wire structure',[1] Tchelitchew wrote to his biographer Parker Tyler shortly before his death. Like the wire and wax head of Edith visible in 4.15, the self-portrait is based on what Tchelitchew called his 'wire basket idea', a form derived literally from a series of wire colanders bought in Montparnasse. The delicate surface structure anticipates the 'interior landscapes', heads delineated with lines of light in dark space, which preoccupied Tchelitchew in the mid to late 1940s.

Edith entitled the piece *The Clown*, describing it in her autobiography as 'a most tragic work'.[2] Both the self-portrait and the mask of Edith were included in the sale of Edith's Tchelitchews in December 1961. Although Edith's mask went to Tchelitchew's American dealer, Kirk Askew (and is now in the collection of Yale University Art Gallery), the self-portrait was in Edith's possession at the time of her death.

1. Quoted in P. Tyler, *The Divine Comedy of Pavel Tchelitchew*, 1967, p. 71
2. TCO, p. 139

4.8

Edith Sitwell

By Pavel Tchelitchew, *c.* 1927

Painted before Tchelitchew's break with Gertrude Stein, this was in all probability the 'first portrait' of Edith by Tchelitchew mentioned in his letter written from Monte Carlo while working on designs for Diaghilev's ballet, *Ode*: 'I am very glad and very touched that you like your portrait. I am still rather anxious about it in spite of the fact that Gertrude Stein is pleased that you like it. She thought it a good likeness! I think I could do it better – I hope to be able to do so one day when you are in Paris for rather longer than the last time.'[1] The portrait was included in the Claridge Gallery exhibition in 1928, reproduced in *The Graphic*, and used as the frontispiece in the special first edition of Edith's *Collected Poems* (1930). It still featured prominently on Osbert's wall when his new flat in York House was photographed by Lewis Morley in 1963.

1. Quoted in Salter, p. 107

4.9

Edith Sitwell

By Pavel Tchelitchew, *c.* 1930

Virginia Woolf went to tea at Pembridge Mansions in July 1930 and noted in her diary: 'Edith Sitwell has grown very fat, powders herself thickly, gilds her nails with silver paint, wears a turban & looks like an ivory elephant, like the Emperor Heliogabalus. I have never seen such a change. She is mature, majestical. She is monumental. Her fingers are crusted with white coral. She is altogether composed ... But though thus composed, her eyes are sidelong & humorous. The old Empress remembers her Scallywag days ... Who was she like? Pope in a nightcap? No; the imperial majesty must be included.'[1]

Virginia Woolf's observations fit well with the parameters for dating this portrait. An ink sketch by Tchelitchew, dated 1929, shows Edith in a similar pose and wearing a turban.[2] The completed portrait appears behind Edith in the photograph (4.15), taken at Pembridge Mansions before Edith left in 1932. It was lot 2 in the sale of Edith's Tchelitchews at Sotheby's in December 1961. After his two large canvases, *Phenomena* (Tretyakov Gallery, Moscow) and *Hide and Seek* (Museum of Modern Art, New York), his portraits of Edith are among Tchelitchew's most important works.

1. V. Woolf, *Diaries 1925-30*, Penguin edn, 1982, p. 308
2. Reproduced in American *Vogue*, 15.11.1948, pp. 130-3. A sheet of similar drawings was sold at Sotheby's, New York, 15.12.1981 (62)

4.10
Edith Sitwell
By Pavel Tchelitchew, 1937

Tchelitchew began his 'Sibyl' portrait of Edith in October 1936. 'This time', she wrote to David Horner, 'it is a straightforward portrait, and I am frightfully pleased with it, and think you all will be.'[1] According to Tchelitchew's biographer (who described the portrait as 'not just physically large, but spiritually ample'), it was undertaken because Tchelitchew wanted 'to pay a signal tribute to Edith Sitwell'.[2]

This was the only one of the six major Tchelitchew paintings of Edith that was not presented to her by the artist. It was acquired by the patron and collector Edward James, who had earlier commissioned Tchelitchew as a designer for *Les Ballets 1933*. James, a major collector of Tchelitchew's work, made even greater claims for the artist than Edith: Picasso, Tchelitchew and Dali, he wrote to Edith, 'are the three most important painters since Renoir and Cézanne'. He predicted that Tchelitchew might become 'the most important painter since Michelangelo, Raphael and Greco'.[3] Edith and Edward James became friends and correspondents, finding mutual ground in a dislike of Charles Henri Ford.

1. Quoted in Pearson, p. 317
2. P. Tyler, *The Divine Comedy of Pavel Tchelitchew*, 1967, pp. 353, 388
3. Quoted in J. Lowe, *Edward James, A Surrealist Life*, 1991, p. 126

4.11
Edith Sitwell
By Pavel Tchelitchew, 1935
(illustrated on page 128)

The most ethereal of Tchelitchew's portraits of Edith was drawn in 1935 and included in his exhibition at Arthur Tooth & Sons that year. Abandoned in Paris at the outbreak of the Second World War, the pastel was not retrieved from Evelyn Wiel at the rue St Dominique flat in 1959. Elizabeth Salter tells the story of its rediscovery four years later in *The Last Years of a Rebel*. She returned to Paris to reclaim the last of Edith's possessions when Evelyn Wiel was taken into hospital. With the help of a neighbour she moved a heavy bookcase and behind it discovered the pastel portrait among a cache of a dozen or so Tchelitchew ink drawings. Unscathed by its long years in the dark, the portrait was brought back to Edith and, apart from being sent to Tchelitchew's retrospective exhibition in New York, never left her sight for the remaining year of her life.

4.12
Charles Henri Ford
By Cecil Beaton, 1930s
(illustrated on page 125)

Edith had been greatly attached to Allen Tanner, Tchelitchew's American companion, and felt a sense of betrayal when Tchelitchew's affections moved on to the young Mississippi writer, Charles Henri Ford (b. 1913), who arrived in Paris in 1931 looking for a publisher for *The Young and Evil*. When this homoerotic work, co-authored with Tchelitchew's biographer Parker Tyler (who himself described it as a 'naughty novel'), was sent to Edith she wrote to Tanner that it was 'like a dead fish stinking in hell' and that in earlier times she would have had Ford's skin made into a bathmat.[1] She continued to correspond with Tanner and to shun Ford until 1940 when she reviewed Ford's poetry favourably in *Life and Letters Today*. A tentatively polite exchange of letters between them gradually became less formal and in 1949 she wrote a foreword to a book of his poems, *Sleep in a Nest of Flames*.

Beaton liked Charles Henri Ford from the start, almost the only English friend of Tchelitchew's to do so. Ford has been described as 'America's surrealist poet' and it may be in this connection that he was photographed in a surrealist costume by Beaton.

1. Glendinning, p. 182

4.13
Pavel Tchelitchew
By George Platt Lynes, *c.* 1935
(illustrated on page 123)

The American-born photographer George Platt Lynes (1907-1955) first visited Paris in 1925 and was introduced to Tchelitchew by Gertrude Stein. Their friendship developed while Platt Lynes freelanced between Paris and New York, Tchelitchew providing him with original backgrounds for some of his photographs. Platt Lynes set up his studio in New York in 1932 and as well as the portraits (see 4.4), ballet and theatre subjects, for which he became well known, he pioneered homoerotic studies of the male nude, anticipating in many respects the work of Robert Mapplethorpe. He photographed Tchelitchew at regular intervals and in 1937 Tchelitchew painted Platt Lynes's portrait.

4.14
Allanah Harper
By Cecil Beaton, *c.* 1926
(illustrated on page 122)

Allanah Harper (1901-1992) was the wealthy daughter of an engineering consultant who worked on the Aswan Dam. She had been at school with Iris Tree (see 2.25) and the Jungman sisters (see 6.8), but only came into contact with the Sitwells in 1925 after hearing Edith read her poems at Lady Mond's house. Her article on the Sitwells in the Belgian review *Le Flambeau* led to a lifelong friendship with Edith, and her letters and unpublished memoir on Edith have been an important source for biographers. She was the co-author with Elizabeth Salter of an anthology, *Edith Sitwell, Fire of the Mind* (1976).

Like the Sitwells, Allanah Harper was 'on the side of the arts' and introduced Edith to a number of useful contacts in Paris. As the founding editor of the Parisian literary review, *Echanges*, she gave useful exposure to both French and English writers and also shared with Edith some of the burden of promulgating Tchelitchew's name among the Parisians. It was partly at her instigation that Cecil Beaton embarked on a career as a portrait photographer.

4.15
Edith Sitwell
By Fox Photos, *c.* 1931

Although the negative has been damaged, the photograph clearly shows Edith with two of her portraits by Tchelitchew: the wire and wax mask and the turbanned portrait (4.9). These, and the two other paintings visible, *The Blue Clown* (above) and *Two Nude Boys* (below) were among the thirty-nine works by Tchelitchew that Edith sold at Sotheby's in 1961.

Edith was relentless in championing Tchelitchew's work. She related to Allanah Harper the bizarre story of a murder tenuously connected with the Sitwell name ('my fourth cousin married as his second wife a woman who is sister to the murdered man's wife') and the fact that the *Daily Express* sent a reporter to interview her, and a photographer. Edith used the visit to suit her own, different, purpose: 'I showed them Pavlik's pictures.' In magisterial tones she told the reporter: 'You have dragged me into this ugly scandal; in return you shall please me by photographing these beautiful pictures and speaking respectfully of the great artist who painted them, in your paper!'[1] The report seems not to have been filed, owing probably to Lord Beaverbrook's staunch defence of his paper against the publicity stunts of a family he branded 'less than a band of mediocrities'.[2]

1. Quoted in Salter, p. 112
2. Quoted in Glendinning, p. 122

4.16
Gold Coast Customs
By Edith Sitwell, 1929

The long poem, 'Gold Coast Customs', is a satire on the speciousness of 'civilised' society, drawing on the customs of the Ashanti, the African artefacts in the British Museum, the horrors of slum life and the *mores* of the fashionable world. The poem's unremittingly bleak vision was altered in later published versions to end on an optimistic note. It was cautiously received. *The Times* described it as 'in the esoteric order', though many years later it earned Edith the nod of approval from Harry Pollitt, the General Secretary of the British Communist Party.[1] The dust jacket bears the portrait of the Ashanti King Munza in full dress, originally engraved by J. D. Cooper to illustrate Georg Schweinfurth's *The Heart of Africa* (1873). The book is dedicated to Helen Rootham and the frontispiece reproduces one of Tchelitchew's paintings of Edith. The title poem was set to music by Humphrey Searle and given a first performance, with Edith and Constant Lambert as reciters, for the BBC in May 1949.

1. See Glendinning, p. 265

4.17
The English Eccentrics
By Edith Sitwell, 1933

Edith began writing *The English Eccentrics* as soon as she moved to Paris in September 1932, working from books sent over by Mr Cox of the London Library. It was published in London in May and in America in September the following year, and was dedicated to Edith's doctor, H. Lydiard Wilson, and his wife. The wrapper and frontispiece were designed by Tchelitchew. The book gives full rein to Edith's collector instinct and was described unsympathetically by *The Times* as having an 'insatiable lust for detail'. According to Edith eccentricity is a particularly English phenomenon, 'because of that peculiar and satisfactory knowledge of infallibility that is the hallmark and birthright of the British nation.'[1] The anecdotes range through miserly vicars, incompetent actors, quacks, soldiers, hunting squires and an ornamental hermit. Victoria Glendinning sees in Edith's description of the relationship between Margaret Fuller, the nineteenth-century American academic, and James Nathan, an echo of Edith's feelings for Tchelitchew. In 1964 Edith attended the London première of an opera based on *The English Eccentrics*, with music by Malcolm Williamson and a libretto by Geoffrey Dunn.

1. ES, *The English Eccentrics*, p. 21

4.18
Edith Sitwell
By Stella Bowen, *c.* 1927-1929

The Australian painter Stella Bowen (1895-1947) was living in Paris with Ford Madox Ford in the 1920s and knew both Gertrude Stein and Tchelitchew before she met Edith. 'I think the most extraordinary thing about Edith Sitwell', she wrote, 'is the big gap that exists between her quite wonderful but alarming façade and the soft and flagrantly human woman whom it conceals.'[1] Stella, who lent her cottage at Guermantes to the Tchelitchew ménage, was a close and perceptive confidante of Edith's tortured relationship with Tchelitchew: 'they were each of them a packet of nerves, infusing therefrom a palpitating and sensuous life into their respective work.'[2]

Stella Bowen's penetrating study conveys the vulnerability she sensed in Edith. 'She has a strange aquiline beauty which it amuses her to decorate with extravagant ornaments and exotic raiment', the artist wrote. 'This picture, however, shows her in what she calls her "linsey-woolsey" mood.'[3] She posed Edith on a coal box under a big mirror in her studio. 'She was a lovely subject for a painter and gave me all the sittings I wanted. We talked hard all the time and when the picture was finished we knew each other very well indeed.'[4] Stella Bowen later painted Edith's hands holding an African mask.[5]

1. S. Bowen, *Drawn from Life*, 1984, p. 172
2. *Ibid.*, p. 173
3. S. Bowen in unidentified article in William Beaumont Morris, 'Of Dame Edith Sitwell' scrapbook
4. S. Bowen, *Drawn from Life*, 1984, p. 176
5. In the collection of Sir Reresby Sitwell Bt

4.19
Edith Sitwell
By John Banting, 1943

John Banting made a habit of collecting and anthropomorphising bones. The painting is based on a bone that he found, decorated with glass eyes and put on a plinth for a joke with a notice 'Portrait of Edith Sitwell. Price £1,000'.[1] It echoes the observation in Virginia Woolf's diary that Edith was 'like a clean hare's bone that one finds on a moor with emeralds stuck about it'.[2]

1. Letter to NPG from Barbara Ker-Seymer, owner of the bone sculpture, 30.1.1987. Bone exhibited in *Dada and Surrealism Reviewed*, Hayward Gallery, London, 1978 (14.84)
2. V. Woolf, *Diary*, 23.3.1927

4.20
William Plomer
By Edward Wolfe, 1929
(page 141, left)

The writer William Plomer (1903-1973) was born in the Transvaal and spent his youth shuttling between South Africa and England. In 1920 he ordered a copy of Edith's *Wooden Pegasus* from Blackwell in Oxford and discerned a poet with a 'new song', one he could admire. In London he heard Edith reading at the Swedenborg Hall, an experience carefully recollected in his autobiography. 'There was a dignity that seemed as if it might sharpen into asperity; an underlying compassion in the voice and in the shape of the eyelids; an easily accessible sense of the ridiculous, the impertinent, and the commonplace.'[1] Plomer became one of Edith's most loyal correspondents and her many letters to him (in the library of Durham University) have been an invaluable source to her biographers. Plomer's own career began with a fiercely satiric first novel, *Turbott Wolfe*, and the anti-establishment magazine *Voorslag*, which precipitated his departure from South Africa in 1926. After two years teaching in Japan he arrived in England and was painted in London by his fellow South African, Edward Wolfe. The artist had settled in England at the age of nineteen and studied at the Regent Street Polytechnic School of Art before going on to the Slade School of Fine Art in 1917. Sitters for his brightly coloured portraits (he became known as 'England's Matisse') included Arnold Bennett and Constance Sitwell, Edith's cousin by marriage. Osbert owned a fine Wolfe drawing of a woman seated at a desk.

1. Quoted in Glendinning, pp. 62-3

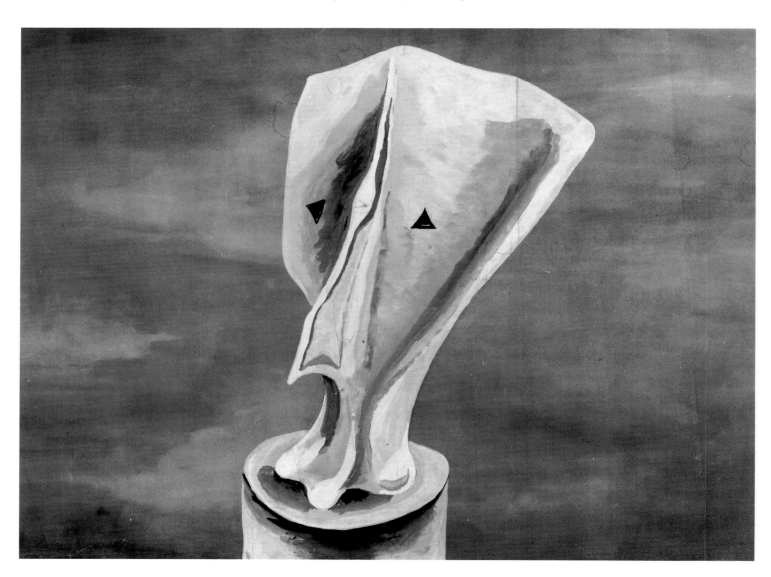

4.21

Thomas Stearns Eliot
By Wyndham Lewis, 1938
(below right)

'One of the few men of letters in my generation whom I should call, without qualification, men of genius'[1], wrote Eliot of Lewis. 'A Prufrock to whom the mermaids would decidedly have sung, one would have said, at the tops of their voices'[2], Lewis wrote of Eliot. It was a mutual admiration that began in 1915 and was sustained with generosity on Eliot's part until Lewis's death. There is a drawing of Eliot by Lewis from 1922-1923 and a painting of 1949 in addition to the completed three-quarter length oil of 1938 for which this is a study. The rejection of Lewis's beautiful portrait of Eliot (now in the collection of Durban Art Gallery) from the Academy in 1938 was the *cause célèbre* that led Augustus John to resign as an Academician and provoked Winston Churchill's remark at the R. A. Banquet that 'it is not the function of the Royal Academy to run wildly after novelty'.

The friendship between Eliot and the Sitwells developed after their meeting at Lady Colefax's poetry reading in December 1917. According to Osbert's unpublished memoir of Eliot, the poet and his wife Vivien dined regularly with the Sitwells at a restaurant in Piccadilly and also frequently met them for tea in a café near Marble Arch. 'Vivienne [*sic*] would be the first to arrive, and then Tom would come from his bank by Underground, and join us in consuming hot tea and muffins. Tea drinking is not a habit of Americans and I often thought that for him it possessed an exotic charm that for us it lacked.'[3] The friendship survived (though not without difficulty) the deterioration of Eliot's marriage to Vivien, but foundered with his second marriage, in 1957, to Valerie Fletcher, Edith feeling that Eliot had betrayed his wheelchair-bound companion, the bibliophile and editor John Hayward.

Professionally Eliot was wary of the Sitwells, refusing to contribute to *Wheels*, though appearing in *Art and Letters*. He deplored Osbert's poetry: 'Heaven preserve me from being reviewed in the company of Osbert'[4] he wrote to John Quinn, but he detected promise in Sacheverell's verse. Eliot's poetry is acclaimed by Edith throughout her critical writings, and he in turn was a loyal defender of Edith in circumstances (such as her insistence that her misquotation of Baudelaire had improved on the original), that a lesser man could only have found compromising.

1. Quoted in J. Meyer, *The Enemy*, p. 120-1
2. Quoted in J. Meyer, op. cit., p. 237
3. Quoted in Pearson, p. 121
4. Quoted in Bradford, p. 103

'Still Falls the Rain'

By Edith Sitwell, *c.* 1941

'Still Falls the Rain' was first published in *The Times Literary Supplement* on 6 September 1941 and subsequently in *Street Songs*; the cancelled verse in the manuscript does not appear in the published version. Edith's celebrated reading of this poem at the Churchill Club in the autumn of 1944 was witnessed by John Lehmann. A warning whistle had sounded just as Edith got up, but she proceeded to read despite the sound of a doodlebug overhead:

'Edith merely lifted her eyes to the ceiling for a moment, and, giving her voice a little more volume to counter the racket in the sky, read on ... She held the whole audience in the grip of her discipline, the morale of her unspoken asseveration that poetry was more important than all the terrors that Hitler could launch against us. Not a soul moved, and at the end, when the doodlebug had exploded far away, the applause was deafening.'[1]

Benjamin Britten's setting of the poem (*Canticle III* for tenor, horn and piano) was dedicated to the memory of the Australian pianist Noel Mewton-Wood and was first performed in 1955.

1. Lehmann, p. 199

Edith Sitwell in the Drawing-room, Renishaw

By Bill Brandt, 1945

Edith spent most of the Second World War at Renishaw with Osbert. The intense cold of the house made overcoats a necessity inside and neither of them would appear downstairs before lunchtime. In the evenings they listened to records on the wind-up gramophone while Edith knitted. Among their visitors during the war years were Evelyn Waugh, John Piper, Bryher and Alec Guinness, who described Renishaw as 'that extraordinary house with its oil lamps and creaking stairs and miles of corridors and haunted rooms'.[1] The photograph appeared in American *Harper's Bazaar* in October 1948 to celebrate Edith's arrival in the United States.

1. Quoted in Pearson, p. 348

4.24
Poetry reading at the Aeolian Hall, 14 April 1943
Photographs from *Picture Post,* 1 May 1943

a) The audience during the first half, listening to
T. S. Eliot reading 'What the Thunder Said'.
Seated in the front row (left to right) are: Arthur
Waley, Princess Elizabeth, Osbert, HM The
Queen, Princess Margaret, Walter de la Mare.
Georgia is visible sitting behind Osbert.

b) The platform during the second half.
Edith reading 'Anne Boleyn's Song'. Behind her
(left to right) are: Osbert, Vita Sackville-West,
Walter de la Mare, Arthur Waley.

The Aeolian Hall poetry reading, in the presence
of The Queen and her daughters, was organised
by Edith and Osbert in aid of Lady Crewe's
French in Britain Fund. The poets, who read in
alphabetical order, included Edmund Blunden,
Gordon Bottomley, T. S. Eliot, Walter de la
Mare, John Masefield, Vita Sackville-West, Edith,
Osbert and Arthur Waley. Sacheverell had
refused to take part, but Georgia was in the
audience. *Picture Post*'s report of the occasion was
lukewarm: 'Here was an unusual opportunity of
hearing good poets read good poetry. Yet it was
impossible to stifle the feeling that perhaps good
actors would have done it better.' Tactfully the
paper did not record the incident, well
documented in private records of the occasion, of
an intoxicated Dorothy Wellesley striking Harold
Nicolson with her umbrella.

Frank Raymond Leavis
By Peter Greenham, 1961-1962

The Sitwells' feud with F. R. Leavis (1895-1978), sparked off by his comment in *New Bearings in English Poetry* in 1932 that 'the Sitwells belong to the history of publicity, rather than of poetry',[1] differed in essence from the feuds with Huxley, D. H. Lawrence and Wyndham Lewis. Leavis had not attacked the Sitwells as Sitwells, but in a single sentence had marginalised their creative ambitions. By implication he had also nullified them as arbiters of literary standards, a role that, largely through his *Scrutiny* magazine, became increasingly his own. Edith told Georgia that she had 'half-murdered Leavis' in *Aspects of Modern Poetry*, which was published in November 1934, but it was a boast that fell flat when the book was ruthlessly exposed in the *New Statesman and Nation* as plagiarising Leavis's *New Bearings*.

Leavis's intellectual weight put him in a different league from the Sitwells and though they ranged against him hostile academic factions and all the forces their social position could muster, it was a battle they could never win. Edith's campaign against Leavis and his wife Queenie degenerated into a lamentable round of snobbery and childish practical jokes. 'The Doctor', as they called him, is still recognised as the most formidable literary critic and teacher of his time in a discipline that tends to look askance at the Sitwells.

At the time of *New Bearings* Leavis was a lecturer and supervisor at Emmanuel College, Cambridge. In 1936 he became a fellow of Downing and his portrait by Peter Greenham was commissioned for his retirement in 1962. 'He was never late and always sat still,' Peter Greenham wrote, 'the most courteous of sitters, much ashamed of interruptions.'[2]

1. F. R. Leavis, *New Bearings in English Poetry*, 1932, p. 73
2. Quoted in 'Portrait of the Critic' by Ian McKillop in *Modern Painters*, 1992, pp. 78-9

John Sparrow
By Derek Hill, 1962

In his *Poetry and Sense* (1934), the barrister and future Warden of All Souls College, Oxford, had written that Edith 'seems never to have thought out her aims clearly, and intellect is always trespassing in her poetry with the most unfortunate results'.[1] This was the unlikely beginning of Edith's long friendship and correspondence with John Sparrow (1906-1992). They met in the summer of 1934 and Sparrow not only wrote a favourable review of Edith's *Aspects of Modern Poetry* when it appeared in November, but continued to defend it in the correspondence column of the *New Statesman and Nation*. His contention was that Edith, rather than plagiarising, was offering a view of poetry contrasting with Leavis: 'no two views could be more radically opposed; the Doctor thinks of poetry as a sort of moral hygiene, Miss Sitwell sees it rather as a means of creating beauty in language.'

The portrait is a smaller, informal version of Hill's commissioned portrait of Sparrow, also in the collection of All Souls.

1. Quoted in Pearson, p. 305

4.27
Geoffrey Grigson
By Fay Godwin, 1970

After savaging *Alexander Pope* in the *Yorkshire Post* in 1930, the poet, critic and editor Geoffrey Grigson (1905-1985) remained one of Edith's principal *bêtes noires*. A year later he wrote a long assessment of Edith's work, concluding that 'her limited class of experience has produced poems little more varied than the uprights of a circular railing and damaged by an unreasonable excess of irrationality'[1]; and he was able to add fuel to the row about *Aspects of Modern Poetry* by suggesting that Edith had probably plagiarised Herbert Read as well as F. R. Leavis. In December 1934 he expressed the opinion that the Sitwells had 'written nothing worth a wise man's attention for five minutes'.[2] The battle rumbled on despite Grigson's attempt at an amnesty in 1946. 'You will not expect me', he wrote, 'to recant in my criticism of the past: I cannot expect you to recant in yours. But if we can agree upon that expectation, we may perhaps agree on keeping, for the future, our judgements relating to each other's work to ourselves.'[3]

Grigson's wide contacts in the arts inevitably overlapped with those of the Sitwells. His support of Dylan Thomas withered when the poet was taken over by Edith and he disapproved of his friend John Piper's visits to Renishaw.

1. G. Grigson in *The Bookman*, August 1931
2. G. Grigson in *New Verse*, December 1934
3. Quoted in Pearson, p. 389

4.28
Cyril Connolly
By Cecil Beaton, 1942

Pearson describes the relationship of Cyril Connolly (1903-1974) with the Sitwells as 'part worshipping, part mocking, part secretly resenting',[1] an ambivalence common to many who knew the trio. A journalist and critic, Connolly first came across the Sitwells in Granada in 1925. 'All of them were wearing black capes and black Andalusian hats and looked magnificent ... we immediately became great friends.'[2] Yet the following year he wrote to Noel Blakiston that 'Edith is tedious, humourless and combative, Osbert advertises, Sashie [*sic*] is the most remote'[3] and by 1932 he had become 'little imperceptible Mr Cyril Connolly' to Edith. As in the case of other intellectuals of the younger generation, it was Edith's war poetry that brought Connolly round again. He described 'The Song of the Cold' as 'a staggering poem, like a symphony composed around one single octave'[4] and the July 1947 issue of *Horizon*, which he co-edited with Stephen Spender, was dedicated to the Sitwells. Shortly before his death Connolly delivered his final verdict: 'the Sitwells were a dazzling monument to the English scene. They absolutely enhanced life for us during the twenties, and had they not been there a whole area of art and life would have been missing.'[5]

Connolly had known Beaton since their schooldays at St Cyprian's in Bournemouth and published some of Beaton's North African wartime experiences in *Horizon* in the same year that Beaton was commissioned to photograph Connolly for *Vogue*.

1. Pearson, p. 189
2. Quoted in Pearson, p. 189.
3. Quoted in Glendinning, p. 102
4. Quoted in Glendinning, p. 248
5. Quoted in Pearson, p. 190

4.29
John Lehmann
By Derek Hill, 1984

'I think when I die', Edith wrote to John Lehmann, 'I shall have to have inscribed on my tomb: "She is still grateful to John Lehmann!"'[1] The writer and editor John Lehmann (1907-1987) was brought into the Sitwell fold by the publication of *Street Songs* in 1942. 'To most of us in London', he wrote in his autobiography, 'it seemed that another great event had happened in English poetry.'[2] As an editor (of *New Writing* in its various forms from 1936 and of *The London Magazine* from 1954) and as a promoter of her work, Lehmann was a useful and influential ally. Under his own imprint he published *The Shadow of Cain* (1947) and Edith's anthology, *The American Genius* (1951); and both Edith and Osbert contributed to other titles he published. But his real value to Edith was as a friend and correspondent for twenty years. Writing to him became a reflex for Edith and her reaction to subjects as disparate as the death of Dylan Thomas and the annoying habits of the members of the Sesame Club can be gauged from her letters to him. His biography of all three Sitwells, *A Nest of Tigers*, was begun during Edith's lifetime with her approval, and published in 1968. The book and its title, taken from a remark Edith made about herself and her brothers, annoyed Sacheverell, who called it 'idiotic'.

1. Quoted in Glendinning, p. 253
2. *Ibid.*, p. 236

Stephen Spender
By Robert Buhler, 1939

In *Aspects of Modern Poetry* Edith dismissed the entire Auden generation of poets as having 'certain mental qualities', but 'not one touch of genius'. Over the years she found that she had been wrong, and not only did she come to admire their work but liked the writers too. (Sir) Stephen Spender (b. 1909) was Edith's closest friend among the 'Pylon' poets. He had admired her poetry as a schoolboy and later wrote enthusiastically about her Second World War poems as 'prodigious hymns' in *Horizon*. Tom Driberg remembered the young Spender at Pembridge Mansions, 'soaring above the smoke and the babel like an innocent pink crane',[1] but it was in the Sesame Club years that Spender and his wife Natasha (to whom 'The Song of the Cold' is dedicated) became almost indispensable to Edith. As co-editor of *Encounter*, Spender published one of Edith's last poems, 'A Girl's Song in Winter', in January 1962.

Herbert Read had noticed a portrait by Robert Buhler at the First British Artists Congress in 1937, but this painting of Spender was the first real landmark in the young artist's portrait career. For a time it was in the collection of Sir Edward Marsh (see 2.35) and was presented by the Contemporary Art Society to the Victoria Art Gallery, Bath, in 1946.

1. Quoted in Glendinning, p. 129

Green Song and Other Poems
By Edith Sitwell, 1946

The leaf design of the cover for *Green Song* (repeated in monochrome as a frontispiece) was the last collaboration of Tchelitchew and Edith before their rupture over *Hide and Seek*. The title poem, dedicated to David Horner in the days when Edith was still making an effort to get on with him, was first published in *Life and Letters To-day* in December 1942.

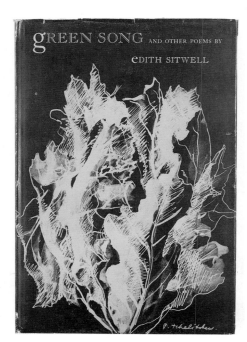

4.32

Dylan and Caitlin Thomas

By Ralph Banbury, c. 1937-1938

It was an index of Edith's affection for Dylan Thomas (1914-1953) and her regard for his poetry that she tolerated in him lapses of behaviour wildly in excess of the 'impertinences' that would have been unforgivable in others. Although she had, by implication, panned the work of the youthful Thomas in *Aspects of Modern Poetry* in 1934, the following December she wrote in *Life and Letters To-day* that he showed 'most remarkable promise', and he was summoned to the Sesame Club in February 1936. 'The first time I saw him', she wrote in her autobiography, 'I felt as if Rubens had suddenly taken it into his head to paint a youthful Silenus.'[1] Her praise in the *Sunday Times* for his *Twenty Five Poems* (1936) was lavish, as was her generosity in practical terms, pulling strings to try and find him a job and sending a cheque for his wedding to Caitlin Macnamara in 1937. After a long hiatus, Thomas and Edith met again at a Society of Authors poetry reading on 14 May 1946. At dinner at the Sesame Club afterwards Dylan Thomas insulted T. S. Eliot and Caitlin called John Hayward a 'great Pansy'. As Dylan remarked later: 'Her parties are always brilliant opportunities for self-disgrace.'[2] The news of Dylan Thomas's death after a titanic drinking session in New York reached Edith as she was on her way to Hollywood. 'I *cannot* believe my dear Dylan, whom I loved, as well as knowing him to be a really great poet, is dead. I just feel a dreadful numbness',[3] she wrote to John Lehmann.

The artist Ralph Banbury escaped a career as an accountant by the unlikely expedient of turning up for work in a pink corduroy suit. Having achieved his dismissal, he studied under Cedric Morris at Dedham and later became a close friend and drinking companion of the Thomases in Soho, where the painting was probably made. The landscape was painted from imagination and the mug in Thomas's hand remained unfinished as the artist could not remember whether it was ceramic or glass.

1. TCO, p. 168
2. Quoted in J. M. Brinnin, *Dylan Thomas in America, An Intimate Journal*, 1988 edn, p. 96
3. Quoted in Glendinning, p. 303

4.33

Letter from Sacheverell to Edith Sitwell

Weston Hall, 25 October 1942

During the long interval in Edith's contact with Dylan Thomas, Sacheverell regaled her with his second-hand account of the Thomases' spectacular activities in two London night clubs:

... I went to London for two days last week, and was told fascinating stories about the exploits of Dylan Thomas, who sounds an utterly impossible but quite fascinating person. His wife, I am told, is dressed like the trainer in a boxing ring, with about seven jerseys one over the other, and is trained to knock him out when he comes home.

The other day she went 'berserker', herself, in a night club, her arms worked like flails; she broke the arm of a young girl called Virginia Gilliatt, who has just been married, and a little casualty clearing station had to be opened in the basement to deal with the persons she had injured. But Dylan Thomas' great exploit was at the 'Gargoyle', a night club owned by David Tennant, and frequented by Dick [Wyndham], Peter Quennell, etc. Constant [Lambert], etc. It is decorated in glass and gold mosaic, with many mirrors, with a staircase leading down into it, so that it is just the place for a drunken entrée, and in fact exactly like the scene at the end of 'Fledermaus' and in the third scene of 'La Vie Parisienne'.

The other night, when the Gargoyle was full of people and the band was playing, Dylan Thomas made his appearance, and came spinning down the staircase so quickly that Ivan Moffat (who told me the story) says his figure could only be seen like a series of circles, as in a comic drawing.

Once on the dancing floor, (he was 'poetically' dressed in tweeds, with curls of hair like Bacchus, shoes, but no socks) he ripped off both shoes and danced barefoot, for a while, in a sinister but distracted fashion. Then his purpose became evident. He moved up to the table where David Tennant was sitting, drinking a valuable bottle of claret, poured it into his own shoe and drank it, finished the bottle, and then with an extraordinary gliding movement, like a sea serpent, traversed the entire floor to the far end of the room, and landed on the divan nestling his head against the thighs of Harold Nicolson, whom he hates. After that, there was general furore, and a sort of pêle mêle struggle, of which the results were long in doubt, owing to the extraordinary bravery and resource of Mrs Dylan T. Eventually, much to the regret of many persons, they were ejected.

It shows infallible taste and instinct, doesn't it?

4·34

**Edith and Osbert Sitwell at the
Gotham Book Mart**

By Lisa Larsen for *Life*, 6 December 1948

In the left foreground is William Rose Benet,
behind him Stephen Spender and behind Spender
are Horace Gregory and his wife Maria
Zwalenska. Seated behind the Sitwells are (left to
right) Tennessee Williams, Richard Eberhart,
Gore Vidal and Jose Garcia Villa. On the ladder
is W. H. Auden. Standing against the bookcase,
on the right, is Elizabeth Bishop and seated in
front, Marianne Moore. Seated at the right is
Randall Jarrell, with the moustache, and Delmore
Schwartz. Charles Henri Ford is in the centre on
the floor.

Charles Henri Ford was the moving spirit
behind the lecture tour that Edith and Osbert
made in America from autumn 1948 to spring
1949. Apart from the coolness between Edith and
Tchelitchew, the trip was a resounding success,
from the cocktail party at Frances Stellof's
Gotham Book Mart, the recital at the New York
Town Hall and a performance of *Façade* at the
Museum of Modern Art to the lectures
throughout the mid-West. 'Every magazine',
growled Wyndham Lewis, who was also in
America, 'has six pages of photographs of them
headed "The Fabulous Sitwells".'[1]

1. Quoted in Glendinning, p. 277

4·35

Marilyn Monroe

By Cecil Beaton, 1956

(illustrated on page 129)

In February 1954 Marilyn Monroe visited Edith in
her apartment on Sunset Boulevard. It was the
idea of *Life* magazine to bring them together, and
an article recording the meeting eventually
appeared in *Time* in 1956. Marilyn wore a green
dress and looked to Edith like a daffodil, 'a little
spring-ghost, an innocent fertility-daemon, the
vegetation spirit that was Ophelia'.[1] In 1956
Marilyn Monroe and her husband Arthur Miller
lunched with Edith at the Sesame Club in
London. Earlier the same year Cecil Beaton had,
after months of negotiations, succeeded in
securing sittings with Marilyn Monroe and
photographed her for *Harper's Bazaar* in a New
York hotel. He, too, was struck by her 'disarming
childlike freshness', forgave her for being an hour
and a quarter late and described her visit as 'an
artless, impromptu, high-spirited, infectiously gay
performance. It will probably end in tears.'[2]

1. TCO, p.183
2. C. Beaton, *The Face of the World*, 1957, p. 184

4·36

Celebrity at a Cocktail

By Tom Keogh, 1948

Osbert and Edith were fêted at numerous parties
in America, but the caricature by Keogh (1921-
1980), a designer for ballet and for *Vogue* and
Harper's Bazaar, is probably based on the Gotham
Book Mart party (see 4.34). *Life* reported that
Edith 'swept around New York looking like a
medieval sorceress' and the *New York Star*
commented on her 'Medusa-like gold headdress'.
On the left of the drawing, leaning on the table
of glasses, is the American poet Marianne Moore,
whom Edith described as 'a delightful woman
with the nature of a bird, very shy but friendly'.[1]
Like Edith, Marianne Moore cultivated an
idiosyncratic appearance and was known by her
cape and tricorn hat. She was one of the last
people to visit Edith before her death. 'They
conversed', wrote Elizabeth Salter, 'these women
of great talent who were bound by genuine
affection, but their conversation reached out and
never quite made a connection.'[2]

1. Salter, p. 69
2. *Ibid.*, p. 196

4.37

Carson McCullers

By Cecil Beaton, 1956

Edith and Osbert met the American novelist Carson McCullers (1917-1967) in 1950 at a party in New York given by Tennessee Williams. Edith then invited her to the dress rehearsal of the *Macbeth* reading at the Museum of Modern Art. McCullers responded by sending Edith two of her novels, *The Heart is a Lonely Hunter* (1940) and *The Member of the Wedding* (1946). The following year Carson and her husband Reeves spent three months in England and saw Edith on several occasions, including a meal at the Sesame Club during which the inebriated Reeves McCullers slid unnoticed under the table. Edith and Carson kept up an affectionate correspondence for the rest of Edith's life, and a painting by Carson was among Edith's possessions at her death.

Carson McCullers suffered from chronic ill-health following a bout of rheumatic fever as an adolescent. When Beaton photographed her for *Harper's Bazaar* in New York in 1956 she had already suffered a stroke and was paralysed in one arm. Despite the supreme physical effort it required, she gave a series of lectures in England in 1962 in order to be able to attend Edith's 75th birthday concert and to see her at Greenhill. Elizabeth Salter recalls her managing 'to convey the atmosphere of the perennial adolescent. Her attitude towards Edith was demonstrative, her southern drawl irresistibly reminiscent of dialogue written by her friend Tennessee Williams.'[1]

1. Salter, p. 163

4.38

George Cukor

Publicity photograph for Paramount Picture Corporation, 1959

The American film director George Cukor (1899-1983) took up the film option on Edith's *Fanfare for Elizabeth* when it was relinquished by Alexander Korda. In early 1951 Edith made the first of three trips to Hollywood and lunched with Cukor, where she met Ethel Barrymore and Merle Oberon. Over the next two years she worked on the film treatment with a professional script-writer, Walter Reich, of whom she eventually despaired, writing to John Lehmann that in Reich's script: 'Anne Boleyn eats chocs behind a pillar, and pinches Jane Seymour's bottom behind Cardinal Wolsey's back.'[1] The film was never made but Cukor became a good friend of Edith's; she wrote in her autobiography of his 'extraordinary subtlety and distinction of mind'.[2] She dedicated her later biography of the adult Queen Elizabeth, *The Queens and the Hive*, to him.

1. Quoted in Glendinning, p. 306
2. TCO, p. 181

4.39

Edith Sitwell

Photograph by Horst P. Horst, 1948

Edith was photographed in colour and in black
and white by Horst in the *Vogue* studio, New
York, on her first visit to America in 1948. Horst
wrote about the photograph: 'I wanted a very
strong picture with a defined shape. I wanted to
make the connection to Old England and
literature. She liked the idea of the big book. She
was amiable but she was not easy to talk to.'[1]
Edith is wearing two of the brooches from the
chinese box (see 4.40) in addition to two
aquamarine rings.

1. V. Lawford, *Horst, his work and his world*, 1985, p. 274

4.40

**Brooches, rings and bracelets belonging to
Edith Sitwell**

Edith's jewellery was one of her trademarks.
There is almost no interview with her that does
not mention her huge aquamarine rings. 'I feel
undressed without my rings', she told a reporter.[1]
The two aquamarine rings, one with rubies on the
shoulders, came from Edith's usual supplier of
aquamarines, Michael Gosschalk of Motcombe
Street, Belgravia. These, the amethyst ring and
the French gold-plated expanding bracelets were
made in about 1950. The fluorite ring, carved in
the shape of two bears, is nineteenth-century
Chinese workmanship, and was also in Edith's
possession by 1950.[2] The box of semi-precious
brooches may have been a gift brought back from
China by Osbert in 1934.

1. ES in 'My Clothes and I', *Observer*, 18.5.1959, p. 19
2. Glendinning, p. 287, jewellery listed on export licence

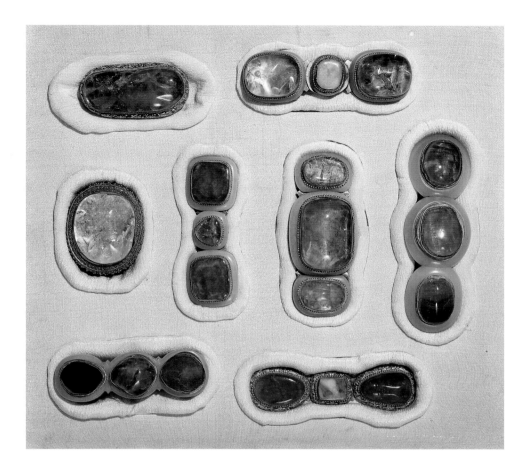

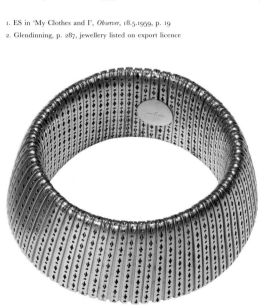

4.41

Ostrich-feather hat

(below left)

Hats are an important part of Edith's iconography. Among favourites are the black tricorne with veils that she wore for Sacheverell's wedding (see 4.4 and 6.4) and the turban in Tchelitchew's Texas portrait (see 4.9). The ostrich-feather hat probably came from the 'wonderful hat department' at Whiteley's, the department store in Bayswater where Edith knew the buyer, Miss Pery. This was also the source for her 'bird-king' hat (see 4.43 and 4.46) which Miss Pery, as Edith told the *Observer*, had immediately recognised as a Sitwellian object, pointing at it and saying 'There she is! There she is!'[1] Edith wore the ostrich-feather hat for her last sitting with Cecil Beaton (see 4.52).

1. ES in the *Observer*, 10.5.1959

Edith Sitwell

By Cecil Beaton, July 1962 (see 4.52)

4.42
Edith Sitwell

By Norman Parkinson, 1939

'I'm not beautiful,' Edith told the *Observer*, 'but I wouldn't look any other way. My hands are my face!'[1] She took great care of her hands ('I always go to Peggy Sage to have them done, except in Italy, where I have to do them myself'), and they were often noticed by other people. After having Edith to tea Virginia Woolf noted in her diary that Edith had 'long frail hands which slide into yours much narrower than one expects like a folded fan'.[2] Parkinson's photograph was taken in connection with an article, 'On Precious Stones and Metals' by Edith in *Harper's Bazaar*, February 1939. This particular pose, not used in the magazine, shows her wearing a Queen Anne bracelet and a ring of pearls and mauve-pink topaz.

1. ES, 'My Clothes and I', *Observer*, 10.5.1959
2. *The Diary of Virginia Woolf*, 1925-30, Penguin edn, 1982, p. 132

4.43
Edith Sitwell

By Jane Bown, 1959

(opposite)

Jane Bown's photograph was commissioned to illustrate an article featuring Edith in a series entitled 'My Clothes and I' (*Observer*, 10 May, 1959). In it she describes the history of the necklace that for no particular reason, has become known as her 'Aztec' necklace. 'This gold collar was made for me by an American woman called Millicent Rogers. She was one of my greatest friends, though I only met her once. She sent it to me, and the British Museum kept it four days and thought it was pre-Columban [*sic*], undoubtedly from the tomb of an Inca – though they couldn't make out how the gold could be stiffened in a way that wasn't in existence in those days. But I have to be careful of the clanking when I am reciting and don't often wear it for that.'[1]

1. ES in 'My Clothes and I', *Observer*, 10.5.1959, p. 19

4.44
Edith Sitwell
By George Platt Lynes, 1950

Edith was photographed in various outfits during this session with Platt Lynes. As with many of Edith's other clothes, the cloak was made out of furnishing fabric and aptly illustrates Stella Bowen's description of Edith being like 'a high altar on the move'.[1]

1. Quoted in Glendinning, p. 296

4.45
Brocade cloak

'I couldn't possibly wear tweeds', Edith told the *Observer*. 'It would be like dressing a lion in rabbit's clothes. People would follow me on bicycles if I did, I'd look so extraordinary.'[1]

Tchelitchew designed 'Plantagenet' dresses for Edith in Paris in the early 1930s, but in later years she either designed her own or went to Madame Astier in the Kings Road, Chelsea. The brocade cloak went with her to America in 1950.

1. ES in 'My Clothes and I', *Observer*, 10.5.1959, p. 19

4.46
Edith Sitwell
By Feliks Topolski, 1959

Topolski made drawings of Edith, as he did of all John Freeman's interviewees, to accompany the credits for the television programme *Face to Face*. The interview was broadcast in 1959 and is generally regarded as one of the most successful in a series that was itself a television landmark. One of the drawings from the sitting is in the Royal Collection[1] and was reproduced in *Topolski's Chronicle* in 1960. The painting (one of several the artist made of Edith),[2] is among twenty portraits of English writers commissioned from Topolski by the University of Texas. It was worked up from the artist's original *Face to Face* drawings of Edith in her 'Bird King' hat and was not shown to her before it was sent to Texas. She was, however, sent a photograph of it and word that she disliked it reached Topolski. He wrote assuring her of his sincerity and respect and she replied with warmth and generosity, explaining that she greatly admired his work in general and only objected to his portrait of her 'for *personal* reasons'. The hunched back reminded her of wearing the 'Bastille' orthopaedic contraption as a child.[3] Topolski wrote again with further reassurance: 'To me you have the rarest PRESENCE ... This aura of yours (I see now in retrospect) must have been what led me to my painting: fragility, therefore style, therefore true authority.'[4]

1. See J. Roberts, *Master Drawings in the Royal Collection*, 1986, pp. 183-4
2. One is now in the collection of the Polish National Museum, Warsaw
3. Both letters are reproduced in *Feliks Topolski Fourteen Letters*, 1988
4. Quoted in Glendinning, p. 339

4·47
Evelyn Waugh
By Cecil Beaton, April 1955

The novelist Evelyn Waugh (1903-1966) had been aware of the Sitwells since his undergraduate days. He was in the audience at the Aeolian Hall performance of *Façade* and by 1930 had become a friend. The account in his diary of staying at Renishaw that summer is one of the most memorable evocations of the Sitwells *en famille*.[1] Edith's conversion to Catholicism in 1955 was an event of particular significance for Waugh, himself a convert of some twenty-five years standing. He wrote to welcome her into the faith and acted as godfather at her reception. He had written to Edith's spiritual adviser, Father Philip Caraman, about his worries that 'the papers may take her up as a kind of Garbo-Queen Christina'[2] but the occasion at Farm Street Church passed without incident. Writing to Edith to thank her for lunch afterwards at the Sesame Club he confided the irresistible truth of his own conversion: 'I know I am awful. But how much more awful I should be without the Faith.'[3]

Waugh had known Cecil Beaton since he bullied him at prep school and seldom let the opportunity slip to needle him in adult life. 'Ostensibly we were friends',[4] wrote Beaton in his diary, admitting that with ambitions in common it suited them both at times to pretend that the hatchet had been buried. The photograph was taken at the Duff Coopers' house at Chantilly.

1. *The Diaries of Evelyn Waugh*, Penguin, 1986 edn, pp. 327-8
2. Quoted in Glendinning, p. 318
3. *Ibid.*, p. 319
4. C. Beaton, *The Strenuous Years*, 1973, p. 70

4·48
Roy Campbell
By Jane Bown, 1951

In the unlikely person of 'noisy, frothing little Mr Roy Campbell'[1] (as she called him in 1931), Edith found a champion willing to take on her battles in print and in person. In return she eulogised Campbell (1901-1957) in her autobiography, cancelling out aspects of his character that other people had found unacceptable in the South African-born poet: 'He has been accused of being a fascist. He was never a fascist.'[2] Campbell was a supporter of Wyndham Lewis, fought for Franco in the Spanish Civil War and remained a belligerent, controversial figure throughout his life. Both he and his wife Mary were Catholics and through them Edith met the Jesuit priest, Father Martin D'Arcy, to whom she disclosed her wish to be received into the faith. The Campbells were godparents to Edith but were unable to attend her reception as Roy was ill.

Jane Bown's photograph was taken the year that Campbell's second volume of autobiography, *Light on a Dark Horse*, was published. The news that he had been killed, six years later, in a car accident in Portugal, was brutally delivered to Edith by a journalist during a press conference in Boston. It was a devastating blow, but at the end of her own life she saw the manner in which Campbell had died as in some way appropriate: 'he, who was all energy, all fire, would have hated to die slowly and helplessly, in bed. He died, as he had lived, like a flash of lightning.'[2]

1 TCO, p. 164
2. *Ibid.* p.166

4·49
Alec Guinness
By Bill Brandt, 1952

Merula, wife of the actor (Sir) Alec Guinness (b.1914) was distantly related to the Sitwells, and Guinness, finding himself with his young family on leave in Sheffield during the war rang Edith up. 'She instantly invited us all to Renishaw for the weekend. She made a great thing about Osbert having to be kept from knowing there was a baby in the house. Babies were supposed to make him ill.'[1] Guinness returned for other visits; Edith knitted him a pair of socks, 'very long and curiously shaped with two left feet'[2], and they began a friendship that deepened with Edith's conversion to Catholicism. Guinness, already a convert, attended her reception at Farm Street and the lunch party at the Sesame Club afterwards. Edith dedicated the poem 'Invocation', published in *Green Song* (1944), to Alec and Merula Guinness.

1. Quoted in Pearson, pp. 347-8.
2. *Ibid.*

4.50

Edith Sitwell

By Mark Gerson, May 1962

Edith was photographed by Mark Gerson for an article she wrote in *Books and Bookmen*, August 1962, to coincide with the publication of *The Queens and the Hive*. Gerson also photographed Leo the cat on his own and sent a print to Edith. He received a warm thank-you letter: 'You have made him look so majestic in the full-face one that I think, no matter how fine your photographs of me may be, it is *Leo* who ought to figure on the cover of *Books and Bookmen*".'[1]

Leo was one of four cats that took up residence with Edith at Greenhill. Since childhood she had been an animal lover, but cats occupied a special place in her affections. 'All poets love cats', she said. After leaving her Paris cat in the care of Evelyn Wiel in 1939 she sent money for his food and expected regular bulletins on his health.

1. ES to Mark Gerson, 26 May 1962

4.51

Edith Sitwell with friends and relatives on the set of *This is Your Life*

By John S. Sherman for the BBC, 6 November 1962

Left to right: Sir Cecil Beaton, Baroness de Bosmelet, Antony Bernard, Tom Driberg, Sacheverell, Osbert (seated), Marjorie Proops, Georgia, Veronica Gilliat, Francis Sitwell, Velma LeRoy, John Robins, Edith, Geoffrey Gorer, Reresby Sitwell.

A month after the 75th birthday concert, organised for Edith by her nephew Francis at the Royal Festival Hall, she was once more propelled into the limelight to feature on the 200th programme in the series *This is Your Life*. The usual format of surprising the subject was waived owing to Edith's state of health and she submitted to the ordeal only because Velma LeRoy, her maid from Sunset Tower, Hollywood, was being flown over specially for the occasion.

4.52

Edith Sitwell

By Cecil Beaton, July 1962

a) page 152
b) page 158
c) page 159
d) page 160

Edith posed in four different hats (for the ostrich-feather hat see page 152) for Beaton's last photographic session, at Edith's penultimate home, Flat 42, Greenhill, Hampstead. The photographs were used in connection with her 75th birthday celebrations and, at her insistence, to promote *The Queens and the Hive*, published in August. 'It is such a comfort', she wrote to Beaton, 'not to appear as a cross between a turkey that has been insufficiently fattened up for Christmas and an escapee from Broadmoor.'[1]

1. Quoted in H. Vickers, *Cecil Beaton*, 1985, p. 457

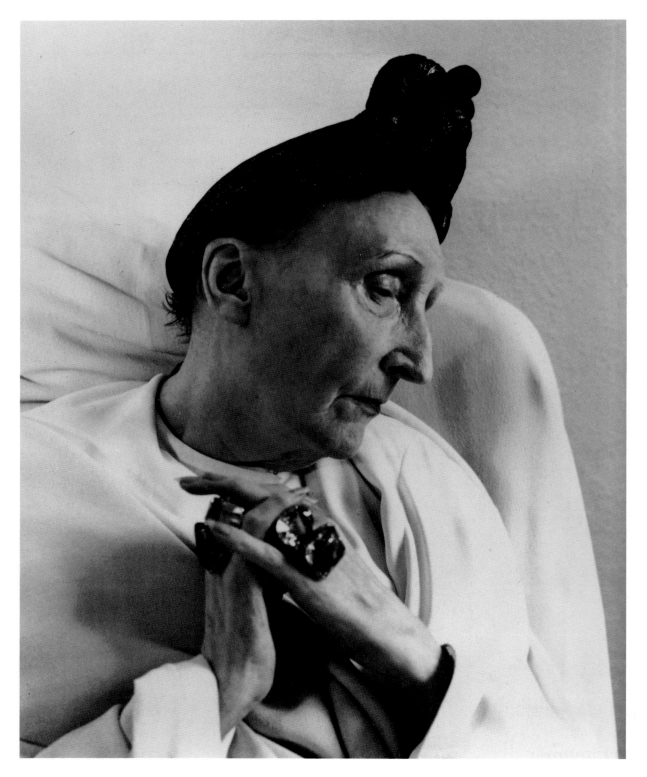

4·53
Edith Sitwell's luggage label

Edith's first two honorary doctorates, from Leeds
and Durham universities, were awarded in 1948.
Oxford, where Edith's friend Maurice Bowra was
Vice Chancellor, followed suit in 1951. Three
years later she was made a Dame Commander of
the Order of the British Empire. Her fourth
honorary doctorate was awarded by Sheffield
University in 1955. Edith rejoiced in the title Dr
Sitwell and each new honour was displayed like a
trophy on her personal stationery.

4·54
Edith Sitwell's Christmas Card

The photograph of Edith's hand was taken by
Lancelot Law Whyte, a Scottish philosopher of
science. He was the author of various works, such
as *The Next Development in Man* (1944), propounding
a 'unitary' philosophy that Edith found
sympathetic to her own belief in 'the
interconnectedness of everything'.[1] One of the few
social visits Edith made in her later years was to
view Whyte's photographs of her at his flat and
she was so pleased with them that she chose one
as her Christmas card for 1958. This copy was
sent to her friend the Portuguese poet Alberto de
Lacerda.

1. Quoted in Salter, p. 89

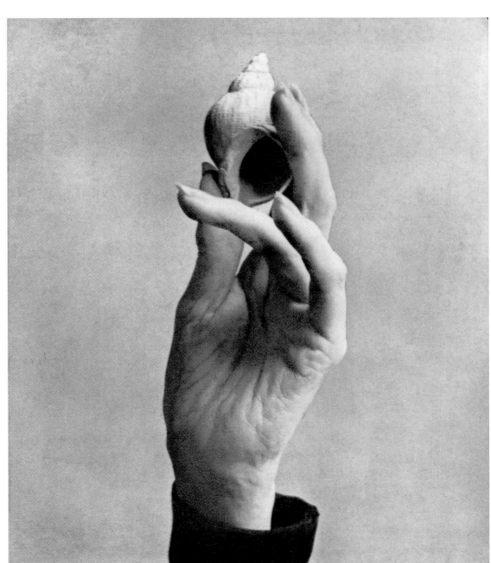

By 1925 the wars of the Sitwells were drawing to a close. The philistine was in retreat, the troops were growing tired of battle, and the trio itself was suddenly in danger of disbanding.

This was the year when Osbert's personal *bête noire*, Sir George, decided he had had enough of offspring and England, and abruptly decamped to his castle in sunny Tuscany with Lady Ida. It was nearly twenty years since he had spotted the crenellated white elephant of Montegufoni (the hill of the owls) on the road to the windswept city of Volterra, and decided there and then to buy it. His workmen had been struggling to make it habitable ever since, and although they never really would, Sir George decided he would take the plunge and live there.

'I shall be known as the Italian Sir George', he remarked as he headed south, leaving behind him a strange vacuum in Osbert's life. True, Sir George had left him Renishaw as his country seat; but Osbert did not want a country seat, and anyhow he currently hated Renishaw, especially as the tricky old gentleman had omitted to leave him the wherewithal to run it. Without Sir George in Derbyshire, one of the principal pillars of Osbert's angry life departed.

Then came a more serious defection. For years now Osbert had been taking Sacheverell's presence at Carlyle Square very much for granted, presumably imagining that they would stay fraternally conjoined until death parted them. But something more exciting than mortality had come between them.

'It had been obvious that my relationship with Osbert couldn't go on much longer and I had been longing to escape', remarked Sacheverell. Obvious to whom, one wonders. Certainly not to Osbert. Sacheverell's engagement to the beautiful Georgia Doble, early in 1925, was a shock to the whole Osbertian system. Although he wisely tried to keep on the best of terms with 'darling Georgia', as he always called her, there is no mistaking the look of stately misery on Osbert's face in the wedding photographs taken outside the Anglican church in Paris where Sacheverell married Georgia that October (see 6.4).

For one who had always seemed so gentle and accepting, Sacheverell was tough to the point of callousness about his brother, and almost overnight their situations were reversed. Suddenly it was Osbert who appeared dependent and at risk. 'I felt dreadful at leaving him', said Sacheverell, 'but of course he managed perfectly without me, although his life was to change totally in the process.'

In fact it was not that easy, for Osbert's world had more or less collapsed around him. At first he reacted fairly predictably. He used to keep a stock of cheap dinner plates near the front door at Carlyle Square. When his rage became insupportable, he found relief in smashing them one by one on his doorstep – after which his housekeeper, the devoted Mrs Powell, who knew Mr Osbert's little ways, would come and sweep them up. The beginning of 1926 saw a lot of broken crockery in Carlyle Square; and when he was short of dinner plates Osbert used authors. Given the chance he was a frightful bully, and his *annus horribilis* of 1926 saw him attacking almost any writer within reach.

He had already had a go at Michael Arlen, complaining to his publisher that in his bestseller, *The Green Hat*, 'the horrible little Armenian' had lifted passages wholesale from his own short story, *The Machine Breaks Down*. The fact that Arlen had emphatically done nothing of the kind barely mattered. Osbert insisted that Arlen needed to be 'taught a lesson'.

Then there was Osbert's former friend and protégé, Aldous Huxley, who was also becoming too successful, and who had been both 'impertinent' and 'treacherous' in basing characters in several of his novels on members of his family. Noël Coward, similarly 'mired' in success, continued to annoy him. And it was now that Osbert tried to get even with all his enemies by writing a brief confessional account of the miseries and slights that bugged him. He called it 'A Few Days in an Author's Life'.

This was the strangest, most uncomfortable piece he ever published, revealing as it does the pain and anger of the man who wrote it. When it appeared the following year one reviewer described it as 'a long-drawn-out whine ... a tedious and tortured tale of trivial complaint'. All the slights and insults of the last three years are there as Osbert, at his most irascible, lists his manifold complaints against the world in general: his troubles with *Façade*; the attentions of 'the Noble Company of Judas', as he called the

Osbert

gossip writers 'chattering' in print about their social and intellectual betters; and another, so far unsuspected opponent, a mysterious Mr X, described as 'our most virulent enemy', who was attempting to 'inhabit the dead body of a great mind' by trying to translate a famous French author. This was in fact C. K. Scott Moncrieff, the first English translator of Proust's *A La Récherche du Temps Perdu*, a book that became a prime influence on Osbert himself when he came to write his own memoirs. His hatred for the poor man is mysterious, except as a symptom of Osbert's growing paranoia and personal unhappiness.

Despite all this, Osbert was attempting to rebuild his private life in the absence of the now happily married Sacheverell. First came a doomed attempt to start a permanent relationship with the young writer Adrian Stokes. Over the next two years Stokes, a troubled young man with hawk-like looks and considerable uncertainty about his sexual inclinations, would make it clear that he was not what Osbert needed. Then in 1926 came a ray of hope with the critical acclaim for Osbert's first novel, *Before the Bombardment*. Despite Sir George's warning – 'It will be an odd sort of book; no love interest and no hero or heroine' – this re-creation of the world of pre-war Scarborough encouraged Osbert's ambitions as a fiction writer, and its further success in the United States encouraged him to think that America might hold the answer to his problems. He sailed to New York in style aboard the SS *Majestic* at the end of 1926, but although he was fascinated by America – he particularly loved both Harlem and the Frick Collection – he also found its 'innocence' and general lack of sophistication unappealing. He missed Europe and its civilisation, and returned to them gratefully, but was still as lonely as ever back in England.

Even Edith started to worry now about her 'dear old boy' as she called him. Sacheverell was increasingly involved with marriage and with his first son, Reresby, born in April 1927, so Edith gamely decided to accompany the solitary Osbert on a duty visit to their parents at Montegufoni early that summer. While in Florence they would call on a writer they had heard so much about but never met: D. H. Lawrence, who was living in a house near Florence with his wife Frieda. It was a visit that would lead to more terrible offence for Edith, but which would give Osbert a curious niche in twentieth-century literature.

They arrived at the Villa Mirenda in time for tea to find Lawrence hard at work on the third and final version of his novel, *Lady Chatterley's Lover*. With his jackdaw's skill at picking up anything or anyone as models for his writing, he had already used Renishaw, which he knew quite well, as the basis for the Chatterley mansion, Wragby Hall: 'a long old house, rather dismal, in a very fine park in the middle of newly developed colliery districts'. Lawrence needed more material for the character of Connie Chatterley's husband, Sir Clifford, and faced with a real-life future baronet, in the person of Osbert Sitwell, he could not resist using him as well. As a result, many of the details of the third 'Sir Clifford Chatterley' and his family are drawn directly from this tea-time meeting and Lawrence's impression of the Sitwells' isolated lives at 'Wragby', 'cut off from their own class by the brooding, obstinate, shut-up nature of Sir Geoffrey, their father, whom they ridiculed, but whom they were so sensitive about.'

Lawrence was clearly intrigued by Osbert, and later wrote to Richard Aldington saying how much he had liked him, but that despite this, he had made him feel 'sort of upset and worried. Of him the same I want to ask: but what ails thee then? Tha's got nowt amiss as a' that!'

It was sad that Lawrence never asked him, although Osbert's answer would have been distinctly unpredictable. Instead he put what he thought were Osbert's problems into his final version of Sir Clifford Chatterley. Interestingly he picks on fear as the crucial element in his character, 'fear' of 'that outer world of chaos' that he could never master. According to Lawrence it was this fear that had led him to become a rebel:

> Rebelling even against his class. Or perhaps rebel is too strong a word; far too strong. He was only caught in the general, popular recoil of the young against convention and against any sort of real authority. Fathers were ridiculous: his own obstinate one supremely so. And governments were ridiculous: our own wait-and-see sort especially so. And armies were ridiculous, and old buffers of generals altogether, the red-faced Kitchener supremely. Even the war was ridiculous, though it did kill rather a lot of people.

5.17
Osbert Sitwell
By Norman Parkinson, 1935
(previous page)

Lawrence had evidently read Osbert's stories, and must have discussed them with him over tea, for he writes of how Sir Clifford, too, had taken to writing stories, 'curious, very personal stories about people he had known. Clever, rather spiteful, and yet, in some mysterious way, meaningless', and how 'morbidly sensitive' he was about them. He describes Osbert's manner to perfection: 'His very quiet, hesitating voice and his eyes, at the same time bold and frightened, assured and uncertain, revealed his nature. His manner was often offensively supercilious, and then again modest and self-effacing, almost tremulous.'

What seems to have struck the novelist most of all was Osbert's sense of isolation. 'He was not in touch. He was not in actual touch with anybody ... perhaps there was nothing to get at ultimately; just a negation of human contact.'

Edith never forgave Lawrence for what she considered a venomous and unprovoked attack upon her brother in this 'disgusting' novel. But Osbert, who certainly read *Lady Chatterley's Lover*, never complained, which suggests that he accepted it as a fair enough portrait. Also, by the time he read it, Osbert's time of loneliness and tribulation was all but over. What he needed was a wife, and when he met his future spouse at a London party early in 1928, he fell in love with him at once.

With his matinée idol's profile, willowy elegance, and pale, rather melancholy features, David Horner was not a young man Osbert Sitwell would have missed. He had been brought up partly in France and partly at Mells Park in Somerset, home of his famous aunt, Frances Horner, Liberal hostess and daughter of the Pre-Raphaelite collector, William Graham. Frances's daughter, Katherine, had married into the Asquiths, thus linking the Horners with the whole Liberal aristocracy of Charterises, Wyndhams, Tennants and Bonham Carters. As these were very much the families Osbert himself had known in his social period before the war, he and David had much in common from the start.

Osbert, much taken, called him 'orchidaceous'. Edith, who came to loathe him, called him 'Blossom'. David in fact was tough, flighty, funny and extremely chic; he was also exactly what Osbert needed. If David didn't save his life, he certainly saved his

prose style and probably his sanity. One sees this fairly clearly in the sudden change in Osbert's writing, which is transformed from all that gloomy, introspective anger. Instead his friendship with David is reflected in the happiest book he ever wrote, his collection of travel sketches that he entitled with good reason *Winters of Content*. It begins in Venice where he and David spent Christmas in 1929, and describes the happy journey to the South, the slow train to Bologna, followed by the night train on to

5.10
David Horner
By Foulsham and Banfield, *c.* 1920s

Naples, and has a loving description of Osbert's favourite city of Lecce, 'the Florence of the baroque'. They reached it just in time to toast the 1920s out and the 1930s in.

The twenties had been the Sitwells' decade but the thirties brought them a period of eclipse. As poets they seemed to peter out, and as personalities they no longer roused the daring adoration of the young. Only their oldest audience, the philistines, stayed faithful. It was partly age. In 1930 Edith was forty-three, Osbert thirty-eight, and Sacheverell thirty-three. Middle age is rarely glamorous, and a new generation of grimmer, more committed poets was already waiting in the wings. As if to underline their fate, it was now that their most committed enemy launched what Sacheverell called 'a sort of literary time-bomb, set to explode in the face of literary London and particularly the Sitwells' – Wyndham Lewis's vast literary satire, which he called *The Apes of God*. A one-time friend, the painter and writer had grown increasingly enraged with everything he felt the Sitwells represented, and he guyed them as the famous Chelsea family, the 'Finnian Shaws'. Osbert, 'Lord Osmund Finnian Shaw', was memorably, and fairly insultingly, depicted:

> In colour Lord Osmund was pale coral, with flaxen hair brushed tightly back, his blond pencilled pap rising straight from his sloping forehead: galb-like wings to his nostrils – the goat-like profile of Edward the Peacemaker. The lips were curved. They were thickly profiled as though belonging to a dark-lipped sultan.

More tellingly, Lewis chose to describe the Sitwells and their followers as 'a sort of middle-aged youth movement', and Osbert's own liberal views as 'a special brand of rich-man's gilded bolshevism'. In the old days Osbert would probably have exploded, but David's influence made him turn to laughter. For the truth was that he no longer really cared, having other things than Wyndham Lewis and the battles of the past to think about.

'Whoever has the chance of seeing Angkor and doesn't is mad', wrote Osbert in one of the great escapist phrases of the thirties. Since setting up home in Carlyle Square with David, contact with Sacheverell and Georgia had all but ceased, and Edith would soon depart for Paris to remain as close as possible

to Pavel Tchelitchew. Osbert could now feel absolutely free to follow his own advice and see Angkor while it lasted. In November 1933 he and David took a French ship from Marseilles to Saigon; saw Angkor, which more than lived up to expectations; and by February they were in Peking, renting a house and visiting Harold Acton.

Osbert loved Peking, and the three months he spent there form the basis of his next book, cheerfully entitled *Escape with Me!*. His chapter on the city still provides one of the last and most readable accounts of the city under the pre-communist regime. Just before they left, Harold Acton took Osbert to visit the ancient college of the imperial eunuchs, and he spent some time in earnest conversation with the oldest of the eunuchs. 'Tell me, young man,' the old castrato asked him, 'do you have a group of people like us where you come from?' Osbert thought carefully before replying. 'Indeed we do', he said. 'We call it Bloomsbury.'

As well as providing the uxorious Osbert with the companionship he needed, David had another great advantage, despite the heartache that it caused. He liked his freedom, and would depart for part of every summer on his own affairs, generally to Switzerland – 'so middle-class!' said Osbert. This left Osbert free to indulge in another branch of life that increasingly

5·13

Osbert Sitwell and David Horner with their Chinese house staff, Peking
By The Photo Specialists Co., 1934

engaged him: his high-flown social life, visiting the houses of the rich whose company he enjoyed. He was in many ways the perfect guest: a considerable raconteur; a celebrity on his own account; and what was known in the jargon of the times as 'a tame cat' – because of his known inclinations he could be a close, indeed an intimate friend of any woman, without the faintest risk of scandal.

Then, at the end of 1936, Edward VIII's abdication brought him renewed fame as a poetic satirist. He had known the King as a fellow Guards officer in the war, but the spectacle of the abdication shocked him deeply. As a devoted monarchist he was appalled by the risks he felt that Edward was taking. As a long-standing enemy of Beaverbrook and Churchill, he was enraged when they, of all people, threatened to support the King and Mrs Simpson with a 'King's Party'. And, as a discriminating snob, he disapproved of the 'common' nature of so many who surrounded the playboy king.

Osbert was still the man of action manqué, and in a fit of weariness and sheer bad temper he took to his bed and wrote what proved to be the most effective poetic satire of his life. He called it 'National Rat Week', and it answered the question posed in its first three lines:

Where are the friends of yesterday
That fawned on Him
That flattered Her?

It was so libellous that it could not possibly be published until long after he was dead, but it made the rounds of Society in samizdat, and soon everyone who mattered seems to have seen it and guessed that he was the author.

'Much talk of rats', wrote Chips Channon in his famous diary. 'Osbert Sitwell has written a poem, not a very good one, called 'Rat Week' in which he lampoons many deserving people. It is cruel, funny and apposite in spirit if not in the letter.'

In the spring of 1937 Osbert returned to London, where he was able to enjoy his grandest social period of all. This was partly on account of 'Rat Week', which enhanced his salon reputation as a man of influence and a rather dangerous wit. The infamous poem had done nothing to upset his closeness with the new inhabitants of Buckingham Palace, rather the reverse, and he began to resemble what Gertrude Stein had once described him as: 'the uncle of a king'.

Though not a royal uncle, he was certainly a personal friend of the king, and of his queen, and during these last two years of peace Osbert, the once dedicated writer, all but disappeared beneath Osbert the courtier, Osbert the wit, Osbert the celebrated social figure who went everywhere and knew almost everyone who counted.

It was now that Osbert made a social conquest marking the apex of his courtier's career. At Londonderry House he was introduced to Queen Mary. 'She was', he wrote to David, 'too charming for words and sent for me afterwards and had a long talk. I saw one or two people I don't like looking very cross', he added. There was more to this meeting, however, than simply getting one up on his rivals, and that 'long talk' would start an important friendship for the future.

But behind the polished, carefully preserved exterior, he was gloomy about the future. Although obsessively convinced that another dreaded war was coming, he found a certain poignancy in watching the approach of Armageddon from the houses of the very rich. 'I myself heard Eden say last night that he didn't expect a war at once, but did not see in the end how one could be avoided!! Rather alarming', he wrote anxiously to David.

If Osbert feared that he was sacrificing his 'genius' as a novelist to this high-flown social life, the reception of his latest novel, in April 1938, might have consoled him with the thought that the sacrifice was worth it, since his social rewards were so much richer than his literary ones. Under the title *Those Were the Days!* he had made one last attempt at the great nostalgic novel, and it clearly had not worked. The reviewers were reasonably polite – except for his old enemy, James Agate, who panned it – but Osbert must have realised from their lack of enthusiasm what he had long suspected. He was not a major novelist, and would never be one now. *Those Were the Days!* marks the end of that particular career, but also hints at the beginning of a richer one to come. From time to time one senses, like the noise of the Underground beneath a London street, that 'rich, rumbling, unmistakable tone' of Osbert's voice, reminiscing about the people and places he remembers. It is quite distinctive. Somewhere beneath the novelist is the presence of the memoirist to come.

By the end of 1938, and knowing that war was now inevitable, Osbert the epicurean was determined to enjoy one final 'winter of content' with David. They embarked for Guatemala, stayed for three months, and found it enchanting – a final glimpse of happiness and warmth before the 'gardens of the West' closed on them both for good. Osbert was deeply pessimistic at the thought of coming back to Europe, which seemed to hold no place for ageing children of the sun. In Antigua he finished off his book on China, and David began a novel. They were both back in Carlyle Square by the nervous spring of 1939.

Selfish as ever, Osbert saw no reason to change his views about the war when it finally arrived. For him it was simply 'the Great Interruption', both tragic blunder and appalling nuisance, which put at risk, or put an end to, almost everything that made his life worth living. It was also, as he saw it, the utterly senseless culmination of all that he had campaigned against and warned against for years: democracy and militarism, cheap rhetoric and political incompetence. He felt no patriotic zeal or enthusiasm for the great events his country was engaged in, and so decided to contract out. Stoically, and more or less bad temperedly, he composed himself to wait until the storm blew over. Yet despite his pessimism, Osbert Sitwell's war would prove to be the most productive period of his life. Ironically, the changes and restrictions of these gloomy years would force him to reach the status of dedicated 'artist' that he had talked about so much, but never quite achieved.

As the war began, almost everything he had dreaded happened. He was cut off from his beloved Europe and almost simultaneously from David, who enlisted in the Royal Air Force. At forty-five Osbert was too old to fight, but Renishaw needed to be lived in to prevent it from being requisitioned. Exchanging the social and intellectual life of London for the humdrum life of a country squire, he left Carlyle Square and moved to Derbyshire for 'the duration'.

Sir George was still in Italy, but soon to escape to Switzerland,

where he would die, unmourned, in 1943. Edith had just returned from Paris and since she had nowhere to live Osbert invited her to join him at Renishaw. For the first time since childhood Osbert and Edith suddenly found themselves living together; surprisingly, they managed rather well, largely because of the space the enormous empty house provided. It was the beginning of what Edith called their 'Robinson Crusoe existence', with 'one aged, fearfully bad-tempered Man Friday', Osbert's old man-servant, Robins, looking after them. There was no electric light, and they were cut off from their friends and all that had made their lives worth living in the past. For Osbert this proved exactly what he needed.

Despite his air of the helpless aristocrat, he had always had an unacknowledged talent for making himself extremely comfortable. He was soon setting up his work-room, with its view across the gardens, with his favourite work-table, painted in Roger Fry's Omega Workshops, his eighteenth-century gout stool and a big Venetian mirror to remind him of Italy. And he suddenly discovered something he had never really experienced before: time and peace of mind.

'For the artist', by which Osbert usually meant himself, 'to be able to work at his best, it is necessary for him to have an endless vista of hours and days, within the space of which he can write or paint without any interruption, except those which are carnal or which he makes himself.'

At Renishaw there seem to have been few carnal interruptions, and that 'endless vista of hours and days' was something which the house could offer at precisely the moment he could make most use of them. He was approaching fifty, and was at the height of his powers as a writer. True the war had cut him off from almost everything he loved and valued, but it had also left him, for the first time in his life, with absolutely no distractions and a regular routine. Industrious as ever, he began to recreate the rich, nostalgic dream-world of his past to set against the drabness of the present.

He seems to have been surprised at first by how much untapped capital he had to draw on: the range and richness of his early life; the number of his friendships and acquaintances;

the battles he, Edith and Sacheverell had fought together; and the story of their rise as writers in the twenties. He could also detect what had previously eluded him: a pattern to it all. Here at Renishaw with Edith, he began to appreciate their ancestral past, their family history and shared characteristics that had helped to make the trio what it was.

At Renishaw, the past was inescapable. He could see, as nowhere else, how the rise and subsequent disaster of his family mirrored the rise and fall of the society he knew. For him this formed a theme to match the ideas Marcel Proust had used when he attempted to recover the precious 'lost time' of his youth in his own great novel. Osbert was very much aware of Proust. He had been sedulously re-reading the translation of his book by the long-dead but still unforgiven Scott Moncrieff, and was determined to follow his example.

He had already been working hard. In 1941 he had published *Open the Door!*, a new collection of short stories, and the following year *Sing High! Sing Low!*, a book of essays. But now he was at work on the first of what would become five volumes of his autobiography. He entitled it *Left Hand Right Hand!*.

Osbert Sitwell's war was not as unremitting and spartan as he liked to pretend. For a period, David, now Squadron Leader

5.25
The South Front, Renishaw
By John Piper, 1942-1943

Horner, was a frequent visitor; and Osbert had befriended a new young artist whose aquatints of Brighton he admired: John Piper. The youthful Alec Guinness was another visitor. He was in the navy at the time, and had become a friend of Edith. It was Edith who invited him to spend some leave at Renishaw with his wife and baby, and he described how Renishaw appeared 'a complete respite from the war' with its great log fires and food from the estate; and how in the evenings, after dinner, Osbert would talk as only Osbert could. 'It was only later on that I realised that he was trying out his stories on me for his book, but he seemed infinitely knowledgeable and wise, with endless anecdotes from a world that I had never known.'

Occasionally, too, Osbert's old courtier life would suddenly revive with an invitation from his cousin, the Duke of Beaufort, to visit Badminton, where Queen Mary was also sitting out the war and feeling lonely. Then for a few days Osbert would have a holiday from Renishaw, talking about the past with this extraordinary old lady, and accompanying her on expeditions round the estate as she indulged in her last royal obsession, the destruction of ivy in the park. Osbert's memories of these visits would one day form the basis for the title essay in his final work, his posthumously published book of reminiscences, *Queen Mary and Others*.

Then, in April 1943, feeling that he had been passive and alone at Renishaw quite long enough, Osbert emerged briefly in his former role as organiser and impresario of the arts, and decided to arrange what he called a demonstration of the power of poetry: a public poetry reading in the presence of Queen Elizabeth and the two princesses at that legendary Sitwellian battlefield, the Aeolian Hall in Oxford Street. Only Osbert with his influence and range of connections could have managed it. T. S. Eliot read from *The Waste Land*. Osbert and Edith both performed, with Edith earning great réclame for her dramatic reading of her newly written 'Anne Boleyn's Song'. And although the reading ended with a touch of chaos with W. J. Turner going on too long, and Dorothy Wellesley smiting Harold Nicolson with her umbrella, it served to show, not only the importance of poetry in wartime London, but also a definite revival in the fortunes of

the Sitwells. Osbert was re-emerging as a mellower version of the artistic 'grandee' he had been in the early twenties, and Edith was increasingly accepted in the role she had tacitly assumed for years: as prima donna *assoluta* of contemporary poetry.

For Osbert, all that truly mattered now was the autobiography. False modesty was never one of his failings, and from the start he had no doubts concerning its importance, describing it to his publishers as 'the book of a lifetime' and saying he believed that it would be a 'classic'. He wrote this in the spring of 1945, on the eve of publication, with the war in Europe almost over, as was his 'exile' from London. He and Edith had had what used to be called 'a good war'. Those long uninterrupted mornings in his work-room, and the lamp-lit evenings, had been exactly what both his nerves and his 'genius' needed. Like Proust himself, Osbert was more at ease with memory than with living.

The reception of *Left Hand Right Hand!* more than justified his expectations. Its tone was absolutely right for the period. A public, sick of the austerity of war, was ready for his extravagant sentences; and readers, longing to return to the remembered happiness of peace, responded to the splendour and excess of his gargantuan nostalgia.

The very breadth and detail of the book were in its favour. The verbally deprived could gorge themselves upon this convoluted prose, and relish the extravagance with which he could recreate a world that every reader felt he could remember. The time was right – and with this one book Osbert found fame and fortune as a national remembrancer.

He should have been extremely happy. After his father's death he had inherited the title and Montegufoni. As a congenital pessimist he had been convinced that the war would destroy the castle; in fact, it had not only survived intact, but had offered sanctuary to some of the most famous paintings from Florence's Uffizi gallery. His money worries were completely over; the house in Carlyle Square was waiting to receive him; and Wing Commander David Horner would soon be demobilised. With Europe just about to open up again, there seemed nothing to prevent this now distinguished author from pursuing many more 'winters of content' and actually enjoying life as well as letters.

To a point it seems as if he genuinely did. The *enfant terrible* had become terribly respectable. He was a close friend of the royal family. In contrast with the days when he ridiculed literary prizes, he would receive the *Sunday Times* gold medal (now sadly discontinued) and £1,000, followed by a C.B.E. in 1956 for services to literature. In 1958 he was made a Companion of Honour and in 1967 a Companion of Literature. He had begun to love Renishaw, and to enjoy his castle in Tuscany, free from the presence of Sir George and all his worries.

The autobiography continued to win unfailing acclaim. *The Scarlet Tree*, published in 1946, was followed by *Great Morning* in 1948 and *Laughter in the Next Room* the year after. Then in the winter of 1948 came prestige of another kind. Together with Edith (since 1948 Dame Edith) Osbert had hit the U.S. lecture trail with great success. Much of this was due, of course, to Edith, whose extraordinary presence – 'so gothic that you could almost hang bells in her', as someone put it – gave her an undisputed star status of her own. But Osbert in his understated way was also a considerable celebrity. In America he was becoming the figure he had so often ridiculed as a young man, the distinguished man of letters. There was no denying the impact of the famous group picture in *Life Magazine*, he and Edith seated like literary royalty in New York's Gotham Book Mart, with some of the brightest hopes of Anglo-American literature in apparent fealty around them: Auden and Spender, Gore Vidal and Tennessee Williams, Marianne Moore, Horace Gregory and Randall Jarrell. The great Sitwellian legend had never been more evident.

'What ails thee then?', as D. H. Lawrence had longed to ask of Osbert Sitwell. For something obviously did, as much as ever. It was partly David, who continued to be as flighty and independent as in the past (although so, in his way, was Osbert). It was partly his health, with bad attacks of gout, 'devils with prongs', which plagued him. It may even have been the absence of Sacheverell, who since the beginning of the war had lived a completely separate life with Georgia at Weston, and who almost never saw him. But the truth was that the anger from his past continued to afflict him.

Perhaps he was congenitally angry, as some are congenitally deaf or astigmatic. The fact of the matter was that the present had largely ceased to interest him. The present was a dreadful disappointment. It was the past alone that mattered. This may have been what enabled him to face life's final indignity with such apparent equanimity. In 1950, when he was diagnosed as suffering from 'a Parkinsonian condition', he treated it as another insult against the artist, and proceeded to ignore it.

Noble Essences, the final volume of his autobiography, appeared in the same year, and for a while his life continued much as usual: more travel; a further book of reminiscences, *Tales My Father Taught Me*, published in 1954; and in the same year another visit to New York. By now the Parkinson's was starting to affect his walk, and Dan Maloney, the young ex-sailor who looked after him, had fearful memories of trying to hold him back as he staggered uncontrollably across the rush-hour traffic of Fifth Avenue. 'That was a damned close shave', Osbert would say afterwards. From then on it was not so much a close shave as a long, Sitwellian decline. As Osbert became progressively more difficult for Maloney to manage on his own, a black male nurse, Witt Harrison, who engagingly addressed him as 'Sir Osbug', also became part of the American support team. Life was imitating art: D. H. Lawrence's portrait of him as the wheelchair-bound Sir Clifford Chatterley of Wragby Hall was coming true.

He was predictably courageous and resilient, and also very rich, but the end was suitably macabre. After David was paralysed in a fall at Montegufoni in 1962, their thirty-year relationship ended, bitterly. Nor were relations ever properly restored between Osbert and Sacheverell, and instead of leaving Montegufoni to his brother he left it to his nephew, Reresby. For the last four years of his life Osbert lived alone in his father's castle, looked after by his friend and secretary, Frank Magro. He died there in 1969 and was buried in the Protestant cemetery in Florence. Frank put a copy of his favourite book, *Before the Bombardment*, in his grave to keep his ashes company. David survived him.

John Pearson

5.1

Renishaw Hall

By Richard Wyndham, c. 1930s

Dick Wyndham (1896-1948) was a cousin of Osbert's army friends 'Bimbo' Tennant and Ivo Charteris. He sold the family collection of Pre-Raphaelite art and devoted himself to painting and travelling, becoming a close friend of Osbert and Sacheverell in the years following the First World War. They enjoyed the dubious credit of introducing him to his difficult protégé, Wyndham Lewis, in Venice in 1922. In the later 1920s Dick Wyndham was often with Sacheverell and Georgia, at Weston, at his own house at Tickerage in Sussex and on numerous trips abroad. In 1928 he collaborated with Sacheverell on *A Book of Towers* and he acted as co-photographer with Costa Achillopoulo for Sacheverell's *Roumanian Journey* (1938).

In September 1925 Sir George and Lady Ida moved permanently to Montegufoni and Osbert became the owner of Renishaw, though with limited discretionary powers and a shortage of cash. In essence little changed in the years before the Second World War. Osbert remained based at Carlyle Square but travelled extensively abroad. In August the family, including Sir George and Lady Ida, reassembled at Renishaw. Dick Wyndham stayed on several occasions, and another painting he made of the house, still in the collection at Renishaw, is dated 1937. Renishaw had little heating and no electric light and by the end of the 1930s the 'ghost wing', on the right of Wyndham's painting, was virtually derelict.

Michael Arlen

By Edmund Dulac, 1925

In *The Green Hat* (1924) by Michael Arlen (1895-1956) Osbert detected plagiarism of his own short story about a plagiarist, 'The Machine Breaks Down'. The charge was totally without foundation but serves as a useful indicator of Osbert's friable and over-sensitive attitude to his writing.

The Green Hat, the tale of a Mayfair *femme fatale*, was a bestseller and made its Armenian author famous, and rich enough to afford a yellow Rolls-Royce. Arlen's literary efforts were patronisingly disparaged by his contemporaries but he made few claims for his writing and was clubbable and well-liked. As with other enemies of the Sitwells, Arlen was in time moved off the blacklist to rank among their friends and was the subject of one of Osbert's 'three-quarter length portraits' in 1931. The artist Edmund Dulac designed a box for a de luxe set of Arlen's *May Fair* and *These Charming People* in the same year as painting his portrait of the author. He also designed covers for *The Michael Arlen Booklets* published in 1927.

Aldous Huxley

By Howard Coster, 1934

Edith met the writer Aldous Huxley (1894-1963) in June 1917 when courting him for *Wheels*, her 'horrible production', as he described it to Ottoline Morrell. Edith succeeded in snaring him, and with nine poems in the second cycle he featured more prominently than any other contributor. Despite an ambiguous attitude to the Sitwells (it was Huxley who called them the Shufflebottoms), he became a close friend and familiar player on the Sitwell stage.

When Huxley's highly successful first novel, *Crome Yellow*, was published in the autumn of 1921, however, it was apparent that the central characters not only resembled the Morrells of Garsington, but in Priscilla Wimbush's debts and Henry's taste for genealogy and antique beds, drew closely on Lady Ida and Sir George. This *lèse-majesté* went unpunished, as apparently did the use of Montegufoni, thinly disguised, in *Those Barren Leaves* (1925). The unpardonable offence, however, came in the form of a short story, 'The Tillotson Banquet', published in 1922, with its cruel depiction of Osbert as Lord Badgery (Hanoverian nose, pig's eyes, pale thick lips). It also trespassed on Osbert's literary territory, making use of the aged Edwardian raconteur, Harry Melvill, whom he had introduced to Huxley in Lucca. Osbert's anger and hurt were channelled into his first prose work, a short story entitled 'The Machine Breaks Down' (1922). This retaliatory version of the Melvill story features Huxley as the smug journalist, William Erasmus, 'tall and thin as a young giraffe, with the small head of some extinct animal' and a magpie yen for other people's ideas. Osbert had found his true literary voice, and his ambivalent debt to Huxley was acknowledged in his autobiography: 'it was only because a friend of mine, a respected contemporary novelist, stole my stories, and because I resented the manner in which he twisted and spoilt them, and because I felt I could write them better myself, that I took to prose.'[1]

By the time of Coster's photograph Huxley was the author of a clutch of novels, including *Brave New World* (1932).

1. LNR, p. 59

5·4

David Herbert Lawrence
By Nikolas Muray, 1923

Even at the end of her life, when D. H. Lawrence (1885-1930) had been dead for more than thirty years, Edith was still spitting her impotent venom at him: 'a plaster gnome on a stone toadstool in some suburban garden'[1]; hardly the intellectual appraisal of a major novelist by a serious literary critic.

Edith had met Lawrence in the early 1920s and admired his poetry. The fact that he and his wife Frieda had rented a villa at Scandicci near Florence seemed propitious for further meetings. The Lawrences called at Montegufoni to see the young Sitwells in 1926, but found only Sir George and Lady Ida, who gave them tea and showed them round the castle, Frieda bouncing on the mattresses to see if they were soft. Lawrence missed the Sitwells again at Renishaw later in the year and it was not until the spring of 1927 that Osbert and Edith went to visit him at the Villa Mirenda. Lawrence was working at the time on the third version of *Lady Chatterley's Lover* and certain characteristics of Sir Clifford Chatterley are unmistakably based on Osbert. The association

of Osbert, indeed of the whole Sitwell family (Sir Clifford is one of three children of an obstinate and ridiculed father) with what Edith called 'a very dirty and completely worthless book',[2] was the root cause of her unforgiving rage against Lawrence. It was an emotion that Osbert may have shared, but he confined its expression to the portrayal of Lawrence as T. L. Enfanlon, a sickly, bearded ascetic who 'loved to pose as the son of a collier', in his novel *Miracle on Sinai*. The ironic upshot of this particular feud was that it ranged the Sitwells on the side of the philistine in literature's most notorious legal battle of the century.

Lawrence had lived a nomadic existence since 1919 and was photographed by the Hungarian Muray in New York in 1920. His cosmopolitanism, however, was no proof against a world overlapping with the Sitwells. The Florentine bookseller Pino Orioli, an old friend of the Sitwells and interpreter for Osbert and Sacheverell during their historic visit in 1920 to Gabriele d'Annunzio at Fiume, was also the publisher in 1928 of a private edition of *Lady Chatterley's Lover*.

1. TCO, p. 108
2. *Ibid.*

5·5

Sir Philip Sassoon
By Howard Coster, 1929

From the age of twenty-four until his death at fifty-one Sir Philip Sassoon (1888-1939) held his father's seat of Hythe in the Unionist cause. His distinguished career took him from private secretary to Earl Haig in 1915 to two terms as Under-secretary of State for Air in the inter-war years, a period crucial in the history of developing air power. His final post, as Commissioner of Works (from 1937) probably best suited his talents and taste, and in this capacity he was responsible for the restoration of Sir James Thornhill's Painted Hall at Greenwich Hospital. In an elegant entry on Sassoon in the *Dictionary of National Biography*, Osbert pays tribute to his creative kindness and asserts that 'no picture of life between the wars is complete without some account of one of [his] houses, filled always with politicians, painters, writers, professional golfers, and airmen.' Among his broad acquaintance were members of the royal family, and it was through Sassoon that Osbert met and made friends with the Duchess of York.

Osbert had fagged for Sassoon at Eton and in later years was his frequent guest at Port Lympne, the house he built on Romney Marsh, and at Trent Park in Hertfordshire, where the photograph by Howard Coster was taken. This house in particular is discussed by Osbert in *The Scarlet Tree*. Although it was close to Ludgrove, his hated prep school, he had failed on subsequent visits to Trent to recognise it as the building he had been made to walk past every Sunday.

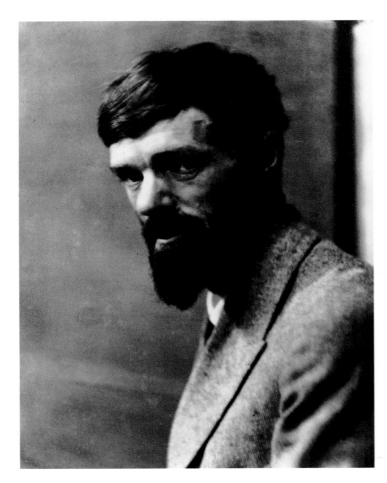

5.6
Lady Aberconway
By Cecil Beaton, 1935

Lady Aberconway (1890-1974) was Osbert's closest confidante for nearly fifty years. Born Christabel Macnaghten, the daughter of a former head of Scotland Yard, in 1910 she married Henry McLaren, who was to succeed his father as 2nd Baron Aberconway (in 1934). Osbert first met Christabel in 1916 or 1917 and wrote in *Laughter in the Next Room* how, some time around 1920, 'a mere acquaintanceship first sloughed its dull and torpid chrysalis, and soared as friendship'.[1] His extravagant tribute continues: 'With the immediate impression she produces on entering a room, of delicacy of texture and sensitiveness of feeling, goes, too, at first sight and most misleadingly, what appears to be an unusual formality, this being produced by a natural precision of demeanour and speech, which, as one grows to know her better, adds an element of surprise to the effect of the discovery of her most unconventional wit and wits, in the same way that one finds out, too, before long, how her discretion covers an unusual and warm understanding of human beings.'[2] Both Sacheverell and Edith at times mistrusted the strong influence that Lady Aberconway exerted on Osbert and she further alienated them by becoming the intimate friend of David Horner.

Beaton and Lady Aberconway were old friends and he photographed her for *Vogue* at her house in London, 38 South Street, Mayfair. *Vogue* noted deferentially 'her dark head the neater in contrast with the amplitude of her skirts; her repose and distinction keeping all this pageantry properly subdued'.[3] Osbert was a frequent visitor to South Street, where in the years before the Second World War Lady Aberconway would perennially arrange for Violet Gordon Woodhouse to play the clavichord for him on his birthday.

1. LNR, p. 130
2. *Ibid.*
3. *Vogue*, 20.2.1935, p. 74

5.7

Dust jacket design for *England Reclaimed*

By Edward McKnight Kauffer, 1927

England Reclaimed (1927) was the first of Osbert's three volumes of eclogues, followed in 1952 by *Wrack at Tidesend* and in 1958 by *On the Continent*. *England Reclaimed* was Osbert's second book to be published by Duckworth, where the young Anthony Powell, one of the signatories on the back of the drawing, had recently begun work. The cover design for *England Reclaimed* is the only instance of Osbert's professional association with the American-born graphic designer Edward McKnight Kauffer, though he describes in *The Four Continents* a morning spent in Sicily with Kauffer and Adrian Stokes. Kauffer had been working as a commercial artist since 1921 and in 1923 designed the cover for a Poetry Bookshop publication of Sacheverell's 'The Parrot' (1923).

5.8

The Man Who Lost Himself

By Osbert Sitwell, 1929

Osbert's first novel, *Before the Bombardment* (1926), met with considerable success and its publication in America occasioned his first trip across the Atlantic to promote the book. Though the publicity for this second novel claimed 'a sense of mystery and beauty which excites and saddens, frightens and amuses us by turn, and a grip of style which is a perpetual revelation'[1], the story of a young novelist who meets his older self is not really a success. A decade later *Those Were the Days* (1938) marked the end of Osbert's novel-writing career and the discovery of his true talent as a writer of memoirs. It has not been possible to establish who designed the covers for *The Man Who Lost Himself*.

1. Dust jacket text, *The Man Who Lost Himself*

5.9

David Horner

By Philip Steegmann, 1926

Osbert met David Horner (1900-1983) in 1921 while Horner was still an undergraduate at Trinity Hall, Cambridge. It was some seven years later, after the death in Paris of Horner's friend Vicomte Bernard d'Hendecourt, that a close relationship began between the two men. In 1930 Horner moved into the house in Carlyle Square and for the next thirty-five years he was an integral part of Osbert's life. Though Osbert was discreet almost to the point of silence in writing of Horner, he dedicated *Laughter in the Next Room*, the fourth volume of his autobiography, to him. Horner himself wrote three books that drew on his experience of life in France: *Through French Windows* (1938), *Was it Yesterday?* (1939) and *The Devil's Quill* (1959). He served with the R.A.F. during the Second World War and for a time was stationed at Watnall Chaworth, within twenty miles of Osbert and Edith at Renishaw. His life remained tied to Osbert, sometimes loosely, sometimes intimately, until a serious accident at Montegufoni in 1962 virtually incapacitated him and set in train events that brought about the end of their friendship in 1964.

Horner's classical good looks were recorded in various forms, from delicate Rex Whistler sketches to the raffish portrait by his friend Brian Connelly, painted in America in 1954.[1] Steegmann shows him as the impeccable twenties dandy, a role Horner sustained well into late middle age. The British-born Steegmann, younger brother of John Steegman [*sic*], art historian and museum director, emigrated to America. In 1951, the year before the artist's death, Horner, Osbert and Edith visited him at his home in New Orleans.

1. Photograph in the collection of Eton School Library

5.10

David Horner

By Foulsham and Banfield, *c.* 1920s
(illustrated on page 165)

Apart from the Bond Street photographers Foulsham and Banfield, David Horner sat to Gordon Anthony, Horst and Lewis Morley (see 5.33). Although Beaton seems not to have photographed Horner, his diary for June 1935 records a mischievous session in Rome with Tchelitchew, Charles Henri Ford and Lord Berners, designing 'the Jubilee celebration for David Horner's reign with Osbert Sitwell in Carlyle Square.'

5.11

Winters of Content
By Osbert Sitwell, 1932

From the early 1920s the Sitwell brothers had
acquired the habit of 'going south in the winter',
ironically seeking an escape from Sir George's
heavy-handed control of their lives right in the
heart of his stamping ground in southern Italy.
At times, avoiding Sir George degenerated into
farce: sliding out of the back of hotels as he
arrived at the front and writing him letters from
the mythical steam yacht *Rover*. But over the years
the pattern of winters spent usually in Amalfi
settled into a regular working routine and one that
Sacheverell's marriage initially seems not to have
disturbed. The winter of 1929-1930 was a time of
particular happiness for Osbert as he shed Sir
George on Christmas Day in Venice and, joined
by David Horner, travelled south via Bologna to
Naples and across to Lecce in the heel of Italy for
the New Year.

    Winters of Content was written largely during,
and about, this idyllic Italian winter. The engraved
half-title by Eric Ravilious is the only instance of a
collaboration between the artist and the Sitwells,
though his close friend Edward Bawden illustrated
Edith's *Popular Song* (1928) as well as Osbert's
Winter the Hunstman (1927) and *Dickens* (1932).

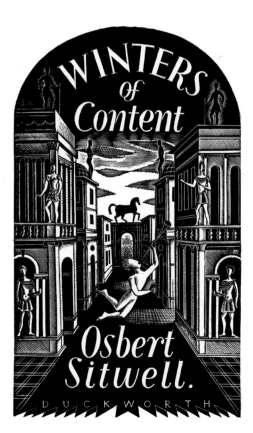

5.12

Harold Acton
By John Banting, *c.* 1930

As a young man the historian and aesthete (Sir)
Harold Acton (1904-1994) had been involved with
the Sitwells over the production of *The Eton Candle*
and was instrumental in Gertrude Stein's
appearance at the Ordinary Society in Oxford in
1926. In *Memoirs of an Aesthete* (1948), he wrote
affectionately of all the Sitwells: of Edith, who
'went out of her way to help over stiles lame dogs
that turned and bit her'; of Sacheverell's style
'flowing like the Yangtze through ever-changing
scenery'; and of Renishaw, 'spacious and gracious
like Osbert himself'. 'They were generous and
hospitable to a fault, loyal friends, excessively
sensitive but free from pettiness.'[1]

    Their paths crossed in London drawing-rooms
in the twenties, in Peking in the thirties (see 5.13)
and in Italy after the Second World War when
Acton settled permanently at his family home,
La Pietra in Florence, almost a neighbour to the
Sitwells at Montegufoni.

    Banting's Cocteau-like drawing was in the
collection of John Sutro, the founder of the
Railway Club of which Harold Acton was an
enthusiastic member.

1. H. Acton, *Memoirs of an Aesthete*, 1948, pp. 205-6

5.13
Osbert Sitwell and David Horner with their Chinese house staff, Peking
By The Photo Specialists Co., 1934
(illustrated on page 166)

In November 1933 Osbert and David Horner sailed from Marseilles on a trip to the Far East that was to last six months and result in Osbert's book *Escape with Me!* (1939). They landed at Saigon and motored to Phnom Penh, then on to the temples at Angkor. They had reached Peking by February and stayed there for three months. After a week in a hotel they rented a house in the Tartar City. They were photographed in the courtyard by a photographer from a company owned by Chang, the Chinese major-domo in charge of the house staff. Osbert reckoned the photographer had made Chang (second from left, front row) look like a 'Chinese Adonis' while transforming his enemy, the cook (second from right, front row) into 'a malicious and idiot gnome'.[1] Harold Acton, resident in Peking as a lecturer at the National University, often joined Osbert's explorations of the city: 'he made me feel that I was participating in an eighteenth-century Grand Tour; in the evenings he luxuriated in the offshoots of his opulent memory, and as I listened to him I enjoyed the sensations of travelling hither and thither in a rococo stage-coach.'[2]

1. OS, *Escape with Me!*, pp. 197-8
2. H. Acton, *Memoirs of an Aesthete*, 1948, p. 352

5.14
Osbert Sitwell and David Horner with unidentified companions
By an unknown photographer, 1934

At the end of May 1934 Osbert and David Horner set off from Peking to see the Great Wall of China on their way home. They travelled by train to Shan-Hai-Kuan where the Great Wall sweeps down to the sea and marks the border of China with Manchuria. There they stayed with 'a hospitable and argumentative Irishman ... whose chief ambition in life was to improve the relations existing between Great Britain and the Japanese'[1] (Japan had, by this date, occupied Manchuria). It is likely that David Horner and Osbert, dressed for the tardy spring he describes in *The Four Continents*,[2] were photographed there with their Japanese companions.

1. OS, *The Four Continents*, 1954, p. 191
2. *Ibid.*, p. 192

5.15
Queen Mary at Badminton
By an unknown photographer, *c.* 1941-1942

Osbert already knew the younger generation of the royal family when he met Queen Mary in 1937. Although Queen Mary's proposed visit to Renishaw in September 1939 was cancelled, Osbert was invited on several occasions to stay with her at Badminton during the war. Queen Mary's exertions for the war effort at Badminton, and her battles against untidiness in nature, are described in detail by Osbert, an unwilling assistant. 'Wooding' at Badminton was a hazardous pastime: 'Queen Mary, attended by a despatch-rider on a motor-bicycle, in person conducted our operations, poking at recalcitrant branches with her walking-stick. The work certainly seemed to be quite dangerous. The despatch-rider of that morning was a new recruit to the post, temporarily replacing a more permanent predecessor who had already been injured: two chauffeurs had been knocked out, and another man, now helping, still wore a black patch over one eye, which, I was told, a splinter had entered.'[1]

After a stay at Badminton in 1942 he sent Queen Mary his essay, 'The Red Folder', based on historic documents they had read together. This may be the 'lovely little book' to which the Queen refers in a message of thanks on the back of the photograph.

1. OS, *Queen Mary and Others*, 1974, p. 45

5.16

Osbert Sitwell

By Desmond Harmsworth, 1938

Desmond Harmsworth (Lord Harmsworth from 1948) knew the Sitwells from at least as early as 1931, when Edith was writing to him, somewhat surprisingly, that she had 'a perfect mania for cooking'.[1] His father Cecil Harmsworth recorded in his diary on 14 March 1930: 'Miss Edith Sitwell to dinner, in one of her famous brocade dresses and with silvered finger-nails!'[2]

The portrait of Osbert was worked up during late 1937 and 1938 in the artist's studio at Lime Lodge, Egham, from drawings made earlier at Carlyle Square. 'The work was done in nightmare conditions', he wrote some forty years later. 'Osbert with a heavy cold had a blanket to his ears and thick-rimmed glasses obscuring his eyes bent over proofs [of his novel *Those Were the Days*] so I never really saw him and painted the picture alone in my studio from memory.'[3] While the painting was in progress Osbert rang the artist up to say that he had to go to Italy, where Sir George was thought to be dying. He telephoned again on his return, and the conversation was recalled by

Harmsworth: 'DH: But how is your father? Osbert: Oh he's all right. DH: That's good, isn't it! Osbert: Well, is it?'[4] The finished portrait was included in the artist's first London exhibition, at Wildenstein's in April 1938. Osbert wrote to congratulate him: 'I do hope you are enjoying a success: though I don't believe that anyone now thinks of pictures or books at all, only of Hitler and gas-masks.'[5]

1. Unpublished letter from ES to D. Harmsworth, 14.12.1931
2. C. Harmsworth, unpublished diary
3. Unpublished letter from D. Harmsworth to 'Victoria', 9.12.1978
4. *Ibid.*
5. OS to D. Harmsworth, 28.4.1938

5.17

Osbert Sitwell

By Norman Parkinson, 1935
(illustrated on page 163)

Parkinson's photograph was probably taken at the same time as the one used in the 1935 Christmas issue of *The Bystander* over the heading 'Osbert Sitwell – Ballet Author'. The reference is to the libretto of a ten-minute ballet, *The First Shoot* or *Shooting Party*, written by Osbert for C. B. Cochran.

5.18

Manuscript notebook containing the masterplan for *Left Hand Right Hand!*

By Osbert Sitwell, *c.* 1941-1945

Osbert had begun work on *Left Hand Right Hand!* by May 1941 when he wrote to Adrian Stokes from Renishaw that he was 'engaged on an endless autobiography'.[1] This large manuscript notebook, written in violet, green and black inks, includes lists of ideas for poems and stories, anecdotes and gossip, all carefully indexed. Page 111, indexed as the 'masterplan', contains the explication of the title:

the lines of the left hand, as one is born with;
the lines of the right hand, as you make it.

Reading his notes, it is clear that from the beginning he had in mind that the work would run to several volumes, the last of which would consist of 'characters of various persons'. He reminds himself ominously to 'instance especially as intellectual weaknesses, the private play of superstition'. On page 110 he notes Sir George's comment that 'for many years past the family has been working up for something'. Osbert's forebears, whom he was conscious some would find intrusive in the story, he sees as crucial. A cancelled passage reads: 'Ancestors stand behind a man and his character like a fan, or the spread tail of a peacock. Everyone is the heir of all the ages.'

The manuscript of the title volume, *Left Hand Right Hand!*, was sent to his secretary, Lorna Andrade, for typing in early 1942, but it was not until spring 1944 that it appeared in print, serialised first in *Atlantic Monthly*, then published in May by Little, Brown of Boston and the following March by Macmillan in London.

1. Quoted in Pearson, p. 349

5.19

Left Hand Right Hand!

By Osbert Sitwell, 1945-1950

The five volumes of Osbert's autobiography constitute his masterpiece. 'This book, I hope,' he wrote to his publisher, 'will be a classic; it is the book of a lifetime.'[1] The first four volumes, *Left Hand Right Hand!* (1945), *The Scarlet Tree* (1946), *Great Morning* (1948) and *Laughter in the Next Room* (1949) cover Osbert's ancestry, his childhood and youth, Renishaw, Scarborough and Montegufoni, his time in the army and the London of the 1920s. Running like a thread through the entire sequence is a mocking, affectionate portrait of Sir George, considerably at odds with the unequivocal dislike Osbert expressed elsewhere. The fifth volume, *Noble Essences* (1950), consists of a series of essays on famous people whom Osbert knew. All the dust jackets in the series were designed by Harry Cowdell at Macmillan (see 5.31); the endpapers reproduce impressions of Osbert's left and right hands.

From the beginning *Left Hand Right Hand!* enjoyed the success that Osbert had hoped for. His old enemy J. C. Squire wrote one glowing review after another in the *Illustrated London News*. More astutely, Harold Hobson pinpointed the care Osbert had taken to maintain both his social standing and his rebel membership of the avant-garde: 'the whole superb charade and mock-battle has been delineated with superficial acerbity but fundamentally profound social admiration'.[2] 'Book succeeds book', *The Times Literary Supplement*

declaimed, 'with the mounting rhythm of a tide', predicting that the completed five volumes would take their place among 'the essential autobiographies of the language'.[3]

1. Quoted in Pearson, p. 363
2. H. Hobson, review of *Noble Essences* from an unidentified publication, 'Sitwelliana' scrapbook
3. *The Times Literary Supplement*, 3.6.1949

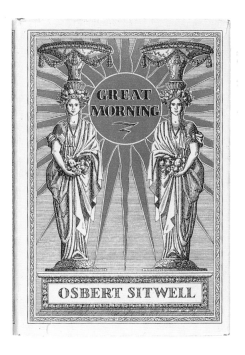

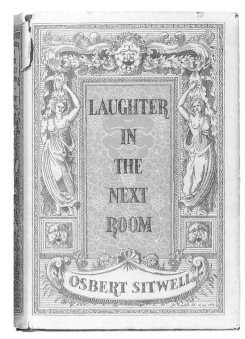

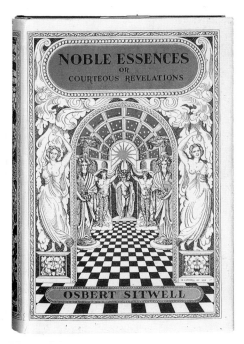

James Agate
By Felix Man, 1939

In the nine-volume, decade-long sweep of *Ego*, the diaries of the *Sunday Times* theatre critic James Agate (1877-1947), there is little indication of the *causus belli* that led Edith to fulminate that she was 'so furious with Agate that I shall certainly cut him dead under circumstances of the greatest ignominy, for him'.[1] Though he had written that there was 'something self-satisfied and having-to-do-with-the-Bourbons'[2] about Osbert, Agate was on dining terms with both Osbert and Edith until the middle years of the Second World War and often quotes Osbert admiringly in his diaries. The breach came with Osbert's anti-war tract, *A Letter to My Son*, published in *Horizon* in March 1943 and issued as a booklet by Home and Van Thal the following year. It was, on the whole, a courageous pacifist manifesto, but injudiciously Osbert made a case for an artistic élite. 'If, in states vowed to death and to fights without a finish, the lot of everyman is, of course, hard, that of the artist is especially abominable. Here, unless some special status is allowed him, as elsewhere, it will mean, in fact, that he becomes a helot.'[3] It was a sentiment roundly demolished by Agate in the *Daily Express*, leading Edith to the bizarre conclusion that Osbert's 'simple character' had laid him open to Agate's 'dirty actions'. Agate was invited by the publishers of *A Letter to My Son* to expand on his position in another pamphlet, and duly produced *Noblesse Oblige: Another Letter to Another Son* (1944). The indomitable Agate,

displayed in all his rotund urbanity by Felix Man, was in many respects the acme of the philistine Osbert had always despised. He continued to mete out praise and criticism of Osbert's work, predicting that *Left Hand Right Hand!* would lead to 'a storehouse of delight' but lamenting that Piper's illustrations had 'the air of a cross between Vlamynck ... and the last shot in the film of Daphne du Maurier's *Rebecca*.'[4]

1. Quoted in Pearson, p. 376
2. J. Agate, *Ego I*, 1935, p. 162
3. OS, *A Letter to My Son*, 1944, p. 19
4. J. Agate, *Ego VIII*, 1946, p. 67

5.21

Osbert, Georgia, Edith and Sacheverell Sitwell outside the High Court
By Universal Pictorial Press, February 1941

For Osbert, as for Edith, litigation was often a first resort. In 1949 their solicitor Philip Frère wrote wearily: 'I seem to spend so much of my time telling you that statements which appear in the Press, and which cause very justifiable annoyance to Osbert or you, as the case may be, are not libellous, that I am beginning to doubt my own judgement.'[1] The *Reynolds News* libel action was a notable exception. On 18 February 1940 the left-wing newspaper ran an unsigned review by Hamilton Fyfe of *Edith Sitwell's Anthology*. 'Among the literary curiosities of the Nineteen-twenties', he began, 'will be the vogue of the Sitwells, sister and two brothers, whose energy and self-assurance pushed them into a position which their merits could not have won.' He continued: 'Now

oblivion has claimed them and they are remembered with a kindly, if slightly cynical, smile.'[2] Counsel advised that there was indeed a *prima facie* case, for libel as these statements were outside the 'fair comment' allowed in reviewing. Osbert refused to settle and, with Edith and Sacheverell, sued for damages, asserting that they were at the height of their fame and that to suggest otherwise would seriously harm their careers. The trial took place in February 1941 with Arthur Waley and Charles Morgan giving evidence of the Sitwells' continuing literary success. Despite accusations of publicity seeking and time wasting during wartime, Mr Justice Cassels decided in favour of the Sitwells and they were awarded £350 each plus costs. They were photographed with Georgia outside the High Court, Edith and Osbert with their gas-masks to hand. Sacheverell's £350 was spent on wine, lunch at the Ritz and a peridot ring for Georgia.

1. Quoted in Pearson, p. 409
2. *Reynolds News*, 18.2.1940

5.22

Photographs by Bill Brandt, 1945

a) Edith and Osbert Sitwell
b) Entrance to the Wilderness, Renishaw
(illustrated on page 11)

The photographs of Edith and Osbert by the
landscape and portrait photographer Bill Brandt
remain among the best-known images of the two
writers (see also 4.23). Here they are posed in the
drawing-room at Renishaw, with the Sargent
group (1.19) and an eighteenth-century silhouette
of the Sitwell and Warneford families by Francis
Torond on the wall behind. This photograph
appeared in *Lilliput* in November 1949 illustrating
a series on writers (entitled 'An Odd Lot') with a
text by Alan Pryce-Jones. 'In a plain age, they
have always maintained coloured standards. Large
houses and large imaginings; good prose and good
food; movement and vision; warm friendship and
blood rows – in public and in private their roles
are as remote from the Century of the Common
Man as the Aztecs.'[1]

On the eastern side of the garden at Renishaw
is the entrance to the 'Wilderness', or Brockshill
Wood, flanked by statues of a warrior and an
amazon. Osbert used Brandt's photograph (b) as
an illustration in *Great Morning* (1948).[2]

1. A. Pryce-Jones in *Lilliput*, November 1949
2. GM, ill. f.p. 57

5.23
Sir George Sitwell in the Cardinal's Garden, Montegufoni
By an unknown photographer, 1935

Montegufoni was still without heating and electric light when Sir George and Lady Ida took up permanent residence there in 1925. During the severest winter weather they stayed at a hotel in Florence, but life on the whole was agreeable; Henry Moat had returned to Sir George's service and the old battle of wills between them resumed to the satisfaction of both parties. 'My mother', wrote Osbert, 'liked the climate, and the life in Florence, and my father enjoyed the absence of life in the house.'[1] Sir George would often sit in the Cardinal's garden, where he had created a box parterre, 'planning and scheming as though death did not exist'.[2] For twelve years life rolled on as renovation works continued, antique furniture accumulated and house parties came and went. Then in 1937 Lady Ida died, in London, after a short illness. Sir George returned to Montegufoni where, after the outbreak of the

Second World War, his health, too, began to fail. Communication with Italy was difficult, but news reached Osbert that his father was being looked after by Olga Woog, a distant relation, and her husband Bernard, who eventually persuaded Sir George to join them in neutral Locarno. There he died on 8 July 1943. Osbert succeeded to the title. 'Being a baronet', he wrote, 'is a delicious experience, like a new toy.'[3]

1. LNR, p. 276
2. *Ibid.*, p. 294
3. Quoted in Pearson, p. 362

5.24
Osbert Sitwell at Montegufoni
By an unknown photographer, 1950s

Osbert had been the nominal owner of Montegufoni since his father bought the castle in his son's name in 1909, but it was not until after Sir George's death, and after the war, that owning it became a reality. From November 1942 the castle had been used to store paintings from the Uffizi Gallery[1] and was occupied successively

by German, New Zealand, English and Indian troops. When Osbert returned in May 1946 he found that good order had been maintained by Guido Masti, the *contadino* whose family had been at Montegufoni for more than a century. In the 'colophon' to *Noble Essences* he describes the tangible reminders of his father's presence there: 'though the tides of destruction and men of several armies had passed through its hall, and albeit, in the next room, in what had been his study, the brown-tiled floor was littered with charters and ancient parchment deeds, torn and trampled, relating to the family estates in Derbyshire and Yorkshire, yet in his bedroom his round air-cushion hung still in the cupboard, and the eighteenth-century rapier, nacre-handled, which he kept as a protection against burglars, still lay on the table.'[2] American lecture tours permitting, autumn or spring at the castle became a pattern for Osbert, Edith and David Horner throughout the 1950s. In November 1965, after the breach with David Horner, Osbert moved permanently to Montegufoni with his secretary and companion Frank Magro.

1. The paintings housed at Montegufoni are listed in Appendix C, LNR
2. NE, p. 305

5.25

Renishaw Hall
Illustrations for Osbert Sitwell's autobiography
By John Piper, 1942-1943

a) The South Front, Renishaw
(illustrated on page 169)
b) Landscape with Mill, Renishaw

After the commission for the curtain for *Façade* (see 3.15), Osbert invited John Piper to stay at Renishaw in July 1942 with a view to commissioning illustrations of the house and surrounds for the autobiography on which he had just embarked (see 5.19).[1] In fact Osbert's intentions were more grandiose and almost certainly influenced by the fact that for the previous eight months Piper had been working at Windsor doing a series of twenty-six water-colours for Queen Elizabeth. Despite Edith's objections (Piper was a friend of her arch-enemy, Geoffrey Grigson, and she registered her annoyance at his presence at Renishaw by staying in bed throughout his stay[2]) more than fifty water-colours and oil paintings were produced during the following year. For the catalogue of the exhibition of a large proportion of these, *The Sitwell Country* at the Leicester Galleries in 1945, Osbert wrote: 'At the moment when the great English houses, the chief architectural expression of their country, are passing, are being wrecked by happy and eager planners, or becoming the sterilised and scionless possessions of the National Trust, a

painter has appeared to hand them on to future ages, as Canaletto or Guardi handed on the dying Venice of their day, and with an equally inimitable art.' Piper was to be the instrument for preserving a record, parallel to the autobiography, of the association between family and house, patron and artist, for generations to come. In the catalogue of the Tate Gallery Piper retrospective in 1983 David Fraser Jenkins writes illuminatingly about the commission and compares the scheme to Lord Egremont's patronage of Turner at Petworth in the 1820s.[3]

Executed in free periods during Piper's stint as a war artist, the illustrations of Renishaw and the estate provided the ideal vehicle for Piper's preoccupation with the picturesque and the sublime. Since illustrations in the autobiography were to be reproduced in monochrome, many of the water-colours were in grisaille and in any case were done in the winter of 1942-1943 in overcast conditions, lending further atmosphere to the 'romantic' effect of the house. A few, like the *Landscape with Mill* (b), include signs of the semi-industrial Derbyshire countryside and irresistibly remind the viewer of Evelyn Waugh's description of the view that Sir George Sitwell could not see: 'In the valley at our feet, still half hidden in mist, lay farms, cottages, villas, the railway, the colliery and the densely teeming streets of the men who worked there. They lay in shadow, the heights beyond were golden ... "You see," he said, "there is *no one* between us and the Locker-Lampsons."'[4]

The vivid gouache of the south front (a),[5]

suggesting the somewhat dilapidated state of the garden during the war years, is close in spirit to one of the larger oils of the north front of the house, though lacking the interminable length of the façade.[6]

1. D. Fraser Jenkins *et al*, *John Piper*, exhibition catalogue, Tate Gallery, London, 1983, p. 107
2. Pearson, p. 397
3. D. Fraser Jenkins, op. cit.
4. LNR, p. 349
5. Repro. LHRH, f.p. 197
6. Repro. D. Fraser Jenkins, op. cit., p. 59

5.26

The Great Court, Montegufoni
By John Piper, 1947
(illustrated on page 185)

It had always been Osbert's intention to ask Piper to do paintings of Montegufoni for his autobiography after the Second World War, and he finally invited the artist to Italy in the autumn of 1947. It was Piper's first work abroad and the seventeen drawings of Montegufoni that he completed are appropriately more intricate and lighter in spirit than those of Renishaw.[1] Osbert describes the Great Court at the heart of the castle 'where the large blue pavers lay reverberant in the heat'. The tower was built in the thirteenth century by a previous owner who had sworn publicly that he would never live out of sight of the tower of the Palazzo Vecchio, but had eventually settled for this compromise.[2] Only four of the drawings, including this one,[3] were used to illustrate *Great Morning* and *Laughter in the Next Room*. Fourteen of the others were exhibited together in *John Piper, The Sitwells' Montegufoni* at the Maclean Gallery, London, in 1981.

1. See D. Fraser Jenkins *et al*, *John Piper*, exhibition catalogue, Tate Gallery, London, 1983, pp. 118, 120-1
2. GM, pp. 172, 174, 175
3. Repro. GM, f.p. 153

5.27
Osbert Sitwell at Renishaw
By Haywood Magee, 1949

a) In his study, the 'boudoir'
b) At the Gothic Lodge

William Sansom, author of the article that
accompanied a four-page spread of photographs
of Osbert by Haywood Magee in *Picture Post*,[1] was
clearly won over by the magic of Renishaw, 'a
northern house filled with elegancies from the
classic South'. He gives a vivid description of late
evening in the library, the oil lamps burning and
'the last northern daylight luminous in the tall
windows', and of Osbert's eclectic conversational
style: 'in five minutes he will have managed to
discuss a prisonscape of Piranesi, the local
postman's alfresco lunch in the park, a swan-farm
in Dorset, the scent of a Henry II rose and a kind
of American ham produced from pigs that like to
live on vipers'. The two photographs illustrated
here were not included with the article and show
Osbert standing in front of the Gothic Lodge
designed by his ancestor, Sir Sitwell Sitwell, and
sitting at the desk in his study. This Sansom sees
as 'the small control room of some wildly
hangared military enterprise', where the weapons
are manufactured for the Sitwell war against
philistinism. At the time Osbert was working on
Noble Essences, and can be seen with a volume
similar to 5.18. Sansom describes him 'copying
from one foolscap book of rough prose into
another more finished, scoring out passages with
violent strokes of purple ink'.

1. 17.9.1949

5.28

Osbert Sitwell

By Horst P. Horst, *c.* 1949

It is likely that Edith had come across the German-born Horst P. Horst in Paris in the early 1930s when the photographer was working for Paris *Vogue*. Though Horst's allegiances differed slightly from the Sitwells' – he was a friend of Noël Coward and of Tchelitchew's arch-enemy Christian 'Bébé' Bérard – they had a wide acquaintance in common and he saw quite a lot of both Osbert and Edith on their trip to America in 1948-1949. The photograph of Osbert was probably taken at Horst's recently finished house on Oyster Bay, Long Island. This may have been the occasion in 1949, recorded in a candid shot by Horst,[1] when the Sitwells' fellow guest was Greta Garbo, 'a being who is, physically', according to Edith, 'of the lily tribe, but with a human heart and mind'.

1. Horst, *Salute to the Thirties*, 1971, pl. 45

5.29

Osbert and Edith Sitwell in New York

By Ruth Sondak for Keystone, 8 November 1948

Osbert's arrival in New York was heralded by Little, Brown bringing out *Laughter in the Next Room* on 5 October 1948. The previous volumes of his autobiography had already proved popular in America and his celebrity status was only narrowly shaded by Edith's. Their first lecture tour was a social and financial triumph. Each lecture netted $1,750, half of which went to the speakers, half to the lecture-agent, W. Colston Leigh, who also covered the Sitwells' expenses. Osbert spoke on 'The Modern Novel – its Cause and Cure' and on 'Personal Adventures'; Edith on 'Modern English Poetry'; and they both read from their own works. Fêted and flattered, they made new friends at every turn; it was a time of rare enjoyment and reaped them the accolade in the *Boston Daily Globe* that they were 'two of the friendliest poets from England ever to set foot on this continent'.[1]

1. *Boston Daily Globe*, 21.12.1948

5.30

The Sitwells

By Dan Maloney, 1950

By the time of the Sitwells' second lecture tour in America in 1950 Osbert had been diagnosed as suffering from Parkinson's disease and needed more consistent care than David Horner was able to give him. A solution to this problem was found by Lincoln Kirstein in the person of Dan Maloney, an artist and ex-member of the U.S. Navy medical corps. Maloney became a valued companion to Osbert on his many subsequent trips to America, regularly taking him to Florida on holiday and introducing him to an extraordinary range of acquaintances.

Maloney was born in Pittsburgh in 1922 and studied at the Cincinnati Art Academy and at the New School of Social Research after serving in the Pacific during the Second World War. *The Sitwells*, painted before Maloney knew Osbert well, was included in Lincoln Kirstein's 'Symbolic Realism' exhibition in London in the summer of 1950.[1] The surrealist composition shows Osbert with an array of masks, and Edith as a herm, wrapped in a cabbage leaf. The central figure, part woman, part tree, may represent 'the spirit of the Sitwells', under which title the painting has sometimes been known.

1. *Symbolic Realism in American Painting*, 1940-1950, Institute of Contemporary Arts, London, 1950 (17)

5.31

Dust jacket design for *The Four Continents*

By Harry Cowdell, 1954

Osbert declared his intention to write *The Four Continents*, subtitled 'More discursions on Travel, Art and Life', in the last pages of *Noble Essences*. Conscious of the wealth of subject matter he had not used in his autobiography – his travels in China, the Andes, Greece, Morocco, Sicily, America, and that ceaseless fount of inspiration, his father – he announced that 'if I am allowed the time' these would be dealt with in another book. *The Four Continents* was published by Macmillan on 16 July 1954 and by Harper and Brothers, New York, on 11 August. In place of the photographic illustrations used in Macmillan's edition, Harper published a series of twelve drawings by Dan Maloney.

The jacket design is by Harry Cowdell (1918-1987), the in-house designer at Macmillan who had joined the firm as a boy in 1932. Cowdell's most widely known work is the oak tree on the cover of the Greenwood edition of Thomas Hardy's works, but he designed many covers for Osbert, including the entire *Left Hand Right Hand!* series and *Collected Stories* (1953), which features a portrait of the author.

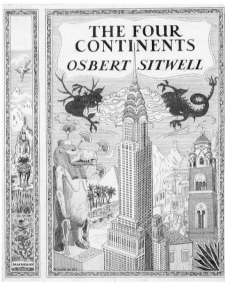

Lincoln and Fidelma Kirstein
By Cecil Beaton, 1957

The great ballet impresario, connoisseur and
writer Lincoln Kirstein (b. 1907), and his wife
Fidelma, were present at the dinner party given
in Edith's and Osbert's honour on their first
evening in America in October 1948. As
Tchelitchew's chief American champion, Kirstein
had a natural affinity with the Sitwells and
became a close correspondent of Edith, Osbert
and David Horner. He had grand plans for Edith
to appear as a regal Elizabethan figure, intoning a
poem entitled 'The Great Seal' at a gala night in
New York in 1950, but the expense proved
prohibitive. He did, however, put on record the
gratitude he felt to Osbert for his support of the
emerging New York City Ballet. In 1950 Kirstein
was in London for the Ballet's first season at
Covent Garden and at the same time organised
an exhibition of American 'Symbolic Realism'.
This, one of the earliest exhibitions at the ICA in
its Dover Street premises, featured the work of
Fidelma's brother Paul Cadmus as well as that of
Osbert's future companion, Dan Maloney. That
same summer Kirstein was on hand when the
cause of Osbert's trembling was finally diagnosed
as Parkinson's disease. He told John Pearson that
Osbert 'acted just as if the whole idea of
Parkinson's were a sort of social affront and that
the doctor had been guilty of bad manners merely
by diagnosing it.'[1]

Beaton's photograph shows the Kirsteins with
three figures by the Polish sculptor Elie Nadelman
(1882-1946). Kirstein wrote two books on
Nadelman's work and passed on his enthusiasm to
Osbert, who also owned two Nadelman figures
and described at some length in *The Four
Continents* a visit to Mrs Nadelman's house in
New York.

1. Pearson, p. 415

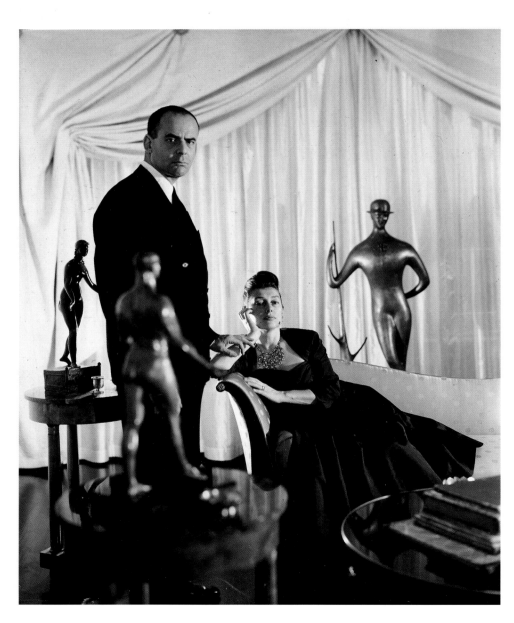

5·33

**Osbert Sitwell and David Horner
at York House**

By Lewis Morley, 1963

a) Osbert
b) David Horner

In March 1963 the lease on 2 Carlyle Square ran out but the resourceful Lorna Andrade found a new London home for Osbert and David Horner in York House, a block of flats off Kensington Church Street. David Horner hated it; the *Daily Telegraph* described it as 'small and soulless'; but it had eight good-sized, light rooms. While the new flat was made ready Osbert and David stayed at the Ritz. 'The operation of removing', Osbert wrote, typically capitalising on an uncomfortable experience by writing an essay on it, 'took not less than ten days, by which time I was so muddled that I nearly got removed myself.'[1] The departure from Carlyle Square was the end of an era noted not only in Osbert's immediate circle but in wider terms too, inducing the *Tatler* to commission an article from Ronald Blythe with photographs by Lewis Morley. Though Blythe regretted the loss of Carlyle Square, 'for 44 years the hub of a celebrated baroque creativity, the urbane H.Q. for many a Sitwellian raid on the Philistine camp', he wrote of 'the luminous feeling of this spacious flat' and the 'exciting clarity'[2] that the bright rooms gave to Osbert's collection. Morley's less anodyne account of the visit was published long after Osbert's death. 'Although large and airy, the flat had already acquired a cocooned quality, reminiscent of a fly in amber. Although there were no cobwebs, there was a musty, unlived-in order. Not unoccupied, but unlived. One existed

in this atmosphere, one did not participate. It was a sanitised Miss Havisham house and I sensed a miasma of emotions, both angry and sad.'[3] It was a perceptive observation, as relations had become increasingly strained since Frank Magro had moved in. 'Sir Osbert was wheeled into the large room by David Horner [whose arm was still in a sling after the fall at Montegufoni the previous year]. He was dressed in varying shades of grey, slumped in his wheelchair, grasping his cane and apparently oblivious to all around him.'[4] Morley describes how Osbert asked to be hauled up from his chair and proceeded, with thoughtful courtesy, to show the photographer around his collection. In the photograph of David Horner, Nevinson's

From an Office Window (2.30) and Dan Maloney's *The Sitwells* (5.30) are visible on the wall above the Chinese gilded flowers in blue glass vases that had been photographed at Carlyle Square forty years earlier (see 2.33). Though Osbert was to spend only a few months at York House, David Horner took over the lease of the flat in 1965 and lived there until his death in 1983.

1. OS, 'Moving House' in *Queen Mary and Others*, 1974, p. 165
2. *Tatler*, 20.11.1963
3. L. Morley, *Black and White Lies*, 1992, pp. 192-5
4. *Ibid.*

Southern Baroque Art was Sacheverell's first prose work, and was to make his reputation as a connoisseur and leader of taste. He considered himself primarily a poet and had already made his literary name as such with the publication of his first volume of poetry, *The People's Palace*, in 1918. Since then he had continued to write and publish verse that was described by even so favourable a critic as Arnold Bennett as 'full of new beauty' but 'damnably difficult'. *Southern Baroque Art* was certainly poetic rather than prosaic. Inspired by Naples, where he had spent the winter of 1920, Sacheverell began writing *Southern Baroque Art* on his return to Scarborough but completed only five or six pages before collapsing with blood-poisoning. A nervous breakdown followed, brought on, Sacheverell claimed, by rage and frustration at his father's refusal to subsidise the Picasso frescoes at Montegufoni. The vision of the baroque, however, remained with him during his illness and in the spring of 1921 he and Osbert set out for Lecce, the town in Puglia that Sacheverell had read was 'the Florence of Rococo Art'. Lecce entranced him with its theatrical façades of golden stone, enhanced by the blinding whiteness of the walls. The image remained indelibly in his mind when he returned to England and to the writing of *Southern Baroque Art*.

Comprising four essays on the baroque – including one on Mexican architecture, which Sacheverell had never seen – it was not an architectural critique and would have been useless as a guide book. It was essentially a poetic interpretation of the spirit of the baroque. 'My aim', Sacheverell wrote, 'has been so thoroughly to soak myself in the emanations of the period, that I can produce ... the spirit and atmosphere of the time and place.' He believed that the unique sensations he experienced through his imagination were the message that he as an artist had to communicate. He continued to believe in this as his particular form of artistic validity until the end of his life. The book had been finished by 1922 but he could not find a publisher for it until he was forced to pay Grant Richards £50 to bring it out in February 1924, when it caused a sensation. The baroque was then a most unfashionable subject, as Kenneth Clark wrote:

Baroque and rococo were still terms of abuse. In Southern Italy they were considered vulgar beyond words. Yet such was the sureness of Sacheverell Sitwell's eye, and the persuasive eloquence of his prose, that in a single volume the whole was changed. *Southern Baroque Art* created a revolution in the history of English taste.

It won Sacheverell admirers among the younger 'Brideshead' generation – Robert Byron, Cyril Connolly and Peter Quennell – and made him, aged not quite twenty-seven, a celebrity in his own right.

Thanks to the notorious first public performance of *Façade* at the Aeolian Hall in June 1923 he was already famous as one of the Sitwell trio. They were headline material even in the popular papers, which did not normally feature the arts. The Sitwells made good copy: they were unconventional aristocrats; they were physically outstanding, all of them being six feet or more; and there were three of them. They were bold, and, in the dandy tradition, invited trouble from the mob. They had become media stars: objects of derision to the middle classes and the old enemy, the philistine, and of adulation to the aesthetes and Society, where art had suddenly become smart. But while Osbert and Edith relished the public controversy, the battles with Noël Coward and other enemies, and the ever-growing pile of newspaper cuttings kept in a huge bowl in the hall at Carlyle Square, Sacheverell did not. He recoiled from controversy and confrontation as much as his brother and sister revelled in it and resented being dragged along in the dust raised by their chariot wheels. He was beginning to find his role as the juvenile lead in the Sitwell comedy irksome.

Increasingly, too, he was finding the atmosphere at Carlyle Square oppressive. Although Sacheverell loved Osbert deeply, he felt the strain of both his dominance of him and his emotional dependence upon him. Like his father and his Sitwell grandmother, Osbert tended to dominate those around him, and his Guards officer background had accustomed him to command. 'You never get used to not being saluted', he once admitted. His unacknowledged homosexuality was an added complication until he found an outlet for love and companionship other than Sacheverell. Sacheverell, on the other hand, was absolutely heterosexual. According to Walton he was 'always in love and

Sacheverell

inevitably right it was that the sensitive poet with his omnivorous antennae for all that was strange or marvellous in the visual arts should depend on the glowing dark beauty of this practical and life-enhancing Canadian ... for the devotion and constant companionship necessary to carry him through his aesthetic adventures.

'My ravishing angel, and Mother and nurse', Sachie called her. It was an accurate description of her role in his life, one that she accepted with enthusiasm, seeing herself as muse and guardian to a genius.

She was already star-struck by his celebrity before they met at a tea-party in Carlyle Square to which she was invited by Osbert who had been impressed by her at a dance given by Arnold Bennett on 4 April 1924. 'I had read *Southern Baroque Art* and I marvelled', she wrote. 'His personality and appearance were not disappointing.' At twenty-six Sacheverell had a distinguished look: he was thin and very tall (six foot four), with his mother's distinctive carriage, his grandmother's Plantagenet features and his own charming, triangular smile. Georgia's effect upon him was the classic *coup de foudre*. 'My senses were numbed. The past and the future ... nothing but a haze ... complete and total blindness ... at the first shock of contact with her.' He took her to *Stop Flirting* at the Strand Theatre and then to supper at the Savoy. Acting, he said afterwards, on 'pure instinct', he determined to marry her. 'It was brave to ask for everything, and for all of life, almost at the first meeting, but such was the counsel of desperation', he was to write sentimentally fourteen years later. 'It was an appeal for help, for the holding out of hands, to which a soul opened and a heart made reply.' Eighteen months later they were married in Paris on 12 October 1925.

Sacheverell's marriage broke up the 'closed corporation', as Osbert had called the trio. Edith's reply to a letter of 'condolence' from Osbert's close friend and confidante, Christabel McLaren, revealed her true feelings about the marriage:

It must make a difference of course – these things always do. At the same time it would really be too dreadful to contemplate if, at least part of our life – the part that really counts (i.e. the artistic side), were not left to us in its entirety.

wanted to get married, probably to get away from Carlyle Square where the atmosphere was often strained'.

The opportunity for escape arose in the spring of 1924 when Osbert introduced Sacheverell to a beautiful eighteen-year-old Canadian girl, Georgia Doble. Georgia was tall, slim, and dark-haired with a slightly olive skin and widely spaced hazel-green eyes. She had beautiful legs, fine ankles and an attractively deep husky voice. She was down-to-earth, highly-sexed, materialistic, ruthless and socially ambitious, but she was also warm-hearted, loyal, vital and amusing. Cyril Connolly wrote of their relationship:

One had only to encounter them for a moment to see how

6.3
'A Modern Poet and his Bride'
The Sketch, 21 October 1925
(previous page)

6.1
Sacheverell Sitwell
By Wyndham Lewis, 1922
(above)

This has more than the personal importance ... How nice Heaven will be – where there is neither marrying nor giving in marriage ... I've only had a short letter from Osbert. I do hope he is alright. I feel rather worried about it ...'

Both Edith and Osbert regarded Georgia as not quite good enough intellectually for their genius of a brother. Osbert never really forgave Sacheverell's desertion of him, or what he regarded as his escape from Carlyle Square. It was to have far-reaching consequences. Although Georgia tried valiantly to merge into the family background and become as Sitwellian as any Sitwell, the quartet could never become what the trio had been. Centrifugal forces exerted by other partners – Georgia herself and later David Horner were destined to give the Sitwell story a final tragi-comic twist. Sacheverell, however, never regretted it. 'Marrying ... gave me my liberty, it made my own life, and let me work in peace.'

For the next five years, however, Sitwell life appeared to continue on in much the same way. Sacheverell and Georgia even spent part of their honeymoon on a working holiday with Osbert at Amalfi, following a tradition that the brothers had established. All three Sitwells, however, were drawing a line under their mutual past. In March 1925 Edith had published 'Colonel Fantock', the poem that described their Renishaw childhood; Sacheverell's autobiographical *All Summer in a Day* came out in 1926; and Osbert's first novel, *Before the Bombardment*, based on the Scarborough they had known before the First World War, was published in the same year.

Sacheverell and Georgia began to establish their independent life with the birth of Reresby, the Sitwell heir, in April 1927, and their move, later that year, to Weston Hall in Northamptonshire, which was to be their home for the rest of their lives. At first they both greatly resented being forced to take this step by 'Ginger', disliking the isolation of the life they led there; but Weston proved the ideal setting for a poet like Sacheverell whose roots lay in nature rather than human experience. Away from their frenetic London social life he worked prodigiously, sitting for hours at his table by the window gazing up across the lawn to the tree-framed horizon. His work during the twenties was varied. He

collaborated with Diaghilev and Gerald Berners on *The Triumph of Neptune*, and with Osbert on the facile and ill-received play *All at Sea*. He published three volumes of poetry and *The Gothick North*, an idiosyncratic compendium of interpretative art criticism and autobiography, and a book on German baroque art. Gertrude Stein's lecture tour of the Oxford and Cambridge literary societies was sponsored by the trio in 1926 and *Façade* was successfully performed at the Chenil Galleries, Chelsea. There were travels with Osbert to Morocco and Greece, and a highly Sitwellian houseparty at Montegufoni in September 1928 for the performance of *Façade* at Siena.

6.7
Georgia Sitwell
By Hay Wrightson, 1927

1930 marked the beginning of the end for 'Sitwellism' as a phenomenon in English cultural life. In August the family gathered, with a glittering succession of literary and social guests, at Renishaw where Cecil Beaton immortalised them in a brilliant series of photographs culminating in a great set-piece of three generations of Sitwells, the 1930s equivalent of the Sargent portrait.

Wyndham Lewis had launched the first attack on them with his satire *The Apes of God*, in which he portrayed his former friends as sham aristocratic amateurs, a theme that was to be taken up by their susbequent critics. The cultural *Zeitgeist* was changing, becoming more left-wing and serious, leaving the Sitwells and their elaborate fantasies stranded. They became the subject of powerful attacks by critics like F. R. Leavis who famously condemned them as belonging to the history of publicity rather than of poetry. In 1933 Sacheverell was so wounded by the hostile critical reception of *Canons of Giant Art*, his best collection of poems so far, that he gave up writing poetry for many years.

Physically, too, the trio were growing further apart. David Horner moved into Carlyle Square to share Osbert's life, gradually excluding Sacheverell from his brother's affections. Edith transferred to Paris to look after Helen Rootham and to pursue her unrequited passion for Pavel Tchelitchew. Sacheverell and Georgia moved in an increasingly social and non-literary set, travelling in great luxury with their new friends, the Duke and Duchess of Westminster, and leading what David Horner, to Georgia's irritation, called their 'pêche-melba life'.

Meanwhile Sacheverell's literary output in the 1930s was bewildering in its diversity. He wrote the first of what he called his 'entertainments of the imagination', *Dance of the Quick and the Dead*; his first and only collection of short stories; a book on Spanish baroque art and another on German baroque sculpture; two studies of English painting, *Conversation Pieces* and *Narrative Pictures*; *The Romantic Ballet in Lithographs of the Time* (with Cyril Beaumont) and *Old Fashioned Flowers* (a new and developing interest); biographies of Mozart and Liszt; and a tribute to Offenbach, *La Vie Parisienne*. He also produced *Roumanian Journey*, written after a visit to the country in 1937, a charming study of the world of peasant costumes and architecture and of the largest and most interesting gypsy population in Europe, all of which were soon destined to disappear under successive waves of totalitarianism. It was the first in a long series of travel books designed to finance his determination to see every work of art or architecture that was worth seeing.

Dance of the Quick and the Dead and its successor, *Sacred and Profane Love*, were woven round Sacheverell's and Georgia's intricate love lives. While Georgia remained his greatest love, Sacheverell also pursued a long affair with Lady Bridget Parsons, a beautiful Anglo-Irish aristocrat (sister to the Earl of Rosse), and a passion for a ballerina, his ideal 'Cinderella', Pearl Argyle. Georgia's sex life was even more active, but she never allowed the affair of the moment to come between her and her 'adored, angel Sachie', as she referred to him in her diary, remaining his protector and the guardian of his muse till the end of her days. Their second son and last child, Francis, was born in September 1935.

Sacheverell escaped fighting in the Second World War as he had in the First, although he was obliged to become an officer in the Home Guard, an occupation that caused him agonies of boredom and resentment. This left him a good deal of time, however, to write and, although he could no longer travel and paper shortages restricted the number of contributions he could make to periodicals, his war years were as productive as any. He published two 'entertainments of the imagination', *Sacred and Profane Love* and *Splendours and Miseries*: extraordinary concoctions of autobiographical fragments interspersed with magpie collections of fascinating information about works of art, Victorian murders, old-fashioned flowers, primitive festivals, and the delvings of his imagination beneath the surface of human life. His fascination with the strange and the macabre resulted in *Poltergeists*, which elicited a letter of congratulation from George Orwell.

British Architects and Craftsmen (1945) showed him to be in the vanguard of taste once again, establishing him as a connoisseur of English art and architecture. It was a continuation and expansion of a theme that he had begun with his two earlier books on English painting and was to continue much later with *Gothic Europe* (1969). In Sacheverell's opinion architecture was, after prose and poetry, England's great contribution to European civilisation. He included under this heading the craftsmen who had executed and complemented the work of Wren and Adam, Kent and Wyatt, and minor masterpieces like eighteenth-century shopfronts and seaside crescents. He connected the great country houses he described with the families who had built them, such as the theatrical Seaton Delaval, designed by Vanbrugh for the violent, beautiful Delavals as a backdrop to their dramatic lives. Experts counted numerous errors of fact but once again Sacheverell had led taste in a new direction, tapping a cultural vein before it came to the surface. It was no coincidence that *British Architects and Craftsmen* was written during the period when Waugh had conceived his romantic celebration of the great English country house in *Brideshead Revisited*. Reviewing *British Architects and Craftsmen* in the *Evening Standard*, Graham Greene praised it for recalling 'so vividly and lovingly with the sense of poetry indispensable to the study of any art, our long and great tradition'. Cyril Connolly later described it as one of the books that had preserved his sanity during the gloom of the immediate post-war period.

As soon as the war had ended Sacheverell planned to escape abroad again. He had found a patron in Winifred 'Bryher' Ellerman, the daughter of a shipping magnate who had been drawn to the Sitwells by her admiration for Edith's poetry. She was equally admiring of Sacheverell's writing and was more than happy to subsidise his journeys by paying for travel tickets and generally lightening his always gloomy financial horizon with Christmas and birthday cheques. He had also found a sympathetic publisher in Harry Batsford who shared his passion for English architecture and had encouraged him to write about it. Batsford had published both his books on English painting and *British Architects and Craftsmen*; during the fifties he was to publish a series of travel books by Sacheverell, including *The Netherlands* (1948), *Spain* (1950), *Portugal and Madeira* (1954) and *Denmark* (1956).

Sacheverell was not a travel writer in the conventional sense; personalities and personal experiences had no place in his books. They were aesthetic adventures in which he gave the reader the benefit of seeing things through his own unerring eye for the beautiful and the curious. In *The Netherlands* he conjured up images of light, grace and colour quite unlike the accepted view of a country of Rembrandts and bulb beds. He wrote of the town houses at The Hague with their marvellous rococo interiors by William III's architect and designer, Daniel Marot; of bedsteps painted with parrots; of Frisian costumes and the 200-year-old orange trees in the Orangery at Enghien. In Portugal and Madeira he succeeded in convincing the Portuguese to look at their architecture in a new light. Whereas the previous fashion had been for the architecture of their 'heroic' period, Romanesque churches and machicolated castles or the extraordinary convoluted Manueline style of the late fifteen and early sixteenth century that celebrated the 'Discoveries' of Portugal's overseas empire, Sacheverell turned the spotlight on to the baroque and rococo designs that were the glory of many Portuguese towns.

His renewed experience of the South broke the block that had prevented him from writing poetry for so long. On a trip to Spain in 1947 he found himself intensely moved by the sight and scent of orange trees in flower in the court of the great mosque at Cordoba. 'It was so lovely that one wanted to weep after all these awful years!' he told Bryher. A month later he wrote of his experience in a new poem, 'The Mezquita'.

The inspiration continued to flow. Later that summer he wrote a group of five poems that in their pure simplicity and technical skill showed that he had not lost his touch, and had in fact refined his style, abandoning the florid imagery of his earlier work. 'The Lime Avenue' described a rainy Renishaw morning; two haunting poems evoked the West of Ireland where he had been staying that August; and 'White Rose' lamented his beloved dancer, Pearl Argyle, who had died tragically young in March that year. A new dancer, Moira Shearer, had come into his life, and it was her beauty and his unrequited passion for her that inspired several poems during these years. He even allowed Edith and Osbert to edit a collection of his poetry, *Selected Poems* (published in 1948), which included his most recent work. It was very favourably reviewed by *The Times Literary Supplement*, which concluded that the collection would 'serve finally to consolidate him as a poet of major signficance. From the work in this volume alone there can be little doubt that posterity will find a place for him.'

Osbert and Edith had welcomed Sacheverell's return to poetry. Osbert wrote of his joy, 'one will once again have poetry to read for the pleasure of sound and of the great sweep of your wings'; while Edith enthused: 'What excitement! Now we can look forward to a long reign of those great poems we have missed so terribly & that nobody else can write.'

Beneath the surface, however, family relations were strained. During the war years Edith had moved in with Osbert to live at Renishaw while David Horner was away on war service. Increasingly in the public minds the Sitwells meant Osbert and Edith, with Sacheverell almost the forgotten man. Edith had enjoyed a literary renaissance with two collections of verse, *Street Songs* and *Green Song*, while the publication of Osbert's five-volume autobiography had made him a 'Great Literary Figure'. Both of them appeared at poetry-readings and kept in contact with influential literary figures like Maurice Bowra, Stephen Spender and Cyril Connolly. Sacheverell, however, had refused to be drawn back into the troika; he shunned the limelight and possibly also invidious comparison with his more successful siblings. His friends, with rare exceptions like Patrick Leigh Fermor and Peter Quennell, were social rather than literary. Being more sensitive and less combative than his brother and sister, he shrank from the bitchy competitiveness of literary society. Georgia increasingly usurped Edith's role as his literary adviser, acting, not always happily, as his intermediary with publishers and upsetting his devoted agent, David Higham.

There were deeper, family reasons for the division between the trio. The death of Sir George in 1943 had severed perhaps the most important bond between his children, their common front against their father. Without this link, subconscious sibling rivalries had risen to the surface. Osbert, inheritor of all the great possessions – Renishaw, Montegufoni and Sir George's considerable fortune, which had been located in Switzerland since his departure from England in 1925 – began to take on, in Sacheverell's eyes, Sir George's role as financial oppressor. Osbert's hidden jealousy of Georgia had turned to dislike after

her tactless behaviour at the time of the reading of the will and Sir George's memorial service in July 1943 when she had, as he told David Horner, trodden 'heavily on every corn that Edith or I had ever possessed ... literary, parental, friendly, every sort'. She had, apparently, made it only too clear that, as Osbert was childless, she and Sacheverell and then Reresby would eventually be masters of Renishaw. Subsequently the financial difficulties into which Sacheverell and Georgia's chronic extravagance had led them was another source of strife between the brothers. In return for financial rescue Sacheverell sold his rights to Renishaw in favour of Reresby. It was a bitter moment, exacerbated by prolonged legal negotiations and the influence of David Horner, who stood to gain from Osbert's alienation from his brother.

Edith, always the most selfless of the three, did what she could to bridge the gap but her personal life and relationship with Osbert were also unhappy. When Horner rejoined the household after the war she found the curious *ménage à trois* increasingly difficult to cope with; while Osbert's developing Parkinson's disease in the early fifties added to the potential tragedy of the situation. Sacheverell and Georgia, invited to Renishaw in August 1959 for the first time in sixteen years, found Osbert and Edith wrecks of their former selves. Both were ill and getting on each other's nerves. Edith, unhappy at the failure of her creative powers and obsessed by Horner's influence over Osbert, sought refuge in alcohol. Eventually, thanks to Bryher's generosity, she moved to London to enjoy her own independent life and her own celebrity. She wrote bestsellers; her extraordinary image with Plantagenet beret and huge rings was familiar everywhere; the triumphant tours she had made in the United States with Osbert in the fifties had made her world-famous. Her seventy-fifth birthday was celebrated with a gala concert, lunch with the Queen Mother and an appearance on *This is Your Life*. When she died in December 1964 both brothers, and Sacheverell in particular, were devastated. 'She was always my friend and mentor from the first days I remember wanting to write – and in fact long before that', he told a friend. Her death inspired him to complete 'Serenade to a Sister' and some of his finest later poems, in which he wrote of her death and of their childhood together

6.12
The Sitwell Family
By Cecil Beaton, 1930
(opposite)

and their 'youth of poetry'. They were privately printed together in a pamphlet entitled simply *To E.S.*

When Osbert died in May 1969 his relationship with Sacheverell, and with Georgia in particular, was at its nadir. After his long affair with David Horner had ended in acrimonious 'divorce' in 1965 the two brothers became closer than they had been for years and Osbert promised to leave Sacheverell Montegufoni, which he had formerly intended to bequeath to Horner. But as Osbert's health deteriorated he came to depend more and more not on his brother but upon his devoted Maltese valet and secretary, Frank Magro. His dislike of Georgia overcame even his love for Sacheverell and after a disastrous visit by the pair to Montegufoni in November 1968 Osbert decided not only never to have his sister-in-law in the house again but to cut Sacheverell out of his will in favour of Reresby. Fortunately for Sacheverell, Osbert died before completing his plan and, although he did not inherit the Tuscan white elephant on which Sir George had lavished so much of his fortune, he did receive the money left in Switzerland, which enabled him to spend his remaining years (now Sir Sacheverell) in relative luxury.

Osbert's 'betrayal' and the loss of Montegufoni inspired his last, long 'entertainment of the imagination', *For Want of the Golden City*, published in 1973. Sacheverell had had high hopes of this, which he saw as his literary testament; the apathy with which it was received disappointed him deeply. It was his last prose work. In it he expressed his bitterness at the final dissolution of the trio. 'The legend of devoted families in the context of brothers and sisters is disproved', he wrote, '… a lifetime of affection and long loyalties, can succumb under pressure of failing faculties and infirmity to other and alien influences.' He consoled himself with Edith's legacy to him: 'the beauty and the poetry/I learned from her/Are antidotes to all self-pity'. He continued writing poetry until he was in his eighties, having it privately printed in a series of 'Brackley booklets' that he sent out to his wide circle of friends. His last collection of poems, *An Indian Summer*, was published in 1982 with a foreword by his old friend and fellow poet, Peter Quennell. He was made a Companion of Honour in 1984 and died, eight years after his beloved Georgia, aged ninety-one in October 1988.

Sacheverell Sitwell is difficult to classify both as a man and as a writer. His personality, a mixture of charm, wit, sensitivity and imagination, remained elusive even to his many friends. James Lees-Milne said of him:

> Sachie was a sort of leprechaun. He wasn't totally a human being. He was a spirit really – almost incorporeal … What was most fascinating about him was his conversation – he flitted from bough to bough, twig to twig so rapidly you couldn't keep pace with him. It was about exotic birds in the West Indies and then you'd find he was talking about architecture in Naples then about nunneries in the Balkans … He was very inspiring and being with him was a treat.

Beneath the dandy exterior there was a vein of melancholy, a sense of the transience as well as the beauty of life. His mother's tragedy had left him with a consciousness of the abyss lurking beneath the surface. He saw death as the end; his 'Agamemnon's Tomb' has been described as one of the finest poems on the subject to have been written in the English language in this century.

As a writer he is if anything more difficult to quantify, not only because of the diversity of his work but because of the unevenness of his writing both in poetry and in prose. His strong points as a poet were his technical virtuosity and mastery of internal rhythm, and a lyrical quality in his 'garden' poetry strongly influenced by the seventeenth century. His avoidance of realism meant that he could never have been a popular poet in his time; he was criticised for being remote in feeling and difficult to understand. He was not interested in the human condition, only in his own aesthetic sensations; a lack of control over his own imaginative processes could lead to obscurity and to an overloading of imagery. The same criticisms could be applied to his prose. His acute sense of the past and of place; his extraordinary memory and powerful imagination; the depth and breadth of his cultural associations made his 'entertainments of the imagination' rich if at times indigestible reading. C. P. Snow wrote of him:

> He is alone in his blend of cultivated civility and macabre imaginative insight … the expression of a unique tension

rejected the idea of beauty as relevant to art. John Betjeman wrote to him on the publication of *Gothic Europe* in 1969: 'what a relief you are after the fearful pedantry & dull art history which kills enjoyment & just gets scholarships for people & breeds more dullards. You are a life-enhancer.'

Sacheverell Sitwell had an original mind unaffected by fashion, a confidence in his own artistic sensibility uninfluenced by commercial reward. He represented, as Evelyn Waugh said, 'pure enjoyment'. Not believing in God, the beauty and humour he found everywhere in life and art was his religion. 'To have been alive and sentient', he wrote, 'is the grand experience.'

Sarah Bradford

between one side of his artistic persona, excessively civilised, a man of taste in the eighteenth-century fashion, world traveller, connoisseur of the visual arts ... and the hidden side, more profound, deeply suspicious of all men's depravity and his own ... His ultimate imagination is much more like Dickens at his darkest ... His sense of human experience has its own outward shape of the baroque, with wild and whirling decorations. Underneath that, there is the feeling for the romantic agony. Underneath that again his gaze is steady, and what he sees is jet-black.

As a cultural influence Sacheverell is considered to be an elitist and anachronistic amateur in a time of deeply researched, narrowly focused specialists and adversarial art critics who have

6.33
Sir Sacheverell Sitwell
By Dudley Reed, 1982

6.1

Sacheverell Sitwell

By Wyndham Lewis, 1922

(illustrated on page 194)

This drawing was probably done in Venice at the same time as the double portrait of Osbert and Sacheverell (3.32) and seems to mark a solution to the problem of achieving a satisfactory likeness, which in Sacheverell's case had been left unresolved. The head here is fleshed out in a penetrating likeness at precisely the same angle.

At this stage Lewis was still on close terms with the Sitwells and was one of Sacheverell's most frequent correspondents. Sacheverell considered him to be the embodiment of the Modern movement in Britain. In Venice he introduced the painter to Richard Wyndham, who became both pupil and patron, before falling from grace; and to William Walton, whose portrait Lewis drew in competition with an unnamed Italian artist.[1]

1. W. Lewis, *Blasting and Bombardiering*, 1937, p. 237

6.2

Georgia Doble

By Maurice Beck and Helen Macgregor, 1924

In early 1924 Georgia Doble (1904-1980) was visiting Europe with her parents (her father, Arthur Doble, was a Canadian banker of Cornish descent), partly to see Georgia's sister, Frances, who, after a year with the Birmingham Repertory Company, was beginning to make a name for herself on the London stage.[1] In February 1924 Frances appeared as 'Eurasia' in Shaw's *Back to Methuselah* at the Court Theatre. The two beautiful sisters made rapid strides in London Society, and on 4 April they attended a ball at Arnold Bennett's house, where Georgia was introduced to Osbert, though not to Sacheverell. The young writer and art historian (Sir) John Rothenstein knew the Doble sisters already and in his autobiography, *Summer's Lease*, takes the credit for persuading Osbert to invite them to Carlyle Square for tea on 16 June.[2] It was then that Sacheverell met and fell in love with Georgia, pursuing her for the rest of the summer. Rothenstein remembers staying at Weston that August and being woken up in the middle of the night by Osbert, Walton and Sacheverell in succession to advise on the situation with Georgia. In the event she was invited for a long weekend before she left for an extended trip to Italy. For the best part of a year the affair was conducted at arm's length, mostly by correspondence from various parts of Italy, with Sacheverell trying to keep things from his parents. After a reunion in London and a great deal of soul searching vis-à-vis his relationship with Osbert, Sacheverell and Georgia were finally engaged a year after they had first met, in June 1925.

As Cecil Beaton realised, the quickest way to make a name for oneself in London Society was to be photographed by one of the fashionable London studios, and Georgia sat to most of the big London names soon after her arrival in Britain. Although not in Helen Macgregor's most experimental mode, the photograph demonstrates the quality that briefly made the studio the most fashionable in British portrait photography immediately prior to Beaton. The pierrot-esque pose, with Georgia in silk tunic and trousers, would have appealed to Sacheverell's love of the *commedia dell'arte*.

1. Ed. J. Parker, *Who's Who in the Theatre*, 8th ed., 1936, p. 523
2. J. Rothenstein, *Summer's Lease*, 1965, pp. 104-5

6.3

'A Modern Poet and his Bride'

The Sketch, 21 October 1925

(illustrated on page 193)

Sacheverell joined Georgia in Paris in early
September 1925, but no date for the wedding
could be fixed until Georgia's father had arrived
from Canada. Further complications ensued, with
money having to be found for Edith to travel to
Paris, Osbert advising a civil marriage in Paris
followed by a religious ceremony in Rome, and
Sir George having to be restrained from joining
the honeymoon 'in case the boy needs me'.[1] The
pair were finally married at St George's Anglican
Church in Paris on 12 October, a date arranged
to suit Osbert who was going to travel on to
Montegufoni with Christabel Aberconway.

Apart from Osbert, Edith and Christabel, the
only other guests were William Walton, Georgia's
parents and her sister Frances. Lady Ida and Sir
George did not feel up to undertaking the journey
from Montegufoni. *The Sketch* reproduced this
photograph full-page under the heading 'A
Modern Poet and his Bride'.

1. Bradford, pp. 153-4

6.4

**Osbert and Edith with Mr and Mrs Doble
at Sacheverell's and Georgia's wedding**

Photographed by the *Daily Mail*, 1925

In the absence of Sir George and Lady Ida,
Osbert and Edith made a formidable pair *in loco
parentis*. This photograph of them with the Dobles
and Walton peering over Osbert's shoulder was
published in the *Daily Sketch* the day after the
wedding, heavily cropped to show only the two
Sitwells – 'poets both'.

Sacheverell and Georgia spent their
honeymoon in the Netherlands before travelling
south to stay with Osbert in Amalfi. This
introduction to Sitwell family life cannot have
been easy for Georgia. She immediately found
herself in the thick of a quarrel with their guest
Peter Quennell, and intellectual matters were also
a worry. When Ada Leverson arrived to stay
Georgia is said to have whispered to her: 'I want
to ask you four questions – quickly now. What is
the difference between Romanticism and
Classicism? Who is Harry Melville? What is
behaviourism and is Julie Thompson received?'[1]

1. Quoted in Bradford, p. 156

6.5

**Sacheverell with (from left to right)
Osbert, Max Meyerfeld, Siegfried Sassoon
and Nellie Burton at Berlin Zoo**

By an unknown photographer, 8 September 1927

In May 1925 a rapprochement had been effected
between Siegfried Sassoon and the Sitwells (see
3.36) when he had seen Sacheverell and Georgia
at the Savoy Grill and gone across to talk to
them.[1] Sassoon subsequently invited Sacheverell
and Osbert to accompany him on a three-week
holiday travelling south through Germany from
Berlin to Budapest, partly, no doubt, in order to
see some of the places Sacheverell had written
about in his pioneering *German Baroque Art* (1925),
originally titled *Later Architecture of the Holy Roman
Empire*. The other guest on this holiday was Nellie
Burton (the landlady of the famous rooming
house in Half Moon Street where Sassoon,
Robert Ross, Lord Berners and others had
lodged), seen here with the rest of the party in
this souvenir postcard from Berlin Zoo taken at
the beginning of the holiday. Georgia was in
Paris, presumably with her parents, and was
reunited there with Sacheverell on 29 September.[2]

1. Bradford, pp. 169-70
2. *Ibid.*, p. 170

6.6
Georgia Sitwell
By Cecil Beaton, 1927

Beaton's first formal photograph of Georgia must
have been taken soon after he met her with
Sacheverell at Wilsford Manor in June 1927 (see
6.9). It shows her sitting in front of Osbert's
Omega screen (2.19), which Beaton used as a
backdrop for the smart young woman-about-town;
and it was almost certainly taken at the same time
as an extraordinary picture of baby Reresby (born
in April) with his black nanny, Mary Cole. This
photograph, or a variant from the same sitting,
was included in Beaton's first exhibition at the
Cooling Galleries in November that year.

6.7
Georgia Sitwell
By Hay Wrightson, 1927
(illustrated on page 195)

Hay Wrightson's ledgers show that Georgia went
to the up-and-coming Bond Street photographer
to have her portrait taken some time in the
autumn of 1927, though she had first been
photographed by him in 1925 as Miss G. Doble.[1]
The rather old-fashioned back-lit image is in
strong contrast to Beaton's photographs of
Georgia of the same period (see 6.6) and seems
designed to show off her newly shingled hair, the
height of late 1920s fashion.

1. Hay Wrightson ledgers, NPG

6.8
Zita and Baby Jungman
By Cecil Beaton, 1926

Zita (born 1904) and Baby (Teresa, born 1908)
Jungman were, as a recent article in the *Sunday
Telegraph* points out,[1] as central to the myth of the
'Bright Young Things' of the twenties as the
Sitwells were to the intelligentsia of the period.
The daughters of Beatrice Guinness by her half-
Dutch first husband, the painter Nico Jungman,
they were extremely well connected, not only
through their mother, a noted Society hostess
known as 'gloomy Beatrice', but also through
their cousins, Tanis and Meraud Guinness, and
other friends such as Eleanor Smith, daughter of
Lord Birkenhead, and Loelia Ponsonby, later
Duchess of Westminster. Zita was credited with
the invention of the Car Treasure Hunt (the first
one was in Bond Street in about 1923); while
Loelia originated the Bring a Bottle Party, both
official activities of the 'Bright Young Things'.
Despite this, Zita was sensitive and dreamy and
immediately captivated Sacheverell when he met
her at Stephen Tennant's house party at Wilsford
in June 1927 (see 6.9). Zita was unfortunately
more attracted to Osbert but in October she
allowed herself to be taken out by Sacheverell in
her car, where they unburdened themselves to
each other in an intense conversation.[2]

Both of the Jungman sisters were the subject
of constant attention from young men, eligible or
otherwise, Baby notably from Evelyn Waugh, who
had hoped to marry 'the Dutch girl' after his first
marriage broke up.[3] Sacheverell's infatuation with
Zita was initially of great annoyance to Georgia
but since she and Sacheverell were constantly
bumping into Zita socially there was little she
could do. On holiday with Osbert, Zita and the
painter Ethel Sands in Morocco early in 1928, she
was relieved to find that Zita, a good Catholic,
had no designs on her husband and she connived
with Sacheverell to try to persuade Osbert to
marry Zita. Even after Zita's marriage to Arthur
James in 1929 Sacheverell continued to write
poems to her and to maintain what had become a
complex triangular relationship. In *The Gothick
North* (1929), Sacheverell's fantastic mixture of art
history, autobiography and musings on the
triumph of the fair-haired northerner, Georgia
and Zita are contrasted as the two halves of
beauty.[4] He continued to flirt with and fantasise
over Zita until his conquest of Lady Bridget
Parsons in 1933, after which they lost touch.[5]

Cecil Beaton took his first photographs of Zita
and Baby in November 1926[6] and, having won

over their mother, probably had some more sittings with them either side of the New Year and was invited to several Guinness parties. Beaton thought Zita 'quite marvellously lovely – great squirrel's eyes, fair hair and nice soft throaty voice'.[7] This double portrait of the sisters appeared in the *Tatler* on 19 January described as 'an example of the new method of photography ... at first sight a bit confusing, because it is never quite clear which side of the picture is the top'.

1. N. Farrell, 'Women who inspired Waugh' in the *Sunday Telegraph*, 20.3.1994, p. 3
2. Bradford, p. 171
3. N. Farrell, op. cit.
4. Bradford, pp. 204-5
5. *Ibid.*, p. 438
6. H. Vickers, *Cecil Beaton*, 1933, p. 74
7. Bradford, p. 168

6.9
Stephen Tennant, Cecil Beaton, Georgia Sitwell and friends at Wilsford Manor
By Cecil Beaton, 1927

Osbert probably met Stephen Tennant, the eccentric and outrageous stepson of Lord Grey of Falloden, through his mother, the former Lady Glenconner, and possibly also through their mutual friend, Rex Whistler, who had been at the Slade School of Fine Art with Tennant. Later described by Osbert as 'the last professional beauty', Tennant epitomised the androgynous and flamboyant young aristocrat of the twenties and was at the centre of the exclusive social circle that became known as the 'Bright Young Things'. Wilsford Manor, his mother's Edwardian house in Wiltshire, was the setting for some of his most memorable parties.

On 18 June 1927 Sacheverell and Georgia were invited down to Wilsford with Osbert for a party that included Tennant's closest friends, Beaton, Whistler and the Jungman sisters (see 6.8), but also Rosamond Lehmann, Edward Sackville-West, Baba Brougham and the writer Eleanor Wylie.[1] On this occasion Beaton persuaded the entire party to lie on the floor beneath a leopardskin rug for a photograph that was published in *Vogue* in November and of which Beaton gave Georgia a signed copy for her album (see 6.19).

The 'boys' (Tennant and Beaton) were invited to Weston in August with Christabel Aberconway, and photographs in Georgia's album show everyone romping around rather self-consciously in eighteenth-century costume. This may have been something of a dress rehearsal for what was planned at Wilsford in October: a series of

tableaux *en fête-champêtre* to be filmed and photographed by Beaton. The October party was smaller, with Walton, the Jungman sisters, Christabel Aberconway and Rex Whistler in addition to the Sitwells, Beaton and Tennant. The seven younger members, posed somewhat histrionically on the ground as Arcadian shepherds and shepherdesses, were (from left to right) Zita Jungman, Walton, Beaton, Tennant, Georgia, Baby Jungman and Rex Whistler.

Osbert, Sacheverell and Christabel Aberconway seem to have avoided the dressing up. According to Laurence Whistler, the man behind the camera was 'William the footman'[2], who had presumably been briefed by Beaton to capture scenes that now appear as remote and archetypal as the Lancrets and Watteaus from which they derive.

1. Bradford, pp. 168-9
2. L. Whistler, *The Laughter and the Urn*, 1980, pp. 100-1

6.10

Georgia Sitwell

By Cecil Beaton, 1930

(opposite)

The photographs that Beaton took of Georgia at the August house party at Renishaw in 1930 could not be more different from those of Edith and the family. Gone is the Zoffanyesque pastiche of both the conversation piece (6.12) and of Edith with the black servant (4.1a). Instead, we are treated to a vision of an anonymous thirties vamp in slinky evening wear and helmet-like head-dress with the ultimate fashion accessory, her borzoi Feo, which had been smuggled in secretly and had to be kept in the stables so that Osbert should not find out.[1] Like the photograph of Edith, a variant of Georgia's appeared in the October *Vogue* with the note: 'Mrs Sachie Sitwell is not only one of the prettiest young marrieds but has in a very short time made herself a position strongly fortified by friendships.'[2]

1. Bradford, p. 219
2. British *Vogue*, 1.10.1930, p. 73

6.11

The Sacheverell Sitwells at Weston

By Fox Photos, 1929

a) Georgia and Edith at Brackley Station
b) Sacheverell and Georgia

A gabled, stone-built manor house dating from the late seventeenth century, Weston Hall had been purchased by a wealthy Northamptonshire man, Sir John Blencowe, for his daughter Susanna Jennens in 1721 and had then descended consistently through the female line in the families of the Barnardistons and Hebers to Harriet, née Wrightson, whose second husband, Colonel the Hon. Henry Hely-Hutchison (veteran of the Peninsular War and Waterloo), was Sir George Sitwell's grandfather. In 1911, on the death of his aunt Lady Hanmer, Sir George had inherited the contents of the house and her money, but it was not until 1923, on the death of another aunt, that he had been able to buy Weston with Sacheverell in mind, considering it an ideal house for a second son. In principle, it was ideal for Sacheverell: nothing, from family portraits to historic clothes and documents, had ever been sold, and eighteenth-century improvements and additions had created an extremely attractive and elegant interior. It was, however, remote, in a 'lost' Northamptonshire village, far away from the stimulus of the London life and culture on which Sacheverell and Georgia thrived, and, moreover, it was run-down. After an initial burst of enthusiasm for his new acquisition and its historical associations, Sir George showed little interest in the house. 'I don't intend to do much here; just a sheet of water and a line of statues', he had confided to Georgia when taking her round the garden.[1] He had no intention of giving it to Sacheverell outright, however, nor of raising his allowance; and it was with considerable misgivings that the young couple finally settled into the house in late 1927 and began the arduous task of transforming it.

These photographs were taken in connection with a double-page spread for a *Hello*-like feature in *The Sketch* that appeared under the title 'A Modern Poet in his Old-World Home: Mr. Sacheverell Sitwell and his Family at Weston Hall' on 28 August 1929. Whether Edith's presence there was by accident or design is not recorded. Osbert was probably in Algeciras with David Horner, otherwise he, too, might well have appeared in the feature.

August 1929 was in fact the first summer holiday that Sacheverell had spent apart from Osbert, and he and Georgia stayed quietly at Weston.[2] Despite increasingly glamorous trips abroad, mostly due to the generosity of friends like the Duke and Duchess of Westminster, their finances at this time were never less than precarious and from May 1931 to April 1932 Weston was virtually shut while they threw themselves at the mercy of various friends, including Lord Berners, with whom they lived at Faringdon and Halkin Street from October to April.[3] When social life started up again at Weston in the spring of 1932 circumstances were still somewhat straitened. Walton's publisher, Hubert Foss, and his wife, Dora, who had come to visit the composer, were among the first batch of guests and supplied a graphic corrective to the usual impression of Sitwell high life. 'Lunch was very late. Sacheverell kept on retiring back stage to see if it was ever coming. There was a butler and a young boy waiting. We started the meal with baked beans which appeared (and tasted) as if they had been an hour in the oven. This course was followed by slices of meat (species unidentifiable) covered with white sauce. The butler, when this was finished, solemnly dealt plates to all and, equally solemnly, removed them and replaced them with small pudding plates. A very small apple pie and a minute jug of cream were then rather gingerly partitioned.'[4]

1. Pearson, p. 262
2. Bradford, p. 205
3. *Ibid.*, pp. 226-7, 233
4. M. Kennedy, *Portrait of Walton*, 1989, p. 67

The Sitwell Family
By Cecil Beaton, 1930
(illustrated on page 199)

Beaton's famous group portrait taken during the August house party at Renishaw in 1930 is probably the only photograph to show the whole family. Apart from the Sargent painting (1.19), to which Beaton's portrait pays a modicum of homage, there is no further evidence that Sir George and Lady Ida posed with their children. While Beaton's personal interest during the holiday was clearly in photographing Edith and Georgia (see 4.1 and 6.10), Osbert, who had assumed the role of master of Renishaw now that his parents spent most of their time at Montegufoni, probably seized on Beaton's presence to create this memorable record of the Sitwell dynasty with its recent additions, Georgia and the three-year-old heir, Reresby. Tucked smugly behind the table with what looks suspiciously like Georgia's handbag in front of him, Osbert fails to steal the scene either from Edith at the centre of the composition or from Georgia, at her most fetching curled up on a stool. Taken in front of the tapestries in the ballroom at Renishaw, Beaton appears to have manoeuvred in extra furniture to create a feeling of opulent intimacy rather than imposing grandeur. Lady Ida perches stiffly and rather distantly on one of the famous Venetian chairs. Rarely seen in photographs, she was to die seven years later, worn out, partly as a result of marital neglect and alcohol.

Sacheverell and Georgia Sitwell with their two sons, Reresby and Francis
By A. V. Swaebe, General Press Agency, 1936

During July and August 1935, when Georgia was expecting her second child, she and Sacheverell had retired to Weston, where together with Francis Bamford they sorted out a cache of correspondence to Mary Heber, a previous owner of the house. When these were published as *Dear Miss Heber* the following year Georgia contributed a preface and Sacheverell the introduction. At the beginning of September they moved down to London, where their second son was born on 17 September. This photograph of the newly enlarged family was presumably taken some months later in the upstairs drawing-room at Weston, probably not long before Reresby, aged nine, was sent away to his first boarding school in May 1936.[1]

Sir George and Lady Ida were in England for the birth of the baby and though delighted with their new grandson did not approve of the name Niccolo, chosen after one of the former owners of Montegufoni and with which Sacheverell had hoped to please his father.[2] By the summer of 1936 the baby was being called Trajan and appeared as such in the dedication of *Dance of the Quick and the Dead* when it was published in October. It was not until the end of the year that he was finally called Francis, with Trajan as his second name.

1. Bradford, p. 258
2. *Ibid.*, p. 255

Mr and Mrs Sacheverell Sitwell in the Drawing-room at Weston Hall
By Etienne Drian, *c.* 1945

Drian was a French artist and illustrator who achieved some fame in the 1920s. In 1937 he is recorded in London, exhibiting at Walker's Galleries until 1939. His style suggests a certain amount of magazine work, but there is no evidence that this drawing was published. Although it might be assumed that Drian returned to France in 1939, Georgia's appearance suggests a post-war date for this attractive record of the Sacheverell Sitwells, who are seen here in the elegant drawing-room at Weston with portraits of Jennens and Barnardiston ancestors.

Sacheverell and Georgia had weathered the war in relative comfort, though the last years had been spoilt by uncertainty and eventual disappointment over Sir George's will. The disappearance of £77,000 of Sir George's money while under the care of his Swiss banker friend, Bernard Woog, meant that neither Sacheverell nor Georgia received anything, though provision had been made for their sons.[1] Despite the patronage of the wealthy novelist and patron, Bryher, the first cracks began to appear in Sacheverell's long and close relationship with Osbert, hastened by friction between his brother and Georgia and the apparent inequalities and uncertainties of their respective finances.

1. Bradford, pp. 320, 331

6.15

Lady Bridget Parsons

By Cecil Beaton, c. 1928

The daughter of the Earl of Rosse, Lady Bridget Parsons (1907-1972) was a friend of, among others, Zita Jungman and Cecil Beaton; and it was during a weekend at Beaton's country house, Ashcombe, in 1931 that Sacheverell met her and began his first major affair.[1] Seriously smitten, Sacheverell pursued her for the next two years, recording in detail in his diary every meeting, both social and clandestine. Lady Bridget was proud, sophisticated and difficult, and while prepared to be flirtatious was also aware of Sacheverell's still-hopeful designs on Zita. Sacheverell was finally rewarded on Tuesday 18 July 1933, 'and', as Sacheverell wrote in his diary, 'again, the next day. Not on Thursday, because of garden party, again on Friday, and again on Tuesday.'[2] By this time Georgia had found out about the affair and Sacheverell had additionally fallen in love with the beautiful ballet dancer Pearl Argyle (see 6.16).

Lady Bridget remained close to Sacheverell for twenty years, though the affair seems to have gradually petered out in the early 1950s. The woman of whom he had written in *Sacred and Profane Love* 'the long stem of her neck, with the unreal attenuation of her waist swelling into her lyre-like hips, her masculine shoulders, her long feline back, her thighs and her legs that had the muscles of a male dancer',[3] was later described as looking like 'the sort of woman you'd ask to take your children to school'.[4] She died – overweight, unmarried and unhappy – in 1972.

Cecil Beaton's friendship with Lady Bridget seems to have produced relatively few photographs, though she did pose with Lord Berners and other friends for some of the spoof pictures in *My Royal Past* (1939). This voluptuous image from the 1920s says a great deal about the cool and remote blonde who held Sacheverell in thrall for so many years.

1. Bradford, p. 224
2. *Ibid.*, p. 242
3. *Ibid.*, p. 294
4. *Ibid.*, p. 438

6.16

Pearl Argyle

By an unknown photographer, c. 1935

Described by Sir Frederick Ashton as 'the most beautiful woman of her generation', the ballet dancer Pearl Argyle (1910-1947) was in her early twenties when she met Sacheverell in the spring of 1933.[1] Simple, direct and from a suburban background, she relished Sacheverell's sophistication and the influence he was able to wield in the ballet on her behalf. While aware that she did not love him, Sacheverell was infatuated by her beauty. His fantasies about her at this time are woven into *Dance of the Quick and the Dead* (1936); and despite the fact that their relationship had begun to cool by 1935, her image pervades *Sacred and Profane Love* (1940) and much of his imaginative and poetic work until his death. In 1936 Pearl married the German film director Kurt Bernhard, and in 1939 she moved with her husband to Los Angeles. She died in 1947 in New York aged only thirty-six.[1]

1. Bradford, p. 336

6.17

Weston Hall

By Rex Whistler, 1929

Despite constant travelling, and long absences in London for the Season, Sacheverell became indivisibly associated with Weston and it was here that most of his prodigious literary output took place in the small first-floor study/dressing-room.

Having frequent weekend guests was one way of compensating for the lack of a London residence, and Rex Whistler was among the first to be invited. After their return from Venice and a visit to the Count Potockis in Poland in September 1929, Sacheverell and Georgia invited Whistler down the following month with the Mosleys, Lord Berners and Walton (now a frequent visitor).[1] Whistler and Berners both painted at Weston, but though Whistler's charming view of the old walled garden was apparently inscribed 'From the kitchen garden.

Oct. 1929', with its minor architectural inaccuracies and unseasonal-looking trees and vegetables, it must have been finished later.[2] The retreating back view of the tall figure with an axe represents Sacheverell, not otherwise known for his practical gardening abilities.[3]

1. Bradford, p. 208
2. L. Whistler and R. Fuller, *The Work of Rex Whistler*, 1960, p. 17
3. Bradford, p. 253

6.18

A View of the South Front, Weston Hall

By John Piper, *c.* 1942-1943

(opposite)

Osbert's commission for John Piper to illustrate his autobiography and record Renishaw (see 5.25) embraced other Sitwell domains, including Wood End and Scarborough, as well as nearby Derbyshire houses such as Hardwick, Sutton

Scarsdale and Bolsover. Although there is no evidence of bad blood between Piper and Sacheverell, the latter wrote to Moira Shearer early in 1951 of Piper's work with the Royal Ballet at Covent Garden: 'the new ballets will be sillier and sillier. Fancy having someone who likes drawing Methodist Chapels as arbiter of taste at Covent Garden.'[1] Piper was evidently unaware of Sacheverell's opinions and in Derek Parker's *Festschrift*, *Sacheverell Sitwell: A Symposium*, (1975), he wrote generously of Sacheverell's contribution to architectural studies.

Piper's gouache of Weston captures it at its most picturesque, with the elegant garden that Sacheverell and Georgia had established.

1. Bradford, p. 354

Georgia Sitwell's photograph albums,
c. 1927-1944
(illustrated on the following pages)

Georgia's photograph albums, covering the period from Reresby's birth in April 1927 to 1944, vividly illustrate the extensive foreign travel and hectic socialising that characterised the early years of her marriage, and are an invaluable supplement to her unpublished diaries. To take a year at random, in 1931 she and Sacheverell spent January cruising on the Dalmatian coast with the Duke and Duchess of Westminster on their yacht, the *Cutty Sark*. In February and March they went on to Egypt and the Sudan, visiting all the major sites, including Tutankhamun's tomb, which they were shown by Howard Carter. In early August they were in Portugal and Spain and later in the month they began a long trip to Scandinavia with Dick Wyndham. The albums also cover the trips to Roumania (1937) and North Africa (1938-1939), made in preparation for Sacheverell's first travel books, *Roumanian Journey* (1938) and *Mauretania* (1940).

Of enduring interest, and constituting a unique document of their times, however, are the photographs of the frequent house parties of the later 1920s and 1930s. Apart from the annual get-togethers at Renishaw and Montegufoni and the 1927 parties at Stephen Tennant's house, Wilsford, those at Denham with the Oswald Mosleys and at Tickerage with Dick Wyndham are particularly noteworthy for their range of fashionable guests. The presence of Cecil Beaton ensured a remarkable range of photographs, of which he presumably distributed small prints afterwards. Bendor and Loelia, Duke and Duchess of Westminster, were frequent travelling companions of Sacheverell and Georgia, though there is a gap in the albums after their divorce until the 1940s, when the family was invited to Eaton Hall in 1944.

As an unofficial record of Sacheverell's and Georgia's changing romantic interests, the albums are also very revealing. The constant presence of Zita Jungman (see 6.8) in the late 1920s is counterbalanced by holidays with Matisse's son-in-law, Georges Duthuit, in the early 1930s. Lady Bridget Parsons puts in frequent appearances in the mid-1930s, while in the later years of the war Georgia's boss in the Northamptonshire county police force, Chief Constable Captain R. H. D. Bolton, crops up at Weston and in Cambridge, succinctly captioned (by Reresby) as 'The Cop'.

Béla, Eddie Sackville-West, Cecil, Eleanor Wylie, Lee, Rosamund Lehmann
Rex   Robert   Stephen   Sachie

Self & Bunny

Cecil

Self & Rueoby

GRETA, TRISTRAM HILLIER. AND ME

LIDO   SEPTEMBER 1933.

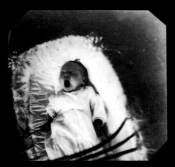

27. WELBECK ST
OCT 10th 1935.

Self + Sorlia at Karnak.

RERESBY + FRANCIS
IN THE NIGHT NURSERY

Constant Lambert + self

THE "BEATTLES" ETC.

Sach + self

6.20

Moira Shearer
By Robin Guthrie, 1944

Sacheverell first saw the beautiful red-haired ballerina and actress, Moira Shearer (b. 1926), when she took over the role of Princess Aurora in *The Sleeping Beauty* from Margot Fonteyn at Covent Garden in the spring of 1946. Although she had become a principal at Sadlers Wells two years previously, it was in effect her first big break. Sacheverell was enchanted, wrote her an extravagant fan letter and three weeks later fell wildly in love with her over lunch.[1]

An intelligent, well-educated Scots girl, Shearer weathered the showers of presents and passionate letters that poured from Sacheverell, while at the same time benefiting from his knowledge and experience of the ballet. Reluctantly accepting her as his inaccessible muse, Sacheverell followed her career closely, sending her poems when she flew off on tour to America and swapping gossip about the Covent Garden ballet world when he was working with Oliver Messel on the abortive film of *The Sleeping Beauty*

for Alexander Korda.[2] His ardour survived Shearer's marriage to (Sir) Ludovic Kennedy in 1950, and although it cooled gradually over the succeeding years they remained close friends and frequent correspondents until his death. Shearer and Pearl Argyle, the two ballerinas whom he loved, haunt much of his later poetic work, from *Cupid and the Jacaranda* (see 6.23) to the poems of the Brackley booklets.

Robin Guthrie's portrait of the young ballerina is one of several he painted at his studio in 5 Albion Street, and this thoughtful study dates from the year in which she became a principal at Sadlers Wells. In 1947, when she had begun filming Powell's and Pressburger's *The Red Shoes* (with which she made herself unforgettable the world over), Guthrie exhibited a painting of her as 'Spring' in the summer exhibition of the Royal Academy (no. 675).

1. Bradford, pp. 333-4
2. *Ibid.*, pp. 353-4

6.21

Patrick Leigh Fermor
By Derek Hill, *c.* 1983

Sacheverell met Patrick Leigh Fermor (b. 1915) in April 1936 at the London house shared by Costa Achillopoulo and Princess Anne-Marie Callimachi, who masterminded Sacheverell's trip to Roumania the following autumn. Still a young man of twenty-one, Leigh Fermor had just returned from extensive travels through Europe, including a year-long stay in Moldavia. His perceptive descriptions of the country aroused Sacheverell's interest and they became lifelong friends. In the autumn of 1939, marking time before he joined the Irish Guards, Leigh Fermor stayed at Weston. Some fifty years later he described life there as a 'marvellous haven' and remembered singing Noël Coward songs to Sacheverell, who listened 'as though it were to some secret and illicit enjoyment.'[1]

Leigh Fermor went on to fabled exploits with the Greek resistance in Crete and, after the war, began a career as a writer. His first book, *The Traveller's Tree* (1950), won the Heinemann and Kemsley prizes and was given a puff by Sacheverell in the *Sunday Times* as 'the most enjoyable book of the year'. He was painted by Derek Hill between the publication of *A Time of Gifts* (1977) and *Between the Woods and the Water* (1986).

1. Quoted in Bradford, p. 286

6.22

Design for the dust jacket of
The Hunters and the Hunted
By Irene Hawkins, *c.* 1947

After *Dance of the Quick and the Dead* (1936),
Sacheverell's 'entertainments of the imagination'
appeared in fairly quick succession, though taking
him longer to write than his travel and art
historical works. Like its four predecessors, *The
Hunters and the Hunted* (1947) is a series of rhapsodic
essays on any number of subjects that caught his
fancy; he had been working on it since the
completion of *Splendours and Miseries* in 1943. Its
title reflects the opening piece about a French
royal hunt, and the work concludes with 'The
Kingdom of the Birds', no less than seventy-five
pages of descriptions of exotic birds that were to
form the basis of *Fine Bird Books* (1953) and *Tropical
Birds* (1948). The book is dedicated to Edith's and
Sacheverell's patron, Bryher.

Irene Hawkins was the most faithful of
Sacheverell's illustrators and had first worked on
the dust jacket of *Edinburgh* (1938), written jointly
with Francis Bamford. Her design reflects the
eclectic nature of the book: on the front cover is a
spotted Appaloosa horse led by an eighteenth-
century groom; on the back a North American
Indian encampment; and on the spine a Shkoder
(Scutari) woman in costume.[1]

1. Ritchie, A47, pp. 122-3

6.23

Cupid and the Jacaranda
By Sacheverell Sitwell, 1952

The writing of Sacheverell's sixth 'entertainment
of the imagination' followed on almost
immediately from *The Hunters and the Hunted* in
1946. Begun in his fiftieth year, it is a
retrospective and autobiographical work looking
back over his life, travels, dreams and the heroes
and friends of his personal world, now in his
imagination 'more fully peopled than the world of
every day'. Never once mentioned by name, but
haunting the whole book, is the ghost of Pearl
Argyle, who had died young in New York in 1947
(see 6.16).

Irene Hawkins's dust jacket is drawn from
photographs of Spanish baroque churches
supplied by Sacheverell: on the front cover is the
Escalera Dorada of Burgos Cathedral, on the
back the Santuario de Ocotlán in Mexico. She
was to design two more covers for Sacheverell:
Truffle Hunt in 1953 and *Selected Works* in 1955.
The relationship came to an end in 1959 when his
publishers, Weidenfeld and Nicolson, would not
allow her to design the jacket for his Japanese
book, *Bridge of the Brocade Sash*.[1] They remained in
touch, however, and in 1975 he published *A Note
for Bibliophiles*, which describes their close
collaboration.[2]

1. Ritchie, p. 156
2. *Ibid*, A105, p. 192

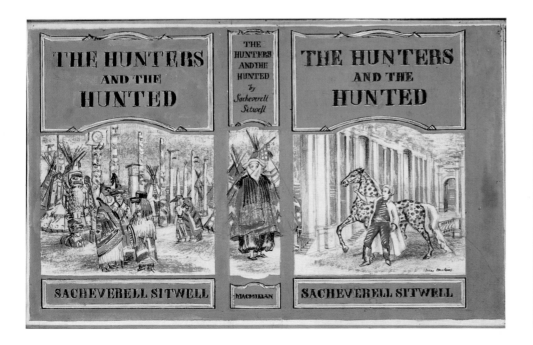

6.24

Denmark

By Sacheverell Sitwell, 1956

Sacheverell wrote some eleven travel books, beginning with the highly evocative *Roumanian Journey* (1938). After the war the publisher Harry Batsford accompanied Sacheverell on a trip to Holland in 1946 with a view to producing a book about the country. The result, *The Netherlands* (1948), written in Sacheverell's discursive and off-beat manner and concentrating on the lesser-known aspects of the country's life and culture, led to four more commissions from Batsford. *Spain* (1950) was the fulfilment of a lifetime's interest and perhaps the most successful of the series; while *Portugal and Madeira* (1954), in which he concentrated on the baroque and rococo heritage of the country, won him recognition from the Portuguese themselves.[1] The trip to Denmark was hurriedly undertaken with Georgia by car in August 1954 after a last-minute decision by Batsford, but the book was not written until the following summer.[2] It took him only three weeks, and reads accordingly in a typically breathless and light-hearted manner. The cover illustrates Benoist's coloured lithograph of the Christiansborg Palace and the Bourse in Copenhagen.[3]

There is no doubt that Sacheverell found these travel books a congenial way of earning a living. The trips provided pleasant and stimulating holidays abroad in places that interested him, and were invariably at his publisher's expense. The success of the series encouraged his publishers to cast their thoughts further afield and books on Brazil, Russia, the Holy Land and Persia were all in the pipeline at this time. In the event, it was the generosity of his patron Bryher, paying Georgia's air fares, that paved the way for his last four travelogues. *Arabesque and Honeycomb* (1957) covered two trips to the Middle East and Iran; while a lengthy stay in Japan in 1958 not only fulfilled a lifelong ambition but produced *Bridge of the Brocade Sash* (1959). His last two 'holiday' books, *Golden Wall and Mirador* (1961) and *The Red Chapels of Banteai Srei* (1962), dealing respectively with South America and Cambodia and India, were, however, poorly received.

1. Bradford, p. 368
2. *Ibid.*, p. 369
3. Ritchie, A60, pp. 145-6

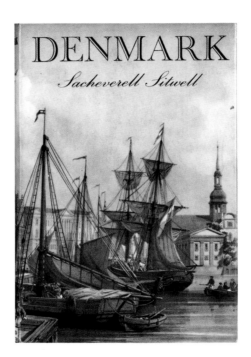

6.25

Sacheverell Sitwell in Home Guard uniform

By an unknown photographer, 1942

On the domestic front, the war years began on a sour note for Sacheverell and Georgia when, in January 1940, *The Sketch* magazine published a picture taken by their friend Costa four years previously, of Christmas round the fire at Weston with the Duchess of Westminster and Lady Bridget Parsons. This tactless display of upper-class sybaritism during a period of crisis was immediately seized on by Edith, but then more seriously by the *Daily Worker* and by William Joyce ('Lord Haw-Haw'), who, in his propaganda broadcast from Germany on 6 February 1940, made a vitriolic attack on Sacheverell and Georgia.[1]

After the 'phoney war' and Dunkirk, Sacheverell had dreaded being given a war job in a ministry, but he was even less pleased to be created adjutant to the general commanding the local Home Guard. Patrick Leigh Fermor (who was a frequent visitor in the early days of the war) and Georgia had to give him moral support and drive him to Brackley for the first day of his new incarnation as a soldier. After some manoeuvres in October 1940 he wrote to Osbert: 'Yesterday (from a military point of view) was the worst horror I have known since I was 21.'[2] Matters scarcely improved when in February 1941 at the time of the *Reynolds News* libel case (see 5.21) he was made second lieutenant in charge of a local platoon at Wappenham and later that year had to take part in a military review, his expression in the march-past apparently one of mute misery. His only excitement was provided by the Admiralty, who invited him to join a naval convoy as a civilian. They left Portsmouth early in 1942 and sailed around the British Isles, which Sacheverell hugely enjoyed.[3]

1. Bradford, p. 288
2. *Ibid.*, p. 291
3. *Ibid.*, p. 301

Sacheverell Sitwell at his desk, Weston
By Cecil Beaton, 1952

The 1950s were an exceptionally prolific decade for Sacheverell, with fourteen new books (seven of them travelogues) and his *Selected Works* (1955). His travels also included a lecture tour of the U.S.A. in late 1952, arranged by Georgia, who had been prompted by the example of Osbert's and Edith's triumphant progress through America (see 4.34). Cecil Beaton, who had also been tempted by this apparently effortless way of supplementing his income, followed closely in Sacheverell's steps the next year and was amused to collect stories of previous lecturers, including Sacheverell, who had apparently 'mumbled, rubbed one leg against another, picked his nails, skipped through his notes and, when asked about his sister, merely said, "Oh horrors".'[1] It was, however, in Chicago in October 1952 that he and Georgia learnt that Reresby had married against their wishes,[2] so he may well have been distracted at the time.

Beaton's published writings indicate that he always remained fond of Sacheverell, and a set of new photographs taken at Weston was probably arranged for inclusion in his new book *Persona Grata* (1953). Kenneth Tynan's text (from which Beaton dissociates himself in the Foreword) describes Weston: 'inside, there are wigstands, needlework carpets, oriental dolls, Turkish paintings, Ingres drawings [sold in 1964], croquet hoops, cocked hats, a Lely, a Van Dyck, parrot-wing pictures, purple freaked passion flowers, and half a dozen dogs. Amid this gallimaufry sits Sacheverell, an inscrutable, insatiable magpie. You are not surprised when he strikes up conversation by briskly remarking: "I went to Bedlam once."'[3]

1. H. Vickers, *Cecil Beaton*, 1985, p. 364
2. Bradford, p. 36
3. C. Beaton and K. Tynan, *Persona Grata*, 1953, p. 87

Letter from Sacheverell to Edith Sitwell, 24 September 1949

Edith was her younger brother's most loyal supporter and, during the years 1936-1948, a constant refrain of her correspondence with him was to encourage him to return to writing poetry. 'Now is the time to write some poetry, you owe it to us ... And the tide is turning', she wrote in 1943.[1] Then again in 1945: 'Now is our time – the tide has turned, we have many and powerful adherents.'[2] Sacheverell for his part never ceased to maintain that he only wrote poetry for Edith's sake. After the disastrous reviews of his *Canons of Giant Art* in 1933, which had caused him to cease writing poetry at all, in 1936 he nervously and apologetically dedicated his *Collected Poems* to her and wrote: 'These poems were written to give [Edith] pleasure and this must be ... their excuse and recommendation.'

Sacheverell did not return to writing poetry again until 1947, when a trip to Spain appeared to unlock his inspiration. This brief thank-you note to Edith for lunch in London concludes: 'I shall write more poems when I get home. Your encouragement has done more to help me than anything else – and, in fact, they are only written to try and interest you, my darling. My love, Sachie.'

1. Bradford, p. 318
2. *Ibid.*, p. 329

6.28
Green Edged Auricula
By John Farleigh
Illustrated in *Old Fashioned Flowers*,
by Sacheverell Sitwell, 1939

Today, when interest in old roses and other old-fashioned garden plants is commonplace, it is often forgotten that Sacheverell was at the forefront of the revival in their interest. His *Old Fashioned Flowers* and the much grander *Old Garden Roses* (1955) were pioneering works. In fact, he himself was no gardener, though an avid collector of old gardening books and seedsmen's catalogues.

Sacheverell's collaboration with his illustrator, John Farleigh (1900-1965), was conducted with great thoroughness and is particularly well documented in their correspondence.[1] At the appropriate season Farleigh would be summoned to Weston – in May 1937 to look at primroses, polyanthus, old roses, fuchsias and tulips, and the following year in April to see the auriculas. These flowers constitute the principal chapters in the book and for each Farleigh provided an outstanding plate in his distinctive style. A section of *Dance of the Quick and the Dead* (1936) had been devoted to Sacheverell's fascination with the auricula, which is here enlarged on; detailed instructions were given to Farleigh for an illustration of an auricula 'theatre', a device for displaying auriculas used by the Spitalfields weavers (who grew these engaging artificial-looking flowers as a hobby).

1. Ritchie, A38, pp. 102-3

6.29
British Architects and Craftsmen
By Sacheverell Sitwell, 1945

Conceived as a sequel to *Conversation Pieces* and *Narrative Pictures*, *British Architects and Craftsmen* is sub-titled 'A Survey of Taste, Design and Style during Three Centuries 1600 to 1830'. It was written during 1943 and 1944, when travelling abroad was out of the question, and with its exhortation to 'consider, rather, our own glorious past and draw profit from it for the future', can be seen in the wartime context of patriotic revival. Like its predecessors, it was a pioneering work that not only embraced architecture in its widest sense from the vernacular in Spitalfields to Wren, Adam, Kent and Wyatt, but also included the craftsmen who carried out their designs.

Its wide-ranging insights and readability have ensured *British Architects and Craftsmen* a permanent niche as a general introduction to the subject. Running into six editions (the last in 1973)[1], it is Sacheverell's most popular book in terms of printed copies. The dust jacket reproduces an aquatint of Thomas Archer's St Paul's, Deptford.

1. Ritchie, A46 (a-h), pp. 116-22

6.30
Sacheverell Sitwell
By Cecil Beaton, *c.* 1965

Beaton remained on cordial terms with Sacheverell and Georgia to the end of his life. In 1958 they were guests at his party at the Café Royal to celebrate the opening of *My Fair Lady* in London and his concurrent exhibition of designs for the show at the Redfern, and they met on holidays with the Rothschilds and elsewhere.

Always ambitious in directions other than photography, Beaton had tired of the faint praise that invariably greeted exhibitions of his drawings and designs, and in October 1953 he took the brave step of enrolling as a student at the Slade School of Fine Art for two days a week. He survived there for little more than a term but it brought home to him 'with an appalling cruelty the difference between the quality of the work I have been doing and that which it will be necessary for me to do if I am to succeed by serious standards'.[1] During the mid-1960s, when Beaton was assembling an exhibition of these 'serious' paintings, Sacheverell became one of the celebrity subjects whom Beaton tackled in his dramatic and often over-life-sized new approach. It is not clear if the painting was included in his exhibition at the Lefevre Gallery in January/February 1966; it may have been the similarly-sized *Poet* (no. 4).[2] Like most of the entirely anonymous portraits in the exhibition, it was not painted from life and indeed shows Sacheverell looking rather younger than he did at this date.

1. H. Vickers, *Cecil Beaton*, 1985, p. 370
2. *Ibid.*, p. 528

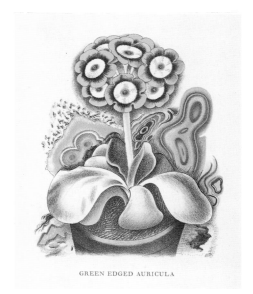

GREEN EDGED AURICULA

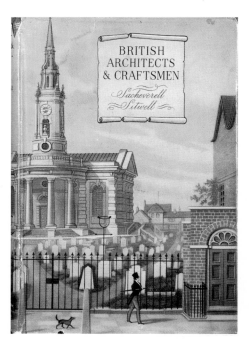

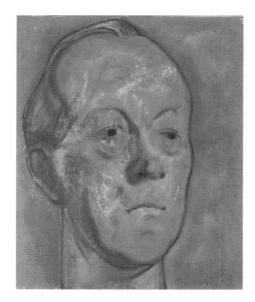

6.31
Sir Sacheverell Sitwell
By Derek Hill, *c.* 1970s

All the artists who painted Sacheverell in his later years were, in one way or another, well known to him personally. From the time of his marriage he had virtually ceased to collect paintings, partly no doubt because his income and lifestyle did not allow him to, and partly because Weston was already full of family portraits and pictures. He always enjoyed the company of artists, however, and book after book demonstrated that he was, if not precisely an art historian, at least one of the most perceptive and intelligent writers on art of his day.

Sacheverell and Georgia had known Derek Hill (b. 1910) since the 1930s when they had all been guests at Cecil Beaton's famous *fête-champêtre* at Ashcombe in July 1937.[1] Hill's painting of forty years later is both one of the most idiosyncratic likenesses of Sacheverell and also one of the most convincing. A smaller companion portrait of Georgia was painted at the same time.

1. Bradford, p. 265

6.32
Sir Sacheverell Sitwell
By Graham Sutherland, 1973

Graham Sutherland (1903-1980) and Sacheverell had known each other since the 1950s. They had many friends in common, especially in Venice where both were frequent guests in the late summer. Sutherland, the most distinguished if controversial portrait painter of his age, was an obvious choice therefore when Georgia decided to commission a portrait of Sacheverell in his seventy-fifth year.

Neither Sacheverell nor Georgia particularly liked the Sutherland when it finally arrived. An inauspicious start had been made when Georgia viewed the painting at the Marlborough Gallery and was shown one of the versions of Sutherland's 1965 portrait of the German Chancellor, Konrad Adenauer, to whom Sacheverell now bore a slight resemblance.[1] Writing in 1981 to Sutherland's biographer, Roger Berthoud, Sacheverell thought Georgia had paid £1,000 for the portrait: 'expensive in my opinion ... I doubt if I have made £1,000 in the whole of my life, writing some sixty or seventy books and reams of poetry since 1918.' It seemed to him 'more the portrait of a footballer than the portrait of a poet'.[2] Expensive or not, the price was extremely modest compared to the £22,500 that Sutherland received in 1975 for his portrait of the geophysicist Pierre Schlumberger. A more thoughtful version of the portrait is in the Graham Sutherland Gallery at Picton Castle.

1. Bradford, p. 430
2. R. Berthoud, *Graham Sutherland: A Biography*, 1982, p. 284

6.33
Sir Sacheverell Sitwell
By Dudley Reed, 1982
(illustrated on page 201)

Dudley Reed's photograph was commissioned to accompany an interview in the *Tatler* for Sacheverell's eighty-fifth birthday. 'You try being 85', he said to the interviewer, Byron Rogers. 'You will not like it very much. I never thought I would live this old. You don't. I think I feel about 60, and I'm determined not to give in to it. I fear loss of memory.'[1] Sacheverell was photographed in the library at Weston in front of Tchelitchew's 1935 pastel of Edith (4.11).

1. *Tatler*, December 1982 and January 1983, p. 108

Childhood at Renishaw

1.1
**Lady Sitwell with Florence and
Sir George**
By George du Maurier, *c.* 1881
Pencil, pen and sepia ink on paper,
15.8 x 22.2
Signed (br): *G du Maurier*
Sir Reresby Sitwell Bt

1.2
Sir George Sitwell
Attributed to Canon Frederick Harford,
issued by A & G Taylor, 1876
Albumen imperial print, 22.5 x 16.5
Stamped on reverse: *A. & G. Taylor
Photographers to the Queen, 153 Regent St N*
Sir Reresby Sitwell Bt

1.3
**Archibald Campbell Tait,
Archbishop of Canterbury**
By James Jacques Tissot ('Coide'), 1869
Colour lithograph, image: 30 x 18.5
Published in *Vanity Fair*, 25 December
1869 as Statesmen No. 38, "An earnest
and liberal Primate"
National Portrait Gallery (D4405)

1.4
**Randall Davidson, Baron Davidson
of Lambeth**
By Sir Leslie Ward ('Spy'), 1901
Colour lithograph, image: 34.5 x 20.8
Published in *Vanity Fair*, 19 December
1901 as "Prelate of the Garter"
National Portrait Gallery (D4406)

1.5
'The Capture of a Spirit'
The Graphic, 7 February 1880
Printed magazine, 42 x 31
Sir Reresby Sitwell Bt

1.6
Electioneering ephemera
Selection of printed cards
Sir Reresby Sitwell Bt

1.7
Lady Ida Sitwell
By Sir William Blake Richmond, 1888
Oil on canvas, 116 x 88.3
Sir Reresby Sitwell Bt

1.8
Sir George Sitwell
By Henry Tonks, 1898
Oil on canvas, 91.5 x 71.1
Signed and dated (bl): *Henry Tonks/1886*
Sir Reresby Sitwell Bt

1.9
**Edith Davis with Osbert, Edith
and Sacheverell Sitwell**
By Cromack, Scarborough, 1898
Bromide cabinet print, 14.6 x 10
Sir Reresby Sitwell Bt

1.10
Edith Sitwell with her Mother
By John Thomson, *c.* 1888
Platinum cabinet print, 14.5 x 10
Francis Sitwell

1.11
Edith Sitwell
By W. D. Brigham, Scarborough, *c.* 1890
Albumen cabinet print, 14 x 9.9
Sir Reresby Sitwell Bt

1.12
**Edith Sitwell at Art Class in
Scarborough**
By an unknown photographer,
c. 1898-1900
Copy print from E. Salter, *Edith Sitwell*,
1979, p. 37

1.13
Edith Sitwell
By W. D. Brigham, Scarborough, *c.* 1904
Carbon cabinet print, 14 x 9.3
Inscribed below print: *Brigham*, and on
reverse: *This portrait of Edith Sitwell at the
age of 17 is the property of her aunt Florence
Alice Sitwell*
Sir Reresby Sitwell Bt

1.14
Osbert Sitwell
By Cromack, Scarborough, *c.* 1896
Bromide cabinet print, 14.4 x 9.9
Sir Reresby Sitwell Bt

1.15
Sacheverell Sitwell
By Cromack, Scarborough, 1899
Bromide cabinet print, 14.7 x 9.8
Sir Reresby Sitwell Bt

1.16
Osbert Sitwell
By Cromack, Scarborough, *c.* 1902
Bromide cabinet print, 14.4 x 9.4
Sir Reresby Sitwell Bt

1.17
Sacheverell Sitwell
By Sarony, *c.* 1908
Carbon cabinet print, 15.9 x 8.3
Sir Reresby Sitwell Bt

1.18
Renishaw Hall
By an unknown photographer, *c.* 1910
Sir Reresby Sitwell Bt

a) From the south
Bromide print, 17.2 x 24.8

b) From the north
Bromide print, 18.1 x 25.3

1.19
The Sitwell Family
By John Singer Sargent, 1900
Oil on canvas, 170 x 193
Signed (bl): *John S. Sargent*
Sir Reresby Sitwell Bt

1.20
Wood End

a) Lady Sitwell in the conservatory
By an unknown photographer, *c.* 1890s
Platinum print, 28.5 x 24
Sir Reresby Sitwell Bt

b) Wood End from the garden
Photographed for the National Buildings
Record, 1981
Bromide print, 25.3 x 20.2
© RCHME Crown Copyright

1.21
**The Esplanade, Scarborough,
at Noon**
By George Washington Wilson, *c.* 1890s
Albumen print, 19.2 x 29
Scarborough Reference Library

1.22
Henry Moat and Reresby Sitwell
By an unknown photographer,
Scarborough, August 1936
Copy print from an original snapshot in
the collection of Sir Reresby Sitwell Bt

Catalogue

1.23

'He gained a fortune but he gave a son'
Portrait of Henry Moat
By Christopher Richard Wynne
Nevinson, 1918
Oil on canvas, 40 x 50.6
Signed and dated (br): *C. R. W. Nevinson 1918*
University of Hull Art Collection

1.24

Montegufoni

a) South front and east baroque façade
By Alinari, Florence, *c.* 1905
Modern print from original negative,
25.5 x 20.3
National Portrait Gallery (EW 738/2)

b) South front entrance
By Alinari, Florence, *c.* 1905
Carbon print, 26 x 20
Studio stamp (br)
Francis Sitwell

c) The Court of the Duke of Athens
(not illustrated)
By Alinari, Florence, *c.* 1905
Carbon print, 25.6 x 19.2
Studio stamp (br)
Sir Reresby Sitwell Bt

d) Montegufoni from the road
(not illustrated)
By an unknown photographer, *c.* 1910
Copy print from an original photograph
in the collection of Sir Reresby Sitwell Bt

1.25

On the Making of Gardens
By Sir George Sitwell, 1909
Published by John Murray, London
Printed book, spine height: 22.3
Inscribed on the half-title page:
Florence Alice Sitwell/ from George
Francis Sitwell

1.26

Sir George Sitwell leaving the Old Bailey
Photograph for the *Daily Sketch*,
12 March 1915
Bromide print, 21.7 x 16.5
John Pearson

1.27

Facsimiles from the *Daily Mirror*, 13 March 1915; the *News of the World*, 14 March 1915; the *Daily Express*, 15 March 1915

1.28

Lady Ida Sitwell
By Bassano, 1904
Sepia platinotype print, 19.5 x 14.5
Sir Reresby Sitwell Bt

Nos. 1.29-1.31 are not illustrated

1.29

On the Making of Gardens
By Sir George Sitwell, 1949
Published by The Dropmore Press
Printed book, spine height: 24
From an edition of 1,000, illustrated by
John Piper, numbered and signed by
Osbert Sitwell and the artist
Sir Reresby Sitwell Bt

1.30

Two letters from Henry Moat to Osbert Sitwell

a) Renishaw Hall, 24 August 1908
Autograph manuscript, headed notepaper,
single folio folded, 17.7 x 11.2

b) Wood End, 9 November 1908
Autograph manuscript, postcard,
8.9 x 11.4
Sir Reresby Sitwell Bt

1.31

Letter from Sir George Sitwell to Osbert Sitwell, *c.* 1917
Autograph manuscript, 17.7 x 11.5
Sir Reresby Sitwell Bt

London and the War

2.1

Sergei Diaghilev
By Elizabeth Polunin, *c.* 1920
Oil on canvas, 69 x 52
Signed (bl): *Elizabeth Polunin*
Polunin Family

2.2

Igor Stravinsky playing *The Rite of Spring*
By Jean Cocteau, 1913
Pen and ink on paper, 15.5 x 18.5
Signed and dated (b): *Jean/1913*
Theatre Museum: Courtesy of the
Board of Trustees of the Victoria and
Albert Museum

2.3

Tamara Karsavina as the Firebird
By Bertram Park, 1912
Toned bromide print, 20.4 x 15.9
Signed on tissue mount (bl): *Bertram Park*
Private Collection

2.4

Poster for the *Ballets Russes* at the Théâtre des Champs-Elysées
By Jean Cocteau, 1913
Lithograph, 188 x 127
Signed in the plate (bl): *JEAN/COCTEAU*
Theatre Museum: Courtesy of the
Board of Trustees of the Victoria and
Albert Museum

2.5

Lydia Lopokova
By Pablo Picasso, 1919
Pencil on paper, 35.5 x 24.1
Signed and dated (tr): *Picasso/Londres 1919*
Syndics of the Fitzwilliam Museum,
Cambridge

2.6

Sacheverell Sitwell
By Maurice Beck and Helen Macgregor,
1924
Bromide print, 28.4 x 22.3
Sir Reresby Sitwell Bt

2.7

Violet Trefusis
By Sir John Lavery, *c.* 1920
Oil on canvas, 38 x 26
Signed (bl): *J. Lavery*
Private Collection

2.8

Lady Cunard with George Moore in her Grosvenor Square Drawing-room
By Sir John Lavery, 1925
Oil on canvas, 62.2 x 75
Signed (bl): *J. Lavery*
Sir Rupert Hart-Davis

2.9

Lady Diana Cooper
By Emil Otto Hoppé, January 1916
Modern print from original negative,
30.5 x 25.5
The Mansell Collection

2.10

Osbert Sitwell
By Emil Otto Hoppé, 1918
Modern print from original negative,
25.5 x 20.3
The Mansell Collection

2.11

Osbert Sitwell
By Geoffrey Gunther, 1918
Pencil, pen and ink on paper, 14.6 x 5.9
Signed (br) in monogram and dated *1918*
The Provost and Fellows, Eton College

2.12

The Winstonburg Line
By Osbert Sitwell, 1919
Published by Hendersons, London
Printed pamphlet, spine height: 22
David Mayou

2.13

Siegfried Sassoon
By Pirie MacDonald, *c.* 1920
Bromide print, 22.6 x 15
Photographer's stamp (br), inscribed below
print: *For Osbert from SS* (monogram)
Sir Reresby Sitwell Bt

2.14

Wilfred Owen
By John Gunston, 1916
Bromide postcard print, 13.8 x 8.8
National Portrait Gallery (P515)

2.15

Ivo Charteris
By Langfier Ltd, *c.* 1915
Carbon print, 36 x 27.4
Inscribed (br): *Ivo Alan Charteris -/ - killed in action/ Sept 17th 1915 -/ Aged 19*
Sir Reresby Sitwell Bt

2.16

Edith Sitwell
By Nina Hamnett, 1915
Pencil and green crayon on paper,
40 x 26.4
Signed and dated (b): *N. Hamnett. 1915*
Art Collection, Harry Ransom
Humanities Research Center,
The University of Texas at Austin

2.17

Osbert Sitwell
By Nina Hamnett, *c.* 1920s
Oil on canvas, 50.5 x 40.6
Inscribed on reverse: *Sir Osbert Sitwell/R. Nevinson* [sic]
National Portrait Gallery (5916)

2.18

Osbert Sitwell
Attributed to Nina Hamnett, *c.* 1920s
Pencil on paper, 25.4 x 19.9
Inscribed (bl): *sketches for/your portrait*
Sir Reresby Sitwell Bt

2.19

Omega Screen
By an unknown artist, *c.* 1919
Oil on canvas, stretched on four panels,
178 x 200 (uneven)
Sir Reresby Sitwell Bt

2.20

Nina Hamnett
By Roger Fry, 1917
Oil on canvas, 82 x 61
Signed and dated (br): *R. F. 1917.*
Courtauld Institute Galleries, London
(Fry Collection)

2.21

Roger Fry
By A. C. Cooper, 28 February 1918
Bromide print, 18 x 15.4
National Portrait Gallery (x4294)

2.22

Edith Sitwell
By Roger Fry, 1918
Oil on canvas, 61 x 41
Signed and dated (bl): *Roger Fry. 1918*
[date indistinct]
Sheffield City Art Galleries

2.23

Alvaro Guevara
By George Beresford, 1920
Modern prints from original negatives
National Portrait Gallery (X6510/1)

2.24

Brian Howard
By an unknown photographer, *c.* 1925
Bromide print, 25.5 x 20
The Provost and Fellows, Eton College

2.25

Iris Tree
By Vanessa Bell, 1915
Oil on canvas, 121.9 x 91.4
Signed and dated (tr): *V. BELL/1915*
Private Collection

2.26

The Editor of *Wheels*
By Alvaro Guevara, *c.* 1919
Oil on canvas, 183 x 122
Tate Gallery, presented by Lord Duveen,
Walter Taylor and George Eumorfopoulos
through the National Art Collections
Fund 1920

2.27

Nancy Cunard
By Alvaro Guevara, 1919
Oil on canvas, 213.7 x 122.2
National Gallery of Victoria, Melbourne,
Australia (Felton Bequest, 1954)

2.28

Wheels
Six anthologies of verse, 1916-1921
Francis Sitwell

a) *Wheels: An Anthology of Verse*
Published by B. H. Blackwell, Oxford, 1916
Printed book, spine height: 20.5

b) *Wheels: A Second Cycle*
Published by B. H. Blackwell, Oxford, 1917
Printed book, spine height: 20

c) *Wheels 1918: A Third Cycle*
Published by B. H. Blackwell, Oxford, 1919
Edited by Edith Sitwell
Printed book, spine height: 20.1

d) *Wheels 1919: Fourth Cycle*
Published by B. H. Blackwell, Oxford, 1919
Edited by Edith Sitwell
Printed book, spine height: 19

e) *Wheels 1920: Fifth Cycle*
Published by Duckworth, London, 1928
Edited by Edith Sitwell
Printed book, spine height: 19

f) *Wheels 1921: Sixth Cycle* [two copies]
Published by C. W. Daniel Ltd, London, 1921
Edited by Edith Sitwell
Printed book, spine height: 21

2.29

A Shell Dump
By William Roberts, 1919
Pen, ink and water-colour on paper,
44.9 x 52.5
Signed and dated (l): *William Roberts. 1919.*
Sir Reresby Sitwell Bt

2.30

From an Office Window
By Christopher Richard Wynne Nevinson,
1917
Oil on canvas, 64.3 x 49
Signed (br): *C. R. W. Nevinson*
Sir Reresby Sitwell Bt

2.31

**The Drawing-room at 2 Carlyle
Square, Chelsea**
By Ethel Sands, *c.* 1920-1925
Oil on canvas, 65 x 47
Signed (bl): *Ethel Sands*
Janet Cooper

2.32

**Photograph of the wardrobe
painted by Ethel Sands in 1924**
By Lewis Morley, 1963
Bromide print, 30.4 x 25.5
National Portrait Gallery (x45390)

2.33

**The Drawing-room, 2 Carlyle
Square**
Copy print from the *Illustrated London News*,
16 October 1926

2.34

Interior of 2 Carlyle Square
By E. J. Mason for *Homes and Gardens*,
January 1936
Bromide prints, 26 x 20.3 each
Sir Reresby Sitwell Bt

a) Dining-room
b) Drawing-room
c) Back room, ground floor
d) Drawing-room (not illustrated)

2.35

Sir Edward Marsh
By Frank Dobson, 1938
Bronze, 38 high
Doncaster Museums & Art Service

2.36

Art and Letters
Nos 1-4 (new series), London, 1918-1919
Four printed magazines, spine height:
24.1 each
Sir Reresby Sitwell Bt

2.37

Who Killed Cock-Robin?
By Osbert Sitwell, 1921
Published by C. W. Daniel Ltd, London
Printed book, spine height: 19
Sir Reresby Sitwell Bt

2.38

Robert Ross
By Elliott and Fry, *c.* 1914
Carbon print, 15.1 x 20.2
National Portrait Gallery (x12885)

2.39

Sir Edmund Gosse
By John Russell and Sons, *c.* 1916
Bromide print, 15.3 x 11.1
National Portrait Gallery (x38473)

2.40

Arnold Bennett
By Howard Coster, 1929
Transferotype, 25.8 x 23
National Portrait Gallery (Ax 2299)

2.41

Woman, Harlequin and Pierrot
By Pablo Picasso, 1918
Pencil on paper, 30.2 x 22.4 (sight)
Signed and dated (bl): *Picasso/18*
Private Collection

2.42

Mother and Child

By Amedeo Modigliani, c. 1914-1916

Pencil on paper, 41.5 x 25.8

Inscribed and signed (tl):

à/Zborowski./modigliani

Francis Sitwell

2.43

At the House of Mrs Kinfoot

By Osbert Sitwell, 1921

Privately published in an edition of 101 by

The Favil Press, Kensington

Printed book, spine height: 18.7

Signed by the author and numbered *6*

Sir Reresby Sitwell Bt

2.44

To the Lord of Song

By William Roberts, c. 1913-1914

Pencil on paper, 9.9 x 9.7 (sight)

Signed (bl): *Roberts* and inscribed (t)

as above

Private Collection

2.45

Robert Nichols

By Augustus John, 1921

Chalk on paper, 30.5 x 24.1

Signed and dated (bl): *John./21*

National Portrait Gallery (3825)

2.46

Virginia Woolf

By Vanessa Bell, 1912

Oil on canvas, 40 x 34

National Portrait Gallery (5933)

2.47

Giles Lytton Strachey

By Nina Hamnett, c. 1917

Chalk on paper, 40.6 x 16.5

Signed (b): *N. H.*

National Portrait Gallery (2215)

2.48

Walter Richard Sickert with his

wife Thérèse Lessore

By Cecil Beaton, 1941

Bromide print, 25.7 x 22.2

National Portrait Gallery (x14204)

2.49

Ada Leverson

By Rita Martin, c. 1911

Bromide print, 14.5 diameter

Inscribed on photographer's pre-stamped

mount (b): *To darling Mama with Ada's love*

Francis Wyndham

2.50

Ronald Firbank

By Augustus John, c. 1915

Pencil on paper, 33 x 31.8

National Portrait Gallery (4600)

2.51

Harold Monro

By Jacob Kramer, 1923

Ink and chalk on paper, 34 x 17

Signed (br): *Kramer*

National Portrait Gallery (4705)

2.52

William Henry Davies

By Augustus John, 1918

Pencil on paper, 29.2 x 22.9

Inscribed, signed and dated (br): *To W. H.*

Davies/from Augustus John/Nov. 1918

National Portrait Gallery (3149)

2.53

Violet Gordon Woodhouse

By Herbert Lambert, 1929

Bromide print, 34.1 x 43.5

Signed and dated on tissue mount (bl):

Herbert Lambert/1929

The Royal Photographic Society

Nos. 2.54-2.74 are not illustrated

2.54

Adolf Bolm and Tamara Karsavina

in *The Firebird*

By Henri Gaudier-Brzeska, 1912

Bronze, 61 high

Incised: *Gaudier/Brzeska* on base

Mercury Gallery, London

2.55

Tamara Karsavina as the Firebird

By Adrian Allinson, c. 1918

Oil on hardboard, 64 x 52.5

Signed (bl): *Allinson*

Theatre Museum: Courtesy of the

Board of Trustees of the Victoria and

Albert Museum

2.56

Programme for the Russian Ballet

season at the Empire Theatre,

London, 1919

Printed booklet, spine height: 24.6

Theatre Museum: Courtesy of the Board

of Trustees of the Victoria and Albert

Museum

2.57

Osbert Sitwell

By Sarony, c. 1911-1912

Carbon cabinet print, 16.2 x 9.9

Sir Reresby Sitwell Bt

2.58

'Babel'

By Osbert Sitwell

Facsimile from *The Times*, 5 May 1916

2.59

Herbert Read

By Jacob Kramer, 1914

Charcoal on paper, 25.5 x 21

Signed (br): *Kramer*

Private Collection

2.60

'Drowned Suns'

By Edith Sitwell

Facsimile from the *Daily Mirror*,

13 March 1913

2.61

The Mother and Other Poems

By Edith Sitwell, 1915

Published by B. H. Blackwell, Oxford

Printed booklet, spine height: 19.3

Inscribed on cover: *Mrs Schumacher with best*

wishes from Edith Sitwell

Francis Sitwell

2.62

Twentieth Century Harlequinade

and Other Poems

By Edith and Osbert Sitwell, 1916

Published by B. H. Blackwell, Oxford

Printed booklet, spine height: 18.7

Francis Sitwell

2.63

Clowns' Houses

By Edith Sitwell, 1918

Published by B. H. Blackwell, Oxford

Printed booklet, spine height: 19.6

Inscribed in ES's hand: *To Helen with my*

very best love and gratitude

Francis Sitwell

2.64

Dinner at the Golden Cross, Oxford

By Gabriel Atkin, 1919

Pen and ink on paper, 18.5 x 23.8

Signed and dated (b): *Gabriel Atkin, 1919.*

Scarborough Art Gallery, Scarborough

Borough Council

2.65

French Art 1914-19

Exhibition catalogue, Mansard Gallery,

Tottenham Court Road, August 1919

Printed booklet, spine height: 17

Sir Reresby Sitwell Bt

2.66

Design for the cover of *Wheels 1920*

By Gino Severini, 1920

Gouache on paper, 19.4 x 13.4 (sight)

Signed (b): *G. Severini*

Francis Sitwell

2.67

Cranks, 1921, An Anthology

Compiled by Obert, Sebert and

Ethelberta Standstill, 1921

Published by Arthur H. Stockwell,

London

Printed pamphlet, spine height: 20

Bertram Rota Limited

2.68

The People's Palace

By Sacheverell Sitwell, 1918

Published by B. H. Blackwell, Oxford

Printed book, spine height: 19.4

Ulysses Bookshop, London

2.69

The Eton Candle

Edited by Brian Howard and Harold

Acton, 1922, published at Eton

Printed book, spine height: 27.1

The Provost and Fellows, Eton College

2.70

John Collings Squire

By John Mansbridge, 1932-1933

Oil on canvas, 62.2 x 74.9

Signed (bl): *John Mansbridge*

National Portrait Gallery (4110)

2.71

Facsimiles from the *Daily Express*

a) 'Asylum School of Poetry' by Louis

J. McQuilland, 20 July 1920

b) 'Poet's Defence of "Asylum School"' by

Osbert Sitwell, 22 July 1920

2.72

Triple Fugue

By Osbert Sitwell, 1924

Published by Grant Richards Ltd, London

Printed book, spine height: 19.5

Private Collection

2.73

Lady Colefax

By Cecil Beaton, 1930s

Resin-coated bromide print, 25.4 x 20.2

Sotheby's, London

2.74

Edith and Osbert in the Drawing-room, 2 Carlyle Square

By an unknown photographer

Copy print from *The Graphic*,
2 March 1929

Façade and the Twenties

3.1

Edith Sitwell

By Maurice Lambert, *c.* 1926-1927

Aluminium cast (1984), 35.4 high

National Portrait Gallery (5801)

3.2

Osbert Sitwell

By Frank Dobson, 1921-1922

Polished brass cast (1994), 32 high

Jason & Rhodes

3.3

Osbert Sitwell

By Frank Dobson, 1921-1922

Painted plaster, 35.5 high

Jason & Rhodes

3.4

Osbert Sitwell

By Hugh Cecil, *c.* 1925

Bromide print, 19.2 x 24.6

Bears photographer's blind stamp

Signed on mount (br): *Hugh Cecil*

Sir Reresby Sitwell Bt

3.5

Photographs by Maurice Beck and Helen Macgregor

a) Osbert, 1924

Bromide print, 29 x 23.5

Signed on mount: *Maurice Beck/Macgregor*

Sir Reresby Sitwell Bt

b) Sacheverell, 1924

Bromide print, 28.6 x 22.8

Signed on mount: *Maurice Beck/Macgregor*

Sir Reresby Sitwell Bt

c) Edith, 1924

Bromide print, 32.9 x 25.6

Signed on mount: *Maurice Beck/Macgregor*

Sir Reresby Sitwell Bt

d) Edith with eyes closed, 1924
(not illustrated)

Bromide print, 32.4 x 26.6

Signed on mount: *Maurice Beck/Macgregor*

Sir Reresby Sitwell Bt

e) Osbert, Edith and Sacheverell, 1924
(not illustrated)

Copy print, courtesy of *Vogue*

© The Condé Nast Publications Limited

f) Osbert, 1924 (not illustrated)

Bromide print, 11.6 diameter

National Portrait Gallery (x12506)

3.6

Mr Osbert and Mr Sacheverell Sitwell

By Max Beerbohm, 1923

Pencil and wash on paper, 40 x 29 (sight)

Signed and dated (bc): *Max/1923*.

Inscribed as above

Scarborough Art Gallery, Scarborough Borough Council

3.7

Mr Osbert and Mr Sacheverell Sitwell

By Max Beerbohm, 1925

Pencil and gouache on paper,
29.6 x 21.7 (sight)

Signed and dated (beneath paint r):
[*Max/Rapallo. 25*]

Inscribed (bl): *Osbert and Mr Sacheverill Sitwell* [*sic*]

Francis Sitwell

3.8

William Walton

By Maurice Lambert, *c.* 1925

Bronze, 29.2 high

Incised with monogram: *ML*

National Portrait Gallery (5913)

3.9

Harlequin and Pulcinella in the Snow

Illustration for frontispiece of *Façade*

By Gino Severini, *c.* 1921

Gouache on paper, 19.5 x 13.7

Signed (br): *G. Severini*

Francis Sitwell

3.10

Façade

By Edith Sitwell, 1922

Published by The Favil Press, Kensington

Printed book, spine height: 18.8

Two copies: one inscribed *Edith Sitwell*, the other: *Darling Mother/with Edith's very best love*

Francis Sitwell

3.11

Curtain design for *Façade*

By Frank Dobson, 1922

Copy print from photograph of original drawing, 1922, published in British *Vogue*, 15 July 1923

Courtesy of *Vogue*, © The Condé Nast Publications Limited

3.12

Autograph manuscript of the 'Valse' from *Façade*

By Sir William Walton, *c.* 1922-1923

6 fols., pencil on paper, 32.6 x 23.7

Signed on final page

Francis Sitwell

3.13

Press cuttings of reviews of the first public performance of *Façade* at the Aeolian Hall, London, 12 June 1923

Facsimiles from the *Daily Express*, 13 June 1923; *The Times*, 14 June 1923; the *Daily Graphic*, 14 June 1923

3.14

***Façade* at the New Chenil Galleries, April 1926**

a) Edith, Osbert and Sacheverell Sitwell

By Pacific and Atlantic Photos Ltd, 1926

Vintage press print, bromide, 25.5 x 20.2

Sir Reresby Sitwell Bt

b) Edith with Neil Porter

Copy print from a publicity photograph

Sir Reresby Sitwell Bt

3.15

Curtain design for *Façade*

By John Piper, 1942

Lithograph, 45.2 x 58.6 (image size)

Signed in pencil (br): *John Piper* and numbered (bl): *41/100*

The William Walton Trust

3.16

Three *Commedia dell'Arte* Musicians

Design for a fresco at Montegufoni

By Gino Severini, 1922

Gouache on paper, 22.6 x 29.2 (sight)

Signed and dated (br):
G. Severini/AD/M.C.M. xxii

Francis Sitwell

3.17

The Serenade

By Gino Severini, c. 1922

Gouache on paper, 25 x 18 (sight)

Signed (br): *G. Severini*

Francis Sitwell

3.18

Design for the dust jacket of
The Thirteenth Caesar

By Gino Severini, 1924

Pen, ink and sepia wash on paper,
14.6 x 12.7 (sight)

Signed (br): *G. Severini*

Francis Sitwell

3.19

Design for the dust jacket of
The Cyder Feast

By Gino Severini, 1927

Pen, ink and sepia wash on paper,
13.7 x 11.9

Signed (b): *G. Severini*

Francis Sitwell

3.20

Noël Coward

By Dorothy Wilding, 1925

Chlorobromide print, 43.2 x 31.7

Signed on tissue mount (bl):
Dorothy Wilding

The Royal Photographic Society

3.21

'The Swiss Family Whittlebot'

By Noël Coward, 1923

a) Facsimile from *The Sketch*,
26 September 1923

b) *Poems by Hernia Whittlebot with an
appreciation by Noël Coward*
Privately printed, 1923
Printed booklet, spine height: 25.5
Theatre Museum: Courtesy of the
Board of Trustees of the Victoria and
Albert Museum

3.22

Constant Lambert

By Christopher Wood, 1926

Oil on canvas, 91.4 x 55.9

National Portrait Gallery (4443)

3.23

The Rio Grande

Miniature score of a poem by
Sacheverell Sitwell, set to music by
Constant Lambert, 1929
Published by the Oxford University Press,
1942
Booklet, spine height: 19.6
Private Collection

3.24

William Walton

By Rex Whistler, 1929

Pencil on paper, 27.9 x 23.5

Signed (br): *Rex Whistler.* Inscribed above
signature: *Willie./-Haus Hirth/AN 27 1929.*

National Portrait Gallery (4640)

3.25

Bath

By Edith Sitwell, 1932

Published by Faber & Faber, London

Printed book, spine height: 23

Francis Sitwell

3.26

Edith Sitwell

By Rex Whistler, 1929

Oil on canvas board, 33 x 24.6

Inscribed on reverse by the artist:
*Edith painted in the tapestry drawing room at
Renishaw, 1929*

Sir Reresby Sitwell Bt

3.27

**Caricature portraits of Osbert,
Edith and Sacheverell Sitwell**

By Rex Whistler, 1929

Pencil, 18.9 x 9.5 each

His Honour Judge Geddes

3.28

**Portrait of the Artist as the Painter
Raphael**

Self-portrait by Wyndham Lewis, 1921

Oil on canvas over hardboard, 76.3 x 68.6

Signed (br): *Wyndham/Lewis*

Manchester City Art Galleries

3.29

Edith Sitwell

By Wyndham Lewis, 1923-1935

Oil on canvas, 86.4 x 111.8

Inscribed (bl): *Wyndham Lewis*

Tate Gallery, presented by Sir Edward
Beddington-Behrens 1943

3.30

Edith Sitwell

By Wyndham Lewis, 1921

Pencil on paper, 38.7 x 28.6

Signed and dated (br): *Wyndham
Lewis./1921* and inscribed (tr):
EDITH SITWELL

National Portrait Gallery (4464)

3.31

Edith Sitwell

By Wyndham Lewis, 1923

Pencil and wash on paper, 40 x 29

Signed and dated (br): *Wyndham Lewis. 1923*

National Portrait Gallery (4465)

3.32

The Sitwell Brothers

By Wyndham Lewis, 1922

Pencil, wash and gouache on light grey
paper, 38 x 26

Signed and inscribed (bl): *Wyndham
Lewis/(The Sitwell Brothers, Osbert &
Sacheveril)* [sic]

Francis Sitwell

3.33

A reading of Ovid (Tyros)

By Wyndham Lewis, 1920-1921

Oil on canvas, 165.2 x 90.2

Scottish National Gallery of Modern Art,
Edinburgh

3.34

Edith Sitwell

By Albert Rutherston, 1928

Black and red chalk on paper, 32.4 x 21.2

Signed, dated and inscribed (bl): *Albert R
1928/ To my friend Alfred Thornton*

Art Collection, Harry Ransom
Humanities Research Center,
The University of Texas at Austin

3.35

A Comedy of Manners, London

Design for a fan

By Albert Rutherston, 1932

Water-colour with pencil under-drawing
on silk laid down on card, 37.5 x 61.6

Signed (br): *Albert R 32* and inscribed
along bottom edge: *A COMEDY OF
MANNERS, LONDON./ T. E. BALSTON
COMMANDIT 1929, ALBERT
RUTHERSTON FECIT 1932*

Syndics of the Fitzwilliam Museum,
Cambridge

3.36

'Sitwelliana'

Selection of caricatures by Siegfried
Sassoon, c. 1925-1950

Pencil and water-colour on paper, various
sizes, including a quarto volume

William S. Reese

3.37

The Triumph of Neptune

Photographs by Sasha, 1926

Theatre Museum: Courtesy of the
Board of Trustees of the Victoria and
Albert Museum

a) Lubov Tchernicheva and Vera Petrova

Bromide print, 24.2 x 19.2

b) Serge Lifar, Lord Berners and
Alexandra Danilova

Bromide print, 24.2 x 19.1

3.38

Lord Berners

(Sir Gerald Tyrwhitt Wilson,
14th Baron)

By Rex Whistler, 1929

Oil on canvas board, 40.2 x 32.9

National Portrait Gallery (5050)

3.39

Cecil Beaton

By Pavel Tchelitchew, 1934

Gouache on paper, 74.6 x 36.8

Signed and dated (br): *P. Tchelitchew/34*

National Portrait Gallery (5306)

3.40

William Walton

By Cecil Beaton, 1926

Bromide print, 29 x 23.9

Stamped and inscribed in Beaton's hand
on reverse: *William Walton the/ Composer/
whose 'Façade' &'/ 'Portsmouth Point' were
played at the recent/ Siena Festival*

National Portrait Gallery (P55)

3.41

**Photographs of Osbert and Edith
Sitwell**

By Cecil Beaton, 1926

a) Osbert

Bromide print, 24.5 x 19.5

National Portrait Gallery (x40367)

b) Edith
Bromide print, 25.2 x 17.3
Sotheby's, London

c) Edith (profile to left, large bead
necklace, not illustrated)
Bromide print, 23.8 x 16.9
Sotheby's, London

d) Edith (deer background, not illustrated)
Bromide print, 15.1 x 20.4
Sotheby's, London

3.42

**Photographs of Edith, Osbert and
Sacheverell Sitwell**
By Cecil Beaton, 1927 (A)

a) Edith
Bromide print, 19.2 x 19
Sotheby's, London

b) Osbert, Sacheverell and Edith
Bromide print, 37 x 32
Signed on mount (br): *Cecil Beaton*
Sir Reresby Sitwell Bt

c) Osbert, Sacheverell and Edith (heads
above each other, profile to left, not
illustrated)
Bromide print, 23.9 x 16.2
National Portrait Gallery (x40365)

d) Sacheverell, Edith and Osbert (profile,
Cubist backdrop, not illustrated)
Bromide print, 23 x 16.4
Sotheby's, London

3.43

**Photographs of Edith, Osbert and
Sacheverell Sitwell**
By Cecil Beaton, 1927 (B)

a) Edith
Bromide print, 24.3 x 19.4
National Portrait Gallery (x40361)

b) Sacheverell
Bromide print, 24.2 x 18.8
Sotheby's, London

c) Edith
Bromide print, 38 x 30.5
Signed on mount: *Cecil Beaton*
Sotheby's, London

d) Osbert, Edith and Sacheverell
Bromide print, 21.2 x 15.6
Sotheby's, London

e) Apotheosis of Edith attended by Osbert
and Sacheverell
Bromide print, 23.8 x 17
Sotheby's, London

f) The Sitwells in Sussex Gardens
(not illustrated)
Bromide print, 23.8 x 16.9
Sotheby's, London

g) Sacheverell, Osbert and Edith (seated,
Sacheverell and Osbert in profile, Edith
turned towards camera, not illustrated)
Bromide print, 17.6 x 20.2
Sotheby's, London

h) Edith and Sacheverell (not illustrated)
Bromide print, 20 x 16.7
Sotheby's, London

3.44

The Sitwells
By Robert Sherriffs, *c.* 1927-1930
Pen and ink on paper, 39.4 x 28.8
Inscribed (b): *Mr Shaw (to the Sitwells)
"Come up here, my dears"*
National Portrait Gallery (D4468)

3.45

**'If the Sitwells indulged in the
simple life'**
By Adrian Allinson, *c.* 1928
Pen, ink and blue chalk on paper,
21.6 x 27.2 (sight)
Signed (br): *Allinson.*
Inscribed (b) as above
Michael Parkin Fine Art Limited

3.46

**Edith, Osbert and Sacheverell
Sitwell**
By Cecil Beaton, 1931
Black and grey inks with pencil on paper,
31.7 x 26.7
Inscribed on fold-over: *Edith/ Sacheverell/
Osbert/ Sitwell/ by Cecil Beaton/ Comb line/ &
tone.* Stamped on reverse: *PUBLISHED
IN/ BRITISH* [VOGUE]
Art Collection, Harry Ransom
Humanities Research Center,
The University of Texas at Austin

3.47

**Design for the dust jacket of
*All at Sea***
By Cecil Beaton, 1927
Pencil, ink and water-colour on paper,
36 x 51
Signed (br): *Cecil Beaton*
Sir Reresby Sitwell Bt

3.48

**The Sitwells with the cast of
*First Class Passengers Only***
Copy print from an unidentified 1927
press cutting in the collection of
Francis Sitwell

3.49

'We Are Hopeless Gramophonists'
By Barbara Ker-Seymer for *Harper's
Bazaar*, Vol. VII, no. 4, January 1933
Magazine, spine height: 33.7
Private Collection

3.50

The Sitwells
By Norman Parkinson, *c.* 1935
Bromide print, 34 x 23
Bears studio stamp (*NP 1 Dover St*)
on reverse
Sir Reresby Sitwell Bt

3.51

**Edith, Osbert and Sacheverell
Sitwell**
By Baron
Sir Reresby Sitwell Bt

a) Bromide print, 36.4 x 29, *c.* 1937
Bears photographer's blind stamp

b) Full-length, *c.* 1937 (not illustrated)
Bromide print, 20.9 x 15.6

c) Profile, with cartoon bubbles, *c.* 1948
(not illustrated)
Bromide print, 36 x 28.5

Nos. 3.52-3.78 are not illustrated

3.52

**Dr Donne and Gargantua,
First Canto**
By Sacheverell Sitwell, 1921
Privately published in an edition of 101 by
The Favil Press, Kensington
Printed book, spine height: 19.2
Signed by the author, unnumbered
Sir Reresby Sitwell Bt

3.53

The Hundred and One Harlequins
By Sacheverell Sitwell, 1922
Published by Grant Richards Ltd, London
Printed book, spine height: 21.7
Bertram Rota Limited

3.54

**Autograph notebook for *Façade* and
*Bucolic Comedies***
By Edith Sitwell, *c.* 1922-1923
Pencil and ink autograph manuscript in
notebook, spine height: 22.5
Harry Ransom Humanities Research
Center, The University of Texas at Austin

3.55

Bucolic Comedies
By Edith Sitwell, 1923
Published by Duckworth & Co., London
Printed book, spine height: 19
Maggs Bros Ltd

3.56

**Constant Lambert's copies of
material relating to performances
of *Façade*, *c.* 1922-1928**
Miscellaneous pieces bound into single
volume, spine height: 33.9
British Broadcasting Corporation

3.57

***Façade* at the New Chenil Galleries**
Facsimile from *The Sphere*, 1 May 1926

3.58

**Programme for *Façade* at the New
Chenil Galleries, 29 June 1926**
Printed pamphlet with autograph
annotations by Constant Lambert,
spine height: 22.1
British Broadcasting Corporation

3.59

Façade
By Edith Sitwell and William Walton
Published by Oxford University Press,
50th anniversary limited edition with
illustrations by John Piper, 1972
Printed book, spine height: 31.6,
with pressed disc of 1929 Decca recording
of *Façade*
Francis Sitwell

3.60

William Walton
By Cecil Beaton, 1930
Bromide print, 25.5 x 20.1
Inscribed on reverse with the
sitter's name
Sir Reresby Sitwell Bt

3.61

**Autograph manuscript of *Two
Songs* on poems by *Sacheverell
Sitwell* for soprano, flute and harp**
By Constant Lambert, 1923
Music manuscript, 2 fols., 36.8 high
Signed on last folio: *Constant Lambert/
Chelsea 1923*
British Broadcasting Corporation

3.62

The Sleeping Beauty
By Edith Sitwell, 1924
Published by Duckworth & Co., London
Printed book, spine height: 19
Inscribed: *Miss Christina Foyle with all good
wishes from Edith Sitwell*
Lawrence Mynott

3.63

Southern Baroque Art
By Sacheverell Sitwell, 1924
Published by Grant Richards Ltd, London
Printed book, spine height: 22.2
Inscribed: *To Georgia Doble from Richmond
Temple with the approval of Sacheverell Sitwell
4.8.24*
Francis Sitwell

3.64

St Francis
By Alessandro Magnasco (1667-1749)
Oil on canvas, 41.5 x 26.5
Sir Reresby Sitwell Bt

3.65

Poor Young People
By Edith, Osbert and Sacheverell
Sitwell, 1925
Published by The Fleuron, London
Printed book with illustrations by Albert
Rutherston, spine height: 25.6
Sir Reresby Sitwell Bt

3.66

Osbert Sitwell
By Albert Rutherston, 1927
Pencil with brown ink on paper,
50.2 x 35.5
Signed and dated (bl): *Albert R 1927*
Art Collection, Harry Ransom
Humanities Research Center,
The University of Texas at Austin

3.67

Gino Severini
By Ida Kar, 1954
Bromide print, 30.6 x 30.4
National Portrait Gallery (x31638)

3.68

**Book-plate for Osbert and
Sacheverell Sitwell**
By Gino Severini, 1923
Engraving, plate size: 12.9 x 16.6
Signed in the plate (b): *G. S.*
Sir Reresby Sitwell Bt

3.69

Out of the Flame
By Osbert Sitwell, 1923
Published by Grant Richards Ltd, London
Printed book, spine height: 21.5
Inscribed: *To dearest Sachie from Osbert
14.6.23*
Francis Sitwell

3.70

The Thirteenth Caesar
By Sacheverell Sitwell, 1924
Published by Grant Richards Ltd, London
Printed book, spine height: 21.6
Francis Sitwell

3.71

The Cyder Feast
By Sacheverell Sitwell, 1927
Published by Duckworth, London
Printed book, spine height: 22.8
Francis Sitwell

3.72

*First Class Passengers Only – A
Social Tragedy in Three Acts*
By Osbert and Sacheverell Sitwell, 1927
Programme for the Arts Theatre Club,
Sunday 27 – Wednesday 30 November 1927
Printed pamphlet, spine height: 21.5
Theatre Museum: Courtesy of the
Board of Trustees of the Victoria and
Albert Museum

3.73

**Edith and Osbert Sitwell's general
amnesty**
Facsimile from *The Times*, 5 June 1928

3.74

Rex Whistler
Self-portrait, *c.* 1934
Oil on canvas, 36.8 x 26
National Portrait Gallery (4124)

3.75

Book-plate for Osbert Sitwell
By Rex Whistler, 1928
Collotype, 10.5 x 7.8
Sir Reresby Sitwell Bt

3.76

Osbert Sitwell
By Rex Whistler, 1935
Pencil and water-colour on paper,
14.9 x 14.9
National Portrait Gallery (5009)

3.77

Arthur Waley
By Rex Whistler, *c.* 1928-1938
Pencil on paper, 29.8 x 24.1
Inscribed by Laurence Whistler (b): *Arthur
Waley recalls: "It was done in his studio
in/Fitzroy St. I don't remember which year.
He was talking,/and it was only when the
drawing was almost done, that/I noticed he was
drawing me." L. W.*
National Portrait Gallery (4598)

3.78

Alexander Pope
By Edith Sitwell, 1930
Published by Faber & Faber Ltd, London
Printed book, spine height: 22.5
Sir Reresby Sitwell Bt

Edith

4.1

Edith Sitwell
By Cecil Beaton, 1930

a) Bromide print, 20.3 x 16.2
Sotheby's, London

b) Bromide print, 22.5 x 17.6
National Portrait Gallery (x4082)

c) (with borzoi, not illustrated)
Bromide print, 24 x 14.2
National Portrait Gallery (x40364)

d) (as hamadryad, not illustrated)
Bromide print, 24 x 13.2
National Portrait Gallery (x40363)

4.2

Gertrude Stein
By Man Ray, 1926
Bromide print, 27.6 x 22.1
Inscribed on support (br): *To Edith/with
much love/from/Gtde.*
Sir Reresby Sitwell Bt

4.3

Gertrude Stein and Alice B. Toklas
By Cecil Beaton, 1938
Bromide print, 19.2 x 19.3
Sotheby's, London

4.4

**Edith Sitwell reading from
Rustic Elegies for a 'Phonofilm',
Clapham Studios**
By an unknown photographer, 1927
Modern print
The Hulton Deutsch Collection

4.5

Edith Sitwell
By Christopher Richard Wynne
Nevinson, 1927
Drypoint etching, 18.9 x 15.1
Signed (r) below plate impression:
C. R. W. Nevinson
Russel I. Kully, Los Angeles

4.6

Pavel Tchelitchew
Self-portrait, c. 1933
Sepia ink, pen and wash on paper,
29.6 x 19
Inscribed and signed (bl): *to my
dearest/ Edith with/ Love – my own face
right/ Pavlik*
Sir Reresby Sitwell Bt

4.7

Pavel Tchelitchew
Self-portrait mask, 1929
Wire and coloured wax, 51 high
Incised with signature and date on the
plinth: *TCHELITCHEW/ 29*
Francis Sitwell

4.8

Edith Sitwell
By Pavel Tchelitchew, 1927
Gouache with sand on paper, 61.9 x 47.3
Signed and dated (br): *P. Tchelitchew./ 27*
National Portrait Gallery (5875)

4.9

Edith Sitwell
By Pavel Tchelitchew, c. 1930
Oil on canvas on board, 79.3 x 66
Signed (br): *P.Tchelitchew*
Art Collection, Harry Ransom
Humanities Research Center,
The University of Texas at Austin

4.10

Edith Sitwell
By Pavel Tchelitchew, 1937
Oil on canvas, 163.2 x 96.5
Signed and dated (br): *P. Tchelitchew/ 37*
The Trustees of the Edward James
Foundation

4.11

Edith Sitwell
By Pavel Tchelitchew, 1935
Pastel on paper, 63 x 48.6 (sight)
Signed and dated (br): *35./ P. Tchelitchew*
Francis Sitwell

4.12

Charles Henri Ford
By Cecil Beaton, 1930s
Bromide print, 25.3 x 20.3
Sotheby's, London

4.13

Pavel Tchelitchew
By George Platt Lynes, c. 1935
Bromide print, 22.8 x 17.7
Signed and inscribed on mount (br):
*Lynes./ To Edith with/ Love/ Pavlik/ 13 May
1935*; studio stamp on reverse
Francis Sitwell

4.14

Allanah Harper
By Cecil Beaton, c. 1926
Bromide print, 21.5 x 26.4
Sotheby's, London

4.15

Edith Sitwell
By Fox Photos, c. 1931
Modern print from original negative,
25.5 x 20.3
The Hulton Deutsch Collection

4.16

Gold Coast Customs
By Edith Sitwell, 1929
Published by Duckworth, London
Printed book, spine height: 18.9
Francis Sitwell

4.17

The English Eccentrics
By Edith Sitwell, 1933
Published by Houghton Mifflin Company,
Boston and New York
Printed book, spine height: 22.5
Bertram Rota Limited

4.18

Edith Sitwell
By Stella Bowen, c. 1927-1929
Oil on panel, 44.4 x 36.5
Mrs Richard Hayward

4.19

Edith Sitwell
By John Banting, 1943
Water-colour with white heightening on
paper, 55.9 x 75.6
Inscribed on reverse: *A Portrait of a
bone-head/ For George Melly/ from John
Banting/ 1970/ Edith Sitwell maybe*
National Portrait Gallery (5962)

4.20

William Plomer
By Edward Wolfe, 1929
Oil on canvas, 142 x 99.4
Signed (br): *Wolfe*
National Portrait Gallery (5172)

4.21

Thomas Stearns Eliot
By Wyndham Lewis, 1938
Oil on canvas, 76 x 51
Signed and dated (br): *WYNDHAM
LEWIS 1938*
Harvard University Portrait Collection,
Harvard University Art Museums, Gift of
Mrs Stanley B. Resor for Eliot House

4.22

'Still Falls the Rain'
By Edith Sitwell, c. 1941
Undated autograph manuscript draft, with
emendations and workings, in notebook,
spine height: 31.8
Harry Ransom Humanities Research
Center, The University of Texas at Austin

4.23

**Edith Sitwell in the Drawing-room,
Renishaw**
By Bill Brandt, 1945
Bromide print, 32.3 x 27.8
National Portrait Gallery (x9231)

4.24

**Poetry reading at the Aeolian Hall,
14 April 1943**
Photographs from *Picture Post*, 1 May 1943
Modern prints from original negatives,
16.4 x 24.1 each
The Hulton Deutsch Collection

4.25

Frank Raymond Leavis
By Peter Greenham, 1961-1962
Oil on canvas, 88.9 x 69.2
Master, Fellows and Scholars of
Downing College

4.26

John Sparrow
By Derek Hill, 1962
Oil on canvas, 36.2 x 43.8
Warden and Fellows of All Souls College

4.27

Geoffrey Grigson
By Fay Godwin, 1970
Bromide print, 28 x 18.2
National Portrait Gallery

4.28

Cyril Connolly
By Cecil Beaton, 1942
Bromide print, 16.2 x 24
National Portrait Gallery (x14049)

4.29

John Lehmann
By Derek Hill, 1984
Oil on canvas, 40.4 x 45.5
National Portrait Gallery (5985)

4.30

Stephen Spender
By Robert Buhler, 1939
Oil on canvas, 75.5 x 62.8
Signed and dated (br): *Buhler. 39*
Victoria Art Gallery, Bath City Council

4.31

Green Song and Other Poems
By Edith Sitwell, 1946
Published by View Editions, New York
Printed book, spine height: 24.2
Francis Sitwell

4.32

Dylan and Caitlin Thomas
By Ralph Banbury, c. 1937-1938
Oil on canvas, 76 x 91.1
Mrs F. L. Hope JP

4.33

**Letter from Sacheverell to Edith
Sitwell**
Weston Hall, 25 October 1942
Autograph manuscript, 2 fols., black ink
on headed notepaper, 22.6 x 17.5
Francis Sitwell

4.34

**Press cuttings from the American
tour, 1948**

a) Edith and Osbert Sitwell at the
Gotham Book Mart. Photographed by
Lisa Larsen for *Life*, 6 December 1948
Press cutting in William Beaumont
Morris's scrapbook 'Of Dame Edith
Sitwell'
Francis Sitwell

b) 'Cocktails with the Sitwells'
(not illustrated)
Facsimile from the *New York Star*,
28 October 1948

c) 'Sitwells Choose Boston for Christmas
in US' (not illustrated)
Facsimile from the *Boston Daily Globe*,
21 December 1948

4.35
Marilyn Monroe
By Cecil Beaton, 1956
Bromide print, 19 x 19.3
National Portrait Gallery (x40269)

4.36
Celebrity at a Cocktail
By Tom Keogh, 1948
Black ink, pencil and white on paper,
47 x 26.7
Signed (tl): *Keogh*; inscribed (b):
CELEBRITY/AT A/COCKTAIL
Art Collection, Harry Ransom
Humanities Research Center,
The University of Texas at Austin

4.37
Carson McCullers
By Cecil Beaton, 1956
Bromide print, 27.8 x 27.7
Sotheby's, London

4.38
George Cukor
Publicity photograph for Paramount
Picture Corporation, 1959
Copy print
Paramount Picture Corporation: Courtesy
of the British Film Institute

4.39
Edith Sitwell
By Horst P. Horst, 1948
(illustrated in colour,
© Horst P. Horst/Hamiltons)
Bromide print, 25.5 x 20.5
Vogue, © The Condé Nast Publications
Limited

4.40
Jewellery belonging to Edith Sitwell

a) Three aquamarine rings, amethyst ring,
carved fluorite ring, two gold-plated
expanding cuff bracelets, Chinese silk-
covered box containing eight semi-
precious brooches
Francis and Susanna Sitwell

b) Gold 'Aztec' necklace
Lady Sitwell

c) Silver gilt 'bahi' bracelet
Mrs A. Kenneth Snowman

4.41
Hats belonging to Edith Sitwell
Francis Sitwell

4.42
Edith Sitwell
By Norman Parkinson, 1939
Bromide print, 10.7 x 7.6
Mrs Wendy Ward

4.43
Edith Sitwell
By Jane Bown, 1959
Bromide print, 50.7 x 40
National Portrait Gallery (x28632)

4.44
Edith Sitwell
By George Platt Lynes, 1950
Bromide print, 23.6 x 19.1
Sir Reresby Sitwell Bt

4.45
**Cloaks and dresses belonging to
Edith Sitwell**
Francis Sitwell

4.46
Edith Sitwell
By Feliks Topolski, 1959
Oil on board, 183 x 122
Signed and dated (bl): *Feliks Topolski 59*
Art Collection, Harry Ransom
Humanities Research Center,
The University of Texas at Austin

4.47
Evelyn Waugh
By Cecil Beaton, April 1955
Bromide print, 28.3 x 23.8
National Portrait Gallery (x14230)

4.48
Roy Campbell
By Jane Bown, 1951
Bromide print, 25.5 x 20.1
National Portrait Gallery (P378)

4.49
Alec Guinness
By Bill Brandt, 1952
Bromide print, 32.3 x 27.8
National Portrait Gallery (x9230)

4.50
Edith Sitwell
By Mark Gerson, May 1962
National Portrait Gallery (x17973, x46700)

a) Bromide print, 25 x 20

b) (head and hands, not illustrated)
Bromide print, 23.4 x 19

4.51
**Edith Sitwell with friends
and relatives on the set of
*This is Your Life***
By John S. Sherman for BBC,
6 November 1962
Bromide prints, 16.5 x 21 each
Francis Sitwell

4.52
Edith Sitwell
By Cecil Beaton, July 1962

a) Bromide print, 20 x 14.2
Francis Sitwell

b) Bromide print, 23.9 x 19
National Portrait Gallery (x40366)

c) Bromide print, 25.9 x 24.3
Sotheby's, London

d) Modern bromide print, 27.8 x 28.1
Sotheby's, London

e) (triple head, ostrich-feather hat, not
illustrated)
Bromide print, 24.4 x 29.2
Sotheby's, London

f) (bird-king hat, half-length, not
illustrated)
Bromide print, 24.1 x 24.1
Sotheby's, London

4.53
Edith Sitwell's luggage label
Printed label, 8 x 15.7
Sir Reresby Sitwell Bt

4.54
Edith Sitwell's Christmas Card
Printed card, 20.2 x 25.2
Inscribed: *For/my dear Alberto/with
love/from/Edith*
Alberto de Lacerda

Nos. 4.55-4.78 are not illustrated

4.55
Portrait of Choura Tchelitchew
By Pavel Tchelitchew, c. 1925-1926
Gouache on paper, 64.7 x 50.4
Studio stamp on reverse
Richard Nathanson, London

4.56
**'Miss Edith Sitwell presents a
Genius?'**
Facsimile from *The Graphic*, 28 July 1928

4.57
Two Figures
By Pavel Tchelitchew, 1929
Water-colour and gouache on paper,
57.3 x 44.5
Signed and dated (br): *P Tchelitchew/29*
Francis Sitwell

4.58
Three Cats
By Pavel Tchelitchew
Sepia ink, pen and wash on paper,
36.2 x 26
Francis Sitwell

4.59
Fan
Decorated by Pavel Tchelitchew, 1934
Gouache on wooden slatted fan, 24 x 46
Inscribed (br): *To Edith/on her/
birthday/Pavlik*
Francis Sitwell

4.60
Phenomena
Exhibition catalogue, Arthur Tooth and
Sons, 1938
Printed booklet, spine height: 26.5
Richard Nathanson, London

4.61
Study for 'Hide and Seek'
By Pavel Tchelitchew, 1941
Oil on canvas, 91.5 x 101.6
Signed and dated (br): *P. Tchelitchew. 41.*
Mrs Richard Hayward

4.62
Edith Sitwell
By Howard Coster, 1937
Modern prints from original negatives,
25.5 x 30.5, 32.7 x 26
National Portrait Gallery (x10964, x1639)

4.63
**Edith and Osbert Sitwell in the
Drawing-room, Renishaw**
By Sheffield Newspapers Ltd, c. 1943
Bromide print, 20.3 x 25.5
Sir Reresby Sitwell Bt

4.64

Denton Welch

Self-portrait, *c.* 1940-1942

Oil on hardboard, 47.6 x 40.3

National Portrait Gallery (4080)

4.65

Maurice Bowra

By Henry Lamb, 1952

Chalk on paper, 35.3 x 25.1

National Portrait Gallery (4667)

4.66

Humphrey Searle

By Michael Ayrton, 1965

Pencil on paper, 55.9 x 29.9

Dated (br): *15.11.1965.*

Fiona Searle

4.67

Dr Edith Sitwell in a recital of scenes from Shakespeare's *Macbeth*

Programme for the Museum of Modern Art, New York, 16 November 1950

Printed sheet, folded, height: 23

The Provost and Fellows, Eton College

4.68

Edith Sitwell reciting from *Macbeth*

By George Platt Lynes, 1950

Bromide print, 22.8 x 19

Private Collection

4.69

Edith Sitwell

By George Platt Lynes, 1950

Bromide print, 23.6 x 19.1

Sir Reresby Sitwell Bt

4.70

'Dr Sitwell finishes script and goes home in silence'

Facsimile from the *Los Angeles Times,* 29 March 1953

4.71

***Saturday Review,* 19 December 1953**

Printed magazine, spine height: 28

Francis Sitwell

4.72

'Elegy for Dylan Thomas'

By Edith Sitwell

Autograph manuscript, blue ink on lined foolscap, folded, 4 fols., 32.6 x 20.4

Inscribed (t): *For/Alberto/with love/ Edith Sitwell. 10 August 1955*

Alberto de Lacerda

4.73

Edith Sitwell's address book, *c.* 1950s-1960s

'Alwych' all-weather cover address book, spine height: 23

Autograph manuscript entries by Edith Sitwell and others

Francis Sitwell

4.74

Edith Sitwell's form (for dealing with pests)

Pre-printed form, 20.2 x 12.6

Sir Reresby Sitwell Bt

4.75

Edith Sitwell on *Face to Face*

BBC photograph, May 1959

Bromide print, 21.9 x 16.5

BBC Photograph Library & Archive

4.76

Edith Sitwell the Sorceress

By Eileen Agar, 1960

Oil on canvas, 56 x 38.1

Signed (br): *AGAR*; inscribed and dated on reverse: *Edith Sitwell the Sorceress 1960*

Bob Simm

4.77

Ephemera from Edith Sitwell's seventy-fifth birthday concert, Royal Festival Hall, 9 October 1962

a) Programme

Printed booklet, spine height: 24.4

Sir Reresby Sitwell Bt

b) Sacheverell, Edith and Osbert, with Francis Sitwell in the background

By an unknown photographer

Modern print from original negative, 25.5 x 20.3

The Hulton Deutsch Collection

4.78

A selection of books by Edith Sitwell

a) *Collected Poems*

Published by Gerald Duckworth and Company Ltd, London, Houghton Mifflin Company, Boston, 1930

Printed book with pen, ink and wash and water-colour illustrations, spine height: 23

Decorated by Rex Whistler, signed by Edith and Sacheverell Sitwell, inscribed by Osbert Sitwell: *Given to Reresby by his Uncle Osbert, 15 April 1967.*

Sir Reresby Sitwell Bt

b) *Jane Barston*

Published by Faber and Faber Ltd, London, 1931

Printed book, spine height: 22.2

Limited edition, illustrations by R. A. Davies, signed by the author and numbered *179*

Lawrence Mynott

c) *Victoria of England*

Published by Faber and Faber Limited, London, 1936

Printed book, spine height: 21.5

National Portrait Gallery

d) *I Live under a Black Sun*

Published by Victor Gollancz Ltd, London, 1937

Printed book, spine height: 19.7

Francis Sitwell

e) *Poems Old and New*

Published by Faber and Faber Limited, London, 1940

Printed book, spine height: 19.3

Inscribed: *For my darling Sachie with Edith's very best love*

Francis Sitwell

f) *Street Songs*

Published by Macmillan & Co. Ltd, London, 1942

Printed book, spine height: 22.2

Inscribed: *For my darling Georgia with very best love from Edith 27 January 1942*

Francis Sitwell

g) *The Song of the Cold*

Published by Macmillan & Co. Ltd, London, 1945

Printed book, spine height: 22.2

Inscribed on flyleaf: *For my darling Georgia with very best love from Edith* and (also in the author's hand) beside a review of *Street Songs* on the back cover: *they oughtn't to spoil me!*

Francis Sitwell

h) *Fanfare for Elizabeth*

Published by Macmillan & Co. Ltd, London, 1946

Printed book, spine height: 22.2

Francis Sitwell

i) *The Shadow of Cain*

Published by John Lehmann, London, 1947

Printed book, spine height: 21.9

Inscribed: *For my darling Sachie with very best love from Edith*

Francis Sitwell

j) *The Canticle of the Rose*

Published by Macmillan & Co. Ltd, London, 1949

Printed book, spine height: 22.2

Inscribed: *For my darling Georgia with best love from Edith*

Francis Sitwell

k) *Gardeners and Astronomers*

Published by Vanguard Press Inc., New York, 1953

Printed book, spine height: 24.1

Francis Sitwell

l) *The Queens and the Hive*

Published by Macmillan & Co. Ltd, London, 1962

Printed book, spine height: 22.2

Inscribed: *For darling Francis with best love from Edith*

Francis Sitwell

m) *Taken Care Of*

Published by Hutchinson and Co. Ltd, London, 1965

Printed book, spine height: 23.5

Francis Sitwell

Osbert

5.1

Renishaw Hall
By Richard Wyndham, *c.* 1930s
Oil on board, 44.3 x 69.5
Signed with initials (bl): *RW*
Francis Sitwell

5.2

Michael Arlen
By Edmund Dulac, 1925
Black and brown ink and wash over
pencil on paper, 23.8 x 18.1
Signed (tr): *Edmund Dulac*
Art Collection, Harry Ransom
Humanities Research Center,
The University of Texas at Austin

5.3

Aldous Huxley
By Howard Coster, 1934
Cream-toned chlorobromide print,
38.5 x 23.4
National Portrait Gallery (x10665)

5.4

David Herbert Lawrence
By Nikolas Muray, 1923
Bromide print, 24.1 x 19.4
Photographer's stamp on reverse
National Portrait Gallery (P208)

5.5

Sir Philip Sassoon
By Howard Coster, 1929
Chlorobromide print, 21.8 x 27.8
National Portrait Gallery (Ax2310)

5.6

Lady Aberconway
By Cecil Beaton, 1935
Bromide print, 25.6 x 20.6
Sotheby's, London

5.7

**Dust jacket design for *England
Reclaimed***
By Edward McKnight Kauffer, 1927
Ink and brown chalk on paper, 30 x 20
Signed (br): *E. McKnight Kauffer*; inscribed
on reverse: *To/OSBERT SITWELL,/our
dear Poet and most constant friend,/who has
RECLAIMED ENGLAND/(published this
day)/and/the English House of
DUCKWORTH/from the Soul-less Routine/
of Modern Industry./October 20th 1927/
signed:/Edward Duckworth/T. Balston/A. G.
Lewis/Anthony Powell.*
Sir Reresby Sitwell Bt

5.8

The Man Who Lost Himself
By Osbert Sitwell, 1929
Published by Duckworth, London
Printed book, spine height: 19.6
Inscribed: *For dearest Sachie & Georgia,/
à Georgia & Sachie/from/Osbert Sitwell*
Francis Sitwell

5.9

David Horner
By Philip Steegmann, 1926
Oil on canvas, 63.5 x 56
Signed and dated (tr): *Philip Steegmann –
p – 1926 –*
Royal Pavilion, Art Gallery and Museum,
Brighton

5.10

David Horner
By Foulsham and Banfield, *c.* 1920s
Bromide print, 20 x 13.1
The Provost and Fellows, Eton College

5.11

Winters of Content
By Osbert Sitwell, 1932
Published by Duckworth, London
Printed book, spine height: 22.6
Inscribed: *For dearest Christabel from
Osbert 1932*
Sir Reresby Sitwell Bt

5.12

Harold Acton
By John Banting, *c.* 1930
Carbon copy ink and pencil on paper,
32 x 24.3
National Portrait Gallery (6255)

5.13

**Osbert Sitwell and David Horner
with their Chinese house staff,
Peking**
By The Photo Specialists Co., 1934
Bromide print, 23.4 x 28
Sir Reresby Sitwell Bt

5.14

**Osbert Sitwell and David Horner
with unidentified companions**
By an unknown photographer, 1934
Bromide print, 14.4 x 19.6
Sir Reresby Sitwell Bt

5.15

Queen Mary at Badminton
By an unknown photographer,
c. 1941-1942
Bromide print, 13.9 x 8.9
Inscribed (br): *Mary R/1942* and on
reverse: *With best wishes/& grateful thanks
for/the lovely little book!/ – /To remind you of
our work at Badminton –*
Sir Reresby Sitwell Bt

5.16

Osbert Sitwell
By Desmond Harmsworth, 1938
Oil on canvas, 66 x 53.3
Signed (br): *Desmond/Harmsworth*; inscribed
on reverse: *Osbert Sitwell by Desmond
Harmsworth/painted 1938/oil on canvas*
Art Collection, Harry Ransom
Humanities Research Center,
The University of Texas at Austin

5.17

Osbert Sitwell
By Norman Parkinson, 1935
Bromide print, 33 x 21
Sir Reresby Sitwell Bt

5.18

**Manuscript notebook containing
masterplan for *Left Hand Right
Hand!***
By Osbert Sitwell, *c.* 1941-1945
Autograph manuscript
Coloured inks on lined paper in bound
volume, spine height: 31.8
Harry Ransom Humanities Research
Center, The University of Texas at Austin

5.19

Left Hand Right Hand!
By Osbert Sitwell, 1945-1950
Published by Macmillan & Co. Ltd,
London
Five printed volumes, spine height:
22 each
Private Collection

5.20

James Agate
By Felix Man, 1939
Bromide print, 28.4 x 20.6
National Portrait Gallery (x1148)

5.21

**Osbert, Georgia, Edith and
Sacheverell Sitwell outside the
High Court**
Copy print from photograph by Universal
Pictorial Press, February 1941

5.22

Photographs by Bill Brandt, 1945

a) Edith and Osbert Sitwell
Bromide print, 34.5 x 29.2
National Portrait Gallery (x22477)

b) Entrance to the Wilderness, Renishaw
Bromide print, 23.2 x 18.7
Sir Reresby Sitwell Bt

5.23

**Sir George Sitwell in the Cardinal's
Garden, Montegufoni**
By an unknown photographer, 1935
Copy print from a photograph in the
collection of Sir Reresby Sitwell Bt

5.24

Osbert Sitwell at Montegufoni
By an unknown photographer, 1950s
Bromide print, 24.2 x 20.2
Sir Reresby Sitwell Bt

5.25

Renishaw Hall
Illustrations for Osbert Sitwell's
autobiography
By John Piper, 1942-1943
Sir Reresby Sitwell Bt

a) The South Front, Renishaw
Ink, water-colour and gouache on paper
mounted on card, 38.2 x 55.5
Signed (bl): *John Piper*

b) Landscape with Mill, Renishaw
Pen, ink and wash on paper mounted on
card, 37.7 x 61.5
Signed (bl): *John Piper*

c) The Apse, the Dining-room, Renishaw
(not illustrated)
Ink, water-colour and gouache on paper
mounted on card, 45 x 59.8

5.26
The Great Court, Montegufoni
By John Piper, 1947
Ink, water-colour and gouache on paper,
50.8 x 35.6
Sir Reresby Sitwell Bt

5.27
Osbert Sitwell at Renishaw
By Haywood Magee for *Picture Post*,
17 September 1949
Sir Reresby Sitwell Bt

a) In his study, the 'boudoir'
Bromide print, 15.2 x 20

b) At the Gothic Lodge
Bromide print, 15.2 x 20.1
Inscribed below print: *For Ian/from/
Osbert Sitwell*

5.28
Osbert Sitwell
By Horst P. Horst, *c.* 1949
Platinum palladium print, 25.4 x 20.3
Signed on mount (br): *Horst*
Hamiltons Galleries Ltd

5.29
**Osbert and Edith Sitwell in
New York**
By Ruth Sondak for Keystone,
8 November 1948
Modern print from original negative,
20.3 x 25.5
The Hulton Deutsch Collection

5.30
The Sitwells
By Dan Maloney, 1950
Oil on board, 24.4 x 19.2 (sight)
Signed and dated (br): *Maloney 50*
Sir Reresby Sitwell Bt

5.31
**Dust jacket design for *The Four
Continents***
By Harry Cowdell, 1954
Pencil, ink and wash on paper, 31.9 x 24.9
Signed and dated (bl): *H. Cowdell del. 1954*
Sir Reresby Sitwell Bt

5.32
Lincoln and Fidelma Kirstein
By Cecil Beaton, 1957
Bromide print, 25.4 x 20.6
Sotheby's, London

5.33
**Osbert Sitwell and David Horner
at York House**
By Lewis Morley, 1963
National Portrait Gallery
(x47399, x45389, x47398)

a) Osbert
Bromide print, 22 x 18.3

b) David Horner
Bromide print, 30.5 x 25.5

c) Osbert (not illustrated)
Bromide print, 29.4 x 23.8

Nos. 5.34-5.50 are not illustrated

5.34
Belshazzar's Feast
Music by William Walton, text selected
and arranged by Osbert Sitwell, 1931
Vocal score, published by Oxford
University Press, London
Printed book, spine height: 25
Private Collection

5.35
Adrian Stokes
By Maurice Lambert, *c.* 1936
Bronze, 31.7 high
Incised in monogram on back of
neck: *ML*
National Portrait Gallery (5841)

5.36
Mr Osbert Sitwell
By Edward Scott-Snell, *c.* 1930s
Pen and ink, 22.5 x 31.7
Signed (br): *Edward Scott-Snell.* and
inscribed (b): *Mr Osbert Sitwell*
Sir Reresby Sitwell Bt

5.37
Osbert Sitwell
By Howard Coster, 1934
Modern print from original negative,
30.5 x 25.5
National Portrait Gallery (x24209)

5.38
'National Rat Week'
By Osbert Sitwell, 1937
The Provost and Fellows, Eton College

a) Autograph manuscript
Pencil on lined paper, single folio,
32.4 x 20.6
Inscribed on reverse: *For David from Osbert*

b) Typescript
Single folio, 25.5 x 16
Signed: *Osbert Sitwell*

c) Printed pamphlet
Folded folio, 18.2 x 25

d) Press cutting from *Cavalcade*,
13 February 1937

5.39
Osbert Sitwell
By Baron, *c.* 1937
Bromide print, 36.4 x 28.6
Studio stamp (br)
Sir Reresby Sitwell Bt

5.40
**'H. M. Queen Mary, the guest of
the Duke and Duchess of Beaufort'**
Copy print from photograph by Dennis
Moss, *Tatler*, 5 October 1938

5.41
Henry Hamilton Fyfe
By Lafayette Ltd, *c.* 1935
Bromide print, 19 x 14
Scottish National Portrait Gallery

5.42
Facsimiles from the *Reynolds News*

a) 'Three anthologies', 18 February 1940

b) 'Poets in the Box: The Sitwells sue
Reynolds News', 9 February 1941

5.43
**Ephemera relating to the *Reynolds
News* libel action, February 1941**
Francis Sitwell

a) Draft manuscript depositions by Edith,
Osbert and Sacheverell Sitwell
Ink with pencil annotations on lined
foolscap – Edith: 19 fols., Osbert: 17 fols.,
Sacheverell: 3 fols.

b) Notes prepared for a witness from
Macmillan & Co. Ltd, London
Carbon copy of typescript, 2 fols., foolscap

c) Judgement, 10 February 1941
Carbon copy typescript, 2 fols., foolscap

5.44
A Letter to My Son
By Osbert Sitwell, 1944
Published by Home and Van Thal Ltd
Printed book, spine height: 19
Francis Sitwell

5.45
**'Who shall save the world for the
artists?'**
Facsimile from the *Daily Express*,
2 September 1944

5.46
**Left to right: Edith Sitwell, Philip
Steegmann, Osbert Sitwell,
Mrs Steegmann, David Horner,
unidentified woman**
By an unknown photographer,
New Orleans, 12 February 1951
Bromide print, 15.7 x 11.4
National Portrait Gallery (x4295)

5.47
Osbert Sitwell
By George Platt Lynes, *c.* 1950
Bromide print, 23.5 x 19
Photographer's stamp on reverse
Sir Reresby Sitwell Bt

5.48
Osbert Sitwell
By Cecil Beaton, 2 May 1953
Bromide print, 23.8 x 21.2
National Portrait Gallery (x14208)

5.49

Osbert Sitwell in his study at Renishaw

By Reresby Sitwell, 6 September 1964
Cibachrome print, 25.5 x 25.5
Sir Reresby Sitwell Bt

5.50

A selection of books by Osbert Sitwell:

a) *Before the Bombardment*
Published by Duckworth, London, 1926
Printed book, spine height: 19.5
Francis Sitwell

b) *Dumb Animal and Other Stories*
Published by Duckworth, London, 1930
Printed book, spine height: 19.3
Bertram Rota Limited

c) *Escape with Me!*
Published by Macmillan & Co. Ltd,
London, 1939
Printed book, spine height: 22.4
Inscribed: *For darling Edith from her devoted
brother Osbert, November 3 1939*
Francis Sitwell

d) *Sing High! Sing Low!*
Published by Macmillan & Co. Ltd,
London, 1944
Printed book, spine height: 22
Francis Sitwell

e) *Wrack at Tidesend*
Published by Macmillan & Co. Ltd,
London, 1952
Printed book, spine height: 22.2
Inscribed: *For darling Sachie and Georgia with
love from Osbert, May 5 1952*
Francis Sitwell

f) *Collected Stories*
Published by Gerald Duckworth & Co.
Ltd, Macmillan & Co. Ltd, London, 1953
Printed book, spine height: 22.4
Inscribed: *For dearest Sachie and Georgia from
Osbert, April 14 '53*
Francis Sitwell

g) *The Four Continents*
Published by Macmillan & Co. Ltd,
London, 1954
Printed book, spine height: 22.4
Inscribed: *For dearest Sachie and Georgia with
love from Osbert, July 2 54*
Francis Sitwell

h) *On the Continent*
Published by Macmillan & Co. Ltd,
London, 1958
Printed book, spine height: 22.1
Inscribed: *To dearest Sachie and Georgia with
best love from Osbert March 7 1958*
Francis Sitwell

i) *Tales my Father Taught Me*
Published by Hutchinson of London, 1962
Printed book, spine height: 21.5
Francis Sitwell

Sacheverell

6.1

Sacheverell Sitwell

By Wyndham Lewis, 1922
Pencil on paper, 37.1 x 27
Signed and inscribed (br):
*Wyndham Lewis 1922. (VENICE)./Drawing
of Sacheverill [sic] Sitwell*
Francis Sitwell

6.2

Georgia Doble

By Maurice Beck and Helen Macgregor,
1924
Bromide prints: a) 29 x 16; b) 28.8 x 19.8
(not illustrated)
Studio stamp on reverse of both prints
Francis Sitwell

6.3

'A Modern Poet and his Bride'

Facsimile from *The Sketch*, 21 October 1925

6.4

**Osbert and Edith with Mr and Mrs
Doble at Sacheverell's and
Georgia's Wedding**

Photographed by the *Daily Mail*, 1925
Bromide press print, 21.3 x 17
John Pearson

6.5

**Sacheverell with (from left to right)
Osbert, Max Meyerfeld, Siegfried
Sassoon and Nellie Burton at
Berlin Zoo**

By an unknown photographer,
8 September 1927
Bromide print, 13.3 x 8.6
Francis Sitwell

6.6

Georgia Sitwell

By Cecil Beaton, 1927
Bromide print, 23.8 x 18.8
Sotheby's, London

6.7

Georgia Sitwell

By Hay Wrightson, 1927
Pink tinted bromide on photographer's
tissue mounted card, 19.8 x 14.2
Signed (bl): *Hay Wrightson*
Francis Sitwell

6.8

Zita and Baby Jungman

By Cecil Beaton, 1926
Bromide print, 17.2 x 23.6
National Portrait Gallery (x40246)

6.9

**Stephen Tennant, Cecil Beaton,
Georgia Sitwell and friends at
Wilsford Manor**

By Cecil Beaton, 1927

a) Bromide print, 14.2 x 24
National Portrait Gallery (x40409)

b) Modern bromide print from original
negative, 21.6 x 30.4
Sotheby's, London

6.10

Georgia Sitwell

By Cecil Beaton, 1930
Bromide print, 21.6 x 19.1
Sotheby's, London

6.11

The Sacheverell Sitwells at Weston

By Fox Photos, 1929

a) Georgia and Edith at Brackley Station
Modern bromide print, 24 x 19.2
John Pearson

b) Sacheverell and Georgia
Modern print from original negative,
19 x 24
The Hulton Deutsch Collection

c) Sacheverell and Reresby (not illustrated)
Vintage bromide print, 24.7 x 19.1
Francis Sitwell

d) Georgia and Reresby (not illustrated)
Vintage bromide print, 24.6 x 19.3
Francis Sitwell

6.12

The Sitwell Family

By Cecil Beaton, 1930
Bromide print, 30.2 x 26.2
Sotheby's, London

6.13
Sacheverell and Georgia Sitwell with their two sons, Reresby and Francis
By A.V. Swaebe, General Press Agency, 1936
Bromide print, 10.5 x 15
Francis Sitwell

6.14
Mr and Mrs Sacheverell Sitwell in the Drawing-room at Weston Hall
By Etienne Drian, c. 1945
Charcoal on paper, 72 x 53.5
Signed (br): *Drian*
Francis Sitwell

6.15
Lady Bridget Parsons
By Cecil Beaton, c. 1928
Bromide print, 25.2 x 19.7
Sotheby's, London

6.16
Pearl Argyle
By an unknown photographer, c. 1935
Bromide print, 22.2 x 17.4
Francis Sitwell

6.17
Weston Hall
By Rex Whistler, 1929
Oil on canvas board, 23 x 30.5
Francis Sitwell

6.18
A View of the South Front, Weston Hall
By John Piper, c. 1942-1943
Ink and gouache on paper, 57 x 74.3
Signed (br): *John Piper*
Francis Sitwell

6.19
Georgia Sitwell's photograph albums, c. 1927-1944
Various sizes
Francis Sitwell

6.20
Moira Shearer
By Robin Guthrie, 1944
Oil on canvas, 44.4 x 33
Signed (bl): *R.G.*, dated *1944* in inscription on reverse
National Portrait Gallery (5974)

6.21
Patrick Leigh Fermor
By Derek Hill, c. 1983
Oil on canvas, 43.2 x 43.2
Signed with initials (br): *DH*
Private Collection

6.22
Design for the dust jacket of
The Hunters and the Hunted
By Irene Hawkins, c. 1947
Gouache on paper, 23.2 x 35.4
Signed (r): *Irene Hawkins*
Francis Sitwell

6.23
Cupid and the Jacaranda
By Sacheverell Sitwell, 1952
Published by Macmillan & Co. Ltd, London
Printed book, spine height: 22
Francis Sitwell

6.24
Denmark
By Sacheverell Sitwell, 1956
Published by B. T. Batsford Ltd, London
Printed book, spine height: 22.2
Inscribed: *To Francis with best love from Daddy, Weston, 22.5.1956*
Francis Sitwell

6.25
Sacheverell Sitwell in Home Guard uniform
By an unknown photographer, 1942
Bromide print, 10.7 x 7.2
Francis Sitwell

6.26
Sacheverell Sitwell at his desk, Weston
By Cecil Beaton, 1952
Modern bromide print from original negative, 28 x 28
Sotheby's, London

6.27
Letter from Sacheverell to Edith Sitwell, 24 September 1949
Autograph manuscript, 1 folio, 17.7 x 11.5
Francis Sitwell

6.28
Old Fashioned Flowers
By Sacheverell Sitwell, 1939
(Illustration: Green Edged Auricula by John Farleigh)
Published by The Curwen Press, London, 1939
Printed books (2 copies), spine height: 25
Sir Reresby Sitwell Bt
Lawrence Mynott

6.29
British Architects and Craftsmen
By Sacheverell Sitwell, 1945
Published by B. T. Batsford Ltd, London
Printed book, spine height: 22.5
Francis Sitwell

6.30
Sacheverell Sitwell
By Cecil Beaton, c. 1965
Oil on canvas, 54.8 x 45
Signed (br): *Beaton*
George Sitwell

6.31
Sir Sacheverell Sitwell
By Derek Hill, c. 1970s
Oil on canvas, 54 x 44
Signed (br in monogram): *DH*
Private Collection

6.32
Sir Sacheverell Sitwell
By Graham Sutherland, 1973
Oil on canvas, 41 x 31.3
Signed (br): *GS. 1973*
William Sitwell

6.33
Sir Sacheverell Sitwell
By Dudley Reed, 1982
Bromide print, 28.9 x 22.9
National Portrait Gallery (x32173)

Nos. 6.34-6.51 are not illustrated

6.34
Album of photographs for the wedding of Sacheverell Sitwell and Georgia Doble
By Alton, Paris, 1925
Nine bromide prints mounted in photographer's card album, 21.5 x 18.1
Francis Sitwell

6.35
Georgia Sitwell
By Madame Yevonde, 1929
Bromide print, 19.9 x 15.1
Signed and dated on support (br): *Yevonde/1929*
Sir Reresby Sitwell Bt

6.36
Georgia Sitwell
By Christopher Richard Wynne Nevinson, c. 1930
Pastel on paper, 38 x 30.5
Signed (br): *C. R. W. Nevinson*
Sir Reresby Sitwell Bt

6.37
Georgia, Francis and Reresby Sitwell, Connaught Square
By an unknown photographer, July 1937
Bromide print, 28.7 x 22.6
Francis Sitwell

6.38
Sir Peter Quennell
By Maurice Lambert, 1927
Bronze, 34.3 high
Private Collection

6.39
Costa Achillopoulo
By John Banting, c. 1930s
Oil on canvas, 39.3 x 29.2
Michael Parkin Fine Art Limited

6.40
'Peaceful English Interior'
Facsimile from *The Sketch*, 10 January 1940

6.41
Georgia Sitwell
By Augustus John, c. 1941
Pencil on paper, 42.8 x 29.8 (sight)
Signed (r): *John*
Sir Reresby Sitwell Bt

6.42
Design for the dust jacket of
Primitive Scenes and Festivals
By Irene Hawkins, 1941
Gouache on paper, 25.3 x 19.8 (sight)
Signed (r): *I. HAWKINS*
Francis Sitwell

6.43

Sacheverell Sitwell

By Bill Brandt, *c.* 1940s

Bromide print, 24.7 x 19

Inscribed (b): *Sacheverell Sitwell.*

Francis Sitwell

6.44

Georgia Sitwell

By Clifford Coffin, 1948

Modern print from original negative,

25.5 x 24.5

Vogue, © The Condé Nast Publications

Limited

6.45

'Brother and Sister: A Ballad of the Paralelo'

Holograph fair copy of a poem by

Sacheverell Sitwell, *c.* 1949

5 fols., in leather binding,

spine height: 33.5

Francis Sitwell

6.46

Sacheverell Sitwell

By Francis Goodman, December 1951

Modern print from original negative,

25.5 x 20.3

National Portrait Gallery (x45471)

6.47

Georgia Sitwell

By Francis Goodman, December 1951

Copy print from original print in

NPG Goodman album

National Portrait Gallery (Ax39596)

6.48

Sacheverell Sitwell

By Cecil Beaton, 1952

Bromide print, 18.9 x 19.3

National Portrait Gallery (x14210)

6.49

Sacheverell Sitwell

By Michael Black, 1985

Bronze, 44.1 high

Incised (back of neck): *Sacheverell Sitwell/
MB* (in monogram) *No 1. 1985*

National Portrait Gallery (5865)

6.50

Visitors' book from Weston Hall

1928-1988

Leather bound volume, spine height: 24.5

Francis Sitwell

6.51

A selection of books by Sacheverell Sitwell

a) *All Summer in a Day*

Published by Duckworth, London, 1926

Printed book, spine height: 22.2

National Portrait Gallery

b) *Canons of Giant Art*

Published by Faber and Faber,

London, 1933

Printed book, spine height: 22.6

Inscribed: *To Edmund Blunden from
Sacheverell Sitwell, 15.VIII.33*

Francis Sitwell

c) *Liszt*

Published by Faber and Faber,

London, 1934

Printed book, spine height: 22

Private Collection

d) *A Background for Domenico Scarlatti*

Published by Faber and Faber,

London, 1935

Printed book, spine height: 19.2

Francis Sitwell

e) *Splendours and Miseries*

Published by Faber and Faber,

London, 1943

Printed book, spine height: 22.5

Inscribed: *For Sacheverell Sitwell with every
good wish Elsa Scammell*

Francis Sitwell

f) *Selected Poems*

Published by Duckworth, London, 1948

Printed book, spine height: 19

Francis Sitwell

g) *Garden Flowers*

In the series *Batsford Colour Books*, general

editor Sacheverell Sitwell

Plates by Jane Loudon, introduction and

notes by Robert Gathorne-Hardy

Published by B. T. Batsford Ltd,

London, 1948

Printed book, spine height: 24.1

Inscribed: *To darling Francis from Sacheverell
Sitwell, Weston, 17 September 1949*

Francis Sitwell

h) *Tropical Birds*

In the series *Batsford Colour Books*, general

editor Sacheverell Sitwell

Plates by John Gould, introduction and

notes by Sacheverell Sitwell

Published by B. T. Batsford Ltd,

London, 1948

Printed book, spine height: 24.1

Inscribed: *To Francis for his birthday, with
love from Sacheverell Sitwell, Weston,
17 September 1949*

Francis Sitwell

i) *The Romantic Ballet*

In the series *Batsford Colour Books*, general

editor Sacheverell Sitwell

Plates from contemporary prints,

introduction and notes by

Sacheverell Sitwell

Published by B. T. Batsford Ltd,

London, 1948

Printed book, spine height: 24.1

Inscribed: *To darling Francis from Sacheverell
Sitwell, Weston, 17 September 1949*

Francis Sitwell

j) *Gallery of Fashion 1790-1822*

In the series *Batsford Colour Books*, general

editor Sacheverell Sitwell

Plates by Heideloff and Ackermann,

introduction by Sacheverell Sitwell, notes

on the plates by Doris Langley Moore

Published by B. T. Batsford Ltd,

London, 1949

Printed book, spine height: 24.1

Inscribed: *For darling Francis with love from
Daddy, Weston, 5 November 1949*

Francis Sitwell

k) *Audubon's American Birds*

In the series *Batsford Colour Books*, general

editor Sacheverell Sitwell

Plates by J. J. Audubon, introduction and

notes by Sacheverell Sitwell

Published by B. T. Batsford Ltd,

London, 1949

Printed book, spine height: 24.1

Inscribed: *To Francis for his birthday with
love from Sacheverell Sitwell, Weston,
17 September 1949*

Francis Sitwell

l) *Truffle Hunt*

Published by Robert Hale Ltd,

London, 1953

Printed book, spine height: 22.1

Francis Sitwell

m) *Fine Bird Books 1700-1900*

By Sacheverell Sitwell, Handasyde

Buchanan and James Fisher

Published by Collins and Van Nostrand,

London and New York, 1953

Printed book, spine height: 49.5

Inscribed: *For darling Susanna with much,
much love from Sachie, Christmas 1976*

Susanna Sitwell

n) *Old Garden Roses, Part I*

By Sacheverell Sitwell and James Russell

With reproductions from paintings by

Charles Raymond

Published by George Rainbird Ltd in

association with Collins, London, 1955

Printed book, spine height: 42.8

Francis Sitwell

o) *Journey to the Ends of Time*

Published by Random House,

New York, 1959

Printed book, spine height: 21.6

Inscribed: *To darling Francis with best love
from S.S., 1 November 1959*

Francis Sitwell

p) *Monks, Nuns and Monasteries*

Published by Weidenfeld and Nicolson,

London, 1965

Printed book, spine height: 25.4

Inscribed: *For my darling Francis with my
best love from his father Sacheverell Sitwell,
25 September 1965*

Francis Sitwell

q) *For Want of the Golden City*

Published by Thames and Hudson,

London, 1973

Printed book, spine height: 24

Francis Sitwell

Index of works